WITHDRAWN

The
Anthropology
OF
Peace
AND
Nonviolence

THE
Anthropology
OF
Peace
AND
Nonviolence

edited by

LESLIE E. SPONSEL & THOMAS GREGOR

LYNNE
RIENNER
PUBLISHERS

BOULDER
LONDON

Published in the United States of America in 1994 by
Lynne Rienner Publishers, Inc.
1800 30th Street, Boulder, Colorado 80301

and in the United Kingdom by
Lynne Rienner Publishers, Inc.
3 Henrietta Street, Covent Garden, London WC2E 8LU

Library of Congress Cataloging-in-Publication Data
The Anthropology of peace and nonviolence / editors, Leslie E.
  Sponsel, Thomas Gregor.
    Includes bibliographical references and index.
    ISBN 1-55587-424-X (hc : alk. paper)
    ISBN 1-55587-450-9 (pb : alk. paper)
    1. Peaceful societies. 2. Peace—Cross-cultural studies.
  3. Nonviolence—Cross-cultural studies. I. Sponsel, Leslie E.
  (Leslie Elmer), 1943– . II. Gregor, Thomas. III. Title:
  Anthropology of peace and nonviolence.
  GN396.A57   1994
  303.6'1—dc20   93-40822
                                                           CIP

British Cataloguing in Publication Data
A Cataloguing in Publication record for this book
is available from the British Library.

Printed and bound in the United States of America

        The paper used in this publication meets the requirements
  ∞   of the American National Standard for Permanence of
        Paper for Printed Library Materials Z39.48-1984.

To the memory of our mentors,

David Bidney (Indiana University)
and Robert Murphy (Columbia University),

two inspiring models for students of humanistic anthropology

✦
Contents

✦
Foreword
Ashley Montagu

This volume, *The Anthropology of Peace and Nonviolence,* is one of the most fascinating and important books I have read in a long time. It is written by a group of distinguished anthropologists, each of whom has had considerable experience, of the most fruitful kinds, among different indigenous peoples. I say "fruitful experience" because these investigators have each not only harvested a crop of observations on the nature of the processes of nonviolence and peace in the cultures they studied, but also have effectively analytically interpreted their meaning. Because these cultures are so various, the responses of their members to the challenges of the world in which they live are equally various, and do not conform to any particular pattern, but are adapted to meet the unique needs of their environment, culture, and history as they have arisen in each society. Because the authors have opened up so many illuminating insights into the nature and dynamics of peace and nonviolence, and not altogether apart from its intrinsic interest, *The Anthropology of Peace and Nonviolence* is a book that for many years will be consulted for its practical as well as theoretical value.

In former years, anthropologists, for the most part, were prepared to rest content with the description of a culture; that is, the way of life of a people. But for many years now, anthropologists have not been satisfied with the mere description, the anatomy, of a culture, important as that may be, but have realized that in order to understand a culture it is necessary to study its physiology, as it were: the interrelatedness of its functions. It is just this that the contributors to this enlightening volume achieve in, among other things, understanding how various are, and how many different and, frequently, unexpected conditions may enter into, the shaping and control of the intra- and intergroup relations we call peace and nonviolence.

Innumerable books and articles have been written on war and peace, but the overwhelming majority were written as if by understanding the causes of war we would be better able to perceive what needs to be done in order to secure a peaceful world. Peace is thought of as a condition that can exist only in the absence of aggression. But this is a negative approach that provides analyses of what is wrong, which are then followed by recommendations as to what needs to be done to set such wrongs right. Peace is perceived in the negative sense as an interlude between wars, but that is not the best way of looking at the problem. As the philosopher Baruch Spinoza remarked in 1670, in his *Theoretical-Political Treatise,* "Peace is not an absence of war, it is a virtue, a state of mind, a disposition for benevolence, confidence, justice." Perhaps we are currently witnessing a change in the state of mind from war to peace in the Middle East with the peace process between the Israelis and the Palestinians.

Surely what most human beings crave is the positive sense of peace— freedom, security, and the attainment of a satisfying life, unencumbered by strife. The driving force of the great desire for peace, and the possibility of its fulfillment, has been hope. However, this has gone so long unrealized that many people suffer from the consequences of what has come to be known as "the giving-up syndrome," an apathy born of despair. Nevertheless, what another philosopher, Immanuel Kant, saw in 1795, in his *Perpetual Peace,* remains within the realm of possibility, if we would but make ourselves acquainted with the available remedies and apply them. But of this, more below. (Also see Montagu 1987.)

At the present time there are more wars being fought in various parts of the world than ever before in the history of humanity. That great blight nationalism, a form of racism, like a deadly virus, has spread over the world. Recently, in the former Yugoslavia, the horrible idea of "ethnic cleansing" has contributed to unspeakable atrocities against the victims and against humanity, although this has been condemned by the United Nations. (See Halpern 1993.) Apparently, the example of the Nuremberg trials of the Nazi leaders of Germany in World War II has not exercised the slightest deterrent effect upon some of the warmakers of the expiring twentieth century.

Clearly, trials, treaties, treatises, and United Nations resolutions have been ineffectual in bringing about peace between nations. This, at least, is what we have learned from past experience. What, then, is needed is no less than a complete revision of traditional approaches toward the attainment of peace. An important step in that direction for anthropology is provided by the introductory chapter and subsequent case studies in the present volume.

Until it is realized that the attainment of peace is essentially a race between education and catastrophe, it is highly unlikely that we shall ever achieve anything resembling peace among the nations. That does not for a moment deny the importance and value of the sciences and humanities in contributing to our better understanding of what needs to be done to bring about the peace on earth that humankind has so long craved. But it is only through education in what the behavioral sciences have revealed concerning human nature, its structure and requirements for healthy growth, development, and fulfillment, that peace will ever be achieved. Our main task should be to implement those findings, especially of the anthropological and psychological sciences, that perceive the principal task of humanity as realizing the innate potentialities of the child, by meeting its basic behavioral needs, its inbuilt value system. I have discussed these basic needs in several of my books, the latest of which, *Growing Young* (Montagu 1989), sets out the many needs requisite for ensuring the growth and development of a healthy human being. By a healthy human being I mean one who is able to love, to work, to play, and to think soundly. (Also see Montagu 1950, 1955.)

By whatever name we call it, war is a crime, the worst of all crimes, the maddest of all follies, and the most destructive of all tragedies. The history of how wars come about has been many times told, but the handful of men who make wars seem to have learned nothing more from them than, as Napoleon Bonaparte cynically remarked, "God is on the side of the army with the heaviest artillery," or as Mao Tse-tung put it, "Political power grows out of the barrel of a gun," or as General von Bernhardi said in 1912, "War gives a biologically just decision between nations."

Then there were "scientific authorities" who added their voices to the chorus of believers in support of the gospel of innate depravity and the belief in the ineradicability of human nature's instinctive drive toward war. From a historical perspective, among the most influential of these authorities were Sir Arthur Keith (1931) of Britain and Raymond Dart (1954, 1959) of South Africa, both of whom were anatomists and physical anthropologists; Sigmund Freud (1922, 1930, 1959) of Austria, the father of psychoanalysis; and Konrad Lorenz (1966), founder of the modern study of animal behavior.

For example, in a famous exchange of letters between Albert Einstein and Sigmund Freud, Einstein asked, "Is there any way of delivering mankind from the menace of war?" To this Freud gloomily replied, "In some happy corners of the earth, they say, where nature brings forth abundantly whatever man desires, there flourish races whose lives go gently by unknowing of aggression and constraint. This I can hardly credit" (Einstein and Freud 1939: 20).

Freud could hardly be reproached for his incredulity, since the evidence for the existence of peaceful peoples was not widely known in his day, while the evidence for the ubiquity of warfare among the peoples of which he had any knowledge was all around him, and this contributed strongly to his firm belief in the destructive nature of humankind. In 1930, in *Civilization and Its Discontents* (p. 86), he wrote, "Men are not gentle friendly creatures wishing for love. . . . A powerful measure for aggression has to be reckoned as part of their instinctive endowment . . . *Homo homini lupus;* who has the courage to dispute it in the face of all the evidence in his own life and history?" During the period of kleptomaniac imperialism, the wars in Europe, the Boer War, the Russo-Japanese War, the wars in the Balkans, and elsewhere, it was difficult for him to shake his belief in a "death instinct."

The belief in original sin, or "innate depravity" as it was called in my youth, was widespread in the Western world, and as an explanatory principle was sufficient to account for every form of violence, and especially for war. It is not difficult to understand how people have become the victims of their belief in an untamable past, and the inevitably of war. (For a critical analysis of the idea of "innate depravity" and related matters, see my book [1976] *The Nature of Human Aggression*.)

But anthropologists have long known that there is much evidence entirely against such a view. As Ralph Beals and Harry Hoijer (1971:408) put it, "Bands, tribes, and confederacies [chiefdoms] appear to represent the most frequent types of political organization found among nonliterate peoples, and it is of interest to note that these political forms are perhaps universal among peoples who have never developed warfare for conquest. The warfare that does exist in such societies is generally a matter of petty raiding for small economic gain or for purposes of vengeance or prestige."

Since, in the literature, there has been much confusion in interpreting such forms of aggression as warfare, it is necessary to point out that war is a state of prolonged armed hostilities between populations, usually for conquest. Such wars, if they can be said to occur at all, are the greatest rarity among traditional indigenous peoples.

In 1978, I edited a book in which seven anthropologists reported on the indigenous cultures they had studied in which there was a marked absence of warfare. In addition to those discussed in the book, there were others already known, like the Hadza of Tanzania, the peoples of Tibet, the Todas and the Birhor of Southern India, the Baiga of Central India, the Lepchas of Sikkim, the Punan of Borneo, and the Arapesh of New Guinea. Since 1978, additional nonviolent societies have been described, such as the Zapotec Indians of Mexico, the Yamis of Orchid Island off the coast of Taiwan, some Micronesian peoples, and others. More recently, a book coedited by Signe Howell and Roy Willis (1989) describes aspects of various nonviolent and peaceful societies. The present volume adds further valuable documentation to the anthropological record of relatively nonviolent and peaceful societies.

I hope I have said enough regarding the existence of peaceful peoples to nullify the claim of those who believe that the disposition to violence is an inborn trait of human beings, and that therefore the attainment of peace remains an unrealistic dream. On the contrary, it needs to be said, with all the positive power of knowledge we today have at our command, that there is nothing in innate human nature that constitutes a barrier to perpetual peace, except willful ignorance. That is one of the messages of the UNESCO-sponsored Seville *Statement on Violence*. That, too, is an important conclusion that this admirable volume reinforces by presenting detailed analyses of relatively nonviolent and peaceful societies.

In the modern world, with complex civilizations, the attainment of peace may seem like a dream, but it is precisely because we are the dreamers of dreams that we have survived, and against all odds have witnessed the victory of truth and goodness over evil and error, the triumph of civility over barbarism, and remain secure in the bond that relates us to all that is best on earth.

✦ References

Beals, Ralph, and Harry Hoijer
1971 *An Introduction to Anthropology.* Fourth edition. New York: Macmillan.

Dart, Raymond, A.
1954 The Predatory Transition from Ape to Man. *International Anthropological and Linguistic Review* 1:207–208.
1959 *Adventures with the Missing Link.* New York: Harper.

Einstein, Albert, and Sigmund Freud
1939 *Why War? A Correspondence between Albert Einstein and Sigmund Freud.* London: Peace Pledge Union.

Freud, Sigmund
1922 *Beyond the Pleasure Principle.* Vienna: International Psycho-Analytical Press.
1930 *Civilization and Its Discontents.* London: Hogarth Press.
1959 *Why War? Collected Papers* vol. 5. New York: Basic Books.

Halpern, Joel M., guest editor
1993 special issue "The Yugoslav Conflict," *The Anthropology of East Europe Review* 11 (1–2):3–126.

Howell, Signe, and Roy Willis, èds.
1989 *Societies at Peace: Anthropological Perspectives.* New York: Routledge.

Kant, Immanuel
1795 *Perpetual Peace.*

Keith, Sir Arthur
1931 *The Place of Prejudice in Modern Civilization.* New York: John Day.

Lorenz, Konrad
1966 *On Aggression.* New York: Harcourt, Brace & World.

Montagu, Ashley
1950 *On Being Human.* New York: Schuman.
1955 *The Direction of Human Development.* New York: Harper & Brothers.

1976   *The Nature of Human Aggression.* New York: Oxford University Press.
1978   *Learning Non-Aggression.* New York: Oxford University Press.
1987   *The Peace of the World.* Tokyo: Kenkyusha.
1989   *Growing Young.* Second edition. Westport, CT: Bergin & Garvey.

Spinoza, Baruch
1670   *Theoretical-Political Treatise.*

✦
Preface

The Anthropology of Peace and Nonviolence is part of a new direction in peace studies. In anthropology, until recently, conflict, aggression, and violence have claimed most of our attention; peace, both interpersonal and intergroup, has received relatively short shrift. For example, Brian Ferguson's recent (1988) bibliography on the anthropology of conflict has 366 pages of references; of these, only four pages are devoted to peace and conflict resolution. To be sure there are signs of change, as represented by a number of recent publications and symposia (for example, Howell and Willis, 1989). In general, however, anthropological interest in peace studies is just beginning.

On the face of it, a disproportionate interest in warfare by anthropologists is strange. For human society to persist, even the most violent of them, there must be order, sociability, reciprocity, cooperation, and empathy—perhaps, even compassion and love. In even the most warlike societies, the vast preponderance of time is spent in the pursuit of ordinary, peaceful activities that embody these qualities. This book is devoted to the proposition that peace is of interest in its own right. Like war, peace has essential preconditions: a structure, an organization, and values, attitudes, and emotions that sustain it. In short, peace is more than the absence of war. What that *more* may be is the subject of this book.

Because this perspective—that peace is more than the absence of war—has seldom been the basis of research and publication, our contributors are, to that extent, pioneers. In *The Anthropology of Peace and Nonviolence* you will find a series of theoretical articles and case studies that help to initiate an anthropology of peace.

Leslie Sponsel sets the stage for our examination of peace in Chapter 1, "The Mutual Relevance of Anthropology and Peace Studies," which emphasizes the contributions and limitations of both fields, the bonds between them, and the need for more attention to the neglected phenomena of peace and nonviolence.

Bruce Knauft, in Chapter 2, offers a new perspective on the evolution of both peace and human culture. Until now, evolutionists have had difficulty explaining why simple human societies are predisposed to cooperate in organized and largely peaceful groups. In "Culture and Cooperation in

Human Evolution," Knauft examines the implications of peace, and suggests that in cultural evolution the cooperating group has been an important unit of adaptation and natural selection.

Robert Dentan's contribution, "Surrendered Men," is one of the very few theoretical articles in the literature that systematically compares different peaceful societies. Remarkably, he finds striking parallels between the peace of simple societies (mainly refugee bands) and "enclaved societies" in complex cultures (such as the Hutterites and Amish).

In Chapter 4, Walter Goldschmidt, like Dentan, uses a comparative perspective. In what is perhaps the first work of its kind, "Peacemaking and the Institutions of Peace in Tribal Societies," he shifts our attention to the organizational basis of peace and the arts of diplomacy in a wide variety of non-Western cultures.

The next six chapters in the *Anthropology of Peace and Nonviolence* are part of a new ethnography of peace. These contributions are case studies, focused on groups with whom the authors have engaged in long-term, ethnographic research. The first three of these chapters are written from the perspective of psychological anthropology. Behind each of them is the premise that peace systems are built not only into political institutions but also into emotion and cognition. Douglas Fry's "Maintaining Social Tranquility: Internal and External Loci of Aggression Control" looks at socialization practices in two Zapotec communities: in one, violence is relatively common; in the other, it is unusual. Chapter 6, "'Why Don't You Kill Your Baby Brother?' The Dynamics of Peace in Canadian Inuit Camps," by Jean L. Briggs, moves into what may be called the dark side of the psychology of peace. Inuit child-training, which results in generally peaceful behavior, brings children very close to aggressive feelings and experiences. The third of these chapters on the psychology of peace, "Ghosts and Witches: The Psychocultural Dynamics of Semai Peacefulness," changes the focus from personality dynamics to cultural symbolism. Clayton Robarchek looks at the individual Semai's orientation to the community to explain why they believe in malevolent ghosts but deny the existence of witches.

The final three case studies focus on the organizational basis of peace and its cultural symbolism. "Peace and Power in an African Proto-State," by George Park, looks at the Kinga of Africa and their different patterns of relative peace and aggression. Behind the peace, Park identifies a covert, sublimated aggression, leading him to question the idea of labeling some societies as aggressive and others as peaceful.

Chapter 9, "Words in the Night: The Ceremonial Dialogue—One Expression of Peaceful Relationships Among the Yanomami," by Jacques Lizot, provides a refreshing approach to the Yanomami by focusing on the ceremonial dialogue as one component of the nonviolent and peaceful side of their society. The ceremonial dialogue reflects exchange and reciprocity, which are so fundamental to the social structure and sociability of the Yanomami.

The final case study, "Symbols and Rituals of Peace in Brazil's Upper Xingu," by Thomas Gregor, examines the symbolism of an unusually complex, Native American peace system. Gregor finds that the ideology of the Xingu peace emphasizes both sociability and deterrence. This dual relationship is expressed in a remarkable ritual that has elements of a game of war.

The final chapter, "Toward a Pedagogy of the Anthropology of Peace and Nonviolence," by Leslie E. Sponsel, reflects our commitment to an overview of the important literature and provides a sample syllabus for the teaching of the anthropology of peace and nonviolence.

Taken together, the contributions to *The Anthropology of Peace and Nonviolence* demonstrate that peace is far more than the absence of war. All of the societies we have examined have special ways of establishing and maintaining peaceful relationships. These include mechanisms of *sociative peace* that bring individuals and groups together in mutually rewarding relationships of cooperation and reciprocity. As Knauft shows, sociative peace has had a profoundly adaptive effect in human evolution. The point is illustrated in a case study by Fry, who looks at how socialization for nonviolence in children produces a society in which adults interact peacefully. Similarly, Gregor describes how the Mehinaku come together to trade, intermarry, and attend one another's rituals.

Most of the groups examined also seem to have methods of practicing *restorative peace*. Examples of this can be seen in Walter Goldschmidt's comparative study, in which he looks at the arts of restorative peace (admittedly often minimally developed). Two chapters—by Park, who writes of the African Kinga, and by Lizot, on the Yanomami—show how breaches in the peace may be transcended or healed.

Perhaps the richest material in our case studies of peace has been instances of the institutions of *separative peace*. In separative peace, tranquil relationships are maintained by physical separation of would-be antagonists, by fear of retaliation, or by psychological fear of aggression. For example, in enclaved societies and refugee bands—as we learn in Dentan's examination—peace is maintained by fission of the group or by authoritarian relationships that deter dissent. Among the Semai—as described by Robarchek—the individual's self-identity is so submerged in the group that conflict is massively threatening. Inuit children learn to feel and contain anger in "dramas" in which their elders engage them. The Mehinaku and the Indians of the Xingu base their peace on deterrence as well as on sociative peace. For the Mehinaku and their neighbors the image of the non-Xingu Indian and fear of witchcraft are constant reminders of the dangers of aggression.

What are we to make of the fact that separative peace is so common in our contributions, while the arts of diplomacy, as Goldschmidt demonstrates, are often so minimally developed? One would wish that a small community of closely related individuals would be held together by perception of mutual interest and the love and respect that emerge from long association. These qualities are abundant enough. But it appears that they are not sufficient. In their human, and therefore imperfect, world, the peace of the peoples we describe is also maintained by institutions that generate (and yet contain) fear, anger, and distrust. How common is this pattern? Certainly, in this volume we have a number of examples. Human relationships are inherently ambivalent. Opposition and antagonism may coexist with, and even help to construct, systems of peace and nonviolence. In an imperfect world, we may well have to settle for an imperfect peace.

We have come to realize that peace is much more than the absence of war. We are just beginning to form typologies of peace, to build theoretical models of peace, and to gather the data to test their validity and utility. It will be some time before we are anywhere near the level of understanding that has already been reached in research on the causes of war. For anthropologists, this is an opportunity. In peace studies, we are still inventing the wheel. The editors hope that the contributions in this volume will stimulate greater interest and research in the anthropology of peace, and that our colleagues and students will join with us in further dialogue.

—Thomas Gregor & Leslie E. Sponsel

✦ References

Ferguson, R. Brian
    1988   *The Anthropology of War: A Bibliography.* New York: Harry Frank Guggenheim Foundation Occasional Paper 1.

Howell, Signe, and Roy Willis
    1989   *Societies at Peace: Anthropological Perspectives.* London: Routledge.

✦ 1

The Mutual Relevance of Anthropology and Peace Studies

Leslie E. Sponsel

"Peace," writes Leslie Sponsel in his introductory article, "is the pivotal issue of the twentieth century." The massive threats of war and violence to human life in our own culture and others demonstrate that the study of peace has a very special status. The study of peace is inexorably linked to questions of values, policy, rights, advocacy, and ultimately to human survival. Anthropology, with its broad time-depth and its willingness to examine the experience of non-Western cultures, is ideally situated to inform us about the nature of human peace. But—as Sponsel also tells us—anthropology as a discipline has a great deal to learn from the study of peace. Peace studies not only reflect on human nature; they also offer prescriptions for social change and challenge the educational and research missions of anthropology.

—THE EDITORS

✦   A few years ago, at the University of Hawaii, I devoted three semesters to organizing and chairing an interdisciplinary faculty seminar about research on nonviolence and peace. The seminar featured more than one hundred speakers from the natural sciences, the social sciences, the humanities, and the professions. Among the diversity of speakers were a physicist, a neurobiologist, a biochemist, an ethnologist, a political scientist, an economist, a psychologist, a historian, a theologian, a philosopher, an artist, a composer, a poet, a physician, a priest, a social worker, and a police officer. To my surprise, most of the speakers at least touched on some aspect of anthropology, even if not necessarily in a very informed or sophisticated manner. (Also in this regard, readers familiar with such works as *The Gaia Peace Atlas* [Barnaby 1988] or the Seville *Statement on Violence* [UNESCO 1986] will recognize anthropological aspects in some of their content.) Simultaneously, in exploring peace studies in this seminar and later as a participant in the development of the Spark M. Matsunaga

Institute for Peace at the University of Hawaii, I began reflecting on the importance of peace studies for anthropology.

These and related experiences have led to the topic of this chapter, the mutual relevance of anthropology and peace studies. In this chapter I briefly consider five questions: (1) What is peace? (2) What is peace studies? (3) What is the relevance of anthropology for peace studies? (4) What is the relevance of peace studies for anthropology? (5) Where do we go from here? The discussion of these questions provides some general background and context for subsequent chapters of this book.

✦ Peace

Peace, broadly conceived, is the pivotal issue of the twentieth century, and how we handle this issue may determine not only whether or not humanity survives into the twenty-first century but also the quality of life for future generations and the biosphere, and even the course of human evolution. To an unprecedented extent, physical, social, and psychological forms of overt violence are ubiquitous, from the individual to global levels.

A few years ago the U.S. surgeon general declared that private violence was of epidemic proportions, including abuse of children, spouses, and grandparents. There is also increasing violence in schools and among street gangs. Drugs have transformed some urban areas into battlefields. Every minute, in the United States, three people are either stabbed, shot, raped, or robbed (FBI 1989).

Globally, more than one trillion dollars are now invested each year in the military in the name of security and peace: that amounts to $2 million a minute. However, this has not reduced violence and warfare. In the twentieth century, ninety-nine million people have been killed in wars; that is ten times the number of war deaths in the two preceding centuries combined. In the four decades since World War II alone, there have been well over one hundred wars. Currently, some forty wars are being fought, involving about a quarter of the countries in the world. Moreover, modern war kills far more civilians than soldiers: in the 1980s, civilians comprised about 90 percent of war deaths. Children under fifteen years of age are used as soldiers in as many as fifty countries.

Another result of modern war is the world's eighty million refugees. And for decades, that portion of humanity that has known about "the Bomb" has been held hostage by the psychological terror of the threat of nuclear war. This terror may have even reached young children (Barnaby 1988: 54, 56, 100, 256). In the early 1990s, even with the end of the Cold War and the disintegration of the Soviet Union, nuclear war remains a possibility. The planet faces yet another nuclear threat in the form of the proliferation of nuclear weapons (Barash 1991: 126–127). We have to add to all this the fact that ethnic conflict and violence now appear to be on the rise, especially in Eastern Europe, bringing with it the horror of "ethnic cleansing" (see Avruch and Black 1991; Boehm 1984; Horowitz 1985; Kuper 1981; LeVine and Campbell 1972; Montville 1990; Rubinstein and Foster 1988a; Staub 1989; Tambiah 1989; and van der Dennen 1987).

Simultaneously, the Third and Fourth Worlds are becoming increasingly militarized (Clay 1987; Nietschmann 1987). In the late 1960s, when I was a beginning graduate student in anthropology, the Mbuti, San, and various other ethnographic celebrities were considered to be traditional cultures living in peace; but since then it has become increasingly evident that many of these Fourth World societies either were or are involved in militarization and violent regional conflicts. As Barnaby states in *The Gaia Peace Atlas:* "About 85 per cent of the armed conflicts since 1945 have begun at the civil level in efforts to overthrow a ruling regime, or disputes over tribal, religious, or ethnic minority issues. Only 15 per cent have involved the armies of two or more countries fighting each other across borders" (Barnaby 1988: 54).

Whereas in 1960 only five Third World countries were arms producers, by 1987 more than twenty-seven such countries were selling fighter aircraft, ships, and missiles on the world market. Among the countries trying to cope with unemployment and balance their trade by selling arms are Argentina, Brazil, China, Egypt, India, Indonesia, Israel, North and South Korea, Mexico, the Philippines, South Africa, and Taiwan (Saul 1987: 20–21; also see Barash 1991: Ch. 4; Frank 1980; World Press 1992; and Worsley and Hadjor 1987).

Such considerations are depressing enough, but there is also the phenomenon of structural violence, which takes a much larger toll than overt physical violence per se (Galtung 1968, 1985). Structural violence refers to more subtle, usually hidden, violence—the violence of ethnocentrism, of racism, of sexism, of ageism, of nationalism, of poverty, of malnutrition, and of disease. Much of the structural violence is the inadvertent result of the use of government funds for militarization rather than food, health, and education. Funds from only half of one day's military spending would allow the World Health Organization to eradicate malaria. Funds equivalent to six months of arms expenditures would be sufficient to eliminate hunger from the planet (Barnaby 1988: 218)! Where are our priorities? It is important to realize that structural violence may flourish in societies that are not involved in actual warfare, and that the toll of suffering and death in such societies may be many times greater than in any war zone (Barash 1991: 8, 376, 398–400). Security is a key concept of political and military strategists, but considerations such as the above lead to the conclusion that the modern world is anything but secure.

Security is usually defined as the protection of a nation from dangers and threats. This encompasses the defense of national territory from foreign

invasion and occupation, the defense of strategic raw materials and economic markets, and the defense of the nation's social and political values
(Barnaby 1988: 42, 210). However, also among the threats to national,
international, and global security are injustice, racism, poverty, malnutrition, illiteracy, and environmental problems. *Security* needs to be reconsid-
ered and redefined realistically. In Barnaby's view, "True security rests on
a supportive and sustainable ecological base, on spiritual as well as material well-being, on trust and reliance on one's neighbors, on justice and
understanding in a disarmed world" (Barnaby 1988: 212). Given the combination of circumstances just described, it is doubtful whether, in our
modern world, there is any other single issue more important than peace.
Peace, if broadly defined, articulates with, indirectly if not directly, a multi-
tude of other phenomena—with concerns, problems, and issues that range
from the individual to the global levels (Barash 1991, Barnaby 1988,
Homer-Dixon et al. 1993).

✦ Peace Studies

Peace studies[1] has flourished in recent decades as a loosely organized,
interdisciplinary and multidisciplinary field of research, education, and
action. The focus has been on all aspects and levels of violence, war, nonviolence, and peace. The emphasis of peace studies is in the social sciences,
especially in political science. Such studies tend to be value-explicit, policy
oriented, and internationally focused. Most participants in peace studies
stress the value of nonviolence, peace, life, creativity, and cooperation over
violence, death, destruction, and competition. Most consider deterrence to
be, in the long term, an illusion that is extremely dangerous. Most scholars
in peace studies stress that investment of money, personnel, equipment,
supplies, and resources in the military is excessive; that it is eroding economic and cultural aspects of national vitality. To illustrate a position within peace studies that is probably typical, although certainly not universal,
Barash (1991: xiv) writes:

> The field itself differs from most social science in that it is value-oriented,
> and unabashedly so. I make no excuses, therefore, for my own bias and
> orientation, which is frankly antinuclear, antiauthoritarian, antiestablish-
> ment, proenvironment, prohuman rights, prosocial justice, pro-peace, and
> left wing. At the same time, I believe that serious emotional and political
> efforts are most effective if they build upon serious intellectual effort,
> including an attempt to understand all sides of complex debates.

This, in the first single-author, general textbook on peace studies. Whether
or not one agrees with Barash, he deserves credit for making his position
explicit. A rare phenomenon!

Furthermore, although some scientists have criticized peace studies as subjective, emotional, and regressive because of the field's explicit values and policy orientation, the emphasis on peace in peace studies is comparable with that placed on health by professionals in the medical sciences (Barash 1991: 25–27). Throughout the history of anthropology, from Franz Boas to Margaret Mead to Stanley Diamond and beyond, there are many examples of scholars who would probably agree, to large degree, with Barash's position.

Since the late 1980s, the field of peace studies has thrived in many countries, levels, and ways. While the roots of peace studies might be traced back to ancient Greek philosophers such as Plato, the beginning of the modern era is marked by Quincy Wright's (1942) classic, *A Study of War*. Modern peace research emerged in the 1940s and it has flourished since the 1960s. In recent years there has been an explosion of government-sponsored institutes and educational activities in peace studies; e.g., the U.S. Institute for Peace, established in 1984. The UNESCO *World Directory of Peace Research Institutions* (1984) lists 282 peace research institutes, in forty-five countries. Since the 1957 founding of the *Journal of Conflict Resolution,* more than a dozen journals, devoted to various aspects of peace studies, have been developed (see Chapter 11).

Education in peace studies has developed mainly since the late 1960s. In 1989, in the United States alone there were more than two hundred undergraduate and thirty-seven graduate programs in peace studies, according to *Peace and World Order Studies: A Curriculum Guide* (Thomas and Klare 1989). This guide contains ninety-three syllabi from courses relevant to peace studies (but none, incidentally, from anthropology). Major syntheses of peace studies are now conveniently available. These include Barash (1991), Barnaby (1988), and *World Encyclopedia of Peace* (1986) (see resource list in Chapter 11).

Peace *action* has a long history, extending back at least into the early nineteenth century. It grew rapidly after World War II, particularly—in the United States—with the civil rights movement of the 1960s, the Vietnam War demonstrations of the 1960s and 1970s, and the nuclear disarmament protests of the 1980s (see Barash 1991: Ch. 3). Today there are over 1,400 peace groups worldwide. Most have developed since the 1950s, but some— notably the London Peace Society founded by the Quakers in 1816—are much older (Barnaby 1988: 154). Also relevant to peace studies are many of the more than five thousand nongovernmental organizations (NGOs) worldwide (Barnaby 1988: 90). Indeed—and this is remarkable—the peace movement is the fastest-growing social movement in recent history (Barnaby 1988: 156).

Of most relevance here is the distinction between the negative and positive concepts of peace. One of these—the negative—tends to be emphasized in the United States; the other—the positive—in Europe (Galtung

1968, 1985). Although these terms are evaluative, the distinction remains valid and useful, regardless of the labels. The *negative* concept of peace is focused narrowly on security, stability, and order, and defines peace as simply the absence of war. Those in peace studies who follow this negative concept emphasize studying violent conflict, especially war, and usually at the national (civil), international, and global levels. Common themes include regional and national conflicts, history of arms control, nuclear weapon systems, geopolitics of nuclear weapons and war, and alternative security systems. Their working assumption is that a knowledge of the causes and functions of war will help to reduce the frequency and intensity of war and to find alternative ways of conflict resolution that will lead to a more peaceful world. This preoccupation with war over peace is found in most of the peace studies literature. For instance, in a review of the contents of the *Journal of Peace Research* from 1964–1980, Wiberg (1981: 113) observes: "For it turns out that out of approximately 400 articles, research communications, etc. published over seventeen years, a single one has been devoted to the empirical study of peaceful societies with a view to find out what seemed to make them peaceful." (The article referred to is by Fabbro 1978.)

The *positive* concept of peace is much broader. Barash (1991: 8) characterizes positive peace as "a condition of society in which exploitation is minimized or eliminated altogether, and in which there is neither overt violence nor the more subtle phenomenon of structural violence." In other words, the positive concept views peace not only as the absence of war but also as the presence of freedom, equality, economic and social justice, cooperation, and harmony (Barnaby 1988: 24). Those who follow the positive concept of peace give more attention to the subjects of nonviolence and peace per se. All levels are considered: individual, group (intra- and inter-), regional, national, international, and global. Common themes include the causes of war; the causes of other forms of violence, including structural violence; nonviolent conflict resolution; economic and social justice; and citizens' peace movements. The working assumption is that it is insufficient to study only violence and war; rather, nonviolence and peace must be studied in addition. Nonviolence and peace must be envisioned; they will never be approximated if we think only about violence and war. To paraphrase the opening words of the constitution of UNESCO, just as war begins in the mind, so peace must begin in the mind (Barnaby 1988: 39). (For an ethnographic illustration of this, see the extraordinary comparison of two of the most violent and nonviolent societies known, respectively the Waorani and Semai, by Robarchek and Robarchek 1992.)

Some consider the breadth of peace studies that stems from the positive concept of peace to be a weakness, rendering the field diffuse. Others, on the other hand, see this breadth as a strength, since they consider the areas covered by their wider net—economic and social injustice—to be a major cause of much of the violence in the world. In their view, an exclusive focus on violence and war is not only myopic but actually a distraction, inadvertent if not purposeful, from many of the underlying problems and issues of peace. These problems and issues include inequities within and between societies. In this view, intellectual scrutiny as well as direct action must be applied on a much broader front if social change is ever to achieve a combination of less violence, more peace, and enhanced quality of life.

✦ Relevance of Anthropology for Peace Studies

Anthropology is relevant for peace studies in many ways and below I list seven of them. More than most disciplines in the social sciences and humanities, anthropology's holistic nature renders it and peace studies especially compatible:

1. Because of its history and holistic approach, like peace studies anthropology has interdisciplinary and multidisciplinary affinities (Tax 1956).
2. Also like peace studies, anthropology is comfortable with global thinking. This results from its traditional concerns with human prehistory and evolution as well as cross-cultural studies.
3. The breadth and diversity of anthropology can counterbalance the relatively narrow focus of more specialized disciplines that contribute to peace studies (Foster and Rubinstein 1986, Rubenstein and Foster 1988a). Anthropology's concern with cross-species comparisons (at least within the order Primates), human prehistory and evolution, cross-cultural comparisons, and ethnographies as microanalyses provides a unique perspective on the human phenomenon—including violence, war, nonviolence, and peace.

For instance, human nature may be seen as inherently violent if looked at from a perspective limited mostly to Western societies in recent history. However, this is not necessarily the conclusion if human nature is viewed through the anthropological lens, which brings breadth and diversity of perspective. Recent field studies of nonhuman primate behavior have revealed that nonviolence predominates over violence (Goodall 1986; Kano 1990; Knauft 1991; Silverberg and Gray 1992; Smuts 1985, 1987, 1989; Strum 1985; Strum and Latour 1987; de Waal 1982, 1986, 1989; and cf. Ghiglieri 1987). So far, archaeological research has not revealed any definitive evidence of war until as late as the Neolithic period: although it must be admitted that absence of evidence is not necessarily evidence of absence (Childe 1941; Eisler 1987; Ferrill 1985; Gabriel 1990; Gowlett 1984; Keeley and Cahen 1989; Milner et al. 1991; Roper 1969, 1975; Vencl 1984; *World Archaeology* 1986). Cross-cultural studies reveal that relatively nonviolent and peaceful societies exist like the Inuit, Hutterites, Mbuti, San, and Semai, among others (Bonta 1993; Fabbro 1978; Howell and Willis 1989; Melko 1973, 1984; and Montagu 1978: 5; cf. Ember 1978; Knauft 1987; Palmer 1965; and Sipes 1973. For further discussion of these matters see Sponsel 1993a. See Ross 1993a, b for recent cross-cultural studies). Unfortunately, such anthropological realizations are not generally recognized by other disciplines, even those of their representatives who are involved in peace studies.

The breadth of anthropology can contribute to peace studies in still more ways. For instance, the other disciplines that compose peace studies tend to focus almost exclusively on warfare and related phenomena within and between nation states of the European tradition (Barash 1991: 32–37, 82–83, 215). But this neglects most of human experience. The state, in the general sense of a level of cultural evolution, did not emerge until about five thousand years ago, and most nation-states are only decades to a few centuries old (although they may have deeper roots in history). The framework of anthropology, however, encompasses all of humanity back to its beginnings, some four to six million years ago. Thus, one of the ways in which anthropology documents hope for peace is by viewing the state (civilization) as just one stage of cultural evolution—a stage that can be transcended like previous stages. This is important because many in peace studies and beyond view the state and war as inevitably correlated (Barash 1991: 420–421). Also, other disciplines that contribute to peace studies, especially political science, tend to define war in a very narrow way as armed aggression, for political goals, between or within nation-states and involving a military sector (separate from a civilian one), with, say, fifty thousand troops and one thousand combat dead (Barash 1991: 32, 82–83, 180–183; cf. Ferguson 1984: 3–5). Such a definition renders warfare a very recent phenomenon within human experience and excludes the classic ethnographic examples of "primitive warfare," such as the Dani or Yanomami. In these and other ways, anthropology can raise significant questions for peace studies; and vice versa.

4. What impresses anthropologists the most is cultural diversity and relativity, the power a particular culture holds over the members of a society, and the extent to which meaning and reality are constructed by culture. For example, a striking example of cultural relativity is Gibson's (1989: 67) observation that both the Buid and the Tausug in the Philippines use the same term for aggression (*maisug*), but they give the term opposite moral judgement: the former rate it negative, the latter positive. Cultural relativity is also apparent in warfare. Consider the tremendous differences in the warfare of the Cheyenne, Dani, Iroquois, Jivaro, Mae Enga, Maori, Nuer, Tausug, Waorani, and Yanomami. Indeed there is so much variability in warfare across cultures that it is difficult to develop a general theory of war, or even an operational definition of war, that allows meaningful cross-

cultural comparisons in any depth (see Otterbein 1985). This point regarding the cultural diversity of war also underlines the important influence of worldview, cultural values, enculturation, gender relations, and role models on violence and nonviolence in a particular society (Howell and Willis 1989; Montagu 1978). Figure 1.1 illustrates in general the primary components of the cultural system that may be explored in detail in teaching and research on nonviolence/peace and violence/war.

Diplomacy, negotiations, and conflict resolution are important components of the peace process that depend on empathy, among other things: empathy in the sense of the ability to grasp and respect the other's viewpoint. For anthropology, this is not a new area: it has long pursued and

Figure 1.1 Heuristic Model of a Cultural System

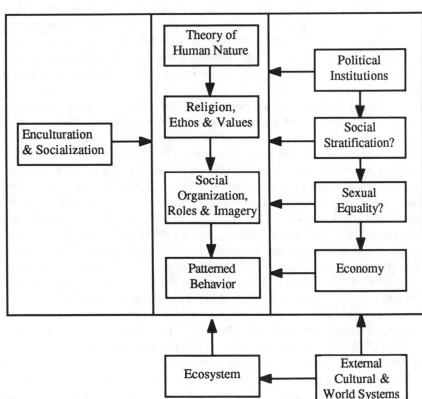

Source: After Sponsel 1989

respected alternative visions. Two central principles for anthropology are cultural relativism and participant observation in ethnography (Herskovits 1972). Anthropology can play a special role when conflicts are cross-cultural (Avruch et al. 1991; Halpern 1993; Montville 1990).

5. The rich ethnographic record that has accumulated in anthropology for over a century provides detailed case studies of cultures that are relatively nonviolent and peaceful as well as those that are relatively violent and warlike (see for example, Robarchek and Robarchek 1992). Most importantly, in the ethnographic record there are precedents of relatively nonviolent and peaceful cultures that may be used as heuristic models for thinking about the causes, characteristics, conditions, processes, functions, and consequences of nonviolence and peace (Bonta 1993; Fabbro 1978; Howell and Willis 1989; Melko 1973, 1984; Montagu 1978: 5; Sponsel 1993b). Unfortunately, since the authenticity of the famous Tasaday has been called into question, although not yet resolved (Headland 1992), they could become of little more than historical interest to peace studies (Sponsel 1990a, 1992). Nevertheless, it is important that various ethnographic cases such as the Semai demonstrate that nonviolence can involve an entire culture rather than being limited to a political strategy (Dentan 1968).

Recently, a number of anthropologists have developed an ethnohistorical approach, marshaling arguments and evidence to indicate that the direct and indirect influences of states and colonialism often triggered, intensified, and/or changed warfare within and among nonstate societies (Blick 1988; Ferguson 1992a; Ferguson and Whitehead 1992a). Three types of war are stimulated by state expansion into the tribal zone: (1) war by indigenous people directed against the state presence, that is, wars of resistance and rebellion; (2) war by indigenous people carried out under the control or influence of state agents; that is, ethnic soldiering; and (3) war between indigenous peoples responding to their own perceived interests in the changing circumstances of the tribal zone, or internecine warfare (Ferguson and Whitehead 1992a: 18). This implies that ethnographic cases of war that were previously thought to be traditional may have actually been developments resulting from external economic, social, and political factors in the processes of contact with states (Ferguson and Whitehead 1992b: 26–27). Another implication of this research is that the ethnographic literature on "primitive" warfare needs to be reassessed, case by case, in ethnohistorical perspective to ascertain to what extent it is a precontact and/or postcontact phenomenon. Indeed, Ferguson (1992b) has argued that Yanomami warfare has been influenced by colonialism and is not purely traditional. Most importantly, this research also implies that pre-state and nonstate societies may have been much more nonviolent and peaceful than previously thought.

It is also important that anthropologists have documented cases in which relatively violent and warlike societies were transformed into relatively nonviolent and peaceful societies, as for example at some stage in the process of the colonial pacification of some indigenous societies in New Guinea, Melanesia, and Africa (Robarchek and Robarchek 1989; Rodman and Cooper 1979; Scheffler 1964; Willis 1989). However, the means that were used by colonials to achieve pacification were certainly not always peaceful or humane (Bodley 1990: 42–56).

Ethnography provides yet another kind of heuristic model; namely, the Ik (Turnbull 1972). They can be considered as showing one scenario for the distintegration of society after a nuclear winter. (For anthropological discussions of nuclear armaments, war, and winter, see Bumsted 1985; Turner and Pitts 1986; Worsley 1985; and Worsley and Hadjor 1986.)

6. The above and other anthropological considerations are indispensable for the construction of any modern theory of human nature—and this, too, is relevant to peace studies. Clearly most people, including those in peace studies, have to some extent developed their own theory of human nature, even if not explicitly, systematically, and critically (Avruch and Black 1990; Berry 1989; Feibleman 1987; Howell and Willis 1989; Kohn 1990; Roosevelt 1990; Stevenson 1987). The importance of a theory of human nature in influencing beliefs and actions should not be underestimated. As Stevenson (1987: 3) observes:

> What is man? This is surely one of the most important questions of all. For so much else depends on our view of human nature. The meaning and purpose of human life, what we ought to do, and what we can hope to achieve—all these are fundamentally affected by whatever we think is the "real" or "true" nature of man.

(See Robarcheck and Robarchek 1992 for an ethnographic illustration of how antithetical emic theories of human nature result in the extremes of the most and least violent societies, the Waorani and Semai, respectively.)

Human nature is also significant in another way. Even if the concept of human nature remains abstract and controversial, it still points to another important contribution that anthropology can make to peace studies and peace; namely, the documentation of the basic evolutionary, biological, and cultural unity of humankind. Dehumanization of an individual or group is often a first step toward their victimization through aggression (Montagu and Matson 1983). Obviously, much of the conflict and violence in the modern world pivots on the recognition and prejudiced interpretation of differences between individuals and groups. In contrast, recognition of the common humanity of others as well as a tolerance and even appreciation of diversity could eliminate some of the problems and reduce many others (Bidney 1963; Brown 1991; Kohn 1990; Montagu and Matson 1983; Staub 1989). A world that is safe for diversity and recognizes unity would be more peaceful.

7. Finally, anthropology is relevant to peace studies because of its enduring critical tradition, from Rousseau (Roosevelt 1990) to Boas (1928), and from Boas to late-modern anthropologists such as Bodley (1985, 1990), Diamond (1974), Hymes (1972), Montagu (1964, 1976), and Pandian (1985). Anthropology has long been at the forefront in challenging ethnocentrism, racism, sexism, and other kinds of prejudice that are based on biological or cultural differences.

Anthropology subjects common beliefs, philosophical questions, theories from the social sciences and other disciplines, and sociopolitical problems and issues to scrutiny via its cross-species, diachronic, cross-cultural, and ethnographic resources. In principle, this applies no less to matters of violence, war, nonviolence, and peace.

As an index of the growing anthropological interest in peace studies, a minimum of 250 U.S. and 150 other anthropologists are involved in some aspect of peace studies according to the *Directory of Anthropologists Working on Topics of Peace, International Security, and Conflict Resolution* (Rubinstein and Foster 1988b). Although no single author has yet synthesized the anthropology of peace studies in a textbook, in the last three decades, and especially in the 1980s, at least a dozen books have appeared dealing with anthropological aspects of peace studies (see Chapter 11). However, except for the two books edited by Howell and Willis (1989) and Montagu (1978), these works from editor-anthropologists tend to follow the negative concept of peace. (See Ferguson 1984, Ferguson and Whitehead 1992b, and Otterbein 1973, 1993 for reviews of the anthropology of war; and Sponsel 1993a for a review of the anthropology of peace.)

✦   Relevance of Peace Studies for Anthropology

Peace studies are relevant to anthropology in at least four ways.

1. Peace studies can be a catalyst for rethinking anthropology, including its history, theory, data, and practice. For example, the history of anthropology has been closely intertwined with various aspects of war. The Bureau of American Ethnology was initiated by the U.S. Congress, following a period of severe warfare between indigenes and colonials, to provide reliable information that could be used by the government for more effective administration of the indigenous population (Hinsley 1979). Evans-Pritchard's (1940) classic ethnographic study of the Nuer was accomplished during a period when the British colonials had machine-gunned the Nuer to submission (see Stauder 1974). Forensic anthropology, human engineering, anthropometry, and human adaptability are areas within the

subfield of physical anthropology that have benefited from developments generated through collaborative research in military and warfare activities (Dupree 1958). Likewise in cultural anthropology, developments associated with collaborative research with the military and war activities include national character studies (Benedict 1946; Mabee 1987; Moss 1963; Suzuki 1980), culture-at-a-distance methodology (Mead and Metraux 1953), and the cross-cultural area files. Cultural anthropologists were involved in the War Relocation Authority, which illegally removed and imprisoned in concentration camps Japanese U.S. nationals during World War II (Starn 1986; Suzuki 1981; Wax 1971. Also see articles in the journals *Applied Anthropology* and *Human Organization* for the period during and just after World War II; Barnett 1956; Leighton 1949; Linton 1945; Smithsonian 1942–1945; and van Willigen 1980). After the war, anthropologists were employed in the administration of islanders in the Trust Territory of Micronesia (Barnett 1956; Fischer 1979). The cross-cultural experience of military personnel during World War II stimulated many to study anthropology in universities, and the GI Bill supported their studies. Experience in the Peace Corps also stimulated many to pursue a career in anthropology. Research on culture change and applied anthropology flourished after World War II (van Willigen 1980). The 1950 UNESCO *Statement on Race* (Montagu 1972) that Mead, Montagu, and other anthropologists helped draft was largely stimulated by the experience of World War II. Similarly, the executive board of the American Anthropological Association drafted *Statement on Human Rights* for the United Nations Commission on Human Rights, toward the development of the Universal Declaration of Human Rights (AAA 1947; Cohen 1989; Washburn 1987). Military funds have supported ethnographic research on indigenous survival knowledge and skills in extreme environments (e.g., Nelson 1969; Nesbitt et al. 1959). The political confrontations in the United States during the era of the Vietnam War led not only to a surge of interest in the anthropology of war (Bohannan 1976; Fried et al. 1968) but also to the scrutiny of the ethics and politics of anthropology (Beals 1969; Davenport 1985; Fluehr-Lobban 1991; Hymes 1972; Wakin 1992). Anthropologists have been involved in the U.S. resettlement and acculturation of refugees from the Indochina conflicts of the last few decades. Elsewhere, anthropology has collaborated with military and other concerns, such as in Nazi Germany (Jell-Bahlsen 1985; de Wolf 1992) and with apartheid in South Africa (Gordon 1988), or has been closely connected with the government and ideology, as in the Soviet Union (Tishkov 1992). In short, it would be feasible (and would prove insightful) to rewrite the history of anthropology in relationship to war and other forms of violence (e.g., Goldschmidt 1979).

    2. Peace studies can provide background for better understanding the militarization of the Third and Fourth Worlds, where most anthropologists have traditionally worked. The rise of advocacy anthropology is in large

part connected with structural and other kinds of violence perpetrated against indigenous peoples, including the violation of their basic human rights (Bodley 1990; Downing and Kushner 1988; Wright 1988). Indeed, *Cultural Survival Quarterly* (Clay 1987) devoted two special issues to the subject of the militarization of indigenous peoples (also see Ehlers 1990; Enloe 1987; and Mirante 1987). War can be an important agent of cultural change, although this aspect has been neglected in anthropological research (e.g., Bodley 1990: 42–56; White and Lindstrom 1989). (The videos *Angels of War, The Meo,* and *The Last Tasmanian*—listed in Chapter 11—illustrate this point quite well.)

3. The positive concept of peace can stimulate a broader and more balanced approach to research and teaching regarding violence/war and nonviolence/peace as integral components of a dialectical process. This would help to counter the systemic bias within the discipline of anthropology: a tendency to focus on violence and war almost to the exclusion of nonviolence and peace, which can lead to a distorted view of human nature, ethnology, and ethnographic cases.

Apparently, most anthropologists who study some aspect of war operate with the restrictive negative concept of peace. Even when the word peace is employed, it is usually conceived negatively as simply the absence of war (e.g., Wolf 1987). Many examples of this systemic bias can be cited. In the extremely useful bibliography on the anthropology of war compiled by Ferguson and Farragher (1988: 275–278), out of 1,888 citations, only sixty-four (3 percent) are on peace, and these are disappointing in their quality, relevance, and currency. Theories of the origin of the state almost inevitably focus on war as a central component (Carneiro 1970, 1978, 1992; Cohen 1984; Lewellen 1983; Paynter 1989; Service 1985; Webster 1977; Wright 1977). The archaeologist Kirch (1984), in surveying the evolution of Polynesian chiefdoms, includes a chapter on resource competition and war, but none on cooperation and peace. In a recent survey of the native cultures of Oceania, Oliver (1989) devotes an entire chapter to "Warfare and Killing"; only six of the seventy-seven pages are on peace (also see Knauft 1990).

The Yanomami, an ethnographic celebrity for the public and the profession, have been consistently depicted as "the fierce people" since the late 1960s in a series of publications by Chagnon, although this phrase, as the subtitle of his famous ethnography, has been dropped in the recent fourth edition (1983, 1992). Nevertheless, it is quite clear from Chagnon's writing that he is operating with the restrictive negative concept of peace. For instance, Chagnon (1992: 7) notes that the Yanomami "are simultaneously peacemakers and valiant warriors. Peacemaking often requires the threat or actual use of force, and most headmen have an acquired reputation for being waiteri: fierce." Chagnon (1992: 8) also states: "But their conflicts are not blind, uncontrolled violence. They have a series of graded forms of violence that ranges from chest-pounding and club-fighting duels to out-and-out shooting to kill. This gives them a good deal of flexibility in settling disputes without immediate resort to lethal violence." Lizot (1985: xiv), a French anthropologist who has worked almost continuously with the Yanomami since 1968, has criticized this Hobbesian view of the Yanomami: "I would like my book to help revise the exaggerated representation that has been given of Yanomami violence. The Yanomami are warriors; they can be brutal and cruel, but they can also be delicate, sensitive, and loving. Violence is sporadic; it never dominates social life for any length of time, and long peaceful moments can separate two explosions." (See also Albert 1989, 1990; Albert and Ramos 1989; Colchester 1987: 8; Good 1991: 73–74; Heider 1988; Ramos 1987; Smole 1976: 16.) In a widely read and cited article in *Science,* Chagnon (1988: 985) takes his negative concept of peace to the extreme with a speculative generalization about the whole of cultural evolution: "Violence is a potent force in human society and may be the principal driving force behind the evolution of culture" (cf. Sponsel 1993a). (See Albert 1989, 1990; and Lizot 1989 for critiques of Chagnon's sociobiological interpretation of Yanomami aggression; and Ferguson's [1992a,b] historical explanation of Yanomami aggression as a product of colonialism.) A radically different ethnographic image of the Yanomami might emerge if Chagnon or others were to pursue fieldwork with the positive concept of peace and focus on nonviolent conflict resolution, prosocial behavior, reciprocity, and related phenomena (see Chapter 9 in this volume).

Actually, many anthropologists have explored the ramifications of the positive concept of peace but they have rarely done so explicitly, or in relation to studies of violence and war, thus their contributions to peace studies have not been adequately recognized (Koch's 1974 study is a notable exception). Anthropologists need more openly to identify and advertise their research on aspects of the positive concept of peace.

If there is any single anthropologist whose work might be identified with peace studies it is Ashley Montagu (1950, 1952, 1955, 1964, 1976 1978, 1987, 1989, etc.). In numerous books, he has consistently challenged social applications of pseudobiological ideas connected with aggression, racism, sexism, and ageism. There are also many other anthropologists whose work is relevant to peace studies, even if it is not explicitly identified as such. Examples include the Vicos Project in Peru (Dobyns, Doughty, and Lasswell 1971); Alcalay (1980, 1981, 1987, 1991) and Kiste (1974), whose work is on the impact of the repeated relocation of the Bikini people to provide space for U.S. bomb-testing in the Marshall Islands; Lewis (1966) on the culture of poverty; and Turner (1957), among the Ndembu, on the political role of religious specialists as mediators in conflict resolution. Much of this work relates to issues of human rights, which have become the focus of advocacy anthropology (Downing and Kushner

1988; Messer 1993; Morris and Hitchcock 1993; Paine 1985; Wright 1988).

In a cross-cultural review of mediation Greenhouse (1985) explores one domain of anthropology's relevance to the positive concept of peace. Conflict resolution is not just a recent development in political science, sociology, social work, or other disciplines involved in peace studies; rather it is a common practice in most if not all human societies (e.g., Podolefsky 1990; Shook 1992). This research is usually considered under the rubric of legal and political anthropology (also see Avruch et al. 1991; Deshen 1992; Gulliver 1979).

In other disciplines, such as animal, primate, and human ethology and psychology, there are signs of what might loosely be termed a paradigm shift from the narrow negative to the broader positive concept of peace (Hinde and Groebel 1991; Kemp 1986; Kohn 1990; and Lackner 1984). Goodall (1986), Kano (1990), Smuts (1985, 1987), Strum (1985), and de Waal (1982, 1986, 1989) have documented the social skills of nonhuman primates in conflict resolution and peace maintenance (also see Silverberg and Gray 1992). A student of pioneer ethologist Konrad Lorenz, Eibl-Eibesfeldt (1989: 399), has taken in the field and analyzed in the laboratory 200 km of film of unstaged human behavior from a most extensive cross-cultural sample. On the basis of his unparalleled field experience, this biologist concludes that war is primarily a cultural institution, and that role models, socialization, and values are primary factors in the expression of violence and nonviolence (Eibl-Eibesfeldt 1989: 399, 403).

4. Peace studies could help anthropology to develop an agenda of priorities for research, teaching, and action (e.g., Ferguson 1986). The profession as a whole lacks any explicit and systematic attempt to identify and pursue an agenda of priorities in research, teaching, and action beyond such general concepts as an enduring commitment to a holistic documentation of the unity and diversity of humankind. It is puzzling how such a paralysis of the profession can persist in the face of the growing gravity and urgency of the contemporary world's economic, social, political, and environmental problems. It is also puzzling how anthropologists can go about "business as usual" when many of the communities they work with are involved in diverse conflicts and crises (Ehlers 1990; Howell 1990: 89–100; Miller 1993; Nordstrom and Martin 1992; Riches 1986; Sluka 1990).

✦ Looking Ahead

Where do we go from here? Toward transcending the systemic bias of the negative concept of peace and developing an agenda of priorities. Below, I offer six suggestions, stemming from this discussion of the mutual relevance of anthropology and peace studies. (Readers who are not anthropologists may construct their own lists for their own professions.)

1. More anthropologists could focus some of their research on aspects of the positive concept of peace and contribute articles to periodicals in peace studies such as the *Journal of Peace Research* and the *Journal of Conflict Resolution.* Publishing in periodicals devoted to peace studies would help to demonstrate to colleagues in other disciplines the relevance of anthropology to peace studies. Likewise, many leads and insights for anthropological fieldwork can be drawn from a perusal of basic texts in peace studies like Barash (1991) and Barnaby (1988). For instance, to pose a question: Are there evolutionary, genetic, physiological (including hormonal), psychological (including neurobiological), ecological, and/or cultural bases for nonviolence and peace?

2. University departments of anthropology could transcend the traditional organization of the curriculum around subfields, topics, and areas to give more attention to courses on contemporary problems and issues as well as other aspects of the positive concept of peace.

3. Every anthropology department in the nation could develop a specific course focusing on the anthropology of nonviolence/peace and violence/war. In programs where a separate course is not feasible, nonviolence/peace and violence/war could be included as a major theme or segment in existing introductory courses on general and cultural anthropology. Another possibility is to teach the history and theory of cultural anthropology through a focus on war and peace. Anthropology already has an enormous and rich literature on violence and war: it awaits discovery and exploration by instructors and students. The topical and geographical bibliography compiled by Ferguson and Farragher (1988) goes a long way toward organizing some of this literature, making it more accessible. Another rich resource is the annotated bibliography on peaceful societies by Bonta (1993). Also, there are many excellent ethnographic films and videos of special relevance to war and peace; most notably the classic about the Dani, *Dead Birds* (see Chapter 11).

4. Introductory textbooks on general and cultural anthropology could include a chapter or appendix on advocacy anthropology, indigenous rights, and related topics, taking advantage of the wealth of published material available from Cultural Survival, Survival International, the Work Group for Indigenous Affairs, and similar organizations (see Messer 1993; Miller 1993; and Wright 1988). The classified indexes of *Cultural Survival Quarterly* are useful for instructors preparing syllabi and lectures and for students writing research reports.

5. The American Anthropological Association (AAA) or the International Union of Anthropological and Ethnological Sciences

(IUAES) could formulate its own anthropological statement on nonviolence/peace and violence/war. Anthropologists could revise the Seville *Statement on Violence* (UNESCO 1986), which, although endorsed by the AAA, leaves something to be desired. A revision could develop additional anthropological points, including some specifically addressing nonviolence and peace. (This statement is reproduced and analyzed in Silverberg and Gray 1992.)

6. The AAA, including its section of the IUAES Commission on the Study of Peace, could try to organize at least one symposium every year (at the annual meetings) focused directly on aspects of nonviolence and peace. Numerous symposia on war and other forms of violence have been presented at annual meetings of the AAA, but there have been only two or three directly focused on nonviolence and/or peace in the ninety years of annual meetings. (Papers revised from a symposium on the "Anthropology of Nonviolence and Peace" held in 1988 at the AAA meetings in Phoenix provided the basis for most of the chapters in this book. Also see Textor 1991.)

✦ **"The Major Challenge"**

In summary, there is no single concern more important than peace, which is surely the pivotal issue of the twentieth century. Fortunately, peace studies has flourished since the 1980s. Unfortunately, there has been relatively little interaction between peace studies and anthropology. There is, however, great potential for productive collaboration.

Most of the anthropological research that is obviously relevant to peace studies focuses almost exclusively on violence and war, following the negative concept of peace. While this work is certainly very important, it is insufficient: nonviolence, peace, and related phenomena also deserve serious systematic attention, as research and teaching foci, following the positive concept of peace. Nonviolent and peaceful societies appear to be rare—not because they are, in fact, rare, but because nonviolence and peace are so rarely considered in research, the media, and other arenas. During this century, only about 1 to 2 percent of human deaths have been inflicted by other human beings; and only about 15 to 25 percent of soldiers in a war ever fired a weapon (Barash 1991: 153, 156). From another angle, Barash (1991: 33) notes that: "Based on the number of national states existing since 1815, there have been approximately 16,000 nation-years, and during this time, war has occupied 'only' 600 of these nation-years, or somewhat less than 4 percent of the possible total." From these and similar considerations, it could be argued that violence and war are abnormal, both statistically and in other ways, rather than an inevitable expression of human nature. In the medical professions, it is important to understand abnormal or pathological conditions and processes, but it is also important to understand healthy conditions and processes. Preventive medicine prescribes such things as appropriate diet, exercise, stress management, and social support for the maintenance of health. Likewise, it as important to understand the characteristics, conditions, causes, functions, processes, and consequences of nonviolence and peace as it is to understand those of violence and war. Of the two, violence and war have been studied the more, perhaps because they better fit Western society, with its values, traditions, and institutions of violence and war, and its emic constructs of human nature and society (Overing 1989; Palmer 1972; Sponsel 1993a).

Peace studies is relevant to anthropology in providing one avenue for rethinking the discipline, understanding the militarization of the societies of the Third and Fourth Worlds, where most anthropologists work, providing insights like the positive concept of peace, and suggesting an agenda of priorities for research, teaching, and action.

This chapter has listed six specific ways in which anthropology could contribute to peace studies: anthropologists could publish in periodicals devoted to peace studies; develop more courses on topics related to the positive concept of peace; develop a course focused on nonviolence/peace and violence/war; add a section on human rights, advocacy anthropology, and related topics to introductory textbooks in general and cultural anthropology; formulate an alternative to the Seville *Statement on Violence,* adding a section on nonviolence/peace as well as giving it a more positive approach; and organize at least one symposium at each annual meeting of the AAA focused directly on nonviolence and peace.

More generally, anthropology is relevant to peace studies with its interdisciplinary and multidisciplinary affinities, global thinking, breadth and diversity, concern for human diversity, including cultural diversity and relativism, in-depth ethnographic case studies, contributions to the theory of human nature, and critical tradition. Anthropology also offers to peace studies some degree of sorely needed optimism about human nature, and alternative visions, including models of societies such as the Semai, which are relatively nonviolent and peaceful.

As Barash (1991: 323–324) states: "The major challenge for Peace Studies is to break away from the existing war system—which includes reliance on peace through strength—and seek to establish a viable ecology of peace whose strength does not derive from violence or the threat of violence." Anthropology can help to meet this and other challenges for peace studies as well as for peace and nonviolence.

✦ Notes

I am grateful to numerous colleagues and students who have contributed to this work in one way or another. The chapter is substantially revised from a previous article (Sponsel 1990b), which in turn was based on a paper presented in Washington, D.C., at the 1989 annual meetings of the American Anthropological

Association in the symposium "Anthropology and the Pedagogy of Peace," organized by Paul Doughty and Vernie Davis. Ram Cheddtri assisted with library and bibliographic research, and this was funded by a grant from the Spark M. Matsunaga Institute for Peace at the University of Hawaii. Ursula Thiele carefully read the proofs of the manuscript.

The late David Bidney, my former professor at Indiana University, stimulated my interest in the humanistic aspects of anthropology. I am especially indebted to Glenn Paige, Professor Emeritus of Political Science at the University of Hawaii and founder of the Center for Global Nonviolence, for his initial and continuing inspiration. Last but not least, the symposium "What We Know About Peace," organized by Thomas Gregor and sponsored by the Harry Frank Guggenheim Foundation, stimulated the revision of this chapter and confirmed my concern for anthropological research on aspects of the positive concept of peace. However, only I am responsible for any deficiencies in the chapter.

1. This section has benefited greatly from the articles in Thomas and Klare (1989), especially the one by Stephenson (1989), and from Barash (1991) and Galtung (1985).

✦ References

Albert, Bruce
   1989   On Yanomami "Violence": Inclusive Fitness or Ethnographer's Representation? *Current Anthropology* 30(5):637–640.
   1990   On Yanomami Warfare: Rejoinder. *Current Anthropology* 31(5):558–563.

Albert, Bruce, and Alcida Rita Ramos
   1989   Yanomami Indians and Anthropological Ethics. *Science* 244:632.

Alcalay, Glenn H.
   1980   The Aftermath of Bikini. *The Ecologist* 10(10):346–351.
   1981   A Tale of Two Islands: Bikini and Enewetak. *The Ecologist* 11(5):222–227.
   1987   Pax atomica: US nuclear imperialism in Micronesia, in *On the Brink: Nuclear Proliferation and the Third World,* P. Worsley and K. B. Hadjor, eds. London: Third World Communications.
   1991   Nuclear Colonialism in the Pacific, in *Women's Voices on the Pacific,* L. Foerstel, ed. 92–102. Washington, D.C.: Maisonneuve Press.

American Anthropological Association
   1947   Statement on Human Rights. *American Anthropologist* 49(4):539–543.

Avruch, Kevin, and Peter W. Black
   1990   Ideas of Human Nature in Contemporary Conflict Resolution Theory. *Negotiation Journal* 6(3):221–228.
   1991   The Culture Question and Conflict Resolution. *Peace & Change* 16(1):22–45.

Avruch, Kevin, Peter W. Black, and Joseph A. Scimecca, eds.
1991   *Conflict Resolution: Cross-Cultural Perspectives.* Westport: Greenwood Press.

Barash, David P.
1991   *Introduction to Peace Studies.* Belmont: Wadsworth Publishing.

Barnaby, Frank, ed.
1988   *The Gaia Peace Atlas: Survival into the Third Millennium.* New York: Doubleday.

Barnett, Homer G.
1956   *Anthropology in Administration.* Evanston: Row, Peterson.

Beals, Ralph L.
1969   *Politics of Social Science Research: An Inquiry Into the Ethics and Responsibilities of Social Scientists.* Chicago: Aldine Publishing.

Benedict, Ruth
1946   *The Chrysanthemum and the Sword: Patterns of Japanese Culture.* Cleveland: World Publishing.

Berry, Christopher J.
1989   *Human Nature.* Atlantic Highlands: Humanities Press International.

Bidney, David, ed.
1963   *The Concept of Freedom in Anthropology.* The Hague: Mouton.

Blick, Jeffrey P.
1988   Genocidal Warfare in Tribal Societies as a Result of European-Induced Culture Conflict. *Man* 23:654–670.

Boas, Franz
1928   *Anthropology and the Modern World.* New York: W. W. Norton.

Bodley, John
1985   *Anthropology and Contemporary Human Problems.* Palo Alto, CA: Mayfield Publishing.
1990   *Victims of Progress.* Mountain View, CA: Mayfield Publishing.

Boehm, Christopher
1984   *Blood Revenge: The Enactment and Management of Conflict in Montenegro and Other Societies.* Philadelphia: University of Pennsylvannia Press.

Bohannan, Paul, ed.
1976   *Law and Warfare: Studies in the Anthropology of Conflict.* New York: Natural History Press.

Bonta, Bruce D.
1993 *Peaceful Peoples: An Annotated Bibliography*. Metuchen, NJ: Scarecrow Press.

Brown, Donald E.
1991 *Human Universals*. New York: McGraw-Hill, Inc.

Bumsted, M. Pamela, ed.
1985 *Nuclear Winter: The Anthropology of Human Survival*. Los Alamos: Los Alamos National Laboratory.

Carneiro, Robert
1970 A Theory of the Origin of the State. *Science* 469:733–738.
1978 Political Expansion as an Expression of the Principle of Competitive Exclusion, in *Origins of the State: The Anthropology of Political Evolution*, R. Cohen and E. Service, eds.: 205–223. Philadelphia: Institute for the Study of Human Issues.
1992 The Role of Warfare in Political Evolution: Past Results and Future Projections, in *Effects of War on Society*, G. Ausenda, ed.: 87–102. San Marino: AIEP Editore.

Chagnon, Napoleon A.
1983 *Yanomamo: The Fierce People*. New York: Holt, Rinehart and Winston.
1988 Life Histories, Blood Revenge, and Warfare in a Tribal Population. *Science* 239:985–991.
1992 *Yanomamo*. New York: Harcourt Brace Jovanovich.

Childe, V. Gordon
1941 War in Prehistoric Societies. *Sociological Review* 32:127–138.

Clay, Jason W., ed.
1987 Militarization and Indigenous People. *Cultural Survival Quarterly* 11(3–4).

Cohen, Ronald
1984 Warfare and State Formation: Wars Make States and States Make Wars, in *Warfare, Culture, and Environment*, R. B. Ferguson, ed.: 329–358. New York: Academic Press.
1989 Human Rights and Cultural Relativism: The Need for a New Approach. *American Anthropologist* 91:1014–1017.

Colchester, Marcus
1987 Book Review: Tales of the Yanomami: Daily Life in the Venezuelan Forest, by Jacques Lizot. *Survival International News* 16:8.

Davenport, W.
1985 The Thailand Controversy in Retrospect, in *Social Context of American Ethnology, 1840–1984*, June Jelm, ed.: 65–71. Washington, D.C.: American Ethnological Society.

van der Dennen, Johan M.G.
1987   Ethnocentrism and In-Group/Out-Group Differentiation: A Review and Interpretation of the Literature, in *The Sociobiology of Ethnocentrism*, V. Reynolds, V. Falger, and I. Vine, eds.: 1–47. London: Croom Helm.

Dentan, Robert K.
1968   *The Semai: A Nonviolent People of Malaya.* New York: Holt, Rinehart and Winston.

Deshen, Shlomo
1992   Applied Anthropology in International Conflict Resolution: The Case of the Israeli Debate on Middle Eastern Settlement Proposals. *Current Anthropology* 51(2):180–184.

Diamond, Stanley
1974   *In Search of the Primitive: A Critique of Civilization.* New Brunswick: Transaction Books.

Dobyns, Henry F., Paul L. Doughty, and Harold Dwight Lasswell, eds.
1971   *Peasants, Power, and Applied Social Change: Vicos as a Model.* New York: Sage Publications.

Downing, Theodore E., and George Kushner, eds.
1988   *Human Rights and Anthropology.* Cambridge, MA: Cultural Survival.

Dupree, Louis, ed.
1958   *Anthropology in the Armed Services: Research in Environment, Physique, and Social Organization.* University Park, PA: Pennsylvania State University Social Sciences Research Center.

Ehlers, Tracy Bachrach
1990   Central America in the 1980's: Political Crisis and the Social Responsibility of Anthropologists. *Latin American Research Review* XXV(3):141–155.

Eibl-Eibesfeldt, Irenaus
1989   *Human Ethology.* Chicago: Aldine de Gruyter.

Eisler, Riane
1987   *The Chalice and the Blade: Our History, Our Future.* San Francisco: Harper and Row.

Ember, Carol
1978   Myths about Hunter-Gatherers. *Ethnology* 17(4):439–448.

Enloe, Cynthia H.
1987   When Ethnicity Is Militarized—The Consequences for Southeast Asian Communities, in *Southeast Asian Tribal Groups and Ethnic Minorities*: 53–57. Cambridge, MA: Cultural Survival.

Evans-Pritchard, E. E.
1940   *The Nuer.* London: Oxford University Press.

Fabbro, David
1978   Peaceful Societies: An Introduction. *Journal of Peace Research* XV(1):67–83.

Federal Bureau of Investigation
1989   *Annual Report on Crime in the USA.* Washington, D.C.: FBI.

Feibleman, James Kern
1987   *The Destroyers: The Underside of Human Nature.* New York: Peter Lang.

Ferguson, R. Brian, ed.
1984   Introduction: Studying War, in *Warfare, Culture, and Environment,* R. B. Ferguson, ed.: 1–79. New York: Academic Press.
1986   Anthropology and War: Theory, Politics, Ethics, in *The Anthropology of War and Peace,* P. R. Turner and D. Pitts, eds.: 141–159. Granby, MA: Bergin and Harvey.
1992a   Tribal Warfare. *Scientific American* 266(1):108–113.
1992b   A Savage Encounter: Western Contact and the Yanomami War Complex, in *War in the Tribal Zone: Expanding States and Indigenous Warfare,* R. B. Ferguson and N. L. Whitehead, eds.: 199–227. Santa Fe, NM: School of American Research Press.

Ferguson, R. Brian, and Leslie E. Farragher
1988   *The Anthropology of War: A Bibliography.* New York: Harry Frank Guggenheim Foundation, Occasional Paper 1.

Ferguson, R. Brian, and Neil L. Whitehead, eds.
1992a   *War in the Tribal Zone: Expanding States and Indigenous Warfare.* Santa Fe, NM: School of American Research Press.
1992b   "The Violent Edge of Empire," in *War in the Tribal Zone: Expanding States and Indigenous Warfare,* R. B. Ferguson and N. L. Whitehead, eds.: 1–30. Santa Fe, NM: School of American Research Press.

Ferrill, Archer
1985   "Prehistoric Warfare," in his *The Origins of War,* 9–31. New York: Thames and Hudson.

Fischer, J. L.
1979   *Government Anthropologists in the Trust Territory of Micronesia. The Uses of Anthropology,* W. Goldschmidt, ed.: 238–252. Washington, D.C.: American Anthropological Association Special Publication 11.

Fluehr-Lobban, Carolyn
1991   *Ethics and the Profession of Anthropology: Dialogue for a New Era.* Philadelphia: University of Pennsylvania Press.

Foster, Mary LeCron, and Robert A. Rubinstein, eds.
1986   *Peace and War: Cross-Cultural Perspectives.* New Brunswick, NJ: Transaction Publishers.

Frank, Andre Gunder
1980   Arms Economy and Warfare in the Third World. *Third World Quarterly* 11(2):228–250.

Fried, Morton H., Marvin Harris, and Robert Murphy, eds.
1968   *War: The Anthropology of Armed Conflict and Aggression.* Garden City, New York: Natural History Press.

Gabriel, Richard A.
1990   "The Archaeology of War," in his *The Culture of War: Invention and Early Development,* 19–34. Westport: Greenwood Press.

Galtung, Johan
1968   Peace. *International Encyclopedia of Social Sciences* II:487–496.
1985   Twenty-Five Years of Peace Research: Ten Challenges and Some Responses. *Journal of Peace Research* 22(2):141–158.

Ghiglieri, Michael
1987   War Among the Chimps. *Discover* 8(11):67–76.

Gibson, Thomas
1989   Symbolic Representations of Tranquility and Aggression among the Buid, in *Societies at Peace: Anthropological Perspectives,* S. Howell and R. Willis, eds.: 60–78. New York: Routledge.

Goldschmidt, Walter, ed.
1979   *The Uses of Anthropology.* Washington, D.C.: American Anthropological Association Special Publication 11.

Good, Kenneth, with David Chanoff
1991   *Into the Heart: One Man's Pursuit of Love and Knowledge Among the Yanomami.* New York: Simon and Schuster.

Goodall, Jane
1986   *The Chimpanzees of Gombe: Patterns of Behavior.* Chs. 12, 13, 17. Cambridge: Harvard University Press.

Gordon, Robert
1988   Apartheid's Anthropologists: The Genealogy of Afrikaner Anthropology. *American Ethnologist* 15(3):535–553.

Gowlett, John
1984   *Ascent to Civilization: The Archaeology of Early Man.* New York: Alfred A. Knopf.

Greenhouse, Carol J.
1985   Mediation: A Comparative Approach. *Man* 20(1):90–114.

Gulliver, P. H.
1979   *Disputes and Negotiations: Cross-Cultural Perspectives.* New York: Academic Press.

Halpern, Joel M., ed.
1993   "The Yugoslav Conflict," Special Issue of *The Anthropology of East Europe Review* 11(1–2):3–126.

Headland, Thomas N., ed.
1992   *The Tasaday Controversy: An Assessment of the Evidence.* Washington, D.C.: American Anthropological Association.

Heider, Karl G.
1988   The Rashomon Effect: When Ethnographers Disagree. *American Anthropologist* 90(1):73–81.

Herskovits, Melville J.
1972   *Cultural Relativism: Perspectives in Cultural Pluralism.* New York: Random House.

Hinde, Robert A., and Jo Groebel, eds.
1991   *Cooperation and Prosocial Behaviour.* New York: Cambridge University Press.

Hinsley, Curtis, Jr.
1979   Anthropology as Science and Politics: The Dilemmas of the Bureau of American Ethnology, 1870 to 1904, in *The Uses of Anthropology,* Walter Goldschmidt, ed.: 15–32. Washington, D.C.: American Anthropological Association Special Publication 11.

Homer-Dixon, Thomas F., Jeffrey H. Boutwell, and George W. Rathjens
1993   Environmental Change and Violent Conflict. *Scientific American* 268(2):38–45.

Horowitz, Donald L.
1985   *Ethnic Groups in Conflict.* Berkeley: University of California Press.

Howell, Nancy
1990   Human Hazards of Fieldwork, in her *Surviving Fieldwork:* 89–100. Washington, D.C.: American Anthropological Association Special Publication 26.

Howell, Signe, and Roy Willis, eds.
1989   *Societies at Peace: Anthropological Perspectives.* New York: Routledge.

Hymes, Dell, ed.
1972   *Reinventing Anthropology.* New York: Pantheon Books.

Jell-Bahlsen, S.
1985   Ethnology and Fascism in Germany. *Dialectical Anthropology* 9:337–347.

Kano, Takayoshi
1990   The Bonobo's Peaceable Kingdom. *Natural History* 11:62–71.

Keeley, Lawrence H., and Daniel Cahen
1989   Early Neolithic Forts and Villages in NE Belgium: A Preliminary Report. *Journal of Field Archaeology* 16(2):157–176.

Kemp, G.
1986   Nonviolence: A Biological Perspective, in *A Just Peace Through Transformation: Cultural, Economic, and Political Foundations for Change,* C. Alger and M. Stohl, eds.: 112–126. Boulder: Westview Press.

Kirch, Patrick V.
1984   *The Evolution of Polynesian Chiefdoms.* New York: Cambridge University Press.

Kiste, Robert C.
1974   *The Bikinians: A Study in Forced Migration.* New York: Holt, Rinehart and Winston.

Knauft, Bruce M.
1987   Reconsidering Violence in Simple Human Societies. *Current Anthropology* 28(4):457–500.
1990   Melanesian Warfare: A Theoretical History. *Oceania* 60:250–311.
1991   Violence and Society in Human Evolution. *Current Anthropology* 32(4):391–428.

Koch, Klaus-Friedrich
1974   *War and Peace in Jalemo: The Management of Conflict in Highland New Guinea.* Cambridge: Harvard University Press.

Kohn, Alfie
1990   *The Brighter Side of Human Nature: Altruism and Empathy in Everyday Life.* New York: Basic Books.

Kuper, Leo
1981   *Genocide: Its Political Uses in the Twentieth Century.* New Haven: Yale University Press.

Lackner, Stephan.
1984 *Peaceable Nature: An Optimistic View of Life on Earth.* New York: Harper and Row.

Leighton, Alexander H.
1949 *Human Relations in a Changing World: Observations on the Use of Social Sciences.* New York: E. P. Dutton.

LeVine, Robert A., and Donald T. Campbell
1972 *Ethnocentrism: Theories of Conflict, Ethnic Attitudes, and Group Behavior.* New York: John Wiley & Sons.

Lewellen, Ted C.
1983 The Evolution of the State, in his *Political Anthropology.:* 41–62. South Hadley: Bergin and Garvey.

Lewis, Oscar
1966 The Culture of Poverty. *Scientific American* 215(4):19–25.

Linton, Ralph
1945 *The Science of Man in the World Crisis.* New York: Columbia University Press.

Lizot, Jacques
1985 *Tales of the Yanomami: Daily Life in the Venezuelan Forest.* New York: Cambridge University Press.
1989 Sobre la Guerra: Una Respuesta a N.A. Chagnon (*Science*, 1988). *La Iglesia en Amazonas* 44:23–34.

Mabee, Carleton
1987 Margaret Mead and Behavioral Scientists in World War II: Problems in Responsibility, Truth, and Effectiveness. *Journal of the History of the Behavioral Sciences* 23:3–13.

Mead, Margaret, and Rhoda Metraux
1953 *The Study of Culture at a Distance.* Chicago: University of Chicago Press.

Melko, Matthew
1973 *52 Peaceful Societies.* Oakville, Ontario: Canadian Peace Research Institute.
1984 Peaceful Societies. *World Encyclopedia of Peace,* Ervin Laszol and Jong Youl Yoo, eds.: II:268–270. New York: Pergamon Press.

Messer, Ellen
1993 Anthropology and Human Rights. *Annual Review of Anthropology* 22:221–249.

Miller, Marc S., et al.
1993   *State of the Peoples: A Global Human Rights Report on Societies in Danger.* Boston: Beacon Press.

Milner, George R., Eve Anderson, and Virginia G. Smith
1991   Warfare in Late Prehistoric West-Central Illinois. *American Antiquity* 56(4):581–603.

Mirante, Edith T.
1987   Ethnic Minorities of the Burma Frontiers and Their Resistance Group, in *Southeast Asian Tribal Groups and Ethnic Minorities:* 59–71. Cambridge, MA: Cultural Survival.

Montagu, Ashley
1950   *On Being Human.* New York: Schuman.
1952   *Darwin, Competition, and Cooperation.* New York: Schuman.
1955   *The Direction of Human Development.* New York: Harper.
1964   *Man's Most Dangerous Myth: The Fallacy of Race.* Cleveland: World Publishing.
1972   *Statement on Race.* New York: Oxford University Press.
1976   *The Nature of Human Aggression.* New York: Oxford University Press.

Montagu, Ashley, ed.
1978   *Learning Non-Aggression: The Experience of Non-Literate Societies.* New York: Oxford University Press.
1987   *The Peace of the World.* Tokyo: Kenkyusha.
1989   *Growing Young.* Westport, CT: Bergin & Garvey.

Montagu, Ashley, and Floyd Matson
1983   *The Dehumanization of Man.* New York: McGraw-Hill.

Montville, Joseph V., ed.
1990   *Conflict and Peacemaking in Multiethnic Societies.* New York: Lexington Books.

Morris, C. Patrick, and Robert K. Hitchcock, eds.
1993   *International Human Rights and Indigenous Peoples.* Dubuque: University of Iowa Press (forthcoming).

Moss, Allyn
1963   Anthropologists in World War II, in *Margaret Mead: Shaping a New World:* 151–159. London: Encyclopaedia Britannica Press.

Nelson, Richard K.
1969   *Hunters of the Northern Ice.* Chicago: University of Chicago Press.

Nesbitt, Paul, Alonzo W. Pond, and William H. Allen
1959 *The Survival Book.* New York: Funk and Wagnalls.

Nettleship, Martin, R. Dale Givens, and Anderson Nettleship, eds.
1975 *War, Its Causes and Correlates.* Chicago: Mouton.

Nietschmann, Bernard
1987 The Third World War. *Cultural Survival Quarterly* 11(3):1–15.

Nordstrom, Carolyn, and Joann Martin, eds.
1992 *The Paths to Terror: Domination, Resistance, and Communal Violence.* Berkeley: University of California Press.

Oliver, Douglas L.
1989 Warfare and Killing, in his *Oceania: The Native Cultures of Australia and the Pacific Islands.* 423–500. Honolulu: University of Hawaii Press.

Otterbein, Keith F.
1973 The Anthropology of War, in *Handbook of Social and Cultural Anthropology,* John J. Honigmann, ed.: 923–958. Chicago: Rand McNally.
1985 *The Evolution of War: Cross-Cultural Study.* New Haven: Human Relations Area Files.
1993 *Feuding and Warfare: Selected Works of Keith F. Otterbein.* New York: Gordon and Breach.

Overing, Joanna
1989 Styles of Manhood: An Amazonian Contrast in Tranquility and Violence, in *Societies at Peace: Anthropological Perspectives,* S. Howell and R. Willis, eds.: 79–99. New York: Routledge.

Paine, R., ed.
1985 *Advocacy and Anthropology.* St. John's, Newfoundland: Institute of Social and Economic Research, Memorial University of Newfoundland.

Palmer, Stuart
1965 Murder and Suicide in Forty Non-Literate Societies. *Journal of Criminal Law, Criminology, and Police Science* 56:320–324.
1972 *The Violent Society.* New Haven: College and University Press Publishers.

Pandian, Jacob
1985 *Anthropology and the Western Tradition: Toward an Authentic Anthropology.* Prospect Heights, IL: Waveland Press.

Paynter, Robert
1989 The Archaeology of Equality and Inequality. *Annual Review of Anthropology* 18:369–399.

Podolefsky, Aaron
1990   Mediator Roles in Simbu Conflict Management. *Ethnology* XXIX(1):67–81.

Ramos, Alcida
1987   Reflecting on the Yanomami: Ethnographic Images and the Pursuit of the Exotic. *Cultural Anthropology* 2(3):284–304.

Riches, David, ed.
1986   *The Anthropology of Violence.* New York: Basil Blackwell.

Robarchek, Clayton A., and C. J. Robarchek
1989   The Waorani: From Warfare to Peacefulness. *The World and I* 4(1):625–635.
1992   Cultures of War and Peace: A Comparative Study of the Waorani and Semai, in *Aggression and Peacefulness in Humans and Other Primates,* James Silverberg and J. Patrick Gray, eds.: 189–213. New York: Oxford University Press.

Rodman, Margaret, and Matthew Cooper, eds.
1979   *The Pacification of Melanesia.* Ann Arbor: University of Michigan.

Roosevelt, Grace G.
1990   *Reading Rousseau in the Nuclear Age.* Philadelphia: Temple University Press.

Roper, Marilyn Keyes
1969   A Survey of the Evidence for Intrahuman Killing in the Pleistocene. *Current Anthropology* 10(4):427–458.
1975   Evidence of Warfare in the Near East from 10,000–4,300 B.C., in *War: Its Causes and Correlates,* Martin A. Nettleship, et al., eds.: 299–343. The Hague: Mouton Publishers.

Ross, Marc Howard
1993a   *The Culture of Conflict: Interpretations and Interests in Comparative Perspective.* New Haven: Yale University Press.
1993b   *The Management of Conflict: Interpretations and Interests in Comparative Perspective.* New Haven: Yale University Press.

Rubinstein, Robert A., and Mary LeCron Foster, eds.
1988a   *The Social Dynamics of Peace and Conflict: Culture in International Security.* Boulder: Westview Press.
1988b   *Directory of Anthropologists Working on Topics of Peace, International Security, and Conflict Resolution.* Gainesville, FL: Commission on the Study of Peace, International Union of Anthropological and Ethnological Sciences.

Saul, John Ralston
1987   The War Business. *World Press Review* 34(6):19–21.

Scheffler, Harold
1964   The Social Consequences of Peace on Choiseul Island. *Ethnology*
3:398–403.

Service, Elman R.
1985   The Origins of Government, in his *A Century of Controversy:
Ethnological Issues from 1860 to 1960:* 173–199. New York: Academic
Press.

Shook, E. Victoria
1992   *Ho'oponopono: Contemporary Uses of a Hawaiian Problem-Solving
Process.* Honolulu: University of Hawaii Press.

Silverberg, James, and J. Patrick Gray, eds.
1992   *Aggression and Peacefulness in Humans and Other Primates.* New
York: Oxford University Press.

Sipes, Richard
1973   War, Sports, and Aggression: An Empirical Test of Two Rival Theories.
American Anthropologist 75(1):64–82.

Sluka, Jeffrey A.
1990   Participant Observation in Violent Social Contexts. *Human
Organization* 49(2):114–126.

Smithsonian
1942–1945 *War Background Studies* 1–21. Washington, D.C.: Smithsonian
Institution.

Smole, William J.
1976   *The Yanomama Indians: A Cultural Geography.* Austin, TX: University
of Texas Press.

Smuts, Barbara
1985   *Sex and Friendship in Baboons.* New York: Aldine de Gruyter.
1987   What Are Friends For? *Natural History* 6(2):36–45.
1989   Primate Detente. *Natural History* 4:91–95.

Sponsel, Leslie E.
1989   An Anthropologist's Perspective on Peace and Quality of Life, in *Peace
and Development: An Interdisciplinary Perspective,* D. S. Sanders and J.
Matsuoka, eds.: 29–48. Honolulu: University of Hawaii School of Social
Work.
1990a   Ultraprimitive Pacifists: The Tasaday as a Symbol of Peace.
Anthropology Today 6(1):3–5.
1990b   The Mutual Relevance of Anthropology and Peace Studies. *Human
Peace Quarterly* 7(3–4):3–9.

1992   Our Fascination with the Tasaday: Anthropological Images and Images of Anthropology, in *The Tasaday Controversy: An Assessment of the Evidence,* Thomas N. Headland, ed.: 200–212. Washington, D.C.: American Anthropological Association.

1993a   The Natural History of Peace: Anthropological Explorations, in *Peace Systems.* T. A. Gregor, ed. (forthcoming).

1993b   Book Review: "Societies at Peace: Anthropological Perspectives," S. Howell and R. Willis, eds. *American Ethnologist* 20(2):396–397.

Starn, Orin
    1986   Engineering Internment: Anthropologists and the War Relocation Authority. *American Ethnologist* 13(4):700–720.

Staub, Ervin
    1989   *The Roots of Evil: The Origins of Genocide and Other Group Violence.* New York: Cambridge University Press.

Stauder, J.
    1974   The "Relevance" of Anthropology to Colonialism and Imperialism. *Radical Science Journal* 1:51–70.

Stephenson, Carolyn M.
    1989   The Evolution of Peace Studies, in *Peace and World Order Studies: A Curriculum Guide,* D. C. Thomas and M. T. Klare, eds.: 9–19. Boulder: Westview Press.

Stevenson, Leslie
    1987   *Seven Theories of Human Nature.* New York: Oxford University Press.

Strum, Shirley
    1985   Baboons May Be Smarter Than People. *Animal Kingdom* 88(2):12–15.

Strum, S., and Bruno Latour
    1987   Redefining the Social Link from Baboons to Humans. *Social Science Information* 26(4):783–802.

Suzuki, Peter
    1980   A Retrospective Analysis of a Wartime "National Character" Study. *Dialectical Anthropology* 5:33–46.
    1981   Anthropologists in the Wartime Camps for Japanese Americans: A Documentary Study. *Dialectical Anthropology* 6:23–60.

Tambiah, S. J.
    1989   Ethnic Conflict in the World Today. *American Ethnologist* 16(2):335–349.

Tax, Sol
  1956   The Integration of Anthropology, in *Current Anthropology*, W. L. Thomas, ed.: 313–328. Chicago: University of Chicago Press.

Textor, Robert B., ed.
  1991   The Peace Dividend As a Cultural Concept: Anticipating the Possible Benefits to American Life from the Human Effort Released By the End of the Cold War. *Human Peace Quarterly* 9(1–3):1–54.

Thomas, Daniel C., and Michael T. Klare, eds.
  1989   *Peace and World Order Studies: A Curriculum Guide* (fifth edition). Boulder: Westview.

Tishkov, Valery A.
  1992   The Crisis in Soviet Ethnography. *Current Anthropology* 33(4):371–394.

Turnbull, Colin M.
  1972   *The Mountain People*. New York: Simon and Schuster.

Turner, Paul R., and David Pitts, eds.
  1986   *The Anthropology of War and Peace: Perspectives on the Nuclear Age.* Granby, MA: Bergin and Garvey.

Turner, Victor
  1957   *The Forest of Symbols: Aspects of Ndembu Ritual.* Ithaca, NY: Cornell University Press.

UNESCO
  1984   *World Directory of Peace Research Institutions.* Paris: UNESCO.
  1986   *Statement on Violence.* Seville: UNESCO.

Vencl, Sl.
  1984   War and Warfare in Archaeology. *Journal of Anthropological Archaeology* 3:116–132.

de Waal, Frans B. M.
  1982   *Chimpanzee Politics: Power and Sex Among Apes.* New York: Harper and Row.
  1986   Conflict Resolution in Monkeys and Apes, in *Primates: The Road to Self-Sustaining Populations,* K. Benirschke, ed.: 341–350. New York: Springer-Verlag.
  1989   *Peacemaking Among Primates.* Cambridge: Harvard University Press.

Wakin, Eric
  1992   *Anthropology Goes to War: Professional Ethics and Counterinsurgency in Thailand.* Madison: University of Wisconsin Press.

Washburn, Wilcomb E.
    1987   Cultural Relativism, Human Rights, and the AAA. *American Anthropologist* 89:939–943.

Wax, Rosalie
    1971   Fieldwork in Japanese American Relocation Centers 1943–45, in her *Doing Fieldwork: Warnings and Advice:* 59–174. Chicago: University of Chicago Press.

Webster, David L.
    1977   Warfare and the Evolution of Maya Civilization, in *The Origins of Maya Civilization*, R. E. W. Adams, ed.: 335–372. Albuquerque: University of New Mexico Press.

White, Geoffrey M., and Lamont Lindstrom, eds.
    1989   *The Pacific Theater: Island Representations of World War II*. Honolulu: University of Hawaii Press.

Wiberg, Hakan
    1981   JPR 1964–1980—What Have We Learned About Peace? *Journal of Peace Research* XVIII(2):111–148.

van Willigen, John
    1980   *Anthropology in Use: A Bibliographic Chronology of the Development of Applied Anthropology*. Pleasantville, NY: Redgrove Publishing.

Willis, Roy
    1989   The "Peace Puzzle" in Ufipa, in *Societies at Peace: Anthropological Perspectives*, S. Howell and R. Willis, eds.: 133–145. New York: Routledge.

Wolf, Eric R.
    1987   Cycles of Violence: The Anthropology of War and Peace, in *Waymarks: The Notre Dame Inaugural Lectures in Anthropology*, Kenneth Moore, ed.: 127–150. Notre Dame: University of Notre Dame Press.

de Wolf, Jan J.
    1992   Ethnology in the Third Reich. *Current Anthropology* 33(4):473–475.

World Archaeology
    1986   "Weaponry and Warfare," in *World Archaeology* 18(2).

World Press
    1992   "Arms Sales," in *World Press,* September, 39(9):13–18.

Worsley, Peter M.
    1985   Proposals for Anthropology in a Nuclear Age. *Current Anthropology* 27:283–284.

Worsley, Peter M., and Kofi Buenor Hadjor, eds.
1987　*On the Brink: Nuclear Proliferation and the Third World.* London: Third World Communications.

Wright, H.
1977　Recent Research on the Origin of the State. *Annual Review of Anthropology* 6:379–397.

Wright, Quincy
1942　*A Study of War.* Chicago: University of Chicago Press.

Wright, Robin
1988　Anthropological Presuppositions of Indigenous Advocacy. *Annual Review of Anthropology* 17:365–426.

✦ 2

Culture and Cooperation in Human Evolution

Bruce M. Knauft

The dominant perspective in the social sciences is what may be called a conflict model. Following Marx, class antagonism is the engine of history. For those with a biological perspective, competition and struggle explain the evolutionary success of species and human institutions. For Freudians, the clash of conflicting emotions underlies both neurosis and normal behavior. There is an opposing tendency in the social sciences, however; one that looks primarily at the *prosocial* capacity of humans to interact cooperatively. Petr Kropotkin's *Mutual Aid,* published some ninety years ago, began this perspective in anthropology. It is a tradition continued by Bruce Knauft in a sophisticated statement of the importance of affiliative behavior. Knauft maintains that the emergence of human culture, with its elaborate patterns of communication, food sharing, and sexuality, created distinctive evolutionary potentials for prosocial behavior. Whereas the individual is the primary unit of selection among animals, humans have the additional capacity for favoring behaviors that benefit the group as a whole. Knauft supports this notion, which opens an important new chapter in the study of human evolution, with data from contemporary hunters and foragers.

—THE EDITORS

✦   For decades and indeed centuries, much has been written about the competing roles of social cooperation and competitive self-interest in human evolution (see Ingold 1986; Stephenson 1990: 7). Even in the Victorian era, the social Darwinism that spread in the wake of *The Descent of Man* (Darwin 1871) was countered by works such as Kropotkin's *Mutual Aid: A Factor in Evolution* (1902; see Gould 1988; cf. Vucinich 1988: ch. 10). In the 1910s, 1920s, and 1930s, the Darwinian legacy went into decline in anthropology, running aground on the speculative excesses of evolutionary and diffusionist reconstruction. The major founding figure of early U.S. anthropology, Franz Boas, was particularly strong and effective in criticizing such excesses by suggesting that the rich local variability of human cultures defied reductionism. For the middle third of the twentieth century, the cultural view of human origins thus frequently deemphasized competition in favor of more prosocial dimensions of behavior, as reflected in Levi-Strauss's (1949) emphasis on primal structures of alliance through kinship, White's emphasis (1949) on the evolutionary importance of human symbolic capacities, and Geertz's (1962) influential essays on the collective nature of culture and the evolution of mind.

Competing perspectives arose more strongly, however, by the 1960s, exemplified in major popular books such as Ardrey's *Territorial Imperative* (1966) and Lorenz's *On Aggression* (1966), which emphasized competitive and aggressive dimensions of a presumed human nature. These rather Hobbesian leanings were countered by an emphasis on cooperative and prosocial dimensions of social interaction in books such as Ashley Montagu's *Learning Non-Aggression* (1978) and *The Nature of Human Aggression* (1976). More recently, there have also been popular rebuttals, such as Lackner's *Peaceable Nature* (1984) and Kohn's *No Contest* (1986) and *The Brighter Side of Human Nature* (1990).

Such works notwithstanding, prosocial and group-cooperative perspectives on human evolutionary theory have diminished sharply in the scholarship of recent decades. This trend was galvanized by Williams' (1966) trenchant critique of group selection and the practical problems of establishing early humans as an exception to his generalizations. By contrast, dominant anthropological approaches to the study of aggression and cooperation in human evolution have been neo-Darwinian, including sociobiology and behavioral ecology. Though having many different dimensions, these perspectives assume that the individual is a self-interested unit of reproductive fitness maximization. In this view, the obvious cooperative features of human behavior are reasoned to arise not directly or altruistically but indirectly through individual self-interest; for instance, as aid to biogenetic relatives (maximizing inclusive fitness; e.g., Hamilton 1964), or as the rational result of competitive self-interest within an interacting social group (reciprocal altruism; see Trivers 1985; Axelrod 1984; cf. Alexander 1988). At the same time, neo-Darwinian perspectives tend to see the violent or aggressive dimensions of social behavior as direct if not natural expressions of competitive self-interest, arising particularly from male competition over access to mates, either within or between groups. This is reflected in works such as Betzig's *Despotism and Differential Reproduction* (1986), in Chagnon's (1988: 985) assessment that violence may be "the principal driving force behind the evolution of culture," and Wrangham's (1987: 68) suggestion that the common ancestor of humans likely had "closed social networks" and "hostile and male-dominated intergroup relations with stalk-and-attack interactions." Such assessments stand in contrast to earlier interpretations such as that by the late Glynn Isaac (1978, 1984) concerning hominid collective affiliation, and selected ethnographic studies on the significance of intense sociality in simple human societies (e.g., Ingold 1987; Testart 1985; cf. Lee and DeVore 1984).

The present perspective does not deny the impetus of biogenetic fitness motivations, nor the tension between group-cooperative processes and the potential manipulation of cultural beliefs as ideology for individualistic ends. The biased weight of neo-Darwinian emphasis, however, behooves us to foreground the real and neglected impact of cultural collectivity in human evolution. This is an important first step toward a more balanced assessment of biogenetic-symbolic interactions in human evolution.

The present approach is consistent with a body of recent work by a growing number of researchers who question the reliance on neo-Darwinian assumptions in the study of human social development and evolution. These analyses are based on a diverse array of evidence from evolutionary theory, ethnography, experimental psychology, and theoretical biology (e.g., Knauft 1987a,b, 1991, 1993: ch. 8; Edgerton 1992; Fialkowski 1990; Moore 1990; Ross 1991; Vining 1986; Caporael et al. 1989; Boyd and Richerson 1985; Kitcher 1985; see Wilson and Sober 1993). From ethnography and demography, queries are raised by the existence of behavior patterns in both state-level and pre-state societies that systematically compromise, rather than maximize, the reproductive success and inclusive fitness of perpetrating actors, thus contravening sociobiological principles. In social psychology, sociobiological assumptions have been questioned on the basis of experiments that document the existence of altruistic tendencies toward strangers in the absence of rationally-expected pay-offs (e.g., Caporael et al. 1989). And from theoretical biology, discontent is informed by increasing realization that the conditions under which self-interested reciprocal altruism can explain social cooperation are more restrictive than previously thought, begging the possibility of supplementary evolutionary processes (such as cultural transmission) that may operate through nonbiogenetic and/or nonindividualistic selection parameters (e.g., Boyd and Richerson 1985; Boyd and Richerson 1988; Boyd and Lorberbaum 1987; Richerson and Boyd 1989; Harpending and Rogers 1987; Durham 1991; Nowak and Sigmund 1989). Wilson and Sober's (1993, cf. 1989; Wilson 1989) recent comprehensive review suggests that the notion of group selection should be strongly reintroduced in the evolutionary study of human behavior. In any event, it seems inappropriate to focus narrowly on the individual or the gene as the unit of fitness maximization and to exclude all systemic levels above that of the organism (or below that of the gene).

In the perspective presently adopted, the oft-presumed isomorphism between cultural and biogenetic pressures is more aptly viewed as a dynamic tension between a primate legacy of individual maximization (e.g., for food and sex) and symbolic processes that subvert this tendency in the interests of group-collective cultural propagation and social coherence (see Boehm 1989; Paul 1987). To consider only the individualistic half of this process in evolutionary scenarios both dehumanizes and obscures the full dynamics of human evolutionary development.

✦ Evolution and Simple Human Societies

It is the argument of this chapter that culture, as the symbolically encoded dimension of social life, has exerted a crucial influence in the evolution of *Homo,* and that this influence has been pronounced in simple society features such as widespread and complex linguistic communication, diffuse rule-of-thumb sharing of food and other items (beyond the parameters of inclusive fitness and reciprocal altruism), and normative rules for governing sexual behavior.

To take seriously the capacities of culture and its progenitors in human evolution requires consideration of observational data—ethnography—from contemporary, simple societies of humans. (Many dimensions of culturally informed behavior do not survive easily or predictably in the archeological record.) These data cannot be viewed uncritically, as virtually all contemporary hunter-gatherers have been influenced by trade and other forms of interaction with "tribal" or state societies, often for quite long periods of time (Headland and Reid 1989; Schrire 1984; Wilmsen 1989; cf. Myers 1988; see Solway and Lee 1990). The growing tendency to omit consideration of hunter-gatherer ethnography in evolutionary analyses seems unnecessary and unwise, however: to neglect the significance of twentieth-century observations of nonintensive foragers because such societies are not "pristine" forgoes crucial information relevant to evolutionary modelling; viz., the influence of human culture. What is needed is to use such ethnographic data critically, being mindful of the historical context in which they have been collected (e.g., O'Connell et al. 1988a,b). In the present case, the general trajectory of historical changes suggests that the patterns presently discussed were if anything more, rather than less, pronounced among simple human societies in the past.

Few would dispute that the following features do indeed distinguish simple human societies from free-ranging nonhuman primates:

- Widespread symbolic communication through language
- Highly developed cooperation in and social coordination of subsistence activities beyond the range of close biogenetic kin
- Diffuse sharing of food and information
- Rule-governed control of sexuality; for instance, in marriage rules, rights, and obligations.[1]

To these features may be added those particularly characteristic of human societies subsisting with dispersed, nonintensive foraging strategies in the absence of animal domesticates:

- Equal access to the means of material production
- General lack of territoriality

My present focus is on those human societies that are socioecological-ly nonintensive/noncomplex and that are "simple" and "egalitarian," i.e., lacking recognizable male leadership roles and lacking regularized delayed economic compensation, such as brideprice or evidence of amassed materi-al wealth (see Knauft 1991). This excludes complex hunter-gatherers and also societies with great reliance on animal domesticates and those relying intensively on riverine or maritime resources. These more evolutionarily recent subsistence adaptations often permitted sedentary residence and for-malized male status differentials or political ranking.[2]

The present focus is thus on those human societies least subject to intensification and centralization in terms of subsistence, residence, demography, and political economy. It is a quite reasonable hypothesis, as suggested further below, that the most prominent features of sociocultural collectivity evident in these societies could have been evident among sim-ple/nonintensive *Homo sapiens* foraging populations from 100,000 years before the present (B.P.) and perhaps among populations of *Homo erectus,* which date to as early as 1.6 million years B.P., until the rise of "complex" hunter-gatherers (beginning about 15,000 B.P.).

✦ Reforming Current Paradigms

Group-cooperative features such as widespread information transfer, dif-fuse sharing of food and other resources, and normative rule-governed con-straints on sexual behavior tend to be neglected if not explicitly omitted from consideration in existing general theories of human evolution. Correspondingly, the affiliative and cooperative dimensions of humanity that are learned through cultural transmission are eschewed by neo-Darwinian perspectives in favor of more individualistic factors. This Hobbesian bias subtly and importantly influences perception of which fea-tures are important in the early trajectory of human development. A reveal-ing illustration of this tendency can be taken from Robert Foley's important book, *Another Unique Species* (1987). Foley provides an excellent synthe-sis of human evolution from a behavioral-ecological perspective, coordi-nating a plethora of data concerning ecological and anatomical stressors, paleoenvironmental trends, predisposing patterns of mammalian and pri-mate evolution, and specific features of hominid anatomic and behavioral adaptation. What is left out of Foley's account—quite explicitly—is con-sideration of human culture:

> Is culture . . . a particularly useful concept in the study of human origins?
> I would argue that it is not. . . . When looked at separately, many of the
> features of human culture can be found in at least rudimentary form in
> non-human animals. . . . Use of the term culture in paleoanthropology

obscures this continuity. In investigating the origins of modern human behaviour it is far more productive to adopt a reductionist approach to deal with the minimalist categories of behaviour, and not to assume, through the use of the term culture, . . . that we are dealing with something different. (Foley 1987:4–5)

Foley's perspective focuses exclusively on the aggregate outcome of individualistic selection pressures but excludes *a priori* the symbolically encoded collective dimension of human society. Reduced to self-interested units of fitness maximization, humans can be only the embodiment of environmentally mediated reproductive competition.

Arguably, however, human culture is revolutionary in compromising if not contravening the imperatives of individualistic Darwinian selection. Boyd and Richerson (1985) have shown that, if imitative learning is strongly selected as a rule-of thumb adaptive strategy (as was likely among early humans—a species highly altricial in infancy and extremely dependent upon socialization), behavioral alterations can spread through imitation and learning at a very fast rate. Added to this, and in causal concert with it, was the highly developed ability of humans to communicate through elaborate symbolic means, the evolution of which is discussed further below. Such features were in all likelihood strongly selected for in *Homo* as a genus highly dependent upon socialization and on information transfer and cooperative action between groups of conspecifics in exploitation of dispersed and patchy resources and in protection against predators (e.g., Kurland and Beckerman 1985). Though the early generalizations on these issues by Isaac (1978, 1984) may not be applicable to all hominids, they remain quite likely applicable to the genus *Homo* and particularly to *H. sapiens.*

Through socialization and symbolic communication, behavioral traits can be learned and spread through cultural transmission at a faster rate than they can be eradicated through standard biogenetic selection. This allows the potential for maladaptive customs temporarily spreading in a human population; but it also allows for the spread of behaviors that can favor the sociocultural group at the relative expense of a given individual's biogenetic propagation (contrast Hamilton 1964). With the rise of extensive symbolic transmission—itself initially selected through standard Darwinian selection—group selection and genuine altruism thus become empirically possible.[3]

It is thus plausible, and indeed likely, that biogenetic selection gave rise to cultural transmission processes that once begun became partially decoupled from standard biogenetic selection. This does not condemn humans to biogenetic dysfunctionality; it simply adds the cultural group to the individual as a separate and competing unit of selection through a different means of phenotypic alteration. As part of this process, the environment to which humans subsequently "adapted" was increasingly a social and cultural one—a cultural world in which symbolic potentials and constraints were important influences on behavior (see Geertz 1973: chs. 2, 3).

In the same way that the individual has been suggested in a neo-Darwinian perspective to be a gene's way of producing another gene (e.g., Dawkins 1976), so, too, an individual in a human cultural environment is to a certain extent a culture's means of reproducing and spreading a given set of symbols—of propagating a collective symbolic system. What results is complex coevolution of distinct behavioral transmission and selection systems—one symbolic, the other biogenetic.

This is not to argue that symbolic/cultural evolution negates or denies the parallel reality of biogenetic processes: patterns of cultural transmission have undoubtedly been in complex coevolution with genetic ones over the long course of human development (cf. Richerson and Boyd 1989; Durham 1991). Though the increased speed and elaboration of cultural selection processes can render their effects especially influential, the tension between them and biogenetic selection is never eradicated. Even the possibility—not to mention the importance—of culture in this coevolutionary process is excluded in most current neo-Darwinian models of human evolution.

I shall illustrate my argument in a more positive and specific way by selectively assessing three factors crucial in human evolution: communication, food-sharing, and sexuality. For each, the evolutionary significance of affiliative cooperation will be assessed.

✦ Communication

Elaborate communication through verbal symbolization is quite likely to have been a major adaptive advantage among *Homo,* ultimately instantiated as human language as we presently know it (Goodenough 1990). Two of the key features of language are that it is learned extragenetically and that it is productive or open in its recombinations; another is the displaced and largely arbitrary relationship between linguistic signifiers and their signifieds (Hockett and Ascher 1964). These properties give language a unique potential for extremely elaborate and widespread communication.

The topic of linguistic origin and development is often neglected in scenarios of hominid and human development or deferred until quite late in the evolutionary chronology.[4] This is unfortunate because the revolutionary nature of human symbolic communication can easily be viewed in conjunction with processes of natural selection during the early evolution of *H. sapiens* and perhaps *H. erectus.* Kurland and Beckerman (1985) have argued that there is a strong selective advantage to sharing information when resources are dispersed and patchy, as they are for most nonintensive foragers. Aiello and Dunbar (1993) have recently reported a robust and important correlation among primates between neocortex size and group size. Projected into our evolutionary past, these factors suggest that large group size and increasing importance of prosocial affiliation were a decisive selective force in the evolution of human language. This trend is consistent with the large home range associated with *Homo* (Foley 1987).

The importance of linguistic communication in human evolution is underscored when juxtaposed against recent suggestions that full language ability as we presently know it may not have arisen until the Upper Paleolithic and the general preponderance of anatomically modern humans (*H. sapiens sapiens*) at 35,000–45,000 B.P. (e.g., Mellars and Stringer 1989; Lieberman 1984; Davidson and Noble 1989; Noble and Davidson 1991; Binford 1989). Even neglecting competing points of view and the origin of anatomically modern humans prior to 100,000 B.P. (Mellars 1988, 1989; Aiello 1993), it seems very likely that complex forms of protolanguage facilitated if not enabled the remarkable development and spread of humans since the time of archaic *H. sapiens* and perhaps since *H. erectus*.[5]

Clear evidence exists for some form of complex symbolic capacity and corresponding behavior at least as far back as *H. erectus,* including fire-hardened hardwood digging sticks, post holes, ocher crayons, and huge amounts of ocher powder in association with Acheulian finds, some dated to several hundred thousand years B.P. (Marshack 1985, 1989a,b). Beads, animal-bone pendants, and other elaborate decorative items have been found from later Mousterian assemblages (e.g., R. White 1989).

Bickerton (1990) has convincingly suggested that complex protolanguage was characteristic of *H. erectus* and that a form of syntactic language was characteristic of *H. sapiens.* The linguistic system of archaic *H. sapiens* if not *H. erectus* may well have included displacement and productivity but lacked full duality of patterning and its accompanying further increase of linguistic referents (Knauft 1991: 398; cf. Parker 1985: 624f.; Parker and Gibson 1979; see Hockett and Ascher 1964). The existence of complex but not-fully-modern protolanguage is consistent with trends generally characteristic of *Homo* such as increased encephalization, increased subsistence flexibility, greatly increased home-range size, and habitation dispersal to nontropical ecozones (Foley 1987; see Aiello and Dunbar 1993).

Protolanguage is also consistent with the complex but relatively standardized toolkit of archaic *H. sapiens* and perhaps *H. erectus;* viz., disk-core Mousterian and perhaps Acheulian technologies that lacked the "second order" objectification of tools such as burins; i.e., tools themselves used to make a myriad of different tools. Conceptually analogous, protolanguage that is complex but lacks duality of patterning omits the second order of internalized linguistic productivity that allows the making of new words through the recombination of existing word-making sounds, and hence the ability greatly to proliferate linguistic referents (cf. Tomasello n.d.). Language could hardly have arisen full-blown, and the cultural features that both allow and reflect complex verbal-symbolic communication would have predated Upper Paleolithic developments. These in all likelihood facilitated the remarkable spread of prehistoric humans to nontropical ecozones.

Significantly, the success of information-sharing for resource exploitation depends on at least a general predisposition to accept the accuracy of referential displacements; i.e., to trust the spoken word. This predisposition would have been crucial to facilitate the diffuse sharing of environmental information that is central to survival among nonintensive foragers. This same capability was quite likely a key element of interspecies advantage among *Homo* generally, facilitating great flexibility and cooperation in resource utilization and permitting the exploitation of extraordinarily large home ranges (Parker 1985: 624f; cf. Foley 1987: 138–141). Common agreement as to lexical meaning both enables and reflects the tremendous power of referents to link individuals in widespread communicative and affiliative networks—networks that stretch well beyond the compass of biogenetic kin. Even the well-known capacity that language affords for lying and deception presupposes a baseline of linguistic referential agreement.[6]

Of additional importance among *H. sapiens* and perhaps *H. erectus* was the advent of religion and the promulgation of religious belief through ritual; e.g., to combat the potential for lying and deception. Ritual has been reliably inferred at least as early as the flower-decorated burials of the Shanidar Neanderthals, 46,000–60,000 B.P. (Solecki 1971; Trinkaus 1983). Red ocher "decoration" has been suggested in conjunction with *H. erectus* at 250,000–300,000 B.P. (Wreschner 1981; Marshack 1981; cf. 1989b). As shown by Rappaport (1971a,b, 1979), human ritual is distinguished from the stereotypic behavior-sequencing of animals in that it *sanctifies* certain beliefs and propositions. As such, ritual reinforces and puts beyond argument or question certain highly general propositions about the spiritual and human world. Correspondingly, through social action as well as autocommunication, ritual activity predisposes deep-seated cognitive acceptance and behavioral compliance with these cosmological propositions.

In terms of our present perspective, religion and ritual are particularly important because they emphasize—in a myriad of culturally specific forms—moral obligations that constrain the individual to the dictates of larger social objectives and spiritual values. The pragmatic social result of these mandates is often if not typically to promulgate group-level goals over and against more immediate and individualistic self-interest. This is not to argue that self-interest is absent from human evolution nor that social and religious norms cannot be contravened; self-interest remains in common if not in constant tension with group-level goals and constraints. The present point, however, is that group-collective beliefs and constraints have long exerted an important influence on both human behavior and on the cognition and motivation that predispose it. Among humans, internalization of values that propagate group-level interests is not only possible but crucial to human societal functioning and survival, as Durkheim (1912) long ago suggested.

✦ Food-Sharing

Cooperative food-sharing outside of mother-infant provisioning is rare in the primate world. Even the reports of chimpanzee meat-sharing—so prominent a few years ago—have been increasingly recontextualized by the weight of accumulated data. As summarized in Goodall's recent scholarly compendium (1986: 299–300), meat is "highly coveted" by chimpanzees: "There is intense aggressive competition around a kill. This aggression comprises (a) attacks on possessors of meat by those who have none, (b) attacks or, more usually, displays or threats by possessors . . . [and] (c) attacks or threats directed by those who have not managed to acquire portions." Though studies have documented some tendency toward turn-taking in chimpanzee sharing under special experimental conditions (e.g., de Waal 1989), and though common and pygmy chimpanzees may be "preadapted" to the possibility of general food-sharing (Itani 1988), the vast majority of this sharing is best characterized as "tolerated scrounging" or, to use primatological parlance, "food taking bouts" (FTBs) (see Kuroda 1984). There is little evidence that nonhuman primates actively initiate sharing of valued resources in the wild, excepting only the provisioning of infants by their mothers.

The behavior of great apes contrasts dramatically with the culturally mandated sharing of large-animal meat that is a hallmark of nonintensive human foragers and that has been documented with exceptional consistency among hunter-gatherers from different world areas (Testart 1985, 1987). This sharing takes place well outside the range of nuclear or close biogenetic kin. Ethnographers have consistently emphasized the social and symbolic, as well as ecological, importance of such sharing; diffuse distribution of major food items (and other items of value) is a prominent if not preeminent tenet of cultural propriety in simple human societies (e.g., [on the !Kung] Marshall 1979, Wiessner 1982; [Mbuti net-hunters] Turnbull 1961, 1965a,b; [Mbuti archers/spearmen] Harako 1976: 76–79; [central Eskimo or Inuit] Balikci 1970: chs. 5–6; [Eskimo] Guemple 1972, Damas 1984; [Guayaki] Clastres 1972; [Ache] Kaplan and Hill 1985a, Kaplan, et al. 1984).

More generally, simple human societies are renowned for the variety of affiliative relationships that link constituents in extensive social support networks, in addition to those predicated on intermarriage (discussed further below). These include trade-partnerships, namesake relations, ritual/totemic affiliations, and fictive kinship. Sharing is also facilitated by residential flexibility and bilateral group cooperation among many foragers—this being particularly true for nonintensive and noncomplex foragers rather than "complex" hunter-gatherers and those employing equestrian/animal domesticate adaptations (Woodburn 1972, 1984; Lee 1979b: chs. 5–6; Turnbull 1984; Meggitt 1962; Yengoyan 1984; Damas 1984; Balikci 1970: chs. 3–5; contrast Price and Brown 1985; Ember 1978).

Stating that widespread social support networks are culturally constituted is not to suggest that human sharing of meat, information, and other items is devoid of natural selection significance. Sharing is economically advantageous, even on an individual level, when rich but unpredictably procured food sources such as large game supply more meat than a single individual can effectively procure, consume, or store (Kaplan and Hill 1985a). However, it is the distinctively cultural norms of cooperation and propriety that explain why, in these societies, meat is shared so completely and diffusely and why gift-giving is so normatively structured. This is particularly true of mandated meat-giving to affines, who often have little biogenetic relationship to the hunter and who are commonly not bound to equal reciprocity (Testart 1985, 1987, 1988; contrast Trivers 1971; see Boyd and Lorberbaum 1987; Boyd and Richerson 1988). In some cases, the hunter himself gets less than a proportional share, or even none, of the prize.

Along the lines of Sahlins' (1972) general model, simple human societies place great emphasis on generalized reciprocity and far less on balanced competition or negative reciprocity. Concomitantly, ethnocentrism and collective military action or warfare tend to be rudimentary or absent in simple human societies (Knauft 1987a, 1991). This contrasts in aggregate terms with more complex, sedentary, food-producing societies, among which subsistence and demographic intensification are associated with increasing property ownership and status inequality, and increasingly competitive politicoeconomic and military rivalry (e.g., Johnson and Earle 1987; Carneiro 1970, 1981; Fried 1967; Upham 1990). Among simple human societies, by contrast, norms of egalitarian status-leveling are particularly strong and unrelenting; self-aggrandizing behavior tends to be strongly devalued; and direct competition and coercive behavior among men is considered improper (see [on the !Kung] Draper 1978, Marshall 1976, and Lee 1979b; [Mbuti] Turnbull 1961, 1965a,b, 1978; [Hadza] Woodburn 1979; [Inuit] Briggs 1970, 1978 and Damas 1984). Many of these societies exhibit what Boehm (1993) has appropriately called a "reverse dominance hierarchy" that actively inhibits the development of leadership dominance. Correspondingly, leadership positions tend to be rudimentary and unformalized in these societies.

✦ Historical Trends

The gradual displacement of this "simple society" pattern through economic intensification and political centralization—concomitant with increasing food production and sedentization—brings to focus the question of historical change: How can cultural models drawn from twentieth-century hunter-gatherers be used to infer characteristics of prehistoric *Homo?* Recent critiques have emphasized that hunter-gatherer ethnography does not capture a timeless ancestral past (Schrire 1984; Headland and Reid 1989; cf. Myers 1988). The general trend of historical changes, however, is to decrease, rather than increase, the features of nonintensive foragers that are presently of concern. Leadership and residential centralization, individualistic property ownership, and status-rivalry competition tend to increase as foragers are impacted by the trade networks and political status differentiation of horticultural and state societies (e.g., Cashdan 1980, 1983, 1986; Hitchcock 1987; cf. classic analysis by Murphy and Steward 1955). Conversely, patterns of decentralized leadership, diffuse and flexible interband alliance, generalized reciprocity, and adult male status equality tend to be greater in relatively more remote and autonomous foragers (e.g., Mbuti net-hunters versus Mbuti archers; !Kung San versus Basarwa). In terms of developmental trajectories, then, the characteristics presently attributed to nonintensive foraging societies are likely, if anything, to have been greater among such societies prior to state and tribal contact than in the historically observed ethnographic record. The present assessment of simple society features on the basis of twentieth-century observational data is, in this sense, methodologically conservative.

The same argument applies, *mutatis mutandis,* to "complex" hunter-gatherer societies, in which status differentiation and/or sedentism are evident in association with incipient socioeconomic intensification (see Price and Brown 1985). The relatively recent evolutionary development of such complex hunter-gatherer societies belies contrastive patterns among nonintensive foragers, the latter having predominated during the much larger part of our genus's history. Politically decentralized and nonintensive foragers thus provide a much better basis for making inferences about long-term human evolution than do complex hunter-gatherers.

✦ Sexuality

Factors that influence male sexual access to reproductively viable females are especially important for the study of human evolution. Among great apes, male sexual access is associated with competitive male dominance hierarchies (e.g., Goodall 1986: chs. 15, 17; Nishida et al. 1985; Smuts et al. 1987; cf. more generally Krebs and Davies 1987; Huntingford and Turner 1987). Among simple and noncomplex human hunter-gatherers, in contrast, competitive male dominance hierarchies and status rivalry are surprisingly attenuated and in most cases actively if not assiduously suppressed by cultural norms (Boehm 1993; Knauft 1991). Cultural control of sexuality in these societies is highly evident in the institution of marriage, in normative monogamy, in widespread classificatory extension of the incest taboo (elaborate exogamy), and in the crucial importance of marital exchange and alliance.

Marriage almost invariably confers rights of sexual access. Although these norms may be broken in simple societies (e.g., Shostak 1981), it remains true that sexual norms do tend to constrain and circumscribe sexual activity for most persons in these groups (e.g., contrast Lee 1979b: ch. 6). In some of these societies, extramarital sexuality is itself culturally controlled and appropriated for alliance purposes—as in Inuit wife-exchange partnership (Balikci 1970: 140–143; see also Lee 1979b: ch. 6; Turnbull 1961). Finally, norms of sexual fidelity in these societies are underscored by the consensual disparagement and scapegoating or ostracism of persons who repeatedly break them (Knauft 1987a: 477–478).

Although many societies tolerate polygyny, or do not actively proscribe it, the cultural and statistical norm for most adults in simple human societies is monogamy (e.g., Lee 1979b: 79; Woodburn 1972; Turnbull 1965a,b; contrast Wrangham 1987; Flinn and Low 1986). Unlike many more complex pre-state societies, polygyny is not a prominent index or symbol of differential adult male status in the simplest human societies, and the linkage of prestige to male heterosexual prerogatives appears notably undeveloped (contrast Betzig 1986). Although cultural marriage rules, rights, and obligations certainly do not determine human sexual behavior in any absolute sense, they do exert an enormous and undeniable influence on it. In addition, they weld sexuality to culturally mandated patterns of economic support and social affiliation.

Perhaps the greatest sociopolitical concomitant of marital organization in evolutionary terms is the advent of culturally defined kin groups and the structuring of affinal alliance relationships (Levi-Strauss 1949 [1969]). Although incest avoidance and exogamy of various kinds have also been documented among nonhuman primates, the structuring of kin groups and social alliance on the basis of marriage proscriptions and prescriptions is enormously important and distinctive among humans. In simple human societies, such kin-group and affinal linkages create a widespread network of economic support, subsistence cooperation, and information sharing that is central to survival and crucial in times of ecological stress (e.g., Lee 1979b: chs. 5–6; Turnbull 1965a,b; Damas 1984;

Woodburn 1972, 1984; Yengoyan 1984; see Gamble 1982 regarding a Paleolithic example).

Of course, illicit sexuality and concomitant social disruption are always a potential threat to cooperation and regional alliance networks. In terms of natural selection, correspondingly, individualistic sexual and reproductive desires are supplemented rather than replaced by cultural imperatives. Biogenetic propensities remain in inextricable tension with cultural values, the latter having their own means of shaping phenotypic behavior and their own means of transmission and spread; learning and socialization can strongly influence but not totally determine behavior.

The importance of culture here is aptly illustrated by the interface between sexuality and social organization in human evolution. One of the key features of recent human evolutionary scenarios is male parental investment, especially the provisioning of meat (e.g., Lovejoy 1981; Hill 1982; Foley 1982; Tooby and DeVore 1987). High male parental investment is consistent with human traits such as relative lack of sexual dimorphism and the relative rarity of polygyny in egalitarian hunter-gatherer societies. Evidence from human and ape sexual morphology (e.g., Nadler and Phoenix 1991) strongly supports the notion that human evolution was characterized neither by a polygynous mating system, similar to that of gorillas, nor by a multimale mating system, similar to that of chimpanzees.

Humans are distinctive in combining high, male parental investment with patterns of social organization that provide unique potentials for sexual cheating. Specifically, nonintensive human foragers generally have large home ranges, are socially gregarious, and maintain a strong sexual division of labor. As a result, men in human societies are frequently distant and absent from their female mates (Rodseth et al. 1991). How, then, can a man be sure that his wife's child is really his own? How can he be sure his parental investment is not a biogenetic waste? The answer is, on the one hand, that rules of sexual propriety are culturally emphasized, enforced, and psychologically internalized in humans; men do tend to believe that their children are in fact their offspring. On the other hand, when they are unsure, cultural norms of cooperative sharing and of sociological, as distinct from genetic, paternity counter the threat of wasted parental investment.

This is not to suggest that male disputes over women and over illicit sex are absent in simple human societies (see Collier and Rosaldo 1981; Knauft 1987a: 477f); rather that these tensions do not preclude coordinated social organization and cooperation based on general adherence to cultural norms concerning sexuality and kinship.[7] The anomaly to the behavioral ethologist of cultural rules that exert real influence upon sexual behavior dissolves, once the neo-Darwinian perspective, based on individualistic competition, is broadened by a view that takes seriously the selection for cooperative capabilities that is strongly instantiated by human culture.

✦ Violence and Sociality

The present perspective on human evolution does not imply a Rousseauian view in which savages are noble and violence is absent. My own data from Gebusi, as well as reanalysis of data concerning !Kung, Inuit, and Hadza, suggest that lethal violence has, on a per capita basis, been quite high in these simple societies (Knauft 1985a,b, 1987a). Rather than being eulogized or associated with kin-group or ethnic oppositions, however, this violence tends to arise sporadically, and sometimes dysfunctionally, out of a pervasive denial of anger and the politics of nonconfrontation in small cooperative domestic groups, particularly with respect to male sexual access to women. Given that violence tends to be disparaged by women as well as men, it is typically an ineffective way of gaining a mate or a wife; by contrast, it is often directed consensually by the community at large against someone who has broken strongly held group norms. Violence that does occur is relatively unrelated to territorial rights, property, and ritual statuses, and is based more on status leveling among men than on status elevation. Further, violence in simple societies rarely results in escalating revenge or collective blood-feuding: the strong desire is to return to norms of group sociality as quickly as possible. It is this normative situation that has most struck ethnographers of simple societies and that tends to be embraced in self-perception by the population itself.[8]

A distinctive emphasis on diffuse sociality thus creates a cultural disposition toward cooperative affiliation that is very important—indeed, preeminent—in simple human societies. It is in this sense that the !Kung are *The Harmless People* (Thomas 1958) and that the Inuit are *Never in Anger* (Briggs 1970). These cultural realities do not negate the existence of violence, but they do facilitate those key cooperative features that are diagnostic of human culture and accentuated among simple human societies. In simple societies, then, the reality of long-term harmony and cooperation in the face of spasmodic violence is not a paradox. Its reality, as Bateson (1972) might have put it, is a function of belief in preeminent cultural values.

*   *   *

This chapter suggests that the distinctive symbolic capacities of human culture have promoted diffuse sociality and cooperative social organization since the inception of *Homo* and through the majority of human evolution. These characteristics are particularly pronounced among simple human societies.

During the course of human evolution, widespread and elaborate transmission of information, diffuse food-sharing, and normative cultural control of sexual behavior allowed humans to occupy a distinctive group-cooperative niche. This is hypothesized to have greatly facilitated features such as the sexual division of labor, diffuse social alliances, and subsistence strategies that were cooperative, flexible, and geographically expansive. These adaptations were highly advantageous and promoted the remarkable spread of *Homo* to diverse, nontropical ecozones. This process begs an understanding of those cultural features that distinguish our evolutionary origin and development from those of other species. Biogenetic selection is supplemented in humans by cultural selection for prosocial and group adaptive behavior, particularly in the simplest human societies that characterize the longest part of our genus's evolutionary history.

Dynamics of cooperative cultural orientation are strongly evident in the ethnographic data concerning nonintensive human foraging societies and are supported by evolutionary inference. These belie the narrow application of neo-Darwinian or sociobiological principles to the study of human evolution. The chapter's emphasis on the cooperative features of culture is intended as a prolegomenon to a more balanced consideration of the tension between collective imperatives and competing individualistic propensities in human evolution.

✦   Notes

An earlier version of this paper was presented at the annual meetings of the American Anthropological Association, Phoenix, 1988. Comments are gratefully acknowledged from Robert Dentan, Walter Goldschmidt, Leslie Sponsel, and an anonymous reviewer. All shortcomings remain my own. This paper is based on research supported by the H. F. Guggenheim Foundation.

1. See in general Woodburn 1982; Ingold 1987; Leacock and Lee 1982; Lee and DeVore 1984; Testart 1985; Lee 1990; contrast the wider purview of Ember 1978.
2. Complex hunter-gatherer adaptations were common during the Mesolithic, e.g., after 8,000 before the present (B.P.), depending on region (e.g., Zvelebil 1986; Price and Brown 1985), with the first known cases arising in Paleolithic Europe and the mid-East at 15,000–10,000 B.P. (viz., the middle Magdelanian and Levant Natufian, see Mellars 1985; Henry 1985) and an exceptional case from the central plain of Russia dated as early as 26,000 B.P. (Soffer 1985; McBurney 1976). Significant complex hunter-gatherer formations have survived and/or developed during the contemporary historical period, permitting ethnographic documentation; e.g., native northwest American fishing adaptations and Great Plains equestrian and other domesticated-animal adaptations, the latter not involving sedentism but potentiating competitive property rights and material status differentiation over animal ownership/disposal. The inclusion of such complex or "nonsimple" hunter-gatherer groups in Human Relations Area Files (HRAF) samples has significantly skewed cross-cultural findings concerning the most decentralized human societies (e.g., Ember 1978; contrast Knauft 1987a).

3. As discussed below, simple human groups are likely to have included non-kin as well as kin. As a result, rule-of-thumb cooperation could not be expected to exist as a function of inclusive fitness alone.

4. The neglected or deferred emphasis on language in human evolution is evident in the scenarios by Wrangham 1987; Tooby and DeVore 1987; Foley 1987; Lovejoy 1981; Mellars and Stringer 1989; Noble and Davidson 1989; and Gibson 1991. There is much current work on specific psychophysiological, biosocial, and archeological dimensions of cognition and language as a relatively recent phenomenon (e.g., Parker and Gibson 1979; Parker 1985; Lieberman 1984; Burling 1986, 1993; Davidson and Noble 1989, 1991; Chase and Dibble 1987; Lewis-Williams and Dowson 1988). These studies focus on the efficient causes and effects of symbolization in terms of individual cognition rather than on either the unique phenotypic transmission properties of language or its social and culture-affiliative implications. As such, they remain somewhat divorced from the longer trajectory of human evolution and from theories of biocultural evolution (exceptions include Aiello and Dunbar 1993; Marshack 1989, 1990; Richards 1987: Ch. 5; Dewart 1989; Whallon 1989; Holloway 1981, 1983).

5. The perils of fossilism—of linking symbolic facility narrowly with relatively elaborate archeological evidence of ritual and art—is highly evident in Lindly and Clark's (1990) review and conclusion that upper Paleolithic assemblages until about 20,000 B.P. generally lack evidence of symbolism. Gamble (1990: 243) notes that even the colonization of North America and the North European Plain after 13,000 B.P. is similarly "marked by very few if any" directly symbolic artifacts. Obviously, the importance of language and protolanguage in human evolution stretch much further back than elaborate visible encoding of symbolism in durable artifacts and should be appraised on the basis of wider contextual evidence. Concern over this issue has often been overshadowed by debates between "replacement" and "continuity" hypotheses concerning the preponderance of anatomically modern humans in Europe during the period 45,000–35,000 B.P. (cf. Trinkaus 1989).

6. The tension between group-collective and self-interested selection pressures arguably links the dominant tendency to accept communication utterances at face value to the occasional suspicion that they may be deceptive.

7. It could be countered that exceptionally intelligent individuals could enhance their reproductive success while *appearing* to conform to community norms. For instance, since the distinction between homicide and capital punishment is often murky in simple human societies (Knauft 1987a: 491–492), community norms could be strategically manipulated by self-interested individuals smart enough unobtrusively to subvert them and get away with it. In the long run, however, this provokes an "arms race" between individual deception (including self-deception) and increasingly intelligent counteraction against deception by the population at large. What results is the simultaneous selection of both self-interested sexual drive and increasingly sophisticated cultural means of internally and externally controlling sexuality. Sexual drive and its control thus become mutually reinforcing. Cultural control over sexuality is thus not diminished but rather driven to new heights by its potential contravention.

8. Sociodemographic features contribute to the ethic of peacefulness in simple human societies. Within a small group of fifty or so persons, a single killing once

every few years can result in a high per capita homicide rate. If the overall rate of day-to-day aggressive behavior is low, however, a sudden homicide every few years may not be perceived either by ethnographers or the indigenous population as betokening a great deal of violence, particularly if it is undertaken to uphold community norms. By contrast, in a sedentary, horticultural society with a great deal of warfare, a group of five hundred persons could sustain a killing ten times as frequently and still have the same homicide rate as the above-mentioned decentralized society. If killing in the sedentary society is merely the most extreme expression of a more general propensity toward assertive intimidation, chronic aggression, and inconclusive display-warfare, then the tribal society is easily perceived as much more violent than its simple-society counterpart—and with respect to social awareness and expectation, it is. This contrast helps explain how simple societies exhibit low overall rates of daily aggression and low valuation and self-perception of aggressive behavior despite a significant homicide rate (Knauft 1987a).

✦ References

Aiello, Leslie C.
1993   The Fossil Evidence for Modern Human Origins: A Revised View. *American Anthropologist* 95:73–96.

Aiello, Leslie C., and R. I. M. Dunbar
1993   Neocortex Size, Group Size, and the Evolution of Language. *Current Anthropology* 34:184–193.

Alexander, Richard D.
1988   *The Biology of Moral Systems.* New York: Aldine de Gruyter.

Ardrey, Robert
1966   *The Territorial Imperative: A Personal Inquiry into the Animal Origins of Property and Nations.* New York: Atheneum.

Axelrod, Robert
1984   *The Evolution of Cooperation.* New York: Basic Books.

Balikci, Asen
1970   *The Netsilik Eskimo.* Garden City, NY: Natural History Press.

Bateson, Gregory
1972   *Steps to an Ecology of Mind.* New York: Bantam Books.

Betzig, Laura L.
1986   *Despotism and Differential Reproduction: A Darwinian View of History.* Chicago: Aldine.

Bickerton, Derek
1990   *Language and Species.* Chicago: University of Chicago Press.

Binford, Lewis R.
1989   *Debating Archaeology.* New York: Academic Press.

Boehm, Christopher
1989   Ambivalence and Compromise in Human Nature. *American Anthropologist* 91:921–939.
1993   Egalitarian Behavior and Reverse Dominance Hierarchy. *Current Anthropology* 34:227–254.

Boyd, Robert, and Jeffry P. Lorberbaum
1987   No Pure Strategy is Evolutionarily Stable in the Repeated Prisoner's Dilemma Game. *Nature* 327:58–59.

Boyd, Robert, and Peter J. Richerson
1985   *Culture and the Evolutionary Process.* Chicago: University of Chicago Press.
1988   The Evolution of Reciprocity in Sizable Groups. *Journal of Theoretical Biology* 132:337–356.

Briggs, Jean L.
1970   *Never in Anger: Portrait of an Eskimo Family.* Cambridge: Harvard University Press.
1978   The Origins of Nonviolence: Inuit Management of Aggression (Canadian Arctic), in *Learning Non-Aggression: The Experience of Non-Literate Societies,* Ashley Montagu, ed.: 54–93. New York: Oxford University Press.

Burling, Robbins
1986   The Selective Advantage of Complex Language. *Ethology and Sociobiology* 7:1–16.
1993   Primate Calls, Human Language, and Nonverbal Communication. *Current Anthropology* 34:25–53.

Caporael, Linda R., Robyn M. Dawes, John M. Orbell, and Alphons J. C. van de Kragt
1989   Selfishness Examined: Cooperation in the Absence of Egoistic Incentives. *Behavioral and Brain Sciences* 12:683–739.

Carneiro, Robert L.
1970   A Theory of the Origin of the State. *Science* 169:733–738.
1981   The Chiefdom: Precursor of the State, in *The Transition to Statehood in the New World,* Grant D. Jones and Robert R. Kautz, eds.: 37–79. Cambridge: Cambridge University Press.

Cashdan, Elizabeth A.
1980   Egalitarianism among Hunters and Gatherers. *American Anthropologist* 82:116–120.
1983   Territoriality among Human Foragers: Ecological Models and an

Application to Four Bushman Groups. *Current Anthropology* 24:47–66.

1985   Coping with Risk: Reciprocity among the Basarwa of Northern Botswana. *Man* 20:454–474.

1986   Competition Between Foragers and Food-Producers on the Botletli River, Botswana. *Africa* 56:299–318.

Chagnon, Napoleon A.
1988   Life Histories, Blood Revenge, and Warfare in a Tribal Population. *Science* 239:985–992.

Chase, Philip, and Harold Dibble
1987   Middle Paleolithic Symbolism: A Review of Current Evidence and Interpretations. *Journal of Archaeological Science* 4:231–243.

Clasters, Pierre
1972   The Guayaki, in *Hunters and Gatherers Today,* M. G. Bicchieri, ed.: 138–173. New York: Holt, Rinehart, and Winston.

Collier, Jane F., and Michelle Z. Rosaldo
1981   Politics and Gender in Simple Societies, in *Sexual Meanings: The Cultural Construction of Gender and Sexuality,* Sherry B. Ortner and Harriet Whitehead, eds.: 275–329. New York: Cambridge University Press.

Damas, David
1984   The Diversity of Eskimo Societies, in *Man the Hunter* 2nd ed., edited by R. B. Lee and I. DeVore: 111–117. New York: Aldine. (Original 1968.)

Darwin, Charles
1871   *The Descent of Man, and Selection in Relation to Sex.* (Reprint, Princeton: Princeton University Press, 1981.)

Davidson, Ian, and William Noble
1989   The Archaeology of Perception: Traces of Depiction and Language. *Current Anthropology* 30:125–155.

Dawkins, Richard
1976   *The Selfish Gene.* Oxford: Oxford University Press.

Dewart, Leslie
1989   *Evolution and Conciousness: The Role of Speech in the Origin and Development of Human Nature.* Toronto: University of Toronto Press.

Draper, Patricia
1978   The Learning Environment for Aggression and Anti-Social Behavior among the !Kung (Kalahari Desert, Botswana, Africa), in *Learning Non-*

Aggression: The Experience of Non-Literate Societies, Ashley Montagu, ed.: 31–53. New York: Oxford University Press.

Durham, William H.
1991 *Coevolution.* Stanford: Stanford University Press.

Durkheim, Emile
1912 *The Elementary Forms of the Religious Life.* (English translation 1964, New York: Free Press.)

Edgerton, Robert B.
1992 *Sick Societies: Challenging the Myth of Primitive Harmony.* New York: Free Press.

Ember, Carol R.
1978 Myths about Hunter-Gatherers. *Ethnology* 17:439–448.

Fialkowski, K. R.
1990 An Evolutionary Mechanism for the Origin of Moral Norms: Towards the Meta-Trait of Culture. *Human Evolution* 5:153–166.

Flinn, Mark V., and Bobbi S. Low
1986 Resource Distribution, Social Competition, and Mating Patterns in Human Societies. In *Ecological Aspects of Social Evolution,* edited by D. I. Rubenstein and R. W. Wrangham: 217–243. Princeton, NJ: Princeton University Press.

Foley, Robert
1982 A Reconsideration of the Role of Predation on Large Mammals in Tropical Hunter-Gatherer Adaptation. *Man* 17:393–402.
1987 *Another Unique Species: Patterns in Human Evolutionary Ecology.* New York: Longman.

Fried, Morton H.
1967 *The Evolution of Political Society.* New York: Random House.

Gamble, Clive
1982 Interaction and Alliance in Palaeolithic Society. *Man* 17:92–107.
1990 Reponse to Lindly and Clark, "Symbolism and Modern Human Origins" (1990). *Current Anthropology* 31:243–244.

Gibson, Kathleen
1991 Tools, Languages, and Intelligence: Evolutionary Implications. *Man* 26:255–264.

Geertz, Clifford
1962 The Growth of Culture and the Evolution of Mind, in *Theories of the Mind,* J. Scher, ed.: 713–740. Glencoe, Ill.: Free Press.

1973   *The Interpretation of Cultures.* New York: Basic Books.

Goodall, Jane
1986   *The Chipmanzees of Gombe: Patterns of Behavior.* Cambridge: Belknap/Harvard University Press.

Goodenough, Ward H.
1990   Evolution of the Human Capacity for Beliefs. *American Anthropologist* 91:597–612.

Gould, Stephen J.
1988   Kropotkin Was No Crackpot. *Natural History* 7:12–21.

Guemple, Lee, ed.
1972   *Alliance in Eskimo Society.* Seattle: University of Washington Press/American Ethnological Society.

Hamilton, W. D.
1964   The Genetical Evolution of Social Behavior I, II. *Journal of Theoretical Biology* 7:1–52.

Harako, Reizo
1976   The Mbuti as Hunters: A Study of Ecological Anthropology of the Mbuti Pygmies. *Kyoto University African Studies* 10:37–99.

Harpending, Henry, and Alan Rogers
1987   On Wright's Mechanism for Intergroup Selection. *Journal of Theoretical Biology* 127:51–61.

Headland, Thomas N., and Lawrence A. Reid
1989   Hunter-Gatherers and Their Neighbors from the Prehistory to the Present. *Current Anthropology* 30:43–66.

Henry, Donald O.
1985   Preagricultural Intensification: The Natufian Example. In *Prehistoric Hunter-Gatherers: The Emergence of Cultural Complexity,* T. Douglas Price and James A. Brown, ed.: 365–384. Orlando, FL: Academic Press.

Hill, Kim
1982   Hunting and Human Evolution. *Journal of Human Evolution* 11:521–544.

Hitchcock, Robert K.
1987   Socioeconomic Change among the Basarwa in Botswana: An Ethnohistorical Analysis. *Ethnohistory* 34:219–255.

Hockett, Charles F. and Robert Ascher
1964   The Human Revolution. *Current Anthropology* 5:135–168.

Holloway, Ralph L.
  1981   Culture, Symbols, and Human Brain Evolution: A Synthesis. *Dialectical Anthropology* 5:287–303.
  1983   Human Brain Evolution: A Search for Units, Models, and Synthesis. *Canadian Journal of Anthropology* 3:215–230.

Huntingford, Felicity A., and Angela K. Turner
  1987   *Animal Conflict.* New York: Chapman and Hall.

Ingold, Tim
  1986   *Evolution and Social Life.* Cambridge: Cambridge University Press.
  1987   *The Appropriation of Nature: Essays on Human Ecology and Social Relations.* Iowa City: University of Iowa Press.

Isaac, Glynn
  1978   The Food-Sharing Behavior of Protohuman Hominids. *Scientific American* 238:90–108.
  1984   The Archaeology of Human Origins: Studies of the Lower Pleistocene in East Africa 1971–1981, in *Advances in World Archaeology* 3:1–89. New York: Academic Press.

Itani, Junichiro
  1988   The Origin of Human Equality, in *Social Fabrices of the Mind,* R. A. Chance, ed.: 137–156. London: Lawrence Erlbaum Associates.

Johnson, Allen W., and Timothy Earle
  1987   *The Evolution of Human Societies: From Foraging Group to Agrarian State.* Stanford: Stanford University Press.

Kaplan, Hillard, and Kim Hill
  1985a Food Sharing Among Ache Foragers: Tests of Explanatory Hypotheses. *Current Anthropology* 26:223–245.
  1985b Hunting Ability and Reproductive Success among Male Ache Foragers. *Current Anthropology* 26:131–133.

Kaplan, Hillard, Kim Hill, Kristen Hawkes, and Magdalena Hurtado
  1984   Food Sharing among Ache Hunter-Gatherers of Eastern Paraguay. *Current Anthropology* 25:113–115.

Kitcher, Philip
  1985   *Vaulting Ambition.* Boston: M.I.T. Press.

Knauft, Bruce M.
  1985a *Good Company and Violence: Sorcery and Social Action in a Lowland New Guinea Society.* Berkeley: University of California Press.
  1985b Ritual Form and Permutation in New Guinea: Implications of Symbolic Process for Socio-Political Evolution. *American Ethnologist* 12:321–340.

1987a   Reconsidering Violence in Simple Human Societies: Homicide among the Gebusi of New Guinea. *Current Anthropology* 28:457–500.
1987b   Divergence between Cultural Success and Reproductive Fitness in Preindustrial Cities. *Cultural Anthropology* 2:94–114.
1988   On Reconsidering Violence in Human Evolution. *Current Anthropology* 29:629–633.
1989   Sociality versus Self-interest in Human Evolution. *Behavioral and Brain Sciences* 12:712–713.
1990   Violence among Newly Sedentary Foragers. *American Anthropologist* 92:1013–1015.
1991   Violence and Sociality in Human Evolution. *Current Anthropology* 32:391–428.
1993   *South Coast New Guinea Cultures: History, Comparison, Dialectic.* Cambridge: Cambridge University Press.
n.d.   The Trajectory of Peace and Violence in Human Evolution, in *The Anthropology of Peace,* Thomas A. Gregor, ed. (ms.)

Kohn, Alfie
1986   *No Contest: The Case Against Competition.* Boston: Houghton Mifflin.
1990   *The Brighter Side of Human Nature: Altruism and Empathy in Everyday Life.* New York: Basic Books.

Krebs, J. R., and N. B. Davies
1987   *An Introduction to Behavioural Ecology* 2nd ed. Sunderland, Mass.: Sinauer Associates.

Kropotkin, Petr A.
1902   *Mutual Aid: A Factor of Evolution.* (Republished 1972, New York University Press.)

Kurland, Jeffrey A., and Stephen J. Beckerman
1985   Optimal Foraging and Hominid Evolution: Labor and Reciprocity. *American Anthropologist* 86:73–93.

Kuroda, Suehisa
1984   Interaction Over Food among Pygmy Chimpanzees, in *The Pygmy Chimpanzee: Evolutionary Biology and Behavior,* R. L. Susman, ed.: 301–324. New York: Plenum Press.

Lackner, Stephan
1984   *Peaceable Nature: An Optimistic View of Life on Earth.* San Francisco: Harper & Row.

Layton, Robert
1986   Political and Territorial Structures among Hunter-Gatherers. *Man* 21:18–33.

Leacock, Eleanor, and Richard B. Lee
    1982   Introduction. In *Politics and History in Band Societies,* Eleanor Leacock and Richard B. Lee, eds.: 1–20. Cambridge: Cambridge University Press.

Leacock, Eleanor, and Richard B. Lee, eds.
    1982   *Politics and History in Band Societies.* Cambridge: Cambridge University Press.

Lee, Richard B.
    1979a   *The Dobe !Kung.* New York: Holt, Rinehart and Winston.
    1979b   *The !Kung San: Men, Women, and Work in a Foraging Society.* New York: Cambridge University Press.
    1990   Primitive Communism and the Origin of Social Inequality, in *The Evolution of Political Systems: Sociopolitics of Small-Scale Sedentary Societies,* Steadman Upham, ed.: 225–246. Cambridge: Cambridge University Press.

Lee, Richard B., and Irven DeVore, eds.
    1984   *Man the Hunter* 2nd ed. New York: Aldine.

Levi-Strauss, Claude
    1949   *The Elementary Structures of Kinship.* (Published in English 1969. Boston: Beacon.)

Lewis-Williams, J. D., and T. A. Dowson
    1988   The Signs of All Times: Entoptic Phenomena in Upper Palaeolithic Art. *Current Anthropology* 29:201–245.

Lieberman, P.
    1984   *The Biology and Evolution of Language.* Cambridge: Cambridge University Press.

Lindly, J. M., and G. A. Clark
    1990   Symbolism and Modern Human Origins. *Current Anthropology* 31:233–261.

Lorenz, Konrad
    1966   *On Aggression.* New York: Harcourt, Brace & World.

Lovejoy, Owen
    1981   The Origin of Man. *Science* 217:304–305.

Marshack, Alexander
    1981   On Paleolithic Ochre and the Early Uses of Color and Symbol. *Current Anthropology* 20:607–608.

1985 *Hierarchical Evolution of the Human Capacity: The Paleolithic Evidence.* New York: American Museum of Natural History.
1989a On Depiction and Language (further responses to Davidson and Noble, 1987, "The Archaeology of Perception"). *Current Anthropology* 30:332–335.
1989b Evolution and the Human Capacity: The Symbolic Evidence. *Yearbook of Physical Anthropology.*

Marshall, Lorna
1961 Sharing, Talking, and Giving: Relief of Social Tensions among !Kung Bushmen. *Africa* 31:231–249.
1976 *The !Kung of Nyae Nyae.* Cambridge: Harvard University Press.

McBurney, C. B.
1976 *Early Man in the Soviet Union.* London: British Academy.

Meggitt, Mervyn J.
1962 *Desert People: A Study of the Walbiri Aborigines of Central Australia.* London: Angus and Robertson.

Mellars, Paul A.
1985 The Ecological Basis of Social Complexity in the Upper Paleolithic of Southwestern France, in *Prehistorical Hunter-Gatherers: The Emergence of Cultural Complexity,* T. Douglas Price and James A. Brown, eds.: 271–297. Orlando, FL: Academic Press.
1988 The Origin and Dispersal of Modern Humans. *Current Anthropology* 29:186–188.
1989 Major Issues in the Emergence of Modern Humans. *Current Anthropology* 30:349–385.

Mellars, Paul, and C. B. Stringer, eds.
1989 *The Human Revolution: Behavioural and Biological Perspectives on the Origins of Modern Humans.* Edinburgh: Edinburgh University Press.

Montagu, Ashley
1976 *The Nature of Human Aggression.* New York: Oxford University Press.

Montagu, Ashley, ed.
1978 *Learning Non-Aggression.* New York: Oxford University Press.

Moore, John M.
1990 The Reproductive Success of Cheyenne War Chiefs: A Contrary Case to Chagnon's Yanomamo. *Current Anthropology* 31:322–330.

Murphy, Robert F., and Julian H. Steward
1955 Tappers and Trappers: Parallel Process in Acculturation. *Economic Development and Culture Change* 4:335–353.

Myers, Fred R.
1988   Critical Trends in the Study of Hunter-Gatherers. *Annual Reviews in Anthropology* 17:261–282.

Nadler, Ronald D., and Charles H. Phoenix
1991   Male Sexual Behavior: Monkeys, Men, and Apes, in *Understanding Behavior: What Primate Studies Tell Us about Human Behavior,* James D. Loy and Calvin B. Peters, eds.: 152–189. New York: Oxford University Press.

Nishida, Toshisada, Mariko Hiraiwa-Hasegawa, Toshikazu Hasegawa, and Yukio Takahata
1985   Group Extinction and Female Transfer in Wild Chimpanzees in the Mahale National Park, Tanzania. *Z. Tierpsychol.* 67:284–301.

Noble, W., and I. Davidson
1991   The Evolutionary Emergence of Modern Human Behavior: Language and Its Archaeology. *Man* 26:222–253.

Nowak, M., and K. Sigmund
1989   Oscillations in the Evolution of Reciprocity. *Journal of Theoretical Biology* 137:21–26.

O'Connell, James F., Kristen Hawkes, and Nicholas Blurton Jones
1988a   Hadza Scavenging: Implications for Plio/Pleistocene Hominid Subsistence. *Current Anthropology* 29:356–363.
1988b   Hadza Hunting, Butchering, and Bone Transport, and Their Archaeological Implications. *Journal of Anthropological Research* 44:113–161.

Parker, Sue T.
1985   A Social-Technological Model for the Evolution of Language. *Current Anthropology* 26:617–639.

Parker, Sue T., and Kathleen R. Gibson
1979   A Developmental Model for the Evolution of Language and Intelligence in Early Hominids. *Behavioral and Brain Sciences* 2:367–408.

Paul, Robert A.
1987   The Individual and Society in Biological and Cultural Anthropology. *Cultural Anthropology* 2:80–93.

Price, T. Douglas, and James A. Brown, eds.
1985   *Prehistorical Hunter-Gatherers: The Emergence of Cultural Complexity.* Orlando, FL: Academic Press.

Rappaport, Roy A.
1971a   Ritual, Sanctity, and Cybernetics. *American Anthropologist* 73:59–76.

1971b The Sacred in Human Evolution. *Annual Review of Ecology and Systematics* 2:23–44.
1979 *Ecology, Meaning, and Religion.* Richmond, CA: North Atlantic Books.

Richards, Graham
1987 *Human Evolution.* New York: Routledge and Kegan Paul.

Richerson, Peter J., and Robert Boyd
1989 The Role of Evolved Predispositions in Cultural Evolution. *Ethology and Sociobiology* 10:195–219.

Rodseth, Lars, Richard W. Wrangham, Alisa Harrigan, and Barbara B. Smuts
1991 The Human Community as a Primate Society. *Current Anthropology* 32:221–255.

Ross, Marc Howard
1991 The Role of Evolution in Ethnocentric Conflict and Its Management. *Journal of Social Issues* 47:167–185.

Sahlins, Marshall D.
1972 *Stone Age Economics.* Chicago: Aldine.

Schrire, Carmel
1984 *Past and Present in Hunter Gatherer Societies.* Orlando, FL: Academic Press.

Shostak, Marjorie
1981 *Nisa: The Life and Words of a !Kung Woman.* Cambridge: Harvard University Press.

Smuts, Barbara B., Dorothy L. Cheney, Robert M. Seyfarth, Richard W. Wrangham, and Thomas T. Struhsaker, eds.
1987 *Primate Societies.* Chicago: University of Chicago Press.

Soffer, Olga
1985 Patterns of Intensification as Seen from the Upper Paleolithic of the Central Russian Plain, in *Prehistoric Hunter-Gatherers: The Emergence of Cultural Complexity,* T. Douglas Price and James A. Brown, eds.: 235–270. Orlando, FL: Academic Press.

Solecki, R.
1971 *Shanidar: The First Flower People.* New York: Alfred Knopf.

Solway, Jacqueline S., and Richard B. Lee
1990 Foragers, Genuine or Spurious? Situating the Kalahari San in History. *Current Anthropology* 31:109–146.

Stephenson, Carolyn
1990   Peace Studies: The Evolution of Peace Research and Peace Education. University of Hawaii Institute for Peace, Occasional Paper 1.

Testart, Alain
1985   *Le Communisme Primitif: Economie et Ideologie*. Paris: Maison des Sciences de l'Homme.
1987   Game Sharing Systems and Kinship Systems among Hunter-Gatherers. *Man* 22:287–304.
1988   Some Major Problems in the Social Anthropology of Hunter-Gatherers. *Current Anthropology* 29:1–31.

Thomas, Elizabeth Marshall
1958   *The Harmless People*. New York: Knopf.

Tomasello, Michael
n.d.   Processes of Communication in Children, Chimpanzees, and Early Humans. (ms.)

Tooby, John, and Irven DeVore
1987   The Reconstruction of Hominid Behavioral Evolution through Strategic Modeling, in *The Evolution of Human Behavior: Primate Models*, Warren G. Kinzey, ed.: 183–237. Albany: State University of New York Press.

Trinkaus, Erik
1983   *The Shanidar Neanderthals*. New York: Academic Press.
1989   *The Emergence of Modern Humans: Biocultural Adaptations in the Later Pleistocene*. Cambridge: Cambridge University Press.

Trivers, R.
1971   The Evolution of Reciprocal Altruism, in *Readings in Sociobiology*, edited by T. Clutton-Brock and P. Harvey. San Francisco: Freeman.
1985   *Social Evolution*. Menlo Park, CA: Cummings.

Turnbull, Colin M.
1961   *The Forest People*. Garden City, NY: Natural History Press.
1965a   The Mbuti Pygmies: An Ethnographic Survey. *Anthropological Papers of the American Museum of Natural History* 50(3):139–282.
1965b   *Wayward Servants: The Two Worlds of the African Pygmies*. Garden City, NY: Natural History Press.
1978   The Politics of Non-Aggression (Zaire), in *Learning Non-Aggression*, edited by Ashley Montagu, pp. 161–221. New York: Oxford University Press.
1984   The Importance of Flux in Two Hunting Societies, in *Man the Hunter* 2nd ed., Richard B. Lee and Irven DeVore, eds.: 132–137. New York: Aldine.

Upham, Steadman, ed.
  1990   *The Evolution of Political Systems: Sociopolitics of Small-Scale Sedentary Societies.* Cambridge: Cambridge University Press.

Vining, Daniel R., Jr.
  1986   Social versus Reproductive Success: The Central Theoretical Problem of Human Sociobiology. *Behavioral and Brain Sciences* 9:167–216.

Vucinich, A.
  1988   *Darwin in Russian Thought.* Berkeley: University of California Press.

Waal, Frans de B. M.
  1989   Food Sharing and Reciprocal Obligations among Chimpanzees. *Journal of Human Evolution* 18:433–459.

Whallon, R.
  1989   Elements of Cultural Change in the Later Palaeolithic, in *The Human Revolution: Behavioural and Biological Perspectives on the Origins of Modern Humans* vol. 1, edited by Paul Mellars and C. B. Stringer. Edinburgh: Edinburgh University Press.

White, Leslie A.
  1949   The Symbol: The Origin and Basis of Human Behavior, in *The Science of Culture,* by L. A. White: 22–39. New York: Farrar, Straus.

White, Randall
  1989   Production Complexity and Standardization in Early Aurignacian Bead and Pendant Manufacture: Evolutionary Implications, in *The Human Revolution: Behavioral and Biological Perspectives on the Origins of Modern Humans* vol. 1, Paul Mellars and Chris Stringer, eds.: 366–390. Princeton, NJ: Princeton University Press.

Wiessner, Polly
  1982   Risk, Reciprocity, and Social Influences on !Kung San Economics, in *Politics and History in Band Societies,* Eleanor Leacock and Richard B. Lee, eds.: 61–84. Cambridge: Cambridge University Press.

Williams, C. G.
  1966   *Adaptation and Natural Selection.* Princeton University Press.

Wilmsen, Edwin N.
  1989   *Land Filled with Flies: A Political Economy of the Kalahari.* Chicago: University of Chicago Press.

Wilson, David S.
  1989   Levels of Selection: An Alternative to Individualism in Biology and the Human Sciences. *Social Networks* 11:257–272.

Wilson, David S., and Elliot Sober
1989   Reviving the Superorganism. *Journal of Theoretical Biology* 136:337–356.
1993   Reintroducing Group Selection to the Human Behavioral Sciences (ms.).

Woodburn, James C.
1972   Ecological, Nomadic Movement and the Composition of the Local Group among Hunters and Gatherers: An East African Example and its Implications, in *Man, Settlement, and Urbanism,* Peter J. Ucko, Ruth Tringham, and G. W. Dimbleby, eds.: 293–306. Hertfordshire, UK: Duckworth Press.
1979   Minimal Politics: The Political Organization of the Hadza of North Tanzania, in *Politics in Leadership: A Comparative Perspective,* William A. Shack and Percy S. Cohen, eds.: 244–266. Oxford: Clarendon Press.
1980   Hunters and Gatherers Today and Reconstruction of the Past, in *Soviet and Western Anthropology,* Ernest Gellner, ed.: 95–117. New York: Columbia University Press.
1982   Egalitarian Societies. *Man* (n.s.) 17:431–451.
1984   Stability and Flexibility in Hadza Residential Groupings, in *Man the Hunter* 2nd ed., Richard B. Lee and Irven DeVore, eds.: 103–110. New York: Aldine.

Wrangham, Richard W.
1987   African Apes: The Significance of African Apes for Reconstructing Human Social Evolution, in *The Evolution of Human Behavior: Primate Models,* Warren G. Kinzey, ed.: 51–71. Albany: State University of New York Press.

Wreschner, Ernst E.
1981   Red Ochre and Human Evolution: A Case for Discussion. *Current Anthropology* 21:631–644.

Yengoyan, Aram A.
1984   Demographic and Ecological Influences on Aboriginal Australian Marriage Sections, in *Man the Hunter* 2nd ed., Richard B. Lee and Irven DeVore, eds.: 185–199. New York: Aldine.

Zvelebil, Marek, ed.
1986   *Hunters in Transition: Mesolithic Societies of Temperate Eurasia and Their Transition to Farming.* Cambridge: Cambridge University Press.

✦ 3

Surrendered Men: Peaceable Enclaves in the Post-Enlightenment West

Robert Knox Dentan

What is it that accounts for peaceful societies? Robert Knox Dentan, who has done field work among what may be the most peaceful society known to anthropology, the Semai, looks at the nature of peace in more complex cultures. His focus is on "enclaved societies," groups such as the Hutterites or Amish, who maintain a distinct culture within a larger society. In the experience of the people of the United States, many of these groups have been astonishingly peaceful, perhaps more so than any other of the peaceful societies known to anthropology. In 350 years, we learn, no Hutterite living within his community has slain another community member.

How can such peace be achieved? Dentan takes a comparative perspective, examining the experience of the Hutterites, the Amish, and more recently formed in-and-out-of-mainstream societies such as the Rainbows and Alcoholics Anonymous. He finds striking correspondences among these groups in the relationship of the individual to the community; in the experience of the group in meeting the outside world; and—for the most part—in an authoritarian tradition. Dentan finds some of these features are characteristic of band societies that are regarded as the most peaceful known to comparative ethnography. What emerges from Dentan's discussion is an unsettling question: Does peace necessarily have a high price? Is the experience of band societies and enclaved groups the only way to achieve peace? Are their experiences relevant to that of the wider society? The reader may be left with the disquieting thought that an imperfect peace is the best we can hope for in an imperfect world.

—THE EDITORS

God worketh only in surrendered men.
　　　　　—Hutterite proverb (Hostetler 1974: 144)

Violence is as American as apple pie.
　　　　　—Stokely Carmichael

✦   In the rising tide of violence in the West are islets of peaceability. How do they survive and maintain themselves? This chapter examines the dynamics of peaceability among North American peaceable "intentional groups": groups whose existence stems from their program (Dentan 1992; Erasmus 1981).

A potentially useful approach to the question is to contrast such "intentional" groups with those that form without conscious planning.[1] Among many foraging peoples and some shifting agriculturalists, nonviolence seems to be a dynamic adaptation to particular political-ecological circumstances (Power 1993: 512). In brief, this unplanned peaceability appears to involve a social organization grounded on mutually independent egalitarian face-to-face primary groups called "bands." Such social organization can arise as an adaptive response to defeat by neighboring peoples when there are relatively unpopulated areas ("refuges") to flee to. These circumstances can lead to a worldview that stresses either "positive" or "negative" peaceability, loving peace or fearing violence, and that entails gentle childrearing. Space does not permit recapping the evidence for how natural-world groups form and survive (for that evidence, see Dentan 1992). For comparative purposes, I will sometimes cross-refer to Semai, a Malaysian people with whom I have been familiar for over thirty years. Semai in this usage represent "refugees," unselfconsciously nonviolent natural-world peoples.

The Peace Groups

The five intentional groups examined fall into two broad categories: "cenobites" and "occasional groups." Cenobites live in permanent communities based on a common religion. The cenobites dealt with in this chapter are Shakers, Amish, and Hutterites. Murder does occur among Amish, but it is extremely rare. In at least some cases, it is also brutal and gruesome, as in a 1993 case in Rockdale Township, PA, where a man beat his wife's head in (Anonymous 1993a). Still, no Old Order Amish person has ever been arrested for a felony (Wittmer 1970: 1064); nor, in over 350 years, has any Hutterite slain another in a bruderhof community (Briggs 1988: 2). Cenobitic pacifism also extends to outsiders.

Two "occasional" organizations are discussed in the chapter: the Rainbow Family and Alcoholics Anonymous (AA). These are acephalous "quasi-groups" (Pospisil 1966: 404–406). They convene regularly to celebrate group unity and group values. They require intragroup peaceability and encourage nonviolence throughout their members' lives. The Rainbow Family of Living Light began its national "gatherings" early in the 1970s. There are local gatherings and national gatherings. The national gathering (held July 1 to July 7) is the central feature of Rainbow social organization. At gatherings, Rainbows are explicitly pacifist. Planning for the 1991 national gathering included work groups on "Peacekeeping" (dealing with verbal and other violence among Rainbows), "Rainbow Peace Projects," "a Peace Pageant," "a Peace Ceremony" and a "Peacenet" computer network. For a few Rainbows, mostly "real vicious warriors" who survived Vietnam, gatherings mark an interlude of peace in otherwise violent lives. All my information about the "family" comes from a doctoral thesis on the topic by a member, Michael Niman (1991).

Among the 1991 Rainbow work groups was one on "twelve-step programs"; e.g., Alcoholics Anonymous (AA); also its offshoots. AA is the other group examined. Although pacificism is not part of the AA program, AA doctrine regards resentment and anger as dangerous emotions likely to make members relapse into drinking. Nonviolence is thus an instrumental goal. I have been a member of AA for over a dozen years.

These five peace groups are among the most successful in terms of membership and social acceptance of any nonviolent enclaved groups known. Except for the Shakers, all seem to be increasing in size. From 1900 to 1980, the Amish population rose from 5000 to 80,000 (Hostetler 1980b: 125) or 108,000 (Kraybill 1989: 264). Hostetler has written: "The Hutterite Brethren are the largest and most successful Christian communal group in the United States" (1980c: 471). The Shakers were historically the most successful cenobites in terms of recruiting converts and amassing communal wealth; still, recruitment officially stopped in the 1960s, and the last eldress (female church leader) died in 1990. As to AA, by 1976 there were over a million members in nearly 28,000 local groups (Alcoholics Anonymous 1985: xi). The organization seems to be growing rapidly and has spawned the fashionable codependency movement. In counting the Rainbows, at a guess about 100,000 participate in national or local gatherings.

Although all these groups were persecuted in the past, all have recently acquired a certain cachet, as public dissatisfaction with the consumerist values of greed and glut grows. Respectability may not be good for the survival of these groups in the long run (see subsection, Repressive Tolerance, near end of this chapter) but so far this seems to be no more than an annoyance or distraction to members (e.g., Fisher 1978: 361–367; Hostetler 1980b: 125; Stoltzfus 1989).

The groups share several characteristics (Ahlstrom 1972: 231; Hardman 1927). Most adhere to a myth of primitive Christianity in which asceticism, egalitarianism, mutual assistance, sharing (communalism or communism), and regular, face-to-face meeting in primary groups are salient (e.g., Brewer 1986: 21; Hostetler 1974; Kessel and Walton 1967). AA claims to be "spiritual" rather than religious (Alcoholics Anonymous 1985: 162–163) but owes a lot to the Oxford Movement, which sought a return to medieval Christianity (Ahlstrom 1972: 621–622, 628–629; Alcoholics Anonymous 1985: 58–59, 64–68, 74–75; Mayer 1954: 277–278). The Rainbow Family rejects organized religion but subscribes to a syncretic New Age spirituality that the family associates with Native Americans. Their mythic charter has much in common with the medieval Christian notion of a "natural state" of society before the rise of hierarchy—a notion (often formalized as the Fifth Epistle of Clement) that played a major role in the peasant movements from which the cenobitic traditions spring (Berger 1979: 196–209; Cohn 1970: 194–197)—a case of reciprocal mutuality.

Cenobites and Rainbows seek to establish a community that follows an explicit code in which "positive peaceability" is salient. All the peace groups with the exception of the Rainbows hold the notion of an initial conversion experience, or "metanoia," that begins with fear or pain and includes an element of surrender and acceptance, bringing those feelings within tolerable limits; and all have difficulty making this experience accessible to their children.

✦ Similarities Between Peace Groups and "Refugees"

Origins in Violence

> *Power and authority are sometimes bought by kindness; but they can never be begged as alms by an impoverished and defeated violence.*
> —Edmund Burke, "On Conciliation" (quoted in Diggins 1993: 11)

I briefly described the common characteristics of nonviolent natural-world peoples (those I call "refugees") at the opening of the chapter. I have documented them and discussed them more fully elsewhere (Dentan 1992). Here I deal with peace-group characteristics that seem similar.

Peaceability among both natural world peoples and peace groups seems to stem from defeat.

> Defeat tamed them . . . those that survived did so by learning virtues of political accommodation or withdrawal from temporal affairs. The bellicose Taborites merged into the Moravian Brethren, the once feared Anabaptists . . . became Mennonites, and the Anti-Cromwellian Fifth Monarchists dissolved into Quakerism. (Barkun 1986: 68–69)

Defeat requires mutual concessions, latent or manifest, by both sides, not just subjecting "passive" losers to the "active" winners' will (Coser 1961). In fact, losers must decide to stop fighting: to withdraw from the contest and abandon their claims. The decision in some ways resembles the "learned helplessness" attributed to battered women (Hoff 1990: 32, 64–66; Walker 1979).

Therefore, defeated people need not think of themselves as "losers." Like Shiite Muslims of Iran and southern Iraq and the cenobites in this study, they may construe their survival as a success in the teeth of the evil forces that defeated them. Like Shiites, Amish celebrate their persecution by the outside world. Surrender, in AA rhetoric, makes one a "winner." A reinterpretation of defeat makes it less demoralizing; it generates "relative advantage"—a sense that the in-group is morally superior to the victors (Wolf 1990). Thus, Amish take pride in being "defenseless Christians" (J. Hostetler and Huntington 1992: 9).

> *I must be a Christian child,*
> *Gentle, patient, meek and mild;*
> *Must be honest, simple, true*
> *In my words and actions too.*
> *I must cheerfully obey,*
> *Giving up my will and way.*
>   —from an Amish school booklet (Kraybill 1989: 30, 1990: 27)

Anabaptists and Camisards

Anabaptism gave rise to the German-American peace groups; the Camisard movement gave rise to Shakers. Both are revitalization movements (Cohn 1970). German peaceability followed the repeated, ruthless repression of egalitarian, communist, Anabaptist revolutionaries in the early 1500s (Blickle 1981; Cohn 1970: 223–286; Hostetler 1974: 6–27; Hutterite Brethren 1989; Johnson 1976: 260; Kraybill 1989: 3–6). It may be worth remarking that Germans gloss the English word *nonviolence* as *Gewehrlosigkeit, defenselessness,* or *Ohnmacht, without power* (Nagler 1982: 139).

Historians estimate that as many as 100,000 revolutionaries were massacred in 1524 and 1525 alone. A couple of thousand were executed in gory ways (Blickle 1981: xvii–xviii; Holloway 1951: 29). Jacob Hutter himself was burnt at the stake in 1536, eight years after the group of refugees from the Tirol, whom he led, had begun to practice communism (Hostetler 1980c: 471). At least some Anabaptist revolutionaries, "the left wing of the Reformation," themselves were violent (Blickle 1981: xvii; Holloway 1951: 29; Hostetler 1974: 7). The Anabaptist leader of the greatest revolt of the late medieval peasant uprisings, "the most thoughtful theoretician of the whole Revolution of 1525" (Blickle 1981: xviii), "signed his letters with the Sword of Gideon and the phrase 'Thomas Muntzer the Hammer. . . .' 'Let not the sword of the saint get cold' was his motto; and his heraldic sign was a red cross and a naked sword." (Johnson 1976: 261; cf. Cohn 1970: 234–251; Mayer 1954: 132).

In the 1500s, some Anabaptist communes more resembled the violence-riddled, terminal stages of failed U.S. therapeutic communities than their (future) U.S. offshoots (Hostetler 1974: 6, 21; Johnson 1976:

262–263; Mayer 1954: 392; Weppner 1983). After the bloody repression, however, they subsided. "Well before they began leaving Europe they had lost their aggressiveness; they were the Stillen am Lande" (Ahlstrom 1972: 231). Pacificism spread quickly a year after the crushing of the main rebellion in 1525 (Hostetler 1974: 6). Peter (1987: 10, 27–28) suggests that Hutterite pacifism was a conscious reaction to military defeat.

Peacefulness did not end the persecution (e.g., Holloway 1951; Hostetler 1974: 11–12), but the sects that survived were pacifist, while resisters "died out," in Hostetler's euphemism (1974: 26). Hutterites fled to reserves in Moravia to found pacifist communities (Hostetler 1974: 29–60, 184–190; Peter 1987: 37–38), accepting refugees from other places and splitting along doctrinal lines. They practiced mandatory sharing (cf. Price 1975) and generally behaved like band communities until renewed persecution, from 1590 to 1621, drove them further east.

Shakers

Shakerism (the United Society of Believers in Christ's Second Appearing) seems partly the product of proselytizing by refugee "French prophets," Huguenot Camisard revolutionaries (Ahlstrom 1972: 494; Foster 1981: 23–24; Holloway 1951: 56; Mayer 1954: 442; but also see Foster 1981: 267n.9). The Camisard movement was a response to prolonged, vicious repression of Protestantism by Louis XIV after the revocation of the Edict of Nantes in 1688. By the beginning of the 1700s, this genocidal persecution, the Dragonnades, provoked revolutionary counterviolence that lasted for years, involved great cruelty by both sides, and forced 200,000 or 300,000 Huguenots to flee to England, Holland, and Prussia (Schwartz 1980: 11–27). In Britain, the nonviolent Shakers were "whipped, beaten with clubs, stoned, kicked, dragged about by their arms and legs" like their French forerunners (Holloway 1951: 59). Many subsequently fled to North America.

The Rainbow Family

The Rainbow Family grew out of popular revulsion against the televised brutalities of the Vietnam War. Its core consists of antiwar activists, whose pracifism permeates Rainbow ideology. "Whacked out Vietnam vets" are another major component. Their military background contributes much of Rainbow vocabulary; e.g., the medical unit was *MASH* until it recently became *CALM,* the Center for Alternative Living Medicine. The vets supply much of the infrastructure of latrines and field kitchens that make gatherings possible.

Alcoholics Anonymous

Increasing evidence suggests that, as children, many alcoholics suffered beating or sexual abuse by adults, an experience of violent defeat and powerlessness as vivid as a human being can have. Although the defeat that leads to AA membership is proximately due to alcohol addiction, inability to participate in normal, or even in alcoholic, society plays a major role in convincing people to join. As long as life outside AA retains some social pleasures, heavy drinkers opt to continue (e.g., Kessel and Walton 1967: 143, 153–154; Schur 1969: 212; Spradley 1970: 12–64; Weppner 1973, 1983: 8–17). This "deviant" and therefore increasingly isolated pattern of living may be a "preadaptation" for membership in the relatively closed society of AA. AA recruits most successfully among those who have "hit bottom," i.e., those whose suffering far outweighs pleasure (e.g., Alcoholics Anonymous 1976: 171–461; Anonymous 1972; Kessel and Walton 1967: 87, 104–106). Indeed, "old timers" may tell reluctant "pigeons" (novices) to "go out and drink again until you're ready." Surrender is the "first step" in the twelve-step program.

✦ Social Organization

Primitivism

The peace groups model themselves on imagined primitives, especially on imagined "primitive Christians." Persecution during the early days of Christianity may have led congregations to adopt the sort of social organization that proved adaptive for foragers and shifting agriculturalists seeking refuge from more powerful neighbors (Dentan 1992). Whatever the historical reality of such "primitive" social organization among Christians, idealizing "primitive" ways is a perennial European and Euroamerican phenomenon that goes back at least as far as Tacitus's contrast of Germanic and Celtic virtues with Imperial Roman decadence (Allen 1913).

The Rainbow Family originated when deracinated middle- and upper-class young people adopted idealized "tribal" peoples as models. Although they disregarded the primitive Christian ideal, which was too close to the oppressive orthodoxy they were rebelling against, their notion of "tribal" peoples served the same function. Indeed, the social and ethical content of the "tribal" and "primitive Christian" ideals is almost identical, sometimes in conscious defiance of ethnographic fact (Dentan 1988b, 1988d; McGlashan 1987, 1988; cf. Holloway, 1951: 21–22). The associated rituals involve items thought to be "tribal," such as feathers, beads, crystals. The language is New Age, Jungian, or sometimes of AA origin. "Neoshamanism" flourishes in journals like *Shaman's Drum.* This "journal of experiential shamanism" contains some interesting ethnography. Neoshamanism is also celebrated in the more mystical and impressionistic *Snake Power, A Journal of Contemporary Female Shamanism.* These movements often involve a concern with peace (e.g., Walker 1991).

Social Characteristics

Whether or not peace groups reproduce primitive Christian or Native American social organization (whatever that really was like), the social organization prevalent among these enclaved groups does resemble that of traditional "band level" peoples. Cenobites live in close-knit communities. In North America, however, the land-base is a reserve rather than a band-style territory. Rainbow gatherings occur in set-aside areas of National Parks or National Forests, reserves as transient as the church basements in which AA meetings stereotypically occur.

Peaceable natural-world "refugees" tend to be xenophobic. German cenobites stress not mixing with outsiders, whom they treat with polite, sometimes affable, reserve (Fisher 1978: 72–73, 116–121). AA and other therapeutic "fellowships," especially those focused on obsessive-compulsive behavior or shared traumas, may isolate themselves structurally by preserving members' anonymity, refusing or limiting outside funding and publicity, closing at least some meetings to outsiders, using a distinctive patois, and in other ways fostering a "we-group" ethos. AA meetings begin with a statement that AA neither endorses nor opposes any causes that engage the attention of "earthpeople." Rainbows stress that they "are not affiliated with any organized religious, political, economic or other group." This insulation seems to have kept them relatively immune to social science (but see, e.g., Gartner 1984; Suler 1984; Weppner 1983).

Political Characteristics

Membership. As in band societies, people may join a peace group by birth or as a result of preexisting social ties, like friendship or workplace association. Affiliation with a particular local group usually rests on proximity or birth. Many social activities, e.g., dances and picnics, recruit only from within the group, and so on. Membership in local German peace groups is flexible, following the fission-fusion pattern characteristic of bands (Barkun 1986: 134–137; Hostetler 1974: 370–372, 1980c: 472; Peter 1987: 61, 81). Rainbows and AAs routinely disperse among outsiders and then gather periodically to celebrate their values, in a manner reminiscent of the fission-fusion pattern of band societies.

Ethnicity is explicitly not a factor in peace group membership. The German groups do not proselytize, and so retain ethnic characteristics. Still, being German seems to have been as unimportant in their lives as it was for German immigrants in general, although one major Amish schism was over language (Hawgood 1940; Nowak 1972: 46–48; Turner 1894: 216–217). As a result of conversions (e.g., Stoltzfus 1989) and adoptions (e.g., Luthy 1989a, 1989b), a third of Amish names are of U.S. origin (Hostetler 1980c: 483). Several people who were antiwar activists during the 1970s joined the Rifton, New York, Hutterite Bruderhof, itself the product of the affiliation of another pacifist movement with the Hutterites (Briggs, 1988: 1; Hostetler 1980c: 473). The Rifton fusion of traditional cenobites with antiwar protesters (who elsewhere became Rainbows) points up the fundamental similarity between the two peace groups. The English origins of Shakerism apparently did not affect its rapid growth by conversion and adoption in the North during the Civil War, when the British sided with the Confederacy. Opposition to the war, however, may have offset ethnic bias.

Although most AAs condemn overt racism or sexism as signs of not "working the program," AA has always attracted and kept a disproportionately large European-American membership, a situation that may be self-maintaining (Caldwell 1983). A sample of about 150 "alcoholism professionals" rated AA more effective for European-Americans than for Native Americans or Afro-Americans. The Cherokee psychologist who conducted the study (Starr 1991) suggests that this judgement may stem from the fact that, for reasons not directly due to alcoholism, social disorganization among minorities is worse, making social therapies less efficient. Professionals who were in AA were more likely than their peers to rate a minority person's alcoholism as severe, though they also thought them as likely as European-Americans to benefit from AA. In their lives outside the organization, AAs seemed more tolerant of Native American alcoholics, and less of Afro-American or European-American ones, than were their colleagues. This confusing congeries of data, which needs replication, may reflect the salience of confession in AA life.

To work, confession requires community. AA began as a middle-class, male-dominated, European-American movement—origins that were perpetuated in the language of the group's Big Book (Alcoholics Anonymous 1976). AA principles of openness and esprit de corps often may not be enough to bridge the existential abysses that divide the levels of U.S. ethnic (and gender) hierarchies. Meetings do represent a cross section of U.S. society, but not a statistically random one. Thus, although all meetings are ideally open to anyone with "a desire to stop drinking," in western New York state, gays, women, Hispanics, and Senecas have formed their own AA groups.

Most Rainbows condemn racial, ethnic, or gender bias, but the Family attracts few Afro-Americans. Rainbows say that, since gatherings are in rural areas, poor urban people rarely hear of them and find them hard to attend. The rule that everyone is welcome draws in some local European-Americans wherever the gathering is held. Native American membership is disproportionately high; and it would be higher, Niman speculates (1991), if Rainbow "Indian worship" (see below) were not simultaneously so ersatz and so pervasive.

Leadership. As in bands, peace group leadership often rests on persuasive ability or perceived superior spirituality. In AA, these are signs of "good sobriety." Distinctions based on age and sex occur, but they may be subordinate to the principle of egalitarianism within the group (see discussion below). Rainbows are particularly sensitive to any violation of absolute equality. Thus, every Rainbow meeting has a council, which anyone may join at any time. Although councils lack enforcement power, they "consense" group decisions on tactics and policy. To assure that everyone has a chance to speak, participants often pass a "focal object" around the council circle. As long as a person is holding the object—often a feather, at least in name, following supposed Amerindian custom—that person has the right to speak at any length and on any topic. Arriving at consensus can take a long time. Of all the peace groups, Rainbows probably most closely approximate the long, inconsequential meetings of unselfconsciously egalitarian societies. The North East Rainbow Family (NERF) in 1991 suggested several changes of procedure to streamline council proceedings. In theory, anyone can speak at any length in an AA "discussion meeting," but in fact "moderators" and self-censorship work against longwindedness, so that meetings rarely last over two hours.

✦ Differences Between Peace Groups and "Refugees"

> *It is our principle to feed the hungry and give the thirsty drink; we have dedicated ourselves to serve all men in everything that can be helpful to the preservation of men's lives, but we find no freedom in giving, or doing, or assisting in anything by which men's lives are destroyed or hurt.*
> —Mennonite Memorial to the Pennsylvania Assembly, 1775

The "peace groups" on which this chapter focuses differ from natural-world peaceable ethnic groups ("refugees") in five ways (cf. Dentan 1992). (1) Pacifism, with a "spiritual" justification, is an explicit part of "peace group" ideology, which stresses conscious and positive peace rather than the unformulated, often negative peace of many refugees. (2) The peace groups are "intentional," i.e., have an explicit program that rationalizes and justifies perpetuating themselves (Chang 1981; Erasmus 1981). Enclaved groups like these seem to need this intentionality, as a mythic charter. (3) AA and the Rainbow Nation are "quasi-groups," social categories whose members assemble periodically but otherwise live scattered among out-siders. AA meetings and Rainbow gatherings serve, among other things, as "time out" from the pressures of life outside (cf. Roy 1960). (4) Each group has "reserves," spaces within which the enclaving dominant group lets the peace group conduct its own affairs without interference, provided that the dominant group's interests are not threatened: "beggar's democracy" (Wittfogel 1957: 121–126). (5) Peaceable refugees, by definition, can often flee their powerful neighbors; whereas peace groups are surrounded. They cannot flee and therefore must devise tactics to fend off extermination, sub-version, or assimilation (Change 1981; Erasmus 1981).

Property

The distribution of wealth among peace groups is more explicit than the sharing that occurs in simple band societies. Among Hutterites and Shakers, Acts 2: 44–54 and 5: 1–11 rationalize and justify group ownership of property. Amish and Rainbows stress sharing and cooperation. The cenobites all refer to Acts 4: 32–37, in which God kills the archetypal liar, Ananias (and Ananias's wife), for trying to avoid giving all their wealth to the church by underreporting their wealth. These ideas belong to the ideo-logical baggage of medieval peasant revolts, including Anabaptists and Camisards (Cohn 1970: 194, 197).

Neither the Rainbow Family nor AA requires members to contribute money. A Rainbow council may "consense" to authorize a Magic Hat Dance to go from camp to camp in a gathering to collect money for large, shared expenses, e.g., buying truckloads of drinking water. Similarly, before the Lord's Prayer, which concludes AA meetings, the moderator passes a basket for voluntary contributions, saying, "We have no dues or fees, but we do have expenses."

Maintaining Identity

Lacking the oppositional frontier processes that create peaceable "refugees," cenobites need "specific mechanisms to maintain the bound-aries between the people and the other 'others'" (Castile 1981: xix). Physical isolation in North America is tricky, though Hutterites and Amish stress and value apartness (Briggs 1988: 1; Hostetler 1980a: 157; Wittmer 1970: 1063). Hutterites manage fairly well to isolate themselves in Canada, although, unlike Amish, they use modern machinery that ties them to the nation-state economy (Hostetler 1974; Holloway 1951: 212–213). Hutterites, like Semai and other peoples persecuted by outsiders, use the presence of outsiders as an opportunity to inculcate xenophobia in children (Peter 1987: 64; cf. Dentan 1978: 128; von Graeve 1989: 4), creating an image of non-Hutterites as bogeymen. Rainbows refer to the outside world as "Babylon," condemning both urbanism and greed in a traditional Jewish and Christian metaphor. AA meetings stress the danger of associating with "wet places and wet people," i.e., drinkers and drinking places. Many AAs socialize almost entirely within "the fellowship."

Group-ideological grounds other than xenophobia also rationalize, regarding group members as fundamentally different from outsiders. Interpersonal rituals and symbols reflect and maintain this separate identity (e.g., Hostetler 1964, 1974: 169–177, 257–260; see discussion of "partial ideology" below). The personal possessions and clothing of Amish, Hutterites, Shakers, and Rainbows manifest lifestyles more austere than most North Americans tolerate.

Belief in dogmatic details is not mandatory for German cenobites, Shakers, Rainbows, or AAs, contrary to first appearances: "We, generally, don't think much in terms of a creed," say Hutterites (Briggs 1988: 2). Similarly, the twelve steps of AA are explicitly "suggestions" (Alcoholics Anonymous 1976: 59; 1985: 74–75), although group pressure to follow them is strong. North American German cenobites may entertain "weird theological aberrations and radical social ideas" (Mayer 1954: 391) as long as they join in group meetings and rituals and otherwise maintain the group identity, which functions like ethnicity (Holloway 1951: 73; Name Withheld 1989; Peter 1987: 67–68; but cf. Brane 1989). Thus, it is less paradoxical than an outsider might think to find among German cenobites

> complete tolerance of conflicting and even mutually exclusive doctrinal views and violent dissensions in matters of cultus . . . [which] rent their body asunder over the language question and split a congregation over the question whether the second band of suspenders constitutes a forbidden luxury. (Mayer 1954: 393; cf. Peter 1987: 30–31)

Their "ethnic totemism" (Schwartz 1975) is "polarization . . . on the basis of select and sometimes minute differences of custom" (Knauft 1985: 327–328). To persist, enclaved peoples require a common set of symbols and rituals. Requiring consensus on the meaning of those symbols might make solidarity harder to maintain (e.g., Johnsen 1980; Knauft 1985: 328–329; Gilsenan 1982: 20, 33; cf. Castile 1981: xix; Tan 1988: 161–164).

A number of practices similarly maintain AA identity. Members refer to nonalcoholic outsiders as "normal people" or "earthpeople." Sayings like "one day at a time" identify AA members to each other, as does the association's "memorable, technical language" (Kessel and Walton 1967: 141). AA bumperstickers (e.g., "One day at a time") and "anniversary" lapel pins identify their users to other AAs. The program stresses the need to maintain the unity and gregariousness characteristic of band societies while concealing members' identities from presumably hostile outsiders (Alcoholics Anonymous 1976: 565; Kessell and Walton 1967: 141, 143).

Relations with Outsiders

We are being schooled into eternal life. We have forsaken the loves of the wor[l]d as well as its lusts, because neither are eternal. We realize war to be the product of earthly loves and relations, we will not fight, nor vote for those who do fight; nor for those who believe in marriage, private property, or who engage in fleshly lusts of whatever description.
—"The Shaker" (Whitson 1983: 197)

The practices that maintain group identity often clash with outsider norms. They stress unity and harmony, not the individualism and competition so salient in the enclaving society. Amish look quaint to mainline North Americans; the total celibacy of Shakers seems bizarre; and both "hippies" and "lushes" are pariah identities. The selectivity of Amish responses to technological innovations produces adaptations that strike outsiders as anomalous; for example, rubber tires are rejected but rollerblades are popular (Anonymous 1993b). The asceticism of North American German cenobites (Hostetler 1974: 255–284), Shakers (Emlen 1987), Rainbows, and AAs (cf. Hardman 1924) conflicts with the invidious consumerism that pervades the mass media (Olshan 1989). Many mainline people in the U.S. regard pacifism as wimpish and bizarre, so that, in periods of heightened jingoism, persecution flares up easily. Thus, all but one colony of Hutterites had to flee to Canada during World War I (Hostetler 1980c: 473; cf. 1980b: 124).

One result of this conflict is that endogamy is preferential (AA) or prescribed (Old Order Amish) and nonconformity leads to ostracism. Amish discourage fraternizing with outsiders (Hostetler 1964; Kollmorgen 1989). Drinkers outside AA are "wet people," and a basic maxim, stressed especially to newcomers, is that sobriety requires socializing with other members and "staying away from wet places and wet people." These exclusivities may conflict with each other as well as with mainline society: at least one Amishman felt he had to become a Mennonite in order to continue his involvement with AA (Hall 1989).

These customs and the constant conflict to which they are a response take their toll. Members lapse, e.g., from Amish or Hutterite to Mennonite (Fisher 1989; Hall 1989; Hostetler 1964, 1980b: 124; Smith 1989), or "slip" (return to alcoholic drinking), or die out, albeit after two centuries of success, like Shakers. All the cenobites lost members at one time and place or another. Of 1,265 Hutterites who arrived in the Dakotas in the 1870s to escape the draft in Russia, only 443 remained in the community (Hostetler 1980c: 472). European Amish have assimilated into the prevailing religions; in the United States about one in four drop out, usually accompanied by family members (Hostetler 1980b: 123). AA's self-estimated lapse rate of 50 percent may be low, although many people return after a slip or simply "go in and out of the program." Rainbow membership seems equally labile. Still, less than 2 percent of Hutterites leave the movement permanently (Hostetler 1980c: 472). The survival and growth of these groups indicates that lapsing is not a major cause of group dissolution in North America, even for the Shakers, whose dissolution seems linked to celibacy and failure to proselytize successfully.

Constructions of Self

For peaceable egalitarianism to last in bands or peace groups, individual autonomy and self-control are vital (Gardner 1991; Dentan 1992). Members must be self-reliant and independent. For example, Hutterites accept people whom the enclaving society would extrude as psychotics or mental defectives, and instead encourage them to work up to their abilities (Eaton and Weil 1955: 157). These autonomous individuals have to shun ambition and eschew prestige or power. The ties that exist between them are personal, consensual, informal, and comprehensible to the participants. People thus can alter or cancel them, unlike the impersonal, inescapable, universalistic, and incomprehensible ties that bind, say, Arab peasants, Japanese businessmen, and U.S. suburbanites together. Everyone is responsible for their own actions. The possibility of escape to the enclaving society makes it hard to maintain authoritarianism without segueing into the totalitarian control characteristic of failed utopias, like Synanon.

This sort of individual autonomy could become *individualism,* the term Alexis de Tocqueville (1840 [1965]) coined to describe early nineteenth-century U.S. society, and ultimately degenerate into the late twentieth-century *egotism* he foresaw.

> Egotism is a passionate and exaggerated love of self, which leads a man to connect everything with his own person, and to prefer himself to everything in the world. Individualism is a mature and calm feeling which disposes each member of a community to sever himself from the mass of his fellow-creatures, and to draw apart with his family and his friends, so that, after he has formed a little circle of his own, he willingly leaves society at large to itself. . . . Egotism blights the germ of all virtue; individualism, at first, only saps the virtues of public life; but . . . is at length absorbed in downright egotism. Egotism is a vice as old as the world; . . . individualism is of separate origin, and it threatens to spread in the same ratio as the equality of conditions. . . . Thus not only does democracy make every man forget his ancestors, but it hides his descendents, and separates his contemporaries from him; it throws him back forever upon himself alone, and threatens in the end to confine him entirely within the solitude of his own heart.

Individualism in this sense makes each person his or her own moral master; freed from oppression, one may deny, repress, or dissociate unacceptable impulses like aggression (Lears 1981: 12–13).

By contrast, among the peace groups, group disapproval tends to control outbreaks of selfishness, individualism, or egotism. Among the cenobites, reiteration of the history of persecution and insistent control of their children's education tends to nullify the generational isolation that Tocqueville discusses. AA's "twelfth step" stresses service to others, and the program in general stresses humility and self-restraint: "This is a 'we' program," members say.

All the groups under consideration, except perhaps the Rainbows, stress self-control.

> Society cannot exist unless a controlling power upon will and appetite be placed somewhere, and the less of it there is within, the more there must be without. . . . Men of intemperate minds cannot be free. Their passions forge their fetters. (Burke 1971 [1982]: 48)

The cenobites, like AAs, stress humility and self-restraint. AAs are encouraged to "turn over" socially unacceptable emotions to their Higher Power, not express them. Rainbows share the U.S. stress on self-fulfillment and self-expression rather than self-control; but people will encircle someone who seems to be "acting out" and, in chorus, hum the syllable *Om* until the person calms down. This practice, called omming, derives from Tibetan Buddhism, in which saying *om* expresses the spiritual power of Buddha and thus creates an atmosphere of peace, compassion, and good (Evans-Wentz 1958: 127n.).

Alcohol constitutes a danger to peaceable societies because it threatens self-control. Cross-culturally, drinking need not lead to violence (Mangin 1957; MacAndrew and Edgerton 1969). However, as the psychoanalytic anthropologist John Dollard used to say, "The superego is the only part of the personality which is soluble in alcohol." Alcoholic loss of self-control can cause social disruption (see, e.g., references in Dentan 1992: 241; Eber 1991; Peranen 1991). The group must respond; but groups that rely on self-control may have no effective, legitimate sanctions other than violence to control drunken loss of self-control (Knauft 1991; Otterbein 1986: 49–60). Thus, drunkenness may disrupt peace both directly and indirectly.

All these groups frown on heavy drinking. Nevertheless, unbaptized Amish teenagers sometimes get drunk and even violent (Kraybill 1989: 138–140). Unbaptized people, however, are "children," not expected to hew to adult standards (Hostetler and Huntington 1992: 10, 31–32). Thus, when two mentally retarded Hutterites repeatedly broke church rules, the community, rather than shunning them, revoked their baptisms: as "children" they were destined for salvation however they behaved (Eaton and Weil 1955: 157). AA's charter is to help members stop drinking, although drunks often come to meetings. Most violence at Rainbow gatherings occurs at A (for Alcohol) Camp, which many Rainbows find an embarrassment. An A Camp is normally on the fringes of the gathering, usually at the front gate, where bikers and locals who have come to "party with the hippies" can congregate and drink. Rainbows encircle violent drunks, omming to reattune the "vibrations" until peaceability resumes.

Confession vs. Reticence

Confession binds peace group members together. All stress "sharing feelings" in ways that are congenial to current pop psychotherapeutic praxis but alien to people in small egalitarian bands, who depend heavily on reticence and self-control to prevent violence (Knauft 1991). Cenobitic confession is a Christian sacrament (Brewer 1986: 13, 20, 50–41; Foster 1981: 75; Holloway 1951: 68–69; Schwartz 1980: 215n.; Weigle 1928: 243): "Confessions provided much of the cement that kept the [Shaker] Family system from falling apart" (Brewer 1986: 71). The catharsis and acceptance that follow confession are therapeutic (Kraybill 1989: 111–114).

After chanting *Om,* Rainbow councils begin with "Heartsong," a gloss of a supposed Amerindian word. During Heartsong, speakers may bare their feelings at some length. Members should pay as much heed to each Heartsong as to group business. No agenda item takes priority. Similarly, AAs hear each other's confessions. The principle is, "Identify (the hearer's experiences with the speaker's), don't compare" (i.e., contrast the two). AA's fourth and fifth "steps" involve revealing particularly intimate secrets. "Speaker's meetings" usually involve confession (*drunkalog*) by a single person. "Closed meetings" may involve joint confessions.

Confession works as social control, like the intimacy and absence of privacy among peaceable "refugees" like the Semai. Moreover, like the long, inconclusive meetings of nonhierarchical peoples, confession vents and reduces resentments against other group members. Indeed, the failure of the French Prophets may have been partly due to the absence of confession (Schwartz 1980: 214n.–215n.). Moreover, since TV dramas have replaced neighborhood gossip, Rainbow gatherings and AA meetings have become oases of empathy in a desert of mutual indifference.

Egalitarianism vs. the Control of Sexuality and Women

The cenobites control in-group conflicts about sex in various ways. Like the Semai, all of them stress self-control over sexual urges, as does AA, but not the Rainbow Family (e.g., Foster 1981: 234–235; Peter 1987: 11, 78). Following common Western praxis, Amish and Hutterites equate the suppression of women with the control of sexuality. They attribute this patriarchy to Pauline Christian tradition (Briggs 1988: 2; Kraybill 1989: 71–73; Holloway 1951: 212; Hostetler 1974: 143, 145–146, 165; Peter 1987: 61–62, 68, 70, 78–81). Since cenobites, like Christians in general, are selective about their beliefs, the fact that Saint Paul endorses women's subordination does not explain why North American German cenobites accept it.

Indeed, it is this same "primitive Christian" rationale that makes AAs negative about "sexism" and leads Shakers explicitly to put the absolute equality of genders at the center of their belief system. To Shakers, Mother Ann Lee, the founder, represents the Second Coming of an androgynous deity whose First Coming, as Christ, was necessarily imperfect because He was merely male (Foster 1981: 41–42; Holloway 1951: 53–59, 64–79). The scriptural justification for androgyny is Matthew 22: 30: "For in the resurrection they neither marry nor are given in marriage but are like angels in heaven." This Christian tradition often unites gender-equality with Platonic love, i.e., strict chastity for both, as among Shakers and others (Foster 1981; Holloway 1951: 34–35, 39, 44, 50, 53–78, 88, 117, 132, 159). If violence among "band level" peoples stems from male sexual rivalry, as sociobiologists claim (Knauft 1987a), then mandatory chastity for everyone, besides maintaining gender-equality, works against violence (cf. Caplan 1987: 285–289). Indeed, Shaker authors explicitly say that the control of sexual conflict is fundamental to avoiding social disorder (Foster 1981: 46–47). Despite their promotion of celibacy, the Shakers made more money, recruited more people, and lasted longer than any of the other cenobites have so far.

Complaints that "male energy" was corrupting council led NERF Rainbows to put four stones in the center of the council circle to form an *X*, alternating "male" and "female" stones. To claim turns at speaking, people line up behind the sexually appropriate stone, or leave a personal possession to mark their place. As the council passes the focal object or "feather" around the circle, it thus goes alternately to men and women, so that the energies "balance."

Such divergence in matters of gender-equality is ancient. At least some German Anabaptists oppressed women far more rigorously than the most patriarchal Amish or Hutterites would dream of (Johnson 1976: 262–263; Mayer 1954: 392). The tenet that souls had no gender, and that chaste men and women were therefore spiritual equals, was endemic in southern France from at least the twelfth to the eighteenth century; i.e., into the time of the Camisard forerunners of the Shakers. Before the Huguenot revolt, women played an important role in Huguenot revitalization movements; during the revolt, men took control. Afterwards, women became important again, but they often felt forced into schisms from the patriarchal French Prophet authority structure (Schwartz 1980: 32–36, 80, 134–141, 210–214).

Rearing Children: Coercion vs. Permissiveness

Patriarchal authoritarianism connects with the difficulty all the cenobites had in transmitting their commitment to the next generation. Such fears need not lead to harsh enculturation: Shaker practice varied, becoming more repressive during periods of increased in-group patriarchy. Nevertheless, cenobites generally are more authoritarian with children than are peaceable "refugees" like Semai.

Rainbow councils discuss "alternative parenting" and "empowering children"; e.g., by involving them in planning a Kids' Village at gatherings. Adult Rainbows also worry that their permissiveness, especially about nudity, may give Babylon an excuse to intervene in the name of preventing child-molestation.

AA has no explicit program of child-training. It does, however, encourage children of alcoholics to join satellite fellowships like AlAnon, Alateen, and ACOL (Adult Children of Alcoholics), organizations that transmit AA values while rejecting traditional authority structures. Group pressure takes the form of constant repetition of the "AA message" by "speakers" or ordinary members during the course of a meeting and by "sponsors" in private. The response to people who have difficulty accepting AA tenets is to urge them to come to meetings more often: "Bring the body and the mind will follow."

In contrast with Rainbow precepts, Semai adults use bloodcurdling threats explicitly to keep children from wandering outside the community—and sometimes, apparently, for the fun of it. The first three Semai phrases my six-year-old daughter learned in 1991 were, "Chop off your head," "Split your heart," and "Gouge out your eyes." Adults and children may avoid looking at or speaking to each other when angry, but the avoidance lapses when the anger does, usually on the same day, and is not culturally elaborated. Amish "shunning" (ostracism) elaborates such spontaneous avoidance (Kraybill 1989: 114–118, 1990: 30–35). Formal shunning is a fundamental Amish tactic introduced by the founder, Jacob Ammann ([1989]; Hostetler 1980b: 123; Newman 1989; Wittmer 1970: 1064).

Corporal Punishment. Aside from such relatively gentle methods, cenobites approve the spanking and whipping of children (Anonymous 1989; Hostetler and Huntington 1992: 23; Kraybill 1989: 29; Stoll 1989; Wittmer 1970: 1064). Authoritarian child-rearing may originate in fear that the outside world may seduce members away (Hostetler 1964, 1974: 162–165; Kraybill 1989: 119). For example, although Hutterites say they use corporal punishment only as "a last resort," a once-lapsed Hutterite man who "interprets the strappings he was given as a child as a sign his father cared for him" says that corporal punishment "is a very sensitive subject for us, and it's a subject that needs the discernment of true, Christian love" (Briggs 1988: 2). Although Amish elder siblings do not discipline their wards physically (Hostetler 1980a: 159), and although switchings are reportedly not "harsh" (1980a: 174), disobedience results in "smackings" with "the hand, a switch, a razor strap, or a buggy whip. Temper tantrums, making faces, name-calling, and sauciness are extremely rare, for the child learns early that his reward for such rebellion is a sound thrashing" (1980a: 161). Outsiders may find such punishments equivalent to child abuse (Warner 1990).

Education. Peaceability seems incompatible with intragroup class structure (e.g., Dentan 1978: 134; Hostetler 1964: 185). Cenobites structure coercive enculturation by age and gender, ostensibly following "primitive Christian" patriarchy (Fabbro 1980: 199). The German cenobitic family is the locus of coercive enculturative authority (Holloway 1951: 19, 212; Hostetler 1964, 1974: 145, 203–206; Hostetler and Huntington 1967: 61). Hutterite communal educational structures are even more authoritarian than the familial ones (Hostetler 1974: 145, 210–220, 321–328; Peter 1987: 12–13, 62–67, 83–102).

The more coercive the group, the more difficulties the group has with the laxity and consumerism of U.S. public schools. Hutterites, who seem to have invented the notion of kindergarten centuries before other German-speakers adopted it, let their children attend public schools with non-Hutterite teachers; but the schools are so isolated that few outsiders attend (Hostetler 1980c: 472). Amish formerly followed the same pattern, until in the 1972 case of *Wisconsin v. Yoder* it was ruled that, beyond primary school, compulsory attendance laws violated their religious freedom (Hostetler 1980b: 125). AA has no position on public education, and Rainbows tend to regard it as repressive.

In fact, the continuation of intentional cenobitic groups, by definition based on ideology, may require coercive enculturation. Schwartz (1980: 279–282) blames the Camisard French Prophets' decline after their flight to London on their failure to pass on their values to their children. Similarly, Hutterite periods of decline seem to coincide with periods of less strict enculturation of children (Peter 1987: 12–14, 40–41); and the Shakers' ambivalence about discipline may have been a factor in their decline (Brewer 1986: 13–14, 74–78, 147–148). The survival of the groups with less authoritarian techniques of enculturation, like Shakers, Rainbows, and AA, depends mostly on recruiting outsiders.

Given the limited ways to structure coercion, patriarchy is an obvious solution to enculturation. Thus the gender-equality characteristic of many band societies, like Semai, is not a necessary correlate of peacefulness among enclaved peoples, although the two phenomena can co-occur. And the permissive child-rearing characteristic of most peaceable peoples outside the West seems to work against the survival of enclaved cenobites.

Peaceable Worldview: Ideologies Total and Partial

Peaceable peoples like Semai contrast themselves with the peoples they fear, creating a counterculture of the sort that other peoples populate with ghosts or witches. The imagined counterculture is much like their own, but with the values inverted. "We" are nonviolent; "they" are not. The result is that Semai are aware of how their more powerful neighbors live and think but, although they in fact have adapted many of their neighbors' ideas and customs to their own needs, reject the idea that their neighbors' worldviews are of any relevance to their own, except as opposites. Their ideology is "total" (Mannheim 1946: 49–40, 58–60); i.e., without intellectual competition.

By contrast, cenobitic ideology grew out of brutal political struggle that involved analyzing and rejecting the beliefs of other Christians, asserting the cenobites' ideological superiority. The Revolution of 1525 started as an ordinary medieval peasant revolt, but it developed its own ideology (e.g., the Swabian Twelve Articles [Blickle 1981: 195–201]). Rationalizing and justifying the rebellion, this ideology was in large part responsible for the spread of the revolution across Germany and for its appeal to miners and the urban lower classes whose economic and social interests were in many ways distinct from those of the peasants (Blickle 1981: xiii–xiv, xx, xxiii; Berger 1979: 195–213). The rise of sectarian "partial" ideology marks the transition between the competition for power within Catholicism, which involved seizing the authority to define heresy, and more "modern" ideological struggles in which quarrels about the nature of reality become politicized: "The politician's feeling for reality took precedence over and displaced the scholastic, contemplative modes of thought and life" (Mannheim 1946: 64).

The people who crushed cenobitic violence occupied positions of power in the precursors of the modern nation-state. They had not yet completely harnessed the rising progressive capitalist economic order, whose disruption of the medieval social order was largely responsible for the revolts in the first place. But, to succeed, the pervasive minimax "rationality" of capitalism, minimizing the risk of loss and maximizing the opportunities for profit, requires political order, so that, although minimax thinking radically disrupts traditional social relations, its practitioners tend to support any political structure that enforces social order. The result was to produce among the cenobites a personal and local attachment to mercantile capitalist agricultural praxis but a rejection of the hostile nation-state and exploitative, "rationalized" social relations. This ambivalence, and the leaders' stress on ideological struggle, made nineteenth-century Marxists see the 1525 Revolution and the subsequent struggle in southern France as precursors of the great revolution they hoped for (Blickle 1981: xii, 3–4).

One difference, then, between North American enclaves and peoples like the Semai is that the former are pacifists, the latter just peaceable. Nonviolence is an explicit part of the cenobites' and Rainbows' "charter" (e.g., Hostetler 1964: 186). Similarly, although nonviolence is not an explicit AA value, members routinely condemn violence as an unacceptable way of trying to control the uncontrollable. Resentments, particularly obsessive ones, are "dry drunks," and these facilitate "slips" back to the drinking of alcohol. The official commentary on the "tenth step" of the basic twelve-step program concentrates heavily on how to deal with anger. Different AA groups have differential success in resolving intragroup hostilities, but all stress the need to "let go of" anger (Kessel and Walton 1967: 142). Without a conscious and overriding commitment to nonviolence, groups otherwise quite similar to North American Mennonites and AA can be extremely violent. For example, one such "group" in the "survivalist right" has a "primitive Christian" charter, seeks a refuge area, maintains a band-style social organization stressing face-to-face involvement, creates group identity out of ethnicity, and so forth. But it remains murderous (Aho 1991; Coates 1987).

Gelassenheit: *Letting Go vs. Pragmatism*

Gelassenheit, roughly glossable as *letting go,* is a central tenet for German cenobites—"the solution to the riddle of Amish culture" (Kraybill 1989: 25). This self-surrender involves letting go of worldly concerns and turning one's life over to God's will. The focus is on what is held to be good personal action (e.g., kindness and hard work), not the outcome of that action (e.g., admiration and material reward). In this sense, letting go resembles the Taoist notion of *wu wei* (not striving). The concept of *wu wei* arose in China during the Warring States period, when ordinary Chinese ran the risk of being slaughtered or brutalized for reasons having nothing to do with their conduct (for a longer discussion, see Dentan 1988a: 870–871, 876–877). Long incorporated into East Asian thinking, it spread into North America in New Age vocabulary as, e.g., "going with the flow," a notion prevalent among Rainbows.

This psychological reprise of historical powerlessness makes people diffident about imposing their will on others, especially by violence. For German cenobites, this means that, toward property, "will-power," and sexual love, they should maintain an attitude of serene detachment, until at last their wills and God's are one (Hostetler 1974: 144–145, 201–202; Hostetler and Huntington 1967: 15; Kraybill 1989: 25–31; Peter 1987: 11–12, 40–41). For Hutterites, although a central tenet is that "personal suffering [is] a necessary condition for following Christ" (Hostetler 1974: 11), the trope of *Gelassenheit* is of relaxing, not of pain or sacrifice. This should be stressed: It is a solution to suffering, not a form of it; an attitude, or state of mind; not an emotion or feeling (Peter 1987: 29).

The First Step of the AA program is a statement of similar surrender, consciously drawn from the same Christian roots as German cenobite self-surrender (Alcoholics Anonymous 1976: 59; Anonymous 1972: 165; Kessel and Walton 1967: 140, 141, 153): "We admitted we were powerless over alcohol—that our lives had become unmanageable." The sense of impotence, vulnerability, and fear (Kessel and Walton 1967: 105–106) that underlie admitting personal powerlessness resembles that of refugees from overwhelmingly powerful invaders, like the Semai in slaving times (cf. von Graeve 1989). AA's traditional public admission of being "sick and tired of being sick and tired" as the sole criterion of membership resembles the Shaker requirement and echoes a phrase from Shaker history. Before her conversion, Mother Ann Lee, the founder of Shakerism, found her life to be "almost unmitigated tribulation" (Ahlstrom 1972: 492). After similar troubles, individuals like "Bill" and "Dr. Bob," the founders of AA, may found nonviolent movements or join groups such as AA.

✦ "Ready-made Symbols Grown on Foreign Soil"

'Tis opportune to look back upon old times and contemplate our forefathers. Great examples grow thin, and are to be fetched from the passed world. Simplicity flies away, and iniquity comes at long strides upon us. We have enough to do to make up ourselves from the present and passed times, and the whole stage of things scarce serveth for our instruction. A complete piece of virtue must be made from the centos of all ages, as all the beauties of Greece could make but one handsome Venus.
—Sir Thomas Browne, "Hydriotaphia: Urn Burial" (n.d [1658]: 141)

Shall we be able to put on, like a new suit of clothes, ready-made symbols grown on foreign soil . . . spoken in a foreign tongue, nourished by a foreign culture, interwoven with foreign history? . . . A man does not sink down into beggary only to pose afterwards as an Indian potentate.
—C. G. Jung (quoted in Campbell 1968: 367–369)

One uses Chinese culture to transform primitives. It is unthinkable to use primitive culture to transform Chinese.
—Mencius (cf. Lau 1970: 103)

A recapitulation. To recapitulate this chapter so far, cenobitic peace groups seem to begin when powerful people defeat less powerful ones. The latter respond with fear, a painful sentiment with which they deal by "letting go," accepting their inability to control the forces that threaten them, a voluntary acceptance that ends their hopeless struggle and seems to bring them relief. Rationalized and justified by ancient Western traditions of an egalitarian and peaceable Golden Age, the resulting pacifism calls for creating an intentional community within the conquering nation state.

To perpetuate this adaptation, people need reserves, usually geographic, where the dominant enclaving society, for whatever reason, normally allows them "beggar's freedom." They need to be able to flee and regroup if this tolerance proves transitory. Band-style social organization is ideal for flight, regrouping, dealing with losses, and incorporating converts. It requires the egalitarianism that the pacifist ideology often entails. Peace groups also need tactics to preserve their identity against the coercive and seductive culture that surrounds them.

Transmitting their values to their children is problematic. Isolation helps, and most peace groups teach children to fear strangers. Unlike peaceable "refugees," enclaved peace groups, however, apparently often resort to forcing children to surrender to external authority, if the groups survive more than a couple of generations. The alternative is to rely on converting outsiders.

Of Probabilities and Possible Misconceptions

Causality in human affairs is hard to establish. Complex patterns of feedback and intervening extraneous variables so affect the causal relationship between two closely connected factors that the only way to state it is as a probability, often without being able to specify numerically what the probability is. Moreover, in most matters, the causal chains between x and y are extremely long. The result, in theory, is to multiply each probability by the next, the upshot being a very low order of probability for the whole sequence (Ellen 1982). Therefore, there are always exceptional cases that do not fit a model and that require special explanation. Faced with such complexity, the most appropriate intellectual response sometimes seems to be to wince. This chapter does not suggest, therefore, that the link between defeat and peaceability is universal, unproblematic, or clear; merely that it seems to hold up in a number of cases, particularly those in which resistance is suicidal.

Essentialism

> *Every normal man must be tempted at times to spit on his hands, hoist the black flag, and begin slitting throats.*
> —H. L. Mencken (quoted as epigraph in Buckley 1991)

Peaceability as an adaptation seems delicate and often transitory. It is not a Platonic essence, somehow, of a people or their religion. Fights do break out among Amish and Rainbows. AA takes official pride in the performance of its members in national wars. The preliminary model sketched above gives no reason to expect that a people with a history of nonviolence have always been, or will always remain, nonviolent, no matter what happens around them. Certainly, such transformations to and from nonviolence have occurred among unselfconsciously nonviolent people, often over a period of only a few years (e.g., Chang 1982; Giliomee 1981; Guenther 1980, 1986; Lee 1984; Lee and Hurlich 1982; Marks 1972; Pratt 1986; cf.

Gardner 1985). The sad cases of Synanon and Matrix House illustrate how easily peaceable, intentional groups can slip into violence (Weppner 1983).

The good news is that, conversely, people with a history of violence need not remain violent. Robarchek (1987) has seen Waorani

> change from an extremely violent society to an essentially nonviolent one (although there are still bands that have not made the change, and an occasional relapse among those that have). . . . [T]he crucial initial changes were social (the creation of a structural level that permitted mediation between hostile bands) and cultural (the conscious and explicit adoption of a new value system).

All the cenobites discussed in this chapter have made such a transition. Attention to the complexities of history suggests that more nuanced approaches are more fruitful than raw essentialism.

Psychological Essentialism

Individualist capitalist ideology is receptive to social science explanations based on quasi-essentialist individual psychology, patterns of childrearing, and so on. Indeed, given the high degree to which the cenobitic traditions structure people's behavior, the apparent psychological homogeneity of Amish compared with other peoples is predictable (Wittmer 1970): "quiet, friendly, responsible, and conscientious" (Hostetler 1980a: 185–186). But the tradition may be situational, as in the case of the "real vicious warriors" who are peaceful only at Rainbow gatherings. Moreover, the same psychologism supports explanations based on "human nature"; e.g., that people are "naturally aggressive," so that peaceability always involves repressed aggression and pervasive peaceability becomes reaction-formation against strong aggressive impulses.

Letting go is as much an intellectual and social phenomenon as a "deep psychological" one. Whatever one's essence, acting quiet, friendly, responsible, and conscientious is socially appropriate in all these peace groups. It is easy, and wrong, to confuse such behavior with "personality" (Sargent and Beardsley 1960).

The Future of Negative Peace in Nation-States

In the epigraphs to this section, Mencius comments smugly that civilized people cannot learn from primitives, a sentiment Jung sadly echoes. We who live in nation-states beset within and without by violence may feel less smug but equally pessimistic about our ability to use other people's solutions to our problems.

The Difficulty of Letting Go. Mainline North Americans fear the green-house effect, carcinogens, nuclear winter, and violence in the streets, phenomena that seem completely out of control. They inculcate these fears into their children, with TV violence, school sessions on ecology, pictures of kidnapped children on milk cartons, and so on. What most North Americans lack, perhaps because their defeat is bloodless and at their own hands, is a way of dealing with these fears other than by despair or trying to reduce the threat. Few of them "let go." Unlike Anabaptists, Camisards, or AAs, whose defeat eventually became too unmistakable to deny, they can, most of the time, avert their attention from the threat; take comfort in the belief that luck, "technology" or "the government" will avert the threats. Invidious striving, not *wu wei,* keeps the economy and the people running.

Conversely, surrender and the detached resignation that letting go entails would be "passive," "unmanly," or "defeatist," all bad words. Self-control" and "responsibility" are less attractive to many people than "self-expression" and "freedom." The myths that rationalize and justify a peaceable way of life are not true, perhaps not even authentic. The peace groups' attitudes and lifestyles are, according to mainline values and the psychotherapeutic apparat that enforces them, mental illness.

Furthermore, the nation-states that currently dominate humanity do not gracefully accept total defeat. Since the Iraq adventure, U.S. triumphalism can scarcely imagine it. A commitment to peaceability runs the unacceptable risk of inviting attack by peoples not so committed. Yet the ordinary origins of the peace groups that this chapter discusses seem to include bloody defeat. The peaceable adaptation to such defeat requires that some nation-state be willing to permit the existence of a reserve within its borders for a peaceful, band-style way of life that is implicitly at odds with mainstream values. Such toleration is uncommon and never unconditional. Enclaved people may follow their customs on their reserves only so long as they do not threaten the entrenched institutions of the enclaving society. That is, peaceability is permissible as long as it is not infectious.

Repressive Tolerance. Tolerance itself can trivialize the potentially subversive praxes of peace groups, making the costs of peaceability seem too heavy to bear. The notion that "all religions are good" segues easily into the notion that they are not significantly different. The Chinese institution of San Jiao (Three Teachings) did away with religious conflicts a millennium ago and made China as secular a civilization as any since the equally tolerant Roman Empire. U.S.-style San Jiao (Protestant/Catholic/Jew) has the same effect (Herberg 1960). Amish become tourist attractions: cute as Easter Bunnies, cuddly as Santa Claus (two other once religiously powerful figures). Twelve-step programs become trendy, broadening the "inspirational" book market. The partial ideologies that maintain peace-group identity grow out of opposition. Without it, they tend to erode.

Moreover, the cenobitic experience seems to testify to the difficulty of transmitting a conscious desire for peace to children who have not experienced the painful defeat that precedes letting go but who encounter, every day, the baubles and benefits of world-conquering capitalism. That problem has been endemic among U.S. intentional groups since the failure of their children to experience grace personally led the Puritans to formulate the Half Way Covenant. Without that commitment to peace, however, cenobitic sects have little chance of enduring; with it, they forgo transforming the society in which they remain undigested lumps. Their dilemma is that they are undermined by the very tolerance that permits them to exist.

Nowadays, for example, financial need is forcing increasing numbers of Amish to cottage industry, making rugs, quilts, rocking chairs, and so on for tourists (Kraybill 1989: 190–199; Olshan 1991). This increased contact with outsiders involves putting aside some of their reserve and otherwise behaving in un-Amish ways. So far, the damage seems under control, although some Amish (including some of my neighbors) have abandoned dealing with tourists.

Folklore (Make That Fakelore)

Another difficulty for sophisticated audiences is that the beliefs of the peace groups seem unbelievable. Rainbows think that their practices, neoshamanism for example, reflect "tribal" or "primitive" ones. Most Rainbows, however, are unfamiliar with "primitive" reality, which they construe as including an ecological sensitivity and pervasive peaceability wildly different from ethnographic or historical fact. (One important source for Rainbows is Longfellow's *Hiawatha,* an epic poem about a people who had no epic poetry, written by a Harvard professor of belles lettres in the meter of the Finnish *Kalevala* in order to give white U.S.A. its own epic tradition.) The reconstruction of "primitive" beliefs within the Western tradition tends to be procrustean, stretching a point here and lopping off another there (e.g., Densmore 1987; Robie 1986, 1987). It can produce fakelore, "a synthetic product claiming to be authentic oral tradition but actually tailored for mass edification" (Dorson 1976: 5). Moreover, all the peace groups interpret intellectualism as a hindrance to spirituality. A persistent critical stance toward group praxis is unacceptable.

For peace-group members, the myths of primitive Christianity or of imagined Native Americans situate the opposition between peace-group life and the enclaving mainline society in history and ethnography. The myths demonstrate for believers that their program is not merely ideological but practical, with empirically proven, beneficial consequences. Denial of the accuracy of these reconstructions therefore makes believers nervous and defensive. They may respond by asserting, correctly, that myths need not be true; and that they can believe whatever they choose—a rarefied and academic stance that undermines the efficacy of the myth (e.g., McGlashan 1988). Or, like some Rainbows, they may simply be uneasy about the lack of fit between their practices and those of Native Americans.

It is important, for reasons of ethnographic accuracy and proper respect, not to transform the lives of real peoples into utopias for the use of others (Berreman 1991: Dentan 1988b; Gordon 1991; Gould 1990; Redford 1991; but cf. McGlashan 1988). When members of powerful society use a self-serving, fakeloric version of another people's history or life as a myth for their own, they may deprive that people of the chance to assert their own, differing version. Moreover, the inaccuracy of fakelore often makes it a bad model. For instance, Amish care for the land exemplifies, in general, how farmers, in a better world, would treat the earth. But "the chicken manure that runs from Lancaster County's Amish farms in Pennsylvania into Chesapeake Bay . . . is killing the oysters in the bay" (Finch 1990: 18). Other peoples' peaceable lives can and should *inform* our utopias: they cannot *be* our utopias.

Nevertheless, outside observers who recognize how myths work should not be unduly upset that—like the myths that rationalize, mystify, and justify other ways of life—the myths of peace groups are bogus, at least in part. As noted above, the idealization of other peoples' lives to criticize Western civilization is a tactic that goes back at least as far as Tacitus (Allen 1913). The translation of other peoples' lives into forms that others can find educational or inspirational requires great care, but it is not a contemptible enterprise. The fact that the intellectual content of these movements is often laughable should not lead anthropologists to treat them any less respectfully than similar movements among non-Western peoples. Anthropologists know little about these movements and need to know more.

Questions: And an Open Question

The persistence of these peace groups and the proliferation of peace-oriented psychotherapeutic cults in North America reflect a yearning that includes a sense of powerlessness and a desire for peace. Although movies like *Witness* (Amish) and *Dances with Wolves* (Native Americans) sentimentalize ways of life that they construe as peaceable, their popularity testifies to the allure of peaceful ways of life. The burgeoning codependency movement models itself on AA or imagined "primitive" peaceable peoples, as do many "support groups." But none of these peace groups has recruited successfully among the urban lower and under classes—the people whose lives are most painfully disrupted by violence. Pacifist ideals that appeal only to those already fairly safe from violence are not going to transform society. The history of the peace groups that this chapter deals with suggests that only violent revolution, followed by brutal repression, would bring peaceability to U.S. slums. Is that a price anyone wants to pay?

Egalitarianism seems to be important in maintaining the peace, although in the areas of age and gender the egalitarianism of these groups is not absolute, even as an ideal. *Anarchism* might be a better term than *egalitarianism* for the ways they govern themselves. Local autonomy is vital. Coercion is rare. Leadership is only by continuing assent. Still, the history of similar groups indicates that their checks against authoritarianism are not always effective. Is decentralization compatible with economies of scale? Is anarchism viable in an industrialized economy except on nonindustrial reserves? How secure are anarchist groups against authoritarianism?

The hope for peace is utopian in the strict sense. Utopians prefer positive peace to peace based on fear. They want it to be associated with equality between the genders and kindness to children. But within nation-states, for the reasons given, successful pacifist cenobites tend to patriarchy (or celibacy) and repressive child-training. Are people willing to embrace chastity in order to secure gender equality? To beat their children and deny them higher education?

Peace groups seem to need mythic charters. Can such a charter be anything but fakeloric? They seem to require letting go and renunciation of capitalist consumerist values. Is that possible in an economy as relatively successful as capitalism? More crucially, all the groups discussed require toleration and reserved spaces. What would the nation-state's response be to a growing and inherently subversive mass movement for peace?

These questions are not rhetorical. The example of peace groups may inspire people. But it does not, I think, offer concrete models for social action in enormous nation-states. Ethnography and history demonstrate the possibility of peaceable living. Peaceable peoples have paid a price for their success. Peace for larger societies will also have costs. The open question is whether pacifists will be willing to pay them.

✦ Note

1. My earlier study (Dentan 1992) was of "refugees," peoples pushed to the margin of polities ruled by more powerful neighbors. Studies of peaceability often reflect ideological bias: that violence is or is not inevitable in human affairs. Believers in the inevitability of violence seize upon data that indicate that people with a reputation for nonviolence are in fact violent; their opponents, data that testify the opposite. The political context tends to favor one or the other view; for instance, during the heyday of leftist opposition to the Vietnam War, the view that, left alone, humans were nonviolent flourished; during the reaction that followed, studies began to argue that people are violent "by nature." Middlebrow mass media

(*Time, Newsweek, The National Review, The Nation*) drastically simplify, polarize, and even misstate these academic debates, but they do not, I think, distort the underlying ideological politics. These hidden agendas stultify arguments about whether humans are "naturally" violent, and this chapter does not address the issue.

✦ References

Ahlstrom, Sydney E.
   1972   *A Religious History of the American People.* New Haven: Yale University Press.

Aho, James A.
   1991   *The Politics of Righteousness. Idaho Christian Patriotism.* Seattle: University of Washington Press.

Alcoholics Anonymous
   1976   *Alcoholics Anonymous* third ed. New York: Alcoholics Anonymous World Services.
   1985   *Alcoholics Anonymous Comes of Age. A Brief History of A.A.* second ed. New York: Alcoholics Anonymous World Services.

Allen, William Francis, ed.
   1913   *"The Life of Agricola" and "The Germania" by Cornelius Tacitus,* revised by K. Allen and G. L. Hendrickson. Boston: Ginn and Company.

Ammann, Jacob
   [1989] The Reforms of Jacob Ammann, in *Amish Roots,* J. A. Hostetler, ed.: 21–23. Baltimore: Johns Hopkins University Press.

Anonymous
   1972   An Alcoholic's Story, in *Readings in Criminology and Penology,* D. Dressler, ed.: 156–166. New York: Columbia University Press.
   1989   Disobedient Children, in *Amish Roots,* J. A. Hostetler, ed.: 111–112. Baltimore: Johns Hopkins University Press.
   1993a Murder Shocks Community of Amish Families. *Buffalo News,* 20 Mar.
   1993b Amish Get around on Rollerblades. *Buffalo News,* 9 Sept.

Antonovsky, A.
   1987   *Health, Stress and Coping.* San Francisco: Jossey-Bass.

Barkun, Michael
   1986   *Crucible of the Millennium.* Syracuse: Syracuse University Press.

Berger, John
   1979   *Pig Earth.* New York: Pantheon.

Berreman, Gerald D.
1991   The Incredible "Tasaday": Deconstructing the Myth of a "Stone-Age" People. *Cultural Survival Quarterly* 15(1):3–45.

Blickle, Peter
1981   *The Revolution of 1525*, T. A. Brady, Jr. and H. C. E. Midelfort, trans. Baltimore: Johns Hopkins University Press.

Brane, C. I. B.
1989   The Silenced Preacher, in *Amish Roots*. J. A. Hostetler, ed.: 199–200. Baltimore: Johns Hopkins University Press.

Brewer, Priscilla J.
1986   *Shaker Communities, Shaker Lives*. Hanover, NH: University Press of New England.

Briggs, Jean L.
1978   The Origins of Nonviolence: Inuit Management of Aggression (Canadian Arctic), in *Learning Non-Aggression*, A. Montagu, ed.: 54–93. New York: Oxford University Press.

Briggs, David
1988   Hutterites Aim to Live Like Early Christians. *Buffalo News*, April 3, section D:1–2.

Browne, Sir Thomas
n.d.[1658]   Urn Burial, in *"Religio Medici" and Other Essays by Sir Thomas Browne*. London: Chapman and Hall.

Buckley, Christopher
1991   *Wet Work*. New York: William Heinemann.

Burke, Edmund
1791   (1982) Letter to a Member of the National Assembly, in *The Portable Conservative Reader*, Russell Kirk, ed.: 47–48. Harmondsworth: Viking Penguin.

Caldwell, F. J.
1983   Alcoholics Anonymous as a Viable Treatment Resource for Black Alcoholics, in *Black Alcoholism*, T. D. Watts and E. Wright, eds. Springfield, IL: Charles C. Thomas.

Campbell, Joseph
1968   *The Masks of God: Creative Mythology*. New York: Viking Press.

Caplan, Pat
1987   Celibacy as a Solution? Mahatma Gandhi and *Brahmacharya*, in *The Cultural Construction of Sexuality*, P. Caplan, ed.: 271–295. London: Routledge.

Castile, George Pierre
1981   Issues in the Analysis of Enduring Cultural Systems, in *Persistent Peoples*. G. P. Castile and G. Kushner, eds.: xvi–xxii. Tucson: University of Arizona Press.

Castile, George Pierre, and Gilbert Kushner, eds.
1981   *Persistent Peoples*. Tucson: University of Arizona Press.

Chang, Cynthia
1981   Anarchy, Enclavement, and Syntropy in Intentional and Traditional Communities, in *Persistent Peoples*, G. P. Castile and G. Kushner eds.: 192–211. Tucson: University of Arizona Press.
1982   Nomads Without Cattle: East African Foragers in Historical Perspective, in *Politics and History in Band Societies*, E. Leacock and R. Lee, eds.: 269–282. Cambridge: Cambridge University Press.

Coates, James
1987   *Armed and Dangerous. The Rise of the Survivalist Right.* New York: Hill and Wang.

Cohn, Norman
1970   *The Pursuit of the Millennium* revised ed. New York: Oxford University Press.

Colby, Benjamin N.
1967   Psychological Orientations, in *Social Anthropology, Handbook of Middle American Indians* vol. 6, Manning Nash, ed.: 416–431. Austin: University of Texas Press.

Coser, Lewis A.
1961   The Termination of Conflict. *Journal of Conflict Resolution* 5:347–353.

Densmore, Christopher
1987   More on Red Jacket's Reply. *New York Folklore* 13:121–122.

Dentan, Robert Knox
1976   Identity and Ethnic Contact: Perak, Malaysia, 1963. *Journal of Asian Affairs* 1 (1):79–86.
1978   Notes on Childhood in a Nonviolent Context: The Semai Case, in *Learning Non-Aggression*, Ashley Montagu, ed.: 94–143. London: Oxford University Press.
1979   *The Semai: A Nonviolent People of Malaysia* fieldwork edition. New York: Holt, Rinehart and Winston.
1988a   Ambiguity, Synecdoche and Affect in Semai Medicine. *Social Science and Medicine* 27:857–877.
1988b   Response (to McGlashan 1987). *Parabola* 13 (1):4–6.
1988c   On Reconsidering Violence in Simple Societies. *Current Anthropology* 29: 624–629.

1988d   Band-level Eden: A Mystifying Chimera. *Cultural Anthropology* 3:276–284.
1988e   Lucidity, Sex and Horror in Senoi Dreamwork, in *Conscious Mind, Sleeping Brain,* J. L. Gackenbach and S. LaBerge, eds: 37–63. New York: Plenum.
1992   The Rise, Maintenance and Destruction of Peaceable Polity: A Preliminary Essay in Political Ecology, in *Aggression and Peacefulness in Humans and Other Primates,* James Silverberg and J. Patrick Gray, eds.: 214–270. New York: Oxford University Press.

Diggins, John Patrick
1993   Burke's Works (Review of C. C. O'Brien, "The Great Melody." Chicago: University of Chicago Press). *New York Times Book Review* (3 Jan):11–12.

Dorson, Richard
1976   *Folklore and Fakelore.* Cambridge: Harvard University Press.

Eaton, Joseph W., and R. J. Weil
1955   *Culture and Mental Disorders.* Glencoe, IL: Free Press.

Eber, Christine E.
1991   Before God's Flowering Face: Women and Drinking in a Tzotzil Maya Community. Ph.D. thesis, State University of New York at Buffalo.

Ellen, James F.
1982   *Environment, Subsistence and System. The Ecology of Small-scale Social Formations.* Cambridge: Cambridge University Press.

Emlen, Robert P.
1987   Shaker Village Views. *Natural History* 96(9):48–57.

Erasmus, Charles J.
1981   Anarchy, Enclavement, and Syntropy in Intentional and Traditional Communities, in *Persistent Peoples,* G. P. Castile and G. Kushner, eds.: 192–211. Tucson: University of Arizona Press.

Evans-Wentz, Walter Yeeling
1958   *Tibetan Yoga and Secret Doctrines* second ed. London: Oxford University Press.

Fabbro, David
1980   Peaceful Societies, in *The War System,* R. A. Falk and S. S. Kim, eds.: 180–203. Boulder: Westview Press.

Finch, Robert
1990   Evolution of Pollution. (Review of R. D. Stone, "The Voyage of the Sanderling." New York: Knopf). *New York Times Book Review* 23 Sept.:18.

Fisher, Gideon L.
1978   *Farm Life and Its Changes.* Gordonville, PA: Pequea Publishers. (Excerpted in Hostetler 1989).

Fisher, Nancy
1989   I Tried Being Mennonite, in *Amish Roots,* J. A. Hostetler, ed.: 188–189. Baltimore: Johns Hopkins University Press.

Foster, Lawrence
1981   *Religion and Sexuality.* New York: Oxford University Press.

Gardner, Peter M.
1985   Bicultural Oscillation as a Long-Term Adaptation to Cultural Frontiers: Cases and Questions. *Human Ecology* 13:411–432.
1991   Foragers' Pursuit of Individual Autonomy. *Current Anthropology* 32:543–572.

Gartner, Audrey
1984   Widower Self-Help Groups: A Preventive Approach. *Social Policy* 15 (Winter):37–38.

Gibson, Thomas
1989   Meat Sharing as a Political Ritual: Forms of Transaction versus Modes of Subsistence, in *Hunting and Gathering Societies,* J. Woodburn, T. Ingald, and D. Riches, eds.: 165–179. London: Berg Publishers.

Giliomee, Hermann
1981   Processes in Development of the Southern African Frontier, in *The Frontier in History. North America and Southern Africa Compared,* Howard Lamar and Leonard Thompson, eds.: 76–119. New Haven: Yale University Press.

Gilsenan, Michael
1982   *Recognizing Islam.* New York: Pantheon.

Gomes, Alberto G.
1988a   The Semai: The Making of an Ethnic Group in Malaysia, in *Ethnic Diversity and the Control of Natural Resources in Southeast Asia.* Michigan Paper on South and Southeast Asia #32, A. T. Rambo, K. Gillogly, and K. L. Hutterer, eds.: 99–105. Ann Arbor: Center for South and Southeast Asian Studies, University of Michigan.

Gordon, Robert
1991   People of the Great White Lie? *Cultural Survival Quarterly* 15(1):49–51.

Gould, Stephen Jay
1990   Shoemaker and Morning Star. *Natural History* 12/90:14–20.

Guenther, Mathias Georg
1980   From "Brutal Savages" to "Harmless People." Notes on the Changing Western Image of the Bushmen. *Paideuma* 26:123–140.
1986   From Foragers to Miners and Bands to Bandits: On the Flexibility and Adaptability of Bushman Band Societies. *Sprache und Geschichte in Afrika* 7:133–159.

Hall, Barbara Yoder
 1989   My Father Saw Himself as a Runt, in *Amish Roots,* J. A. Hostetler, ed.:
         189–193. Baltimore: Johns Hopkins University Press.

Hardman, O.
 1924   *The Ideals of Asceticism.* New York: Macmillan.

Hawgood, John A.
 1940   *The Tragedy of German-America.* New York: Putnam.

Herberg, Will
 1960   *Protestant, Catholic, Jew: An Essay in American Religious Sociology*
         revised ed. Garden City, NY: Anchor Books.

Hoff, Lee Ann
 1990   *Battered Women as Survivors.* London: Routledge.

Holloway, Mark
 1951   *Heavens on Earth. Utopian Communities in America 1680–1880.*
         London: Turnstile Press.

Hostetler, Herbert
 1989   Solomon Cried Like a Child, in *Amish Roots,* J. A. Hostetler, ed.:
         238–239. Baltimore: Johns Hopkins University Press.

Hostetler, John A.
 1964   Persistence and Change Patterns in Amish Society. *Ethnology*
         3:185–198.
 1974   *Hutterite Society.* Baltimore: Johns Hopkins University Press.
 1980a   *Amish Society* third ed. Baltimore: Johns Hopkins University Press.
 1980b   Amish, in *Harvard Encyclopedia of American Ethnic Groups,* Stephan
         Thernstrom, Ann Orlov, and Oscar Handlin, eds.: 122–125. Cambridge:
         Harvard University Press.
 1980c   Hutterites, in *Harvard Encyclopedia of American Ethnic Groups,*
         Stephan Thernstrom, Ann Orlov, and Oscar Handlin, eds.: 471–473.
         Cambridge: Harvard University Press.
 1989   *Amish Roots.* Baltimore: Johns Hopkins University Press.

Hostetler, John A., and Gertrude Enders Huntington
 1967   *The Hutterites of North America.* New York: Holt, Rinehart and
         Winston.
 1992   *Amish Children: Education in the Family, School, and Community* sec-
         ond ed., New York: Holt, Rinehart and Winston.

Hutterite Brethren
 1989   The Founders Were Cursed and Slandered, in *Amish Roots,* J. A.
         Hostetler, ed.: 20–21. Baltimore: Johns Hopkins University Press.

Johnsen, John Hilmer
 1980   Doctrinal Diversity in Two Religious Organizations. Ph.D. dissertation,
         anthropology, SUNY/University at Buffalo.

Johnson, Paul
1976   *A History of Christianity*. New York: Atheneum.

Kessel, Neil, and Henry Walton
1967   *Alcoholism* revised ed. Harmondsworth: Pelican.

Klama, John
1988   *The Myth of the Beast Within*. London: Longman.

Knauft, Bruce M.
1985   Ritual Form and Permutation in New Guinea: Implications of Symbolic Process for Socio-political Evolution. *American Ethnologist* 12:321–340.
1987a Reconsidering Violence in Simple Human Societies: Homicide Among the Gebusi of New Guinea. *Current Anthropology* 28:457–482.
1987b Managing Sex and Anger: Tobacco and Kava Use among the Gebusi of Papua New Guinea, in *Drugs in Western Pacific Societies*. ASAO Monograph 11, Lamont Lindstrom, ed.: 273–289. Lanham, MD: University Press of America.
1991   Violence and Society in Human Evolution. *Current Anthropology* 32:391–428.

Kollmorgen, Walter M.
1989   We Don't Visit Together, in *Amish Roots*, J. A. Hostetler, ed.: 258–259. Baltimore: Johns Hopkins University Press.

Kraybill, Donald B.
1989   *The Riddle of Amish Culture*. Baltimore: Johns Hopkins University Press.
1990   *The Puzzles of Amish Life*. Intercourse, PA: Good Books.

Lau, D. C., ed. and trans.
1970   *Mencius*. Harmondsworth: Penguin.

Lauer, Carol
1988   Variability in the Patterns of Aggression of Pre-school Children. Paper presented at the annual meeting of the American Association for the Advancement of Science, Boston, 11 February.

Lears, Jackson T. J.
1981   *No Place of Grace*. New York: Pantheon.

Lee, Richard B.
1984   *The Dobe !Kung*. New York: Holt, Rinehart and Winston.

Lee, Richard B., and Susan Hurlich
1982   From Foragers to Fighters: South Africa's Militarization of the Namibian San, in *Politics and History in Band Societies*, Eleanor Leacock and Richard Lee, eds.: 327–345. Cambridge: Cambridge University Press.

Luthy, David
  1989a The Peight Family, in *Amish Roots,* J. A. Hostetler, ed.: 183–184.
         Baltimore: Johns Hopkins University Press.
  1989b Rosanna of the Amish, in *Amish Roots,* J. A. Hostetler, ed.: 184–186.
         Baltimore: Johns Hopkins University Press.

MacAndrew, Craig, and Robert B. Edgerton
  1969   *Drunken Comportment: A Social Explanation.* New York: Aldine.

Mannheim, Karl
  1946   *Ideology and Utopia. An Introduction to the Sociology of Knowledge.*
         New York: Harcourt, Brace.

Marks, S.
  1972   Khoisan Resistance to the Dutch in the Seventeenth and Eighteenth
         Centuries. *Journal of African History* 13:55–80.

Marshall, Lorna
  1961   Sharing, Talking, and Giving: Relief of Social Tensions among !Kung
         Bushmen. *Africa* 31:231–249.

Mayer, F. E.
  1954   *The Religious Bodies of America.* St. Louis, MO: Concordia.

McGlashan, Alan
  1987   The Dream People. *Parabola* 12 (3):11–15.
  1988   Response [to Dentan 1988a]. *Parabola* 13 (1):6–7, 132–133.

Miller, Perry
  1965   *The Life of the Mind in America from the Revolution to the Civil War*
         books 1–3. New York: Harcourt, Brace and World.

Nagler, Michael N.
  1982   *America without Violence.* Covelo, CA: Island Press.

Name Withheld
  1989   Discipline of an Indiana Congregation, in *Amish Roots,* J. A. Hostetler,
         ed.: 87–88. Baltimore: Johns Hopkins University Press.

Newman, Sadie C.
  1989   A Pennsylvania Discipline, in *Amish Roots,* J. A. Hostetler, ed.: 86–87.
         Baltimore: Johns Hopkins University Press.

Nietschmann, Bernard
  1987   The Third World War. *Cultural Survival Quarterly* 11(3):1–16.

Niman, Michael
  1991   The Rainbow Nation. Doctoral dissertation, American studies, State
         University of New York at Buffalo.

Nowak, Michael
  1972   *The Rise of the Unmeltable Ethnics.* New York: Macmillan.

Olshan, Marc Alan
    1989   Strangely Primitive, in *Amish Roots*, J. A. Hostetler, ed.: 260–261.
            Baltimore: Johns Hopkins University Press.
    1991   The Opening of Amish Society: Cottage Industry as Trojan Horse.
            Human Organization 50:378–384.

Otterbein, Keith F.
    1986   *The Ultimate Coercive Sanction.* New Haven: Human Relations Area
            Files.

Paul, Robert
    1978   Instinctive Aggression in Man: The Semai Case. *Journal of
            Psychological Anthropology* 1:65–79.

Peranen, Kai
    1991   *Alcohol in Human Violence.* New York: Guilford.

Peter, Karl A.
    1987   *The Dynamics of Hutterite Society. An Analytical Approach.* Edmonton:
            University of Alberta Press.

Pospisil, Leopold
    1964   Law and Societal Structure among the Nunamiut Eskimo, in
            Explorations in Cultural Anthropology, W. H. Goodenough, ed.:
            395–432. New York: McGraw-Hill.

Power, Margaret
    1993   Review of J. Silverberg and J. P. Gray, eds., "Aggression and
            Peacefulness in Humans and Other Primates." New York: Oxford
            University Press. *American Anthropologist* 95:511–512.

Pratt, Mary Louise
    1986   Fieldwork in Common Places, in *Writing Culture,* J. Clifford and G. E.
            Marcus ed.: 27–50. Berkeley: University of California Press.

Price, J. A.
    1975   Sharing: The Integration of Intimate Economies. *Anthropologica*
            17:3–26.

Redford, Kent H.
    1991   The Ecologically Noble Savage. *Cultural Survival Quarterly* 15
            (1):46–48.

Robarchek, Carole J., and Clayton A. Robarchek
    1988   Reciprocities and Realities: World Views, Peacefulness and Violence
            among Semai and Waorani. Paper presented at the 87th annual meetings
            of the American Anthropological Association (Nov. 16–20, Phoenix,
            AZ).

Robarchek, Clayton A.
    1977   Frustration, Aggression and the Nonviolent Semai. *American
            Ethnologist* 4:762–779.

1979a Learning to Fear: A Case Study in Emotional Conditioning. *American Ethnologist* 6:555–567.
1979b Conflict. Emotion and Abreaction: Resolution of Conflict among the Senoi Semai. *Ethos* 7:104–123.
1986 Helplessness, Fearfulness, and Peacefulness: The Emotional and Motivational Contexts of Semai Social Relations. *Anthropological Quarterly* 59:177–184.
1988 Ghosts and Witches: The Psychocultural Dynamics of Semai Peacefulness. Paper presented at the 87th annual meetings of the American Anthropological Association (Nov. 16–20, Phoenix, AZ).

Robarchek, Clayton A., and Carole J. Robarchek
1992 Cultures of War and Peace: A Comparative Study of Waorani and Semai, in *Aggression and Peacefulness in Humans and Other Primates,* James Silverberg and J. Patrick Gray, eds.: 189–213. New York: Oxford University Press.

Robie, Harry
1986 Red Jacket's Reply: Problems in the Verification of a Native American Speech Text. *New York Folklore* 12:99–117.
1987 (Reply to Densmore). *New York Folklore* 13:123.

Ross, Marc Howard
1981 Socioeconomic Complexity, Socialization, and Political Differentiation. *Ethos* 9:217–247.
1992 Social Structure, Psychocultural Dispositions and Violent Conflict: Extensions from a Cross-Cultural Study, in *Aggression and Peacefulness in Humans and Other Primates,* James Silverberg and J. Patrick Gray, eds.: 271–294. New York: Oxford University Press.

Roy, Donald F.
1960 "Banana Time" Job Satisfaction and Informal Interaction. *Human Organization* 18:158–168.

Sargent, Stansfeld, and Katherine Pease Beardsley
1960 Social Roles and Personality Traits. *International Journal of Social Psychiatry* 6: 66–70.

Schwartz, Hillel,
1980 *The French Prophets.* Berkeley: University of California Press.

Schwartz, Theodore
1975 Cultural Totemism: Ethnic Identity, Primitive and Modern, in *Ethnic Identity: Cultural Continuities and Change,* George De Vos and Lola Romanucci-Ross, eds.: 106–131. Palo Alto, CA: Mayfield.

Schur, Edwin M.
1969 *Our Criminal Society. The Social and Legal Sources of Crime in America.* Englewood Cliffs, NJ: Prentice-Hall.

Sipes, Richard G.
1973 War, Sports and Aggression: An Empirical Test of Two Rival Theories. *American Anthropologist* 75:64–86.

Smith, C. Henry
1989   They Were Sure I Was Foolish, in *Amish Roots*. J. A. Hostetler, ed.:
        186–188. Baltimore: Johns Hopkins University Press.

Sponsel, Leslie E.
1990   Ultraprimitive Pacifists: The Tasaday as a Symbol of Peace.
        Anthropology Today 6 (1):3–5.

Spradley, James P.
1970   *You Owe Yourself a Drunk. An Ethnography of Urban Nomads*. Boston:
        Little, Brown.

Starr, Edward
1991   Impact of Alcoholic's Race on Treatment Evaluations. Ph.D. disserta-
        tion in psychology, State University of New York at Buffalo.

Stoll, Joseph
1989   How Not to Spank, in *Amish Roots,* J. A. Hostetler, ed.: 112–113.
        Baltimore: Johns Hopkins University Press.

Stoltzfus, Eli
1989   Tourists Often Ask Me, in *Amish Roots,* J. A. Hostetler, ed.: 175–176.
        Baltimore: Johns Hopkins University Press.

Suler, John
1984   The Role of Ideology in Self-Help Groups. *Social Policy* 15
        (Winter):29–36.

Tan Chee Beng
1988   *The Baba of Melaka*. Kuala Lumpur: Pelanduk.

Tocqueville, Alexis de
1840 (1965) Of Individualism in Democratic Countries. Contributions to *Indian
        Sociology* 8:10–12.

Turner, Frederick Jackson
1894   The Significance of the Frontier in American History, in *Annual
        Report of the American Historical Association for 1893*:199–
        227.

von Graeve, Bernard
1989   *The Pacaa Nova*. Lewiston, NY: Broadview Press.

Walker, Barbara G.
1991   Ritual for World Peace. *Woman of Power* 19 (Winter):5.

Walker, L. E.
1979   *The Battered Woman*. New York: Harper.

Warner, Gene
1990   Hurt by Misuse of Child Abuse Law, Adoptive Mom Says. *Buffalo
        News,* 19 August: B1, B20.

Weigle, Luther A.
1928 *American Idealism.* New Haven: Yale University Press.

Weppner, Robert S.
1973 An Anthropological View of the Street Addict's World. *Human Organization* 32:111–121.
1983 *The Untherapeutic Community. Organizational Behavior in a Failed Treatment Program.* Lincoln: University of Nebraska Press.

Whitson, Robert Edward
1983 *The Shakers: Two Centuries of Spiritual Reflection.* New York: Paulist Press.

Wilson, James Q., and Richard J. Herrnstein
1985 *Crime and Human Nature.* New York: Simon and Schuster.

Wittfogel, Karl
1957 *Oriental Despotism. A Comparative Study of Total Power.* New Haven: Yale University Press.

Wittmer, Joe
1970 Homogeneity of Personality Characteristics: A Comparison Between Old Order Amish and non-Amish. *American Anthropologist* 72:1063–1068.

Wolf, Charlotte
1990 Relative Advantage. *Symbolic Interaction* 13:37–61.

✦ 4

Peacemaking and the Institutions of Peace in Tribal Societies

Walter Goldschmidt

Walter Goldschmidt examines a topic that has been all but neglected in the anthropological fascination with warfare. Once at war, how do tribal peoples make peace? Once at peace, how do they maintain it? At the outset, Goldschmidt warns that the answers will not come easily: "All who have investigated the ethnography of war have complained about the poverty of material available, but I can assure you that it is magnificent compared with the ethnography of peacemaking." The techniques of peacemaking that Goldschmidt identifies include ritual, the use of intermediaries, compensation, and other devices. A successful outcome of such efforts seems to depend on whether the former combatants are able to find a basis for peace that is in their mutual interest—such as trade or alliance. In general, however, this chapter makes clear that tribal peoples are no closer to the secret of peace than are we ourselves. The art of peace seems everywhere to be undeveloped. When it works, there may be a substantial price paid in terms of individual liberty and the relationship of the individual to the group, as Robert Dentan explained in the preceding chapter on "enclaved" societies. War is a powerful organizer of human energies; and it is difficult to contain. From this perspective, the second half of Goldschmidt's chapter is cause for optimism about the human condition: institutions that allow the safe expression of aggression and conflict may—says Goldschmidt—successfully preserve the peace.

—THE EDITORS

✦ When I investigated why men in tribal societies were—and are—willing to endanger life and limb in the pursuit of war, I discovered that a great deal of cultural energy was devoted to inducing them to engage in an activity that is often described as long periods of tedium interspersed with moments of terror (Goldschmidt 1986, 1988). More particularly, where warfare is an endemic activity, the cultural values focus on valor; and the rewards given to the warrior, both material and social, are substantial. I turned to the examination of peacemaking with the expectation that the same kind of rewards might be made available to those who sought to establish amicable relationships with their neighbors. I thought that wergild, which is the regular payment made to the victim or his relatives for a harm done, represented such a reward system. I was also impressed by a story that Spencer and Gillen (1927: II,444) tell of an avenging party they accompanied, in which the alien band that was the object of their wrath sued for amity by offering the attacking warriors access to their women—for women are frequently part of the booty received by successful combatants.

As we shall see, the goods over which men fight and that may be part of the spoils of war are often used in the suit for peace, whether paid as wergild or as indemnity; that is, the rights to things and privileges, which so often constitute the *causus belli,* are also used as instruments of peace. But my investigations have led me to believe that the war-settlement processes described for tribal societies do not offer much encouragement. Indeed, they have led me into another direction; namely, to examine institutions that reduce violence among tribal peoples. So this chapter falls into two parts: a review of the peacemaking processes reported in the ethnographic literature and an examination of what I call the institutions of peace.

My review of the literature concentrated on three areas, all recognized as being characterized by endemic warfare: the North American Plains, lowland South America (the Amazon Basin and the Gran Chaco), and island New Guinea. I have not made a thorough search of the literature, but have examined enough material to get a fair knowledge of the practices encountered. My selection was not necessarily the best for my purposes. It might have been better to seek out areas where warfare is not endemic and to discover why it should be absent, but I doubt that this would have revealed much, since ethnographers do not usually record the absence of such behavior, let alone explain such absence.

The data on peacemaking procedures are sparse. All who have investigated the ethnography of war have complained about the poverty of material available, but I can assure you that it is magnificent compared with the ethnography of peacemaking, which if present at all is usually relegated to a paragraph or two at the close of the discussion on war. Rarely does the rubric *peace* appear in an index.

Although I am not directly addressing the causes of war among tribal peoples, it is necessary to give them some attention. Much of the ethnographic literature treats tribal warfare as a kind of game; more deadly than some of our contact sports but essentially of the same nature. Occasionally this sportive character does appear, and we shall examine it in our discussion of the Dani, but it is a mistake to assume that warfare, even when it appears to have a sportive element, lacks economic or geopolitical consequences. Occasionally, as among the Mae Enga, it is specifically directed to the issue of territory or the control of economic resources or trade routes, but more often such matters are implicit.

Finally, in this introductory section, I want to point up what I consider the major theoretical issue that the ethnography of war (and of peace, of course) addresses: the issue of human nature. There are those who argue that war is the consequence of mankind's inherently bellicose nature—that war is an inevitable result of human instincts. A chapter in an earlier book addressed this issue directly (Goldschmidt 1988). There I showed that men had to be induced to engage in warfare; that a great deal of cultural energy was devoted to getting men to fight; yet even in the most belligerent of tribes many men found excuses to avoid battle. There are others who argue that war is a product of modern life; it is the unfortunate consequence of the modern nation-state; the implication being that humans are naturally peaceloving in character and that wars are foisted upon them by an evil leadership. The ethnographic data gives those who believe warfare to be an "unnatural" excrescence as little comfort as it does the biological determinists. At the conclusion of this chapter I will stake out the middle ground between these two points of view, for I believe that any practical effort to reduce the incidence of warfare in the modern world must be based on a proper assessment of what motivates humans as members of society.

✦ The Peacemaking Process

The North American Plains

Warfare was endemic on the North American Plains. The area was unstable. From the 1630s, when the North American Indians first got horses from the Spanish, until 1890 and the Battle of Wounded Knee, the area was in constant turmoil. The horse altered the ecological situation. The plains were invaded from all sides and the different tribes never succeeded in establishing firm and permanent boundaries. Such equilibrium as might have been attained was repeatedly disrupted by the introduction of ever more effective weaponry, by the increasing pressure of the foreigners who were coming in, and most significantly by the growing opportunities for trade. The warfare among these tribes involved both the control of territory and the prosecution of commerce.

Despite the salience of war—or perhaps because of it—the Indians did have devices for avoiding and concluding hostilities. Marian Smith (1951) describes sham battles in which men displayed their strength and boldness in bloodless contests. Signals of peaceable intent were used by parties wanting to avoid or disengage from conflict; the peace pipe was, as popular literature has it, actually smoked in solemn ceremonies as ratification of an entente; and the exchange of gifts followed most such agreements.

The fragility of these accords is indicated by Hill's Navaho informants:

If the treaty was to be made with the Hopi, a Blessingway chanter was sent to open negotiations. This man entered the village singing. At times, this worked; at other times he was killed. This man arranged for a conference between the Hopi peace chiefs and the Navaho herdsmen. On the date set, a series of smoke signals were given by both peoples, announcing and answering the arrival of the Navaho so that they might come safely to the village. The delegates of each party rolled cigarettes. . . . Harmless insects were put in the tobacco to make the Hopi friendly. (1936: 19)

But Hill's informants also said (as reported earlier in the book):

The Hopi would treat them [the Navaho peacemakers] well and feed them. When the Navaho had been fed the Hopi would throw them off the mesa. In revenge the Navaho would organize a war party. After the attack they would go home and the Hopi would prepare a return attack on the Navaho country. Then each people would consider themselves satisfied and a treaty would be made until some one was thrown off the mesa, or until a Navaho killed a Hopi in the cornfields. The Navaho were usually the ones who broke the treaties. (1936: 3)

Compensation to erase a wrong was a frequent means of maintaining internal harmony among Plains Indian peoples, according to letters published by Chittenden and Richardson in 1905. The Blackfoot, for instance, gave horses and robes to their enemies; and a murderer (or thief) could "redeem" his body when confronted by the relatives of the slain by the payment of horses. Or a man might offer himself to expiate a crime, but if "no one has the sad courage to take his life, as often happens, then he is 'washed of the murder' and need pay nothing" (Chittenden and Richardson 1905: vol. 3: 1090).

Treaties and Treaty-making. Of equal significance to the maintenance of internal harmony was the establishment of peaceful relationships between neighboring tribes. The fluid and competitive pattern of relationship among them meant that treaties were established and broken repeatedly to meet the altering aims of the various groups. Mishkin (1966: 60) discusses a Crow-Assiniboine treaty that took place about 1844 by means of which the Crow received permission to hunt in Assiniboine territory unmolested and could pass through it to trade with the Hidatsa for corn. In return, the Crow, who were richer in horses, would provide the Assiniboine with mounts and also help provision them through hunting buffalo in their territory.

The Assiniboine also established amity with the Gros Ventre. We are told the motivation but not the manner in which it was brought about. According to Denig (1952), the Assiniboine preferred to import corn and be left to pursue their hunting. "Neither the one or the other party have many horses, therefore, the principle object of the war not being obtainable by

either, both were pleased to meet on friendly terms and exchange com-
modities in place of scalps" (1952: 145). The peace lasted for four years to
the advantage of the Assiniboine, but though the Gros Ventre desired to
maintain the peace, according to Denig, "the Assiniboines were not united
enough among themselves for this end" (146). Some warriors were dissatisfied with the peace offerings and began to steal the Gros Ventre horses. "A
number of the members of the former group have approached the Gros
Ventre with the peace pipe only with the intention of taking horses from the
Gros Ventre camp" (146).

This problem of internal dissatisfaction with existing peace treaties
among these acephalous societies is a recurrent one. Father De Smet,
whose letters were mentioned above, describes the effort of the great Crow
chief, Rotten-Belly, to make peace with the Blackfeet because of the great
number of losses the Crow were sustaining. He selected twenty-five young
soldiers to offer peace terms, guided by a Blackfoot prisoner captured earlier, to serve as a delegation "loaded with presents, consisting of horses,
arms, and ornaments of every kind" (Chittenden and Richardson 1905: vol.
3: 1037). Two of the young men had earlier lost brothers to the Blackfeet
and, though they had promised to forget their grievance, they used the
opportunity to get revenge. They met two Blackfoot hunters and offered
them the calumet (ceremonial pipe) as a sign of friendship. After assuring
the two Blackfeet of their peaceful intentions, and receiving gifts of a gun
and a horse from the hunters, the two Crows suddenly killed them. This
ended the effort to establish peace between the two tribes. Denig describes
another case in which a Crow-raised Gros Ventre woman who had established herself as a great warrior went back to her tribe to sue for a peace
treaty, only to be killed by her relatives when they discovered who she was,
thus ending any hope of peace between the two tribes.

Plains Indian fears of duplicity perhaps lie behind the following
account of an effort to arrive at a peace accord between the Salish, Piegan,
and other tribes of the northwestern plains. The tale was told by the explor-
er David Thompson, as quoted by Tyrrell (1916: 546–549). A conference
was called by the Salish to discuss the proposal with their allies. Thompson
and his interpreters attended. After the Salish chief had described the purpose of the meeting,

> an old Spokane throwing aside his robe showed a breast well marked with
> scars, and in a tone of bitterness, said, So our enemies have proposed
> peace, how often have they done so, and whenever we trusted to their
> mouths, we separated into small parties for hunting the Bison, and in this
> situation they were sure to attack us, and destroy the Women and children,
> who is there among us that has not cut off his hair several times, and
> mourned over our relations and friends, their [flesh] devoured, and their
> bones gnawed, by Wolves and Dogs. A state of peace has always been a
> time of anxiety, we were willing to trust and sure to be deceived; who is

there among us all that believes them. . . . Do as you please, I now sleep
all night, but if you make peace I shall sleep in the day, and watch all
night. (Tyrell 1916: 548)

This refrain of dismay and distrust was repeated by several others and
in the end the alliance was rejected (which Thompson also advised) and, as
a result, during the following bison-hunting season, many Salish were
killed.

Eavesdropping, in print, on this two-hundred-year-old debate among
the leaders of already doomed tribes, with its pious expression of the wish
for peace, its distrust of the enemy, and its dismaying conclusion that could
but lead to further disaster, one cannot help but be reminded of current
international discourse—with the same tired excuses and the same likely
outcome.

It would be unfair to the North American tribes if I failed to record the
single impressive recorded success in treaty negotiations. This took place
between the Kiowa, Apache, Arapaho, and Cheyenne in 1840. The negotiations are remarkable for two facts. The first is that it involved elaborate
exchange of gifts, with subsequent trading. What is important about these
exchanges is that they were economically relevant: the Cheyenne, who
were poor in horses, obtained mounts in great numbers; the other tribes
acquired goods ultimately deriving from the whites, especially guns and
ammunition. The tribal leaders were explicit in their request for these
goods and the peace treaty in fact established a pattern of trading that continued thereafter. The second remarkable feature of the deal is that the
action was not taken by the Cheyenne until they had first cleared it with the
Dog Soldiers, their strongest band of warriors (Grinnell 1915: 61). As
Jablow (1951: 77) points out, this did not block "the warriors' path to glory
and wealth," as Llewellyn and Hoebel (1941: 43) phrase it, but gave them
many horses with which to continue their traditional activities. It merely
redirected them from their erstwhile enemies to the Spanish settlements of
the Southwest. More broadly, it is clear that the internecine warfare among
these tribes was stopped because they were now in the presence of a greater
and more powerful external force; one from which they had much to gain
but even more to fear.

Peacemaking among the Plains Indians is fragile and uncertain;
liaisons are established only when there is an overriding economic interest
or when there is a common enemy against which they find it advantageous
to unite.

South American Indians

The information on peacemaking among the Indians of South America is
even less revealing than that for those to the north. Of the dozen peoples

examined in my review, only the Timbira seem to have had an active interest in peacemaking, esteeming their chiefs for their ability to negotiate conflict resolution and concluding warfare with the exchange of valuables. The Yanomamo establish alliances by feasting, trading, and exchanging women (Chagnon 1977: 101). But these alliances are brittle. They are arranged when a tribe is so weak that it needs an alliance as protection against another. The Lengua settle wars by arranging that wergild be paid for all those who have fallen in battle, using neutral tribes as go-betweens. An instance is on record in which the Chulupi, having been decimated by the Toba, sued for peace by lavishing them with elaborate tribute and virtually becoming their vassals (Human Resources area files [HRAF]).

For the Abipone, Bororo, Jivaro (Karsten 1967), Mundurucu (Murphy 1957), Nambiacuari, Toba, Tocano, and Tupinamba, the sources offer nothing with respect to peacemaking with alien tribes, though some internal settlements are resolved by the payment of wergild (HRAF). Sometimes such payments are ritualized. The Jivaro shaman, for instance, buries a lance (said to contain the animosity between the conflicting parties) in a place hidden deep in the forest so that the antagonists cannot uncover it (Stirling 1938). Apparently some of this animosity manages to spill out, inasmuch as the feuds are generally resumed.

Melanesia

Camilla Wedgewood summarized the data on Melanesian warfare and devoted some attention to peacemaking procedures. She concluded that there existed "a rudimentary form of international law among such simple agriculturalists as the people of the West Pacific" (1930: 31). She found that, though there was much variation in peacemaking procedures from one tribe to another, they usually "fall into two distinct parts; the making of compensation for injuries inflicted during the fighting; and the performance of some ceremonial, such as the exchange of gifts or food, which symbolically unites the erstwhile opponents" (1930: 25).

The massive amount of ethnographic material that has come from this region in the subsequent sixty years bears out these generalizations, as to both the variation in detail and the underlying comparability. For example, among the Maring (Rappaport 1967) women are exchanged between enemies as part of the peace negotiations, ideally one woman from one tribe for each man slain in the other. Among the Kiwai (Landtman 1927), in contrast, the peacemaking feasts that each enemy tribe gives its opponent includes giving their hosts access to their women "to put out the fire."

Sometimes the peacemaking procedures appear rather perfunctory; at other times they are elaborate. Fox (1924) describes the procedure for San Cristoval:

When peace is made a friend from a village which is at peace with both the combatants is usually sent, one who has relations by marriage in each, if possible a *mau* [parallel cousin], and there is a preliminary payment of money . . . after which fighting ceases. Then a day and place are fixed, and the two parties meet, fully decorated and armed for war, and engage in sham fighting. This sometimes ends in actual fighting.

Fox quotes from a missionary account of 1869:

We waited where we overtook Taki [the leader of the Wango party] till the main body from Wango came up. They charged past in fine style, looking very well in their holiday dress, each with his left hand full of spears and one brandished in the right. It looked much more like a fighting party than a peace party; but it is the custom to make peace with the whole army, to convince the enemy that it is only for his accommodation that they are making peace, and not because they are afraid to fight him. . . . [The opposing Fagani warriors] rushed brandishing their spears to within ten or twelve paces of the Wango party, who had joined into a compact body, and so seated themselves as soon as they saw the movement. Kara, a Fagani man, made his speech, first running forwards and backwards, shaking his spear all the time, and at the end he took out ten strings of Makira money and gave it to Taki. Fagani went back across the stream and the Wango went through the same performance, Taki making the speech. . . . He gave four strings of money. (1924: 311–312)

Peacemaking also involves a great deal of oratory and the payment for all damages on both sides: men killed, men wounded, pigs killed, and insults uttered. Water even is fouled by men urinating in it. It involves a sacred oath on a specially constructed altar and finally a pig-feast at which the payments are actually made (Fox 1924: 311–313).

On Malekula, peace is also arranged by two men from opposing sides who are friends. They fix a day for a peace dance, at which time a pig is given to those suffering the most damage or, if there were equal casualties, small pigs are exchanged. The soldiers on each side paint and decorate themselves as if for war. They also carry clubs and the plants of a species of wild taro, which is a symbol of peace. The two sides confront one another and go through what appears to be a mock fight, though no weapons are used, the soldiers dodging imaginary missiles. At length, one or another of the leaders signals by raising one or more sprouted coconuts to indicate the number of pigs that he will give, the length of the sprout indicating their size. When the combatants are satisfied with the settlement, each warrior who has killed a man goes to a relative of the person he has killed, giving him an arrow or a cartridge saying that it is the missile with which he was going to kill him. After payments are made, there is a feast. After the feast an altar of sorts is set up with the emblem of the women's secret society as a visible curse that such "unhallowed effeminacy" shall fall upon whosoever shall break the peace (Deacon 1934: 225–226).

The Maring, according to Rappaport (1967), have "formal enmity relations" with neighboring groups, establishing a principle of reciprocity in vengeance that is very difficult to break. Once established, there is a pattern of alternation between open hostilities and truce in a twenty-year cycle, the war recurring after an elaborate pig-feast ritual. Since it is not easy to arrange for the scores between the combatants to end up even, "each round of fighting contains within it the seeds of the next" (Rappaport 1967: 113). Apparently, these agreements to have hostile relationships can be disengaged, but this is not frequently done, and the "details of the procedure are vague and conflicting" (218).

Even where there is an ethic of peaceableness, or at least where there is an acceptable sentiment that other forms of conflict are preferable, escape from the cycle of war is difficult. With respect to Choiseul, Scheffler (1965) writes:

> Despite their avowed emphasis upon taking revenge for wrongs, the Choiseulese generally preferred to settle disputes peacefully when possible. It was probably true, as they say, that some men "wanted only to fight" and that no man admitted that he never wanted to fight. But it was probably true also that men often found it to their advantage not to fight. It was better to settle things peacefully with fines, exchanges of *ziku* or *kesa* [valuables], "because then no one was killed." (1965: 223)

Despite these sentiments, the pattern of vengeance, which not so much demanded an eye for an eye as the inflicting of greater damage than that received, led to continuing conflict. While, as elsewhere, each conflict carried the seeds of the next, it is also the case in Choiseul that the complex overlapping social groups, together with the existence of group headmen or managers who had great influence though no real authority, served to contain the feuding and warfare to a considerable degree. Scheffler concludes his discussion of these military operations as follows:

> War was a considerable drain upon all of a group's resources and could lead to the end of the group as an active political unit. Such considerations led men to take simple revenge when they would rather have had massive retaliation; since no manager could go to war without the consent of his followers they were able to dissuade him from the more drastic course of action, and the followers and would-be allies could exert similar pressures and thus keep the conflict from ramifying. But as in any vengeance system, there was always the danger of counter-vengeance and the possibility of escalation into warfare. Furthermore, since secrecy with regard to actual strength was a major stratagem, miscalculation was always possible and sometimes the relative strengths of the parties could only be determined in

conflict itself, so that, in effect, conflict had to be enlarged before it could be resolved. Warring occurred then, but not as often as it might have if pride and prestige were the only considerations. When war did eventuate, its organization entailed its resolution. The organization of warfare involved expansion of the conflict through a multiplication of the number of parties; and as the number of parties increased, so did the likelihood of conflicts of allegiance, and in these resided the possibility of peace. (1965: 239)

The Kapauku, whose elaborate mechanisms for economic exploitation have been fully described by Pospisil (1958), do not find warfare profitable. Pospisil (1963: 89) quotes one leader as saying, "War is bad and nobody likes it. Sweet potatoes disappear, pigs disappear, fields deteriorate and many relatives and friends get killed." Yet the Kapauku are caught in the same web of internecine conflicts that we have found elsewhere in Melanesia. Pospisil's informant goes on to say: "But nobody can help it. A man starts a fight and no matter how much one despises him, one has to go and help because he is one's relative and one feels sorry for him."

When the warring parties become weary of the fight, the headman of one side will propose a peace through a neutral person, which is generally responded to, and if the casualties are even, an agreement may be reached and a pig-feast is held, along with dancing and speechmaking. But since matters are rarely even, and since a wounded person may subsequently die, this does not necessarily end matters, unless blood money restores the balance.

Heider (1970) gives little attention to the process by which peace is achieved among the Dani in his extensive discussion of their warfare. He shows that the Dani have two forms of war: one, a formalized and structured conflict played out according to strict rules, in which few lives are lost and which has no apparent political or social consequences; the other, consisting of secretly prosecuted and very bloody raids in which whole villages may be wiped out or routed, and which generally result in the taking over of territory and the alteration of social alliances. Heider does not himself suggest it, but it seems reasonable to assume that the former is a kind of ritualized expression of intergroup hostility, taking the place of war rather than being warfare itself. These ritualized fights might even be seen as a kind of institution of peace, to be discussed below.

By contrast, warfare among the Mae Enga is explicitly in the interest of the expansion of territory. This applies even to war among closely related clans. Thus, in forty-one of the seventy-one cases of warfare over a fifty-year period collected by Meggitt, the dispute involved land; and of the thirty-four for which the outcome could be determined, the victors seized some territory in nineteen; and in six there was the complete eviction of the defeated (Meggitt 1977: 14). This does not mean that the interests of vengeance are absent; only that the demographic and social consequences are severe. There is a tendency for the loser to find reason to pay off the victor to avoid loss of land. This does not necessarily lead to peace, as the losers may renew the quarrel once they have strengthened themselves. Where there is a stalemate, both sides may be interested in ending the conflict and this can lead to a successful peace negotiation. As among the Choiseulese, the pressure to stop the war is apt to come from the allies of the principal parties who have less than a wholehearted commitment to it. This also allows the "owners of the quarrel" to save face by shifting the somewhat degrading responsibility for engaging in negotiation. Once the Big Men of the group decide to negotiate, they must persuade the warriors to agree. When they do, the leaders send intermediaries from a neutral group to their adversaries. Then the Big Men of this group must persuade their warriors of the advisability to negotiate. This leads to proposals and counterproposals handled by the go-between; each principal party remaining distrustful of the other. However much the leaders wish to conclude hostilities, they adopt an aggressive and ostensibly unyielding position at the meeting. Tensions run high at such sessions, but they are often reduced by the leaders of neutral groups making innocuous or amusing speeches. Eventually the oratory shifts to the details of the number killed and wounded and the compensation required. Though some of the kinsmen of the slain will insist that only blood can erase the blood lost, they usually yield under pressure and the knowledge that they will be benefitted by the settlement.

Limitations of the Peacemaking Process

The details of warfare and peacemaking vary widely. Military engagements sometimes have important potential economic or territorial effects; at other times, they have no discernible consequences. The warriors may gain loot or get access to women, or neither; they may even be forbidden to do so. Peacemaking procedures may be initiated by the victor or the vanquished; may come as a result of a stalemate or out of weariness or as the result of pressure from allies. The score may be evened out by the transfer of women, by the slaying of a person from one group, or by giving over a man or a woman to the other; or only sexual access may be exchanged. The transfer of valuables is frequent, but the amount may be substantial or token; it may be paid as reparation or, contrariwise, it may be tribute paid by the vanquished to the victor. The payment may be a net calculation or it may require each party to make restitution to the opponent. The peace may lead to trade relationship, to other forms of friendly engagement, or may leave the parties to the dispute in a relationship that continues to be suspicious if not openly hostile.

The ritual side of peacemaking also varies. It may involve an elaborate display dance of such excitement that it can revive the conflict or it may be a symbolic burial of the hatchet; or, again, it may be no more than a sedate conference, with the principals quietly smoking the sacred tobacco. The one ceremonial aspect that seems to be universal is a postnegotiation feasting.

None of the procedures are very effective. The literature on the peacemaking process among tribal peoples offers no model for coping with our own problems of endemic international conflict. The practices they display are obvious; the means are meager; and the results discouraging. Even where peace is the aim proclaimed by the leadership, and even where it is the earnest desire of the population, the procedures do not create an ambience of amity. Only where such amity has a direct and obvious advantage to both parties, such as to engage in trade or to make an alliance against others, is there any hope of making peace—and even then it is slim and the peace fragile. However, as we shall see in the next section, the interest of trade or exchange does constitute a major factor in establishing intertribal amity.

The reason that peace is so difficult to achieve in these societies is, however, highly instructive. In the cultures that we have been examining, the prosecution of war is perceived as a virtue. The young men are inculcated with the qualities that are necessary for soldiering: bravery, suspiciousness, and even bloodthirstiness. Empathy and forgivingness are not perceived as virtues, but as the vices of weakness and cowardice.

It should be reiterated that we have been examining a sample of peoples who are known to engage in aggressive warfare and that peaceful relationships run against the grain of such cultures. More specifically, they are in direct conflict with the idea of what makes a man a man. Even when the population is war weary, even when there is a genuine need for peace, the peace is fragile precisely because there remain those who feel that their masculinity, by which we mean their social identity, is lost if they do not press their cause, as indicated by the fact that men will often accept reparations only when others press them to do so. For instance, both the Mae Enga and the Cheyenne could not forge a treaty without the approval of their warriors, and the same is implicitly indicated in other cases. The Boran of East Africa understand this. According to Baxter (1977: 83–84), the older men are ritually made to give up their spears and to serve only the purposes of peace: they realize that the inducement of their young to engage in war, which they deem to be necessary for economic reasons, leads to the constant threat of useless conflict. But most peoples do not understand this and do not have this minor institutionalized means for the restraint of their warriors.

Having focused our attention on these war-oriented societies, we find that warfare among them is not the absence of peace, but that peace is the absence of war. Cultural force, then, overrides such human propensities as desire for comfort and ease, for amity, and for the pleasures of friendly intercourse. These cultural forces appeal to the individual's desire for a sense of personal worth, which I consider to be a human universal—defined, as is always the case, in terms of their own cultural values.

✦ The Institutions of Peace

Values differ from one culture to another. A sense of personal worth can be established on the basis of values other than militaristic ones; human competitiveness can be channeled into other pursuits, and in this section I will examine briefly what I call the institutions of peace. These are socially constructed patterns of behavior in which antagonism and competitiveness are expressed in ways that are neither lethal nor violent. I shall examine three such instances: the White Deerskin Dance, the potlatch, and the *kula*. While none of these institutions eliminated war, they do reduce the level of military conflict.

The White Deerskin Dance

The Hupa, Karok, and Yurok are three tribes that share the lower Klamath-Trinity watershed in northwestern California. They also share a biennial, world-renewal ceremony that has been called the White Deerskin Dance after the principal valuables that are displayed at it (Goldschmidt and Driver 1940; Kroeber 1925). It is one of the most deeply felt religious rites among all these peoples, its stated purpose being to cleanse the world of the sins that humans have committed. Stated more closely to their poetic idiom, the dance is to push back the miasma of sin that threatens to engulf the world; to put the world back on an even keel. The ritual lasts for about ten days. Its central feature is the repetition of a dance in which the singers line up, dressed in valuable paraphernalia, displaying on poles the decorated skins of albino deer. During one portion of each such unit, two pairs of men dance in front of the line, carrying great obsidian or chert chipped blades, some almost a meter in length, that are the second most important of the many highly valued and deeply sacred objects that make up their ritual regalia. As these dancers, always young men, glide past each other, holding the blades in front of them, they pass as closely as possible, quite conscious of the danger that the blades will shatter should they actually make contact.

It is the social structuring of the dance rather than its ceremonial aspects that convey the significance of the ritual (Goldschmidt 1951). These societies have no official roles of leadership nor any firmly structured social units such as clans or phratries. They are societies in which social power is acquired through wealth; in which wealth is transferred not only by inheritance and bride price but also in compensation for a wide variety of legal wrongs and even, under duress, in the purchase of the necessities of life. The result is that there is a great deal of potential social mobility. This mobility is not merely upward, for men can and do change their social affiliations, which are negotiable social networks. The combination of this fluid state, the absence of all authoritarian roles, and the high degree of litigiousness all conspire to create a situation of interpersonal tension. They need an institution that will keep the world in tolerance and harmony.

Rich men in each community sponsor a unit of the dance. There may be a half-dozen such men in any one year; they are not always the same, but they must be men who are known as wealthy and important. The dance serves to display their wealth and their power. No man owns enough ceremonial goods to make a full display, so that his paraphernalia is augmented by items loaned by those with whom he is on friendly terms—often men from one of the other tribes. Thus, the rite is not merely a competitive display of wealth: it is also a public statement of social affiliations (for the ownership of the ceremonial goods is known to all the cognoscenti)—affiliations that are subject to change as new hostilities arise and old rivalries are dissolved. The importance of knowing the strength of affiliations of men of power can be understood when we realize that the only sanction for the many legal confrontations is the potential feud between the principals to the dispute, the outcome of which depends upon the strength of their social (and military) support.

A comparative analysis of the elements of the ritual made by Harold Driver (Goldschmidt and Driver 1940: 126–128) indicates that the rite is historically derived from the war dances found more widely in the region— dances that are part of the peacemaking process. The Karok, as a matter of fact, refer to this rite as a war dance. Certainly, the obvious symbolism of the blades is that they are icons of war, and perhaps the symbol of the deerskins is that of peaceableness. I might also point out that the ritual described earlier for the people of San Cristobal is so comparable in its general character as to have given me a sense of déjà vu when I read it.

We see, therefore, that the competitive aspect of social interaction of the kind that elsewhere leads to warfare is sublimated by or displaced into this ritualized and highly competitive display of wealth. It does not eliminate all hostile physical confrontation or all intertribal war, but certainly it does reduce them.

The Potlatch

That the potlatch is a peaceable mode of hostile confrontation is expressed directly by the Kwakiutl, who call it "fighting with property," a phrase that Helen Codere used to entitle her monograph on the subject. In her words:

"Fighting with property" instead of "with weapons," "wars of property" instead of "wars of blood," are Kwakiutl phrases expressing what has proved to be a fundamental historical change in Kwakiutl life occurring within the period known to history. . . . The general conclusion is that the binding force in Kwakiutl history was their limitless pursuit of a kind of social prestige which required continual proving to be established or maintained against rivals, and that the main shift in Kwakiutl history was from a time when success in warfare and head hunting was significant to the time when nothing counted but successful potlatching. (Codere 1951: 118)

Codere goes on to say that potlatching was not merely a metaphor for war, which it was, but that it was also a substitute, being "planned like campaigns against the enemy" (Codere 1951: 119).

The potlatch is of course many things; no institution of importance is ever monovocalic in its references and inferences, and it is doubtful that it could serve the function here described if it did not have the capacity to call forth a wide range of sentiments and beliefs. Of the Tlingit potlatch, de Laguna (1952) says:

The primary aim of the potlatch cycle is to reunite the community after the tragedy of death, by affirming the kinship bonds between the members, by symbolizing the participation of the ancestral dead, by replacing the deceased (if a chief) by his successor, by bringing forward the children in whom other honored names live again, by dedicating anew the totemic crests and symbolically offering them as emblems of comfort to the bereaved, and finally by physically rebuilding the village through renovation of the deceased chief's house or erection of a new house for his successor. Yet the same potlatch cycle provides occasion for creating and airing of ill-feeling, since the etiquette of rank may be used to shame an enemy, or an inadvertent slight be interpreted as an intentional insult. The meeting provides the arena where potential heirs compete for coveted honors and where the victor triumphs over his rivals. The patterned joking which occurs at the more convivial stages of the series may be manipulated to pay a direct compliment, to provide good-humored fun, or to make a nasty remark about one's relatives. Other potlatches have as their primary purpose the wiping away of an insult or the reaffirmation of social status which has been jeopardized. (de Laguna 1952: 4–5)

We see in this the affirmation of the resolution of many potential conflicts, not only internal to the givers of the potlatch, but between them and their rivals, though perhaps not quite so overtly as among the Kwakiutl. What de Laguna does not say, but which Viola Garfield (1947) and my own research (Goldschmidt and Haas 1946) has shown, is that these rites are also affirmations to territory held by the hosting group; an affirmation that the very presence of rivals gives support to—and certainly this is a means of avoiding conflict.

The Tlingit potlatch is not, like the White Deerskin Dance, derived from peace rituals, which exist separately. But both Swanton (1908) and de Laguna indicate in passing that it is used specifically to avoid militaristic confrontation, though the Tlingit are less explicit in this than are the Kwakiutl. Far more important than such explicit uses, from my point of view, is the fact that the potlatch serves as a general context in which individuals may display their virtue and value, in which contests for social standing and social power and the control of resources may take place in a peaceful manner. Catharine McClellan (1954: 75–96) makes it clear that, though both the Tlingit themselves and their ethnographers tend to portray Tlingit society as made up of people of fixed rank, there is actually a good deal of social mobility. The potlatch does not merely affirm existing social standing, as Drucker and Heizer (1967) assert; it constantly reestablishes and often rearranges it.

The Kula

Like the potlatch, the *kula* is polysemic. Jerry Leach (1983: 5), in his review of the "explanations" of this international Melanesian institution, divides them into three categories: recirculation of resources, prestige competition, and social communication. This prismatic analysis breaks its several functional involvements into meaningless entities, for the *kula* is and must be all these things at the same time—as most of the scholars he analyzed fully understood. Leach admits, "Few theorists have advanced only one of these interpretations." The function of *kula* in the service of peace was first articulated by Lenoir (1924) and picked up by Fortune (1932) in his analysis of Dobuan potlatch. Fortune wrote: "Through all M. Lenoir's misconceptions he has . . . grasped the fact that the exchange of the ornaments, useless in itself, makes strongly for peaceful relationships between potentially hostile internationals" (1932: 210). A few pages earlier, Fortune says that "refusal to make such exchanges between Dobu and Tubetube would mean war" (204). And Macintyre (1983: 376) quotes the Tubetube standard phrase, "In the beginning kune [ceremonial valuables] and war went together."

Our knowledge of Melanesian societies indicates that warfare was endemic throughout the area, as we saw in our examination of peacemaking pursuits. It is quite clear that peace is difficult to establish in all of the societies reported on and impossible to maintain. This was repeatedly expressed in the data reviewed in the previous section. The potlatch-like activities of the Big Men in the area (e.g., among the Siuai of Bougainville [Oliver 1955]) indicate the interrelationship between wealth, status, rivalry, and warfare.

The *kula* exchange created an extensive entente cordiale among the circle of peoples engaged in it. For it to succeed in taking over the function of headhunting, as apparently was the case at least in Tubetube (Macintyre 1983), it had to offer an alternate route to leadership to that of fighting. It is a solution that would have pleased Pospisil's informant, Awiitigaj, whose expression of preference for trade over warfare has already been quoted. It is also not without significance that *kula* involved physical danger, for the ocean voyages made in small canoes were no child's play. But these natural dangers did not suffice; the *kula* traders had to create additional imaginative dangers to call forth the bravery of these erstwhile warriors; to the natural terrors inherent in the expeditions, they added the fearsomeness of the witch *yoyova* and other nameless dangers of the deep (Malinowski 1922: 238). Thus, to engage in *kula*, men did not have to abandon their "masculine" virtues associated with war and, indeed, the potential of fighting was not entirely eliminated. This is indicated by the essentially adversarial role of the exchange partners—a pattern of hostility carefully brought under control by an elaborate protocol that governed their exchange behavior (Malinowski 1922).

The *kula* therefore can be seen as deflecting the competitive element in social interaction from aggressive war to hostile trading. Within each of the engaged tribes, *kula* participation gave social standing and power. Apparently, the details of the manner in which prestige roles could be attained within the several participating peoples varied, but this was an internal matter. What was common was that status and power rested on the attainment of *kula* privilege and its mastery, with the acumen and bravery that that entailed. From the perspective of our interest, it is the international function that is important. Here, of course, the relationship between *kula* and economically significant trade is the essential ingredient. It is now generally recognized that however ceremonial and "irrational" the exchange of *vaygu'a* was, it was followed by trade that functioned to improve the economic well-being of all. This function could not have been performed without the modicum of peace that the *kula* institution provided, and the character of the *kula* enabled its leaders to have peace with honor.

The relationship between peacemaking and commerce in goods, whether explicitly for profit or in the idiom of prestations, was seen to exist in all the areas we examined in our discussion of that peacemaking process. The *kula* can be seen as a kind of anticipation, so to speak, of the material concerns that war repeatedly entails, and by ritualizing and sacralizing exchanges, it serves to deflect naked physical aggression.

Wealth and the Redirection of Conflict

Most of the world's societies invest a great deal of meaning in particular classes of objects. We call these things wealth, but more basically they are the symbolic embodiment of prestige, markers in the universal status game; i.e., status symbols. The three institutions we have been examining all focus on such goods, though in different ways. The items themselves vary, but it is possibly significant that they all include goods that men can wear, that can enhance the person's physical image, just as they enhance his symbolic image. The manner in which these items are used and the institutions surrounding them are quite different. Even the sense in which they may be said to be "owned" varies. The Californians have a strong sense of individual ownership and even like to claim the items as family heirlooms: there is a strong sense of personal identification with these objects and these Native Americans could not conceive of giving them away. In contrast, most of the potlatch goods are acquired specifically to be used as gifts. This giving is not to be confused with generosity. It is not an expression of affection or amity, but rather clearly of hostility and rivalry. There is a special irony to this contrast in that the Northwest Coast Indians give away goods to affirm their rights to basic resource property; whereas in Northern California, ceremonial goods may actually be used in exchange for material resources or may be lost through legal action involving resource property. *Kula* wealth represents yet a different pattern; the armbands and necklaces can hardly be said to be "owned" by anyone. Such "ownership" as does exist consists in the right to engage in the exchange, for the objects themselves are destined to move inexorably in their eternal circuit from one person to another.

A deeper layer of consistency underlies these separate patterns. In each instance, the culture has invested in specific sets of objects the mana that derives from human creativity. This potency is in turn projected into those individuals who make a claim on the leadership through their "ownership" of (or right to control) these goods. Thus the manipulations of these sacred symbols of personal worth enable men to receive the honor and power they seek without recourse to arms—though, it must be admitted, the weapons always stand in readiness in the background. It is in this sense that the rivalry inherent in social life is reformulated into peaceful pursuits. The White Deerskin Dance does push back the miasma created by human cupidity, though it is never fully dissipated.

Thorstein Veblen, in his *The Theory of the Leisure Class,* argues that the predatory use of wealth among the industrial barons of the modern world derived from the militaristic pursuits of the "barbarian stage" of mankind (Veblen 1967). Leaving aside his antiquated evolutionism and his expression of social disdain, he was making an important point: Hostile impulses often displayed as military confrontation can be expressed in a less lethal form of predation; namely, by commerce in goods that proclaim personal worth. This, it seems to me, is what these institutions of peace accomplish for those peoples who have found this solution to their patterns of conflict.

✦ Implications

Warfare is not the inevitable consequence of instinctive aggression; that is, it is not built into human nature. It is, however, the indirect consequence of certain universal human propensities. If we are to use anthropological knowledge to help find the solutions to the issues of war and peace, we must make a realistic appraisal of what these human propensities are and how they can be diverted away from violence. In this closing section, I want briefly to articulate what I perceive these to be, summarizing the thesis developed in my book *The Human Career* (Goldschmidt 1990).

Human beings everywhere seek ego gratification that can only be supplied by the accolades of their fellow men. This is, fundamentally, a very social quality, for it induces people to act in accordance with established values; that is, with the kinds of behavior that the community presumes to be desirable. Yet there is an antisocial side to this same phenomenon: the obverse of this need for social approval is competitiveness. Both needs can be met when the competition, and the hostility that accompanies it, are directed outward. All that needs to be added to this scenario to render it a veritable formula for war is for the society to place a high value on aggressiveness and ferocity. There can be good reasons why these qualities should be valued, as, for instance, when the community is threatened by others. Unfortunately, these qualities can also pay off for the individual who can translate his bloody-mindedness into power and social standing. The potency inherent in the combination of physical strength and ruthlessness gives those with these qualities particular force in any social system, even where external threats do not exist, and thus constitute a threat to the more amiable qualities of humanity. These militaristic attributes can only be suppressed by strongly reinforced values of peaceableness.

Institutions of peace can, however, redirect these aggressive impulses into more amicable kinds of ego-gratifying actions. To do so, they require not only the existence of material goods that serve as social markers, as symbols of value, but also the ennoblement of other human attributes— empathy, generosity, restraint of impulses, and the like—all of which are in the repertoire of human behavior.

One final comment: Is it possible, one may well ask, for modern nations to engage in the equivalent of the potlatch or other nonviolent forms of social competitiveness? There is some positive evidence. In the first decades after World War II, something like an international potlatch was taking place, a giant give-away in the form of the Marshall Plan and the East-West competition in assisting (and courting) Third World countries. This competitive struggle for the hearts of the world through programs of international aid had some of the qualities of the potlatch. We even had, for a while, a practice not unlike that of the Northwest Coast Indians, whose greatest act of conspicuous consumption was not the bestowal of ever more useless gifts upon their rivals but the throwing of giant, mana-laden, highly valued copper shields into the sea. Sputnik initiated a period in which we and the Soviets were throwing expensive, power-laden objects into the great sea of space. It was a competition that evoked the highest values in our respective cultures, far more noble than human aggressiveness. We have by these means vanquished our foe; in the process we have depleted our accumulated wealth—not unlike the victorious clans in a Tlingit potlatch. We must now restrain the warrior impulse within us as we undertake the more mundane task of rebuilding our economic surplus—not unlike the Mae Enga and other tribes of New Guinea.

✦ References

Baxter, P. T. W.
  1977   Boran Age-sets and Warfare, in *Warfare among East African Herders,* K. Fukui and D. Turton, eds.: 69–95. Kyoto: National Museum of Ethnology (Osaka).

Chagnon, Napoleon A.
  1977   *Yanomamo: The Fierce People* second ed. New York: Holt, Rinehart and Winston.

Chittenden, H. M., and A. T. Richardson, eds.
  1905   *Life and Letters of Father Pierre-Jean De Smet, S. J.* New York: Harper.

Codere, Helen
  1951   *Fighting with Property: A Study of Kwakiutl Potlatching and Warfare, 1792–1930.* American Ethnological Society monograph XVIII. New York: J. J. Augustin.

de Laguna, Frederica
  1952   Some Dynamics in Tlingit Society. *Southwest Journal of Anthropology* vol. 8: 1–12.
  1972   *Under Mount Saint Elias: The History and Culture of the Yakutat Tlingit.* Smithsonian Contributions to Anthropology vol. 7. Washington: Smithsonian Institution Press.

Deacon, A. Bernard
  1934   *Malekula: A Vanishing People in the New Hebrides.* London: Routledge.

Denig, Edwin T.
  1952   Of the Assiniboines. *Bulletin of the Missouri Historical Society* 8: 121–150.
  1930   Indian Tribes of the Upper Missouri, *Annual Report of the Bureau of American Ethnology,* J. N. B. Hewitt, ed. Washington: Government Printing Office.

1953   Of the Crow Nation. Bureau of American Ethnology, Bulletin 151, John
        C. Ewers, ed. Washington: Smithsonian Institution.

Drucker, Philip, and Robert F. Heizer
1967   *To Make My Name Good: A Reexamination of the Southern Kwakiutl
        Potlatch.* Berkeley and Los Angeles: University of California Press.

Fortune, R. F.
1932   *Sorcerers of Dobu: the Social Anthropology of the Dobu Islanders of the
        Western Pacific.* New York: Dutton.

Fox, C. E.
1924   *The Threshold of the Pacific: An Account of the Social Organization,
        Magic & Religion of the People of San Cristoval in the Solomon Islands.*
        London: Kegan Paul.

Garfield, Viola E.
1947   Historical Aspects of Tlingit Clans in Angoon, Alaska. *American
        Anthropologist* 49: 438–452.

Goldschmidt, Walter
1951   Ethics and the Structure of Society. *American Anthropologist* 49:
        506–524.
1986   Personal Motivation and Institutionalized Conflict, in *Peace and War:
        Cross-cultural Perspectives,* M. L. Foster and R. A. Rubinstein, eds.
        New Brunswick, N.J.: Transaction Books.
1988   The Inducement to Military Conflict in Tribal Societies, in *The Social
        Dynamics of Peace and Conflict: Culture in International Security,* R.
        A. Rubinstein and M. L. Foster, eds. Boulder: Westview Press.
1990   *The Human Career: The Self in the Symbolic World,* Cambridge, MA:
        Basil Blackwell.

Goldschmidt, Walter R., and Harold E. Driver
1940   The Hupa White Deerskin Dance. University of California *Publications
        in American Archaeology and Ethnology* 35 (8): 103–142.

Goldschmidt, Walter R., and Theodore H. Haas
1946   The Possessory Rights of the Indians of Southeast Alaska. (mimeo.)
        Washington: Bureau of Indian Affairs.

Grinnell, G. B.
1915   *The Fighting Cheyenne.* New York: Scribners.

Heider, Karl G.
1970   *The Dugum Dani: A Papuan Culture in the Highlands of West New
        Guinea.* Viking Publications in Anthropology 49. Chicago: Aldine.

Hill, W. W.
1936   *Navaho Warfare.* New Haven: Yale University.

Jablow, Joseph
  1951   *The Cheyenne in Plains Indian Relations: 1975–1984.* Monographs of
          the American Ethnological Society 19.

Karsten, Rafael
  1967   Blood Revenge and War Among the Jivaro Indians of Eastern Ecuador,
          in *Law and Warfare,* P. Bohannan, ed. New York: Natural History
          Press.

Kroeber, A. L.
  1925   *Handbook of the Indians of California.* Bureau of American Ethnology
          Bulletin 78. Washington: Smithsonian Institution.

Landtman, Gunnar
  1927   *The Kiwai Papuans of British New Guinea.* London: Macmillan.

Leach, Jerry W.
  1983   Introduction in *The Kula: New Perspectives on Massim Exchange,* J. W.
          Leach and E. Leach, eds. Cambridge: Cambridge University Press.

Lenoir, Raymond
  1924   Les Expeditions Maritimes, Institution Sociale en Melanesie
          Occidentale. *L'Anthropologie* XXXIV: 387–410.

Llewellyn, Karl, and E. Adamson Hoebel
  1941   *The Cheyenne Way: Conflict and Case Law in Primitive Jurisprudence.*
          Norman: University of Oklahoma Press.

Macintyre, Martha
  1983   Kune on Tubetube and in the Bwanabwana region of the Southern
          Massim, in *The Kula: New Perspectives on Massim Exchange,* J. W.
          Leach and E. Leach, eds. Cambridge: Cambridge University Press.

Malinowski, Bronislaw
  1922   *Argonauts of the Western Pacific.* London: Kegan Paul.

McClellan, Catharine
  1954   The Interrelations of Social Structure and Northern Tlingit
          Ceremonialism. *Southwestern Journal of Anthropology* 10: 75–96.

Meggitt, Mervyn
  1977   *Blood Is Their Argument: Warfare among the Mae Enga Tribesmen of
          the New Guinea Highlands.* Palo Alto, CA: Mayfield.

Mishkin, Bernard
  1966   *Rank and Warfare among the Plains Indians.* Seattle: University of
          Washington.

Murphy, Robert F.
  1957   Intergroup Hostility and Social Cohesion. *American Anthropologist* 58: 1018–1035.

Oliver, Douglas L.
  1955   *A Solomon Island Society: Kinship and Leadership among the Siuai of Bougainville.* Cambridge: Harvard University Press.

Pospisil, Leopold
  1958   *Kapauku Papuans and Their Law.* Yale University Publications in Anthropology 54. New Haven: Yale University.
  1963   *Kapauku Papuan Economy.* Yale University Publications in Anthropology 67. New Haven: Yale University.

Rappaport, Roy
  1967   *Pigs for the Ancestors.* New Haven: Yale University.

Scheffler, Harold W.
  1965   *Choiseul Island Social Structure.* Berkeley and Los Angeles: University of California Press.

Smith, Marian W.
  1951   *American Indian Warfare.* Transactions of the New York Academy of Sciences (2nd series) vol. 13: 348–365.

Spencer, Baldwin, and F. J. Gillen
  1927   *The Arunta: A Study of a Stone Age People.* London: Macmillan.

Stirling, M. W.
  1938   *Historical and Ethnographical Material on the Jivaro Indians.* Bureau of American Indians Bulletin 117. Washington: Smithsonian Institution.

Swanton, John R.
  1908   Social Conditions, Beliefs, and Linguistic Relationships of the Tlingit Indians. Annual Report of the Bureau of American Ethnology: 391–486. Washington: Government Printing Office.

Tyrell, J. B., ed.
  1916   *David Thompson: Narrative of His Explorations in Western America 1784–1812.* Toronto: Champlain Society.

Veblen, Thorstein
  1967   *The Theory of the Leisure Class.* New York: Penguin.

Wedgewood, Camilla H.
  1930   Some Aspects of Warfare in Melanesia. *Oceania* 1: 5–33.

✦ 5
Maintaining Social Tranquility: Internal and External Loci of Aggression Control
Douglas P. Fry

What accounts for peaceful societies? In Chapter 2, Bruce Knauft accounted for peaceful behavior in terms of the adaptive advantages conferred by sociability and cooperation; in Chapter 3, Robert Dentan examined the historical experiences of enclaved societies and refugee bands. Here, Douglas Fry takes another perspective. In *Maintaining Social Tranquility* he argues that early experiences may create barriers to the expression of aggression in later life. The focus of Fry's work is a comparison between two Zapotec communities in Oaxaca, Mexico. One is markedly more violent than the other. The difference is explained by different socialization processes. In the nonviolent community, parents model peaceful behaviors and warn their children about the consequences of physical aggression. In the more violent community, parents teach their children to anticipate the use of force, and model it for them in the use of corporal punishment. Substantial cross-cultural data support the importance Fry gives to socialization. Later in this volume, Jean Briggs also makes the point (in an unexpected way) in her analysis of the Inuit treatment of children (Chapter 6). Peace begins in the nursery.

—THE EDITORS

✦   In this chapter, I consider conflict prevention and conflict management in two Zapotec communities that exhibit different levels of physical aggression. One community is quite peaceful; the other is markedly more aggressive. A comparison of conflict-control mechanisms in the two locations—both in Oaxaca, Mexico—can help highlight some of the ways in which tranquility is maintained in the more peaceful community.

Table 5.1 frames the discussion of conflict prevention and control mechanisms. Although the distinctions presented in the table between *internal, external-informal,* and *external-formal* are of heuristic value, of course, in reality these are not absolute, mutually exclusive categories. The Zapotec employ a variety of formal (cf. Nader 1969) and informal (cf. O'Nell 1981, 1986) means to prevent and resolve conflicts (also cf. Black

1984: 2–6; Draper 1978: 31). The two communities are basically similar regarding the operation of formal control mechanisms, and also regarding some informal controls, but differ in interesting ways when it comes to *internal,* individual mechanisms of control. In other words, the people of these communities *internalize* different attitudes and worldviews regarding the expression of aggression and the resolution of conflict.

Table 5.1   Continuum of Internal-to-External Conflict-Management Processes

Level 1 Internal (individual) Locus	Level 2 External-informal Locus	Level 3 External-formal Locus
Denial of anger Denial that a conflict exists Avoidance of conflict situations and/or disputants Internalization of values incom- patible with the expression of violence (e.g., respect, equality) Positive image of others in the community Fear of witchcraft Beliefs that anger, hostility, and/or aggression are associated with illnesses Fear of gossip and so on	Gossip Witchcraft Intervention by nonauthor- itarian other(s) Ostracism and so on	Local authority structure (community police and judicial authorities); hearings, fines, jail District and State authorities; hearings, legal fees, fines, prison sentences

Note: Level 1 is largely self-imposed, although culturally constructed. Levels 2 and 3 are both largely imposed by others.

The internalization of different views, attitudes, and values in turn contributes to marked behavioral differences between the two communities. Specifically, the data presented in this chapter suggest that different internalized cultural patterns contribute to the variation between these two communities in amounts and types of aggression; that is, members of the more violent community share a cultural schema that at times includes physical aggression, while members of the tranquil community possess an internalized cultural schema that more directly discourages aggressive behavior. I argue that nonviolence is optimally maintained in the more peaceful community through internal and external controls operating in unison, mutually reinforcing each other, in contrast to what occurs in the more violent community, where internal controls against the expression of aggression are much less developed. After presenting some background information on the two communities, I will examine these propositions in the light of several different data sets.

✦   The Communities

La Paz and San Andrés[1] have been in existence since at least the 1500s and have similar recent histories. They are Zapotec-speaking communities that lie six to seven kilometers apart in the Valley of Oaxaca. While Zapotec is spoken on a daily basis, most men and some women also speak Spanish. Over the last several decades, the populations of both communities have been increasing. La Paz has a population approaching two thousand people, while San Andrés has a population of almost three thousand. The overwhelming majority of marriages in both locations continues to be endogamous.

Private landholdings are used for subsistence farming of maize, beans, and squash, and for growing the cash crop, *maguey*. About three-quarters of the farmers in each location plant *maguey*. San Andrés informants report that, typically, a person from their community owns between one and three hectares; informants from La Paz report that in their community the average holding is between three and five hectares. These informant estimates are substantiated by data obtained on economic questionnaires, wherein a sample of La Paz households was found to own more land (almost four hectares per family) than a San Andrés sample (just over two hectares per family). Furthermore, a substantial number of citizens in San Andrés (37 percent) own virtually no land (one hectare or less), while this is much less often the case in La Paz (16 percent). These differences in land ownership result largely because, although both communities have roughly the same amount of farmable land, San Andrés has a larger population than La Paz. Also, variation in the amount of land owned is slightly larger within La Paz than within San Andrés.

Unlike the rural Mexican communities studied by Friedrich (1972), Greenberg (1981, 1989), and Nash (1967), San Andrés and La Paz lack rival political factions and political bosses (*caciques*) (cf. O'Nell 1969: 32). There are no *mestizo* subgroups in either location, and stratified class structures are lacking. La Paz has no *barrio* divisions. The larger San Andrés is divided into two *barrios* of approximately equal size, although there are no marked social or economic differences between them. The two neighborhoods are linked by a cross-cutting network of kinship ties (cf. Kearney 1972: 23). People pass regularly from one barrio to the other to run errands, go to the fields, and pay visits. Further ethnographic descriptions of one or both of these communities can be found in Fry (1986, 1987, 1988, 1990, 1992), K. Fry (1989), and O'Nell (1972, 1975, 1979, 1981).

✦   Differences Regarding Nonviolence

Multiple lines of behavioral data indicate that striking differences exist regarding the expression of aggression in these two communities. O'Nell

(1979: 302) explains that while animosities and quarrels arise in La Paz, "relatively few of these problems have led to physical violence." During celebrations or parties, where many people are inebriated, fighting often breaks out in San Andrés; but in La Paz during similar occasions of heavy drinking, fighting is much less common (Fry 1986: 333–346). Fistfights among drunks in San Andrés regularly result in bruises, scrapes, and cuts before the combatants are separated by other people. In La Paz, however, fights occur less frequently and tend to end with one participant leaving the altercation of his own accord. Besides the lower frequency of fighting in La Paz, this difference in the termination of fistfights also reflects the reluctance of people from La Paz to participate in physical violence. Even while sober, San Andrés citizens engage in physical aggression; but in La Paz such occurrences were never observed. Judicial records in the district archives show a much higher assault rate for San Andrés than for La Paz (Paddock 1982, pers. com. 1986).

Additionally, several wife-beatings were witnessed in San Andrés, but none were seen in La Paz (Fry 1986). In San Andrés, patterns of jealousy have become institutionalized in various ways. San Andrés men attempt to control their wives and assure fidelity through fear, containment, and sometimes force. In La Paz, however, women are much closer to being equals with men—perhaps due in some part to women's long-standing economic contribution to the family through pottery-making—and mutual respect is a valued quality in husband-wife relationships (cf. K. Fry 1989). In La Paz, even in cases of infidelity, a circumstance where wife-beating might be socially condoned, husbands do not necessarily beat their wives. An informant told me of one case of adultery that resulted in the birth of a child while the husband was away from town working. When the husband returned to La Paz, rather than becoming violent, he wept and ordered his wife to give the infant up for adoption in a neighboring town (cf. Fry 1986: 314–327).

The district archives show San Andrés to have had a higher homicide rate than La Paz for the 41 years for which records were available between 1920 and 1968: 18.1 homicides per 100,000 persons per year in San Andrés compared with 3.4 homicides per 100,000 persons per year in La Paz (Paddock 1982, pers. com. 1986).

Information regarding the occurrence of homicides gathered from informants in the communities during 1981–1983 corresponds with the district archive data. La Paz informants reported no murders within memory, while O'Nell (1969) describes a murder that occurred in 1935 in La Paz (cf. Fry 1986). On the other hand, details of homicides in San Andrés suggest that murders occur every three to five years (cf. Fry 1986: 346–354). In 1986, a reliable La Paz informant noted that there still had not been a murder in La Paz for a very long time. In San Andrés, meantime, a man had been ambushed and killed just a couple days before our return visit; and another recent death, which one account held to have been an accident, was said in a different version to have been a homicide. Most of the recent murders in San Andrés resulted from disputes over women. Fighting among men at parties in San Andrés frequently has its roots in jealousy, which can be sparked, for example, if a man repeatedly dances with another man's wife. Generally, San Andrés men take care not to arouse jealousy in their peers, and wives are careful to avoid arousing jealousy in their husbands.

In La Paz, jealousy is considered an emotion of youth that is not appropriate in grown men (Fry 1986: 320–321, 1988). In contrast to San Andrés, for example, unrelated men and women talk casually with each other. The husband who does express jealousy becomes the subject of disapproving gossip. This difference between the two communities is reflected by the fact that citizens of La Paz regularly discuss the "ridiculous" manner in which San Andrés men are prone to jealousy.

San Andrés is religiously homogeneous. On the other hand, the most serious source of conflict and hostility within La Paz appears to be religious in nature. A conflict between the Catholic majority and a small group of Evangelists has been smoldering with periodic eruptions for the last couple of decades. But these tensions over religion in La Paz have not resulted in loss of life (cf. O'Nell 1979: 302).

Thus overall, while San Andrés is not the most violent community in the vicinity, it has a substantially higher level of violence than La Paz. A comparative analysis of the two communities, therefore, can highlight certain mechanisms that, while they maintain peace in La Paz, are weaker or absent in San Andrés.

✦ Formal Controls

O'Nell (1981: 356) defines formal control mechanisms as those that are explicitly codified, institutionalized, and involve penal sanctions. In San Andrés and La Paz, a formal legal system exists, similar in many respects to the local judicial systems described by Nader (1969) and Parnell (1978, 1988) for the Sierra Juarez region of Oaxaca. Since most interpersonal disputes in San Andrés and La Paz do not progress to the state or national legal systems, the community judicial system is the most important level of formal social control for the citizens of these communities under most circumstances (cf. O'Nell 1981: 356–358).

As is typical in Mesoamerican peasant communities, citizens of San Andrés and La Paz are elected to fill positions (*cargos*) in civil/religious hierarchies. The term *cargo* means burden and in both communities serving a position is considered a sacrifice that one makes for the good of the community. San Andrés is a municipality (*municipio*) in and of itself, while La

Paz is a subunit of a municipality (an *agencia*). However, La Paz functions very much as if it were a *municipio,* as O'Nell (1972: 295) also observes.

The highest-ranking local official in San Andrés is the mayor (*presidente*). The mayor in La Paz is referred to as the *agente* (although sometimes *presidente*). One role of a mayor is to listen to grievances and disputes within the community. In both communities, a judge (*sindico*) assists the mayor in hearing legal cases. Disputes involve a variety of matters: animals destroying crops, a teenage boy with amorous intentions detaining a teenage girl in the street, a claim that a neighbor has moved a property-marker in a field, and so on.

Nader (1969) points out that the goal of Sierra Zapotec law is to restore personal relations to equilibrium. Correspondingly, Morrissy (1978) reports that the local authorities in a Valley Zapotec community close to San Andrés and La Paz dispense justice in such a way as to restore the balance between disputants.[2] The authorities in both San Andrés and La Paz operate toward similar ends (cf. Fry 1986; O'Nell 1981). The local authorities levy fines and imprison wrongdoers in the local jail (usually for only a day or two), but often they simply listen sympathetically to what a complaining citizen has to say. When the authorities see one party as clearly being in the wrong, they are likely to lecture the wrongdoer, impose a fine, and/or require a payment of restitution. The authorities take into account the attitude of a citizen appearing before them. A respectful, humble, apologetic defendant is likely to get off much easier than an argumentative, self-righteous one. In a San Andrés case where a young, drunk husband hit his wife hard enough to leave a large lump on her head, the husband was respectful and conciliatory, and the authorities required him to pay to the municipality an amount equal to several days' wages; that is, a moderate fine. In summary, the formal authority structures and concepts of justice are very similar in the two locations, and therefore differences in levels of aggression cannot be traced to markedly different *formal* social control mechanisms in the two communities.

✦ **Exploration of Internal and External Loci of Control**

A main difference between the two communities is that the people of La Paz internalize values and attitudes that consistently run counter to the expression of aggression and the prolonging of conflict, while by contrast, the citizens of San Andrés internalize other attitudes and values. The internalization of particular values and attitudes in La Paz provides an internal, or individual, locus of conflict-prevention that does not exist to the same degree in San Andrés.

Below, I explore four topics that illustrate how different loci of control predominate in these communities. The first topic involves divergent community images and worldviews. The second topic considers differential use of some internally oriented conflict-management tactics. For both topics, information was gathered through behavior observations and informal interviews with a variety of informants.[3] The third topic involves different patterns of child discipline, and stems from structured questionnaire interviews with forty-nine respondents as well as general behavior observations. The fourth topic considers differences in children's aggression, and is based on ethological behavior observations of forty-eight children between the ages of three and eight.

Community Images and Worldviews

A number of researchers writing about societies with low levels of aggression have discussed the role of internalized values and/or worldviews that favor nonviolence (cf. Hollan 1988:52). For example, the Semai "have an image of themselves, developed during enculturation as nurturant, dependent, affiliative, and nonaggressive. . . . Such an image largely precludes aggression as a behavioral alternative" (Robarchek 1980: 113). Robarchek (1979: 111) also writes that "conflict runs counter to fundamental Semai values and calls into question both the cultural ideal and the carefully nurtured image of one's fellows as friendly, helpful, cooperative and generous." Draper (1978: 33) suggests that among the !Kung, social norms are strongly internalized and that these people "devalue aggression; they have explicit values against assaulting, losing control, and seeking to intimidate another person by sheer force of personality."

In both San Andrés and La Paz, the social ethics of respect (*respeto*), equality (*somos iguales*), and cooperation (*cooperación*) are especially valued (cf. O'Nell 1979, 1981, 1986; Selby 1974). The people believe that they should treat their fellow townspersons respectfully (cf. Nader 1969), fulfill their social obligations, and serve their community when asked to do so. Certain behaviors are incongruous with the maintenance of respect: stealing, destroying another's property, committing adultery, and physically attacking others are disrespectful acts to be avoided. Although the citizens of both communities regularly espouse the virtues of respectful conduct, Fry (1986: e.g., 298–361) provides various examples of how people from San Andrés are generally more likely to argue, insult, lie, cheat, come to blows, and damage another's property than are the people of La Paz. This is not to say that all people from San Andrés lack respect; but overall the community patterns are noticeably different. The people of La Paz manage to live in closer correspondence with the ideals of respect and equality than do the citizens of San Andrés.

Fried (1953: 286) notes that "there are, besides the ideal norms mentioned by informants, usually alternative patterns or acceptable substitutes, although these may not be so clearly formulated by them as the ideal norms." This seems to be the case in San Andrés. The citizens of San Andrés hold a community image of themselves as basically good, but, unlike the Zapotec of La Paz, many citizens also lament that some individuals lack proper respect and may act violently. One informant on different occasions said: "There are one, or two, or maybe three really bad people in town," "Men are really jealous here," "Most people are good, but not all." Another informant complained that people in San Andrés fight, are not religious, commit adultery, and lack respect: "In the old days they had more respect, but not now. Especially when they are drunk, men lack respect. Sometimes feuds or disputes develop between men, and one person may kill the other" (Fry 1986: 3–4). Such statements reflect a typical ambivalence among the people of San Andrés. It seems that many citizens would like to view their community in a more positive light, yet when faced with recurring evidence to the contrary concede that some people are disrespectful bastards (*cabrones*) who may act violently.

I recorded the opinions of six persons from San Andrés on the nature of the people of La Paz. They agreed that La Paz is a good and friendly place, and some stated that La Paz is just like San Andrés. On the other hand, not a single person from La Paz said that their San Andrés neighbors were just like themselves. To the contrary, they employed the adjectives quarrelsome, dangerous, jealous, unfriendly, and disrespectful when describing the people of San Andrés. One fifty-year-old man from La Paz referred to the people of San Andrés as "unfriendly, egotistical barbarians, who are always swearing." Another man voiced concern that, by living in San Andrés, I was placing myself in peril—that they might kill me. He told me that in San Andrés "they kill people and then leave the bodies in the street!"

A La Paz informant referred to his own townspeople as peaceful or pacifists (*pacíficos*). Generally, the people of La Paz express a consensus that their community is a friendly, peaceful place. Several men emphasized that in La Paz they do not fight, and one man expressed the sentiment that all of La Paz is like one family. Overall, the citizens of La Paz maintain a self-image of themselves as respectful, peaceful, nonjealous, and cooperative.

In San Andrés, however, there appears to be a countervailing set of attitudes, to the effect that sometimes aggression is justified, as voiced in sentiments that avenging a close relative's death may be honorable; that killing a sexual rival is certainly understandable; that fighting, especially when drunk, is to be expected with regularity. Thus, the people of San Andrés internalize ambivalent belief and value systems regarding aggression and do not hold a consistently nonviolent image of their community.

Why is La Paz a peaceful place? One factor is that the people of La Paz more consistently internalize attitudes and images of themselves that countermand the expression of aggression. Unlike the people of San Andrés, the citizens of La Paz do not talk of the presence of disrespectful bastards or violent persons in their community; and unlike San Andrés, La Paz lacks a widely held countervailing belief or value system that condones violence. The La Paz Zapotec have ideals, values, and beliefs that run more consistently counter to the expression of aggression than do the people of San Andrés.

Conflict-Management Strategies: Denial, Avoidance, and Escalation Prevention

O'Nell (1981, 1986) describes a variety of social-control mechanisms operating in La Paz, some of which are externally oriented (e.g., gossip), and others more internally focused (e.g., denial of anger, denial that a problem exists, and avoidance of another person). Some mechanisms have both external and internal dimensions. For example, the belief in La Paz that hostility, anger, and violence may be caused by certain illnesses may operate as an internal check on conflict. Externally, such beliefs also may reduce conflict in La Paz, because a person suffering from an illness has a socially acceptable excuse for aggression and can be forgiven by others.[4]

A variety of mechanisms help preserve the peace in both La Paz and San Andrés. However, the internalized patterns of conflict avoidance, denial, and escalation prevention are more consistent in La Paz. The following event illustrates all three mechanisms: One night, when an angry, inebriated La Paz man came looking for a householder, the man simply avoided the problem by pretending not to be at home. He let his unmarried sister deal with the intoxicated visitor while he remained locked inside his house. The next day, the drunk denied to family members that he had had any angry feelings toward this neighbor the night before. Both parties simply let the matter drop.

One La Paz man explained to me that it is usually better to abandon a complaint against another person if the problem is not resolved in a timely manner (Fry 1986: 307). He said he had not pursued a grievance against a fellow community member because "it was not good to prolong a dispute and make someone angry at you for a long time."

While one informant from San Andrés expressed a similar attitude, many disputes and feuds are nonetheless prolonged by the citizens of San Andrés. For example, one man confided that he was waiting until a new set of local authorities took office in order to press a claim to a plot of land. And San Andrés men sometimes harbored grudges for years. For instance, according to the people of San Andrés, along with disputes over women, motives for murder include ongoing interpersonal feuds and avenging previous killings.

In San Andrés, it is typical for brawlers to fight until other persons break up the fight, demonstrating a reliance on informal external control.

By contrast, when individuals from La Paz exchange blows, chances are that one disputant will flee the area of his own accord, thus illustrating internal control and the principle of avoidance. Overall, individuals from La Paz take greater measures to prevent and avoid conflicts, and to deny that they exist; individuals from San Andrés are more willing to harbor grudges, become involved in personal feuds, and escalate existing disputes.

Patterns of Parental Child Discipline

Steinmetz (1977), in a study in the United States, found that intergenerational patterns of conflict resolution occur within families. She reported that if parents use *discussion* to resolve conflicts between themselves and with their children, then their children also tend to adopt this approach. She also found that *verbal aggression* and *physical aggression* were adopted by children if these conflict-resolution styles were used by their parents.

Psychologists have suggested that when a parent or other adult employs physical punishment on a child, the child may use the adult as a behavioral model (cf. Bandura 1973; Huesmann 1988). Additionally, several anthropologists have noted that physical punishment of children is sometimes absent or very rare in cultures with low levels of aggression (e.g., Briggs 1978: 60, for two Canadian Inuit groups; Dentan 1968: 59, 1978: 132, and Robarchek 1980: 113–114, for the Semai; Draper 1978: 37, for the !Kung San; Levy 1978: 228–229, for the Tahitians; Sorenson 1978: 24, for the Fore). On the basis of such findings, I predicted that parents in La Paz would employ less physical punishment than parents from the more aggressive San Andrés, and that parents from La Paz would use verbal means of disciplining their children more often than San Andrés parents.

I present attitudinal and observational data regarding child discipline not only to examine these predictions, but also because the child-discipline findings provide another example of the greater manifestation of internal control in La Paz in comparison with a more external focus in San Andrés.

The assessment of attitudes toward the use of physical punishment was approached from several angles during structured interviews with samples of fathers from both communities (Fry 1993).[5] For instance, respondents were asked how they would respond if two of their own children were fighting. For the San Andrés sample, the majority of the respondents (71 percent) included punishment in their answer, while less than half of the respondents from La Paz (40 percent) included punishment in their response (difference-of-proportions test: $z = 1.99$; $p = .023$, 1-tailed).

In both communities, boys are frequently assigned the chore of taking the bulls, goats, and sheep to graze or drink. Respondents were asked what a father should do if his son, by not caring properly for the bulls, let them eat another farmer's alfalfa. In San Andrés, the majority of the fathers (65 percent) included punishment in their answers to this question, while less than one-quarter of the sample from La Paz (20 percent) suggested punishment—a very significant difference (difference-of-proportions test: $z = 2.71$; $p = .003$, 1-tailed).

A set of seven child-discipline questions were asked regarding sons and then the same questions were repeated pertaining to daughters. All questions began: "What should a father or mother do if their son/daughter . . ." and then the questions were completed by one of the following: (1) "tells a lie?" (2) "does not do his/her work?" (3) "fights with others?" (4) "hits his/her father or his/her mother?" (5) "takes things belonging to the neighbors?" (6) "does not obey his/her parents?" and (7) "does not respect his/her parents?"

Fathers from San Andrés favored the use of physical punishment significantly more often than did the La Paz fathers (Mann-Whitney U test: $z = 3.73$; $p = .0001$, 1-tailed; see Table 5.2). Regarding negative nonphysical responses (e.g., scolding), no significant difference was found to exist between the samples (Mann-Whitney U test: $z = .28$; $p = .39$, 1-tailed). Finally, a highly significant difference between the two samples was found regarding positive nonphysical responses (Mann-Whitney U test: $z = 3.68$; $p = < .0001$, 1-tailed). That is, fathers from La Paz favored the use of positive verbal responses significantly more often than did their counterparts from San Andrés (Table 5.2). Thus the primary disciplinary method suggested by the San Andrés fathers was to administer physical punishment to their children, reflecting an external locus of control. One San Andrés man advocated: "The idea that we have here . . . is to hit him, give him a blow in order that he then obeys."

By sharp contrast, the preferred disciplinary method for La Paz fathers was to respond positively and nonphysically. La Paz respondents advocated talking to their children in order to correct misbehavior, and they emphasized the importance of teaching and showing children the correct patterns of behavior that were expected of them. This La Paz pattern is congruent with the suggestion that values and attitudes favoring nonviolence are internalized in La Paz. This approach emphasizes prevention of child misconduct by teaching children appropriate behavior. While physical punishments were sometimes advocated in La Paz, this means of correction generally played a subordinate role to alternative approaches. Thus, most La Paz fathers agreed with the verbal explanations such as, "Listen son, if you do not obey . . . I am not able to assist you. . . . You, as my son, ought to [have] respect. . . . I am your father. . . . You ought to respect my words, because you know that your father and your mother are the ones that raise you."

Furthermore, ethnographic observations correspond with these questionnaire findings and indicate that substantial differences exist in how children are actually disciplined in San Andrés and La Paz. Beatings and other types of severe punishment were witnessed in San Andrés. In

Table 5.2   **Preferred Disciplinary Styles in San Andrés and La Paz for Fourteen Types of Child Misconduct**

	San Andrés	La Paz
Physical Punishment Responses[a]		
Mean:	62.6	23.0
Standard Deviation:	34.1	20.9
Range:	(0–100)	(0–64)
Negative Nonphysical Responses[b]		
Mean:	17.9	19.9
Standard Deviation:	21.1	27.9
Range:	(0–79)	(0–83)
Positive Nonphysical Responses[c]		
Mean:	30.7	70.9
Standard Deviation:	30.7	30.7
Range:	(0–100)	(8–100)

Notes: a. Common physical punishment verbs included hit, punish, punish with a stick, and pull ears.

b. Common negative nonphysical verbs included scold, lecture/advise, obligate/compel, and threaten.

c. Common positive nonphysical verbs included tell/say, correct with words, educate, talk to, teach/show, and explain.

contrast, comparably severe punishments were *never* observed in La Paz. The proposition that La Paz children seldom actually are beaten gains additional credence from O'Nell's (1969:263) independent observation that in La Paz, "the physical disciplining of a child might be undertaken with a *vara* (cane), reported to be so by fathers *but never observed*" [emphasis added].

In La Paz, on two occasions, mothers were seen threatening their children with sticks, but in neither of these cases did the parents actually hit the children. By contrast, in San Andrés I observed at least eleven separate child beatings with sticks, ropes, or belts. In one case, a child began screaming and came running around the corner of the house, pursued by an adult male: "He had a belt and swung it striking her on the backs of her legs. She screamed, still running. A woman with a baby in her arms . . . [attempted] to stop the man from chasing the girl, but he raised his arm with the belt as if to hit her and the baby, and she stepped aside" (Fry 1986: 288). Apart from these beatings, on at least five occasions, San Andrés children were seen running from adults with sticks. This tally of San Andrés beatings does not include the regularly occurring beatings that older children administered to their younger siblings or other forms of physical punishment seen in San Andrés (but not in La Paz), such as when parents threw rocks at their children, kicked them, or struck them very forcefully by hand.

The pattern of child discipline in La Paz may help children develop their own internal controls against acting aggressively. Parents explain the consequences of misdeeds to children and convey in words and actions ideals such as respect, cooperation, humility, and nonviolence. One father said, "If my boy sees that I also do not have respect for other persons, well . . . he thus acquires the same sentiment. But if I have respect for others, well he imitates me. It is done like this. Above all, the father must make himself an example, by showing how to respect." On the other hand, the heavy reliance on physical punishment in San Andrés may not be nearly as conducive to the internalization of self-restraints against aggression. Not only do San Andrés socializing agents model physical aggression during punishment episodes, but social ideals that run counter to violence may simply not be conveyed from parent to child under such circumstances.

Patterns of Children's Aggression

Various researchers have differentiated play aggression from serious aggression among children (Aldis 1975; Blurton Jones 1972; Fry 1987; Smith and Lewis 1985). Parents in both communities report that serious fighting among children is bad and should not be encouraged. In La Paz, play aggression appears to be more closely linked to real aggression and is also discouraged to some degree. On several other occasions, I heard La Paz parents telling children to cease playfighting. O'Nell (1969: 251) notes that out of twenty-one La Paz fathers questioned, only four said that they approved of play aggression, and the majority disapproved of both play fighting and real fighting. Once a La Paz woman noticed that I was observing several boys playwrestling, and she came over to me to explain that the boys were *only* playing. In La Paz, both types of behavior are seen as being within the realm of parental influence and control. When asked how he would respond if his children were fighting, a La Paz man answered, "Advise them. Tell them not to do it, that it is bad for brothers and sisters to fight. This is not good."

Parents in San Andrés however, while also saying that they disapprove of children's aggression, nonetheless affirm the view that a certain amount of fighting and playfighting is part of the nature of children. Paralleling the ambivalent community image that people from San Andrés regularly express, we also see an ambivalence regarding what constitutes acceptable children's behavior in San Andrés. Observations show that citizens from San Andrés do not necessarily break up or discourage fights among children when they see them. San Andrés parents hold an attitude that little or nothing can be done about such behavior in children—illustrated by a mother's idle remark as her sons threw rocks at each other, "The boys are always fighting."

I employed ethological behavior observation techniques to record the agonistic interactions of samples of twenty-four children from each community.[6] The mean age of the children in San Andrés was 5.5 years (SD = 1.7) and in La Paz 5.6 years (SD = 1.7), which is not a significant difference by a Mann-Whitney U test ($z = .15$; $p = .88$, 2-tailed).

As reported in Fry (1988, 1992), the rate of play aggression was significantly higher in San Andrés than in La Paz by a binomial test ($z = 7.20$; $p < .00005$, 1-tailed). The sample from San Andrés averaged 6.9 episodes of play-aggression per hour, while the rate for the La Paz sample was 3.7 episodes per hour. Likewise, the rate of serious aggression was significantly higher in San Andrés than in La Paz ($z = 2.81$; $p = .0025$, 1-tailed). Aggression occurred at an average rate of .78 episodes per hour among the San Andrés youngsters and .39 episodes per hour among the La Paz children.

Thus systematic behavior observations indicate that even by the age range of three to eight years, children in La Paz show greater restraint against fighting and playfighting than do San Andrés children. As described, adults from La Paz only rarely fight, and should they become involved in a physical confrontation are likely to separate of their own accord. This pattern of restraint and avoidance is mirrored by La Paz children. I suggest that these differences in children's behavior once again reflect the internalization of different beliefs and values regarding the expression of aggression in these two communities. The Zapotec children of San Andrés and La Paz imitate the behaviors of their elders, especially their parents. They increasingly engage in behavioral patterns that are accepted, expected, and/or rewarded by other community members. Through socialization, La Paz children of this age range already begin to develop internal controls against physical agonism, both of the play and serious varieties. The fact that adults are busy and cannot constantly attend to what children are doing suggests that the La Paz children engage in less agonism, not simply because La Paz adults externally monitor their activities, but because they are internalizing the self-restraints against physical aggression that typify their community.

*   *   *

In summary, during socialization, the people of La Paz internalize certain attitudes, beliefs, self-images, and community-images that act as a first level of aggression control, contributing to the overall peacefulness in the community. Restraint against acting aggressively comes from within. Citizens of La Paz may deny their feelings of anger, avoid conflict situations, reassure themselves that all the people in their community are good and peaceful persons, reaffirm the ethic of respect, and, when disputes do arise, people from La Paz—again at an internal level of control—tend to employ restraint to prevent the spread, escalation, or lengthy duration of the conflict.

Compared with La Paz, San Andrés has a less developed *internal* locus of aggression control. Citizens of San Andrés internalize a different set of beliefs, values, attitudes, self-images, and community-images that allow for the overt expression of aggressive behavior; that is, people from San Andrés have a series of beliefs and attitudes that contradict the ideals of respect, cooperation, and nonviolence. Thus, most citizens from San Andrés lack the *strong* internal restraint against expressing violence and escalating or prolonging conflicts that people from La Paz generally exhibit. The prevention and control of conflict in San Andrés is relatively more dependent on external mechanisms of control, both formal and informal, that La Paz also possesses as "backup" mechanisms for occasions when internal control mechanisms do not work. Thus, one reason La Paz is less violent than San Andrés is because La Paz has an additional line of defense against the overt expression of aggression, namely, internal control mechanisms, which prevent and/or reduce the severity of conflicts. This interpretation is substantiated by the data presented on (1) community images and world views; (2) patterns of conflict avoidance, denial, and restraint; (3) disciplinary beliefs and practices; and (4) patterns of child agonism.

The focus in this chapter on conflict-control mechanisms does not imply that other factors are unimportant to the etiology of nonviolence or aggression. To the contrary, I am in agreement with Huesmann's (1988) multidimensional approach to the study of aggression and with Dentan's (1978: 133–134) perspective that nonviolence can be attributed to various conditions—enculturation, economics, ecology, history, and social structure—existing or operating in combination (cf. Fry 1986, 1988, 1992).

Besides the internalization of different beliefs, attitudes, and conflict-management strategies, what other factors contribute to differences in peacefulness between San Andrés and La Paz? Certain community comparisons are summarized in Table 5.3. To begin with, many common explanations for conflict in rural Mexico can be ruled out. Explanations based on political factions (cf. Friedrich 1972), disputes between *barrios* (cf. Greenberg 1981, 1989), rivalries between healers (cf. Nash 1967), *machismo* (cf. Romanucci-Ross 1973), inequities in wealth (cf. Greenberg 1981; Nash 1967), social stratification, and interethnic tensions (cf. Flanet 1977) would seem to contribute little or nothing to our understanding of why La Paz is more peaceful than San Andrés, because both communities lack political factions, political bosses, rivalries among healers, multiple ethnic groups, *machismo,* and marked social stratification or substantial inequities.

La Paz has only one *barrio;* San Andrés has two. However, San Andrés is not split along *barrio* lines: the relations among people from the different *barrios* are not different from the interpersonal relations within *barrios.* And land is distributed more or less evenly between the *barrios.* San Andrés informants consistently reflect the belief that everybody is about equal regarding landholdings: "We all have the same amount of land,

Table 5.3   Comparisons Between San Andrés and La Paz

San Andrés	La Paz
Zapotec-speaking	Zapotec-speaking
Population: 3,000±	Population: 2,000±
Endogamous	Endogamous
Subsistence crops & *maguey*	Subsistence crops & *maguey*
Average holdings: 2± hectares	Average holdings: 4± hectares
37% own less than 1 hectare	16% own less than 1 hectare
No *caciques* or political factions	No *caciques* or political factions
Two *barrios*, no *mestizos*	One *barrio*, no *mestizos*
Largely autonomous local govt.	Largely autonomous local govt.
Uniformly Catholic	Majority Catholic, some Evangelist
Tortilla-making for resale (recent)	Pottery-making tradition (female)
Women lack respect, freedom	Greater respect, freedom for women
Prevalent jealousy	Jealousy rare
Periodic wife-beatings	Wife-beatings rare
Fistfights regular	Fistfights uncommon
Horseplay common	Horseplay exceedingly rare
Swearing common	Swearing rare
Ambivalent community image	Nonviolent community image
18.1/100,000 homicide rate	3.4/100,000 homicide rate
Children disobedient	Children obedient
Children more aggressive	Children less aggressive
Physical punishment	Positive verbal discipline

almost nothing." Interestingly, as mentioned earlier, La Paz actually has a wider range of size of landholdings than San Andrés. Thus the variation is greater in La Paz, and patterns of equity in land distribution do not explain differences in peacefulness. Furthermore, neither community is facing a situation wherein some individuals have differential access to resources as occurred in the communities studied by Greenberg (1981, 1989) and Nash (1967).

While various factors can be eliminated as probable contributors to the differential peacefulness between these two communities, access to land and jealousy merit further consideration. Earlier in the chapter I noted that the citizens of La Paz have more land on the average than do the people of San Andrés: about one-third of San Andrés families own one hectare or less, in contrast with La Paz, where about only one-sixth of the families own one hectare of land or less. Consequently, more pervasive shortages of land in San Andrés over the last several generations may have contributed to—and may continue to contribute to—greater tensions and competition than in La Paz. Such tensions sometimes shatter the peace. However, I should reiterate that when disputes over land do occur in San Andrés, they are between individuals, not larger community factions, which contrasts with the situations described by Friedrich (1972) and Greenberg (1981, 1989). Furthermore, while indicating that occasionally land disputes are motives for homicide in San Andrés, an informant discounted the idea that killing is generally viewed as a viable strategy for attaining land: "One man kills another over the land and then he has to flee or is put in jail. Both feuding men are gone, but the land remains!"

Sex-role socialization patterns also appear to contribute to different levels of community tranquility. Specifically, jealousy regularly contributes to violence in San Andrés in a way that rarely occurs in La Paz. In San Andrés, most of the recent murders involved disputes among men over women. One man was killed after publicly declaring his affection for a married woman—a mistake he committed while quite inebriated. In La Paz, by contrast, jealousy is considered an emotion of youth and is rarely expressed by adult men. While the origins of differences in patterns of male jealousy between these two neighboring communities remain unclear, there can be little doubt that socialization processes continue to perpetuate these differences from one generation to the next as children learn community-appropriate sex-role behavior (cf. Fry 1988).

It would be simplistic to propose that the peacefulness of La Paz in comparison with San Andrés can be accounted for by any single variable. In all likelihood, La Paz is more tranquil than San Andrés due not only to the enhanced, internal, conflict-control mechanisms described in this chapter, but also because jealousy does not permeate La Paz and land resources are not as scarce in La Paz as in San Andrés. Other factors may be important as well.

✦ Notes

I thank Carl O'Nell for graciously facilitating this field project in a number of ways. I also appreciate John Paddock's willingness to provide district archival data on homicide rates. The chapter has benefitted greatly from suggestions offered by Kathy M. Fry, Richard Henderson, M. Melissa McCormick, Susan Philips, Norman Yoffee, and the editors, Thomas Gregor and Leslie Sponsel. I thank these scholars for their input, but of course do not hold them accountable for any remaining short-comings. I am also grateful to the National Science Foundation (grant #81-17478) and the Wenner-Gren Foundation for Anthropological Research (grant #4117) for supporting this research, and to Carlos Vélez-Ibáñez for making available the resources at the Bureau of Applied Research in Anthropology at the University of Arizona.

　　1. San Andrés and La Paz are pseudonyms. Carl O'Nell, who worked previously in La Paz, also uses La Paz as a pseudonym for this community.

　　2. The restoration of equilibrium and normal relations between disputants—rather than the eye-for-an-eye type of justice—appears to be the goal in various societies, such as the !Kung (Draper 1978:38–39) and the Semai (Robarchek 1979), although this ideal can be accomplished through informal as well as formal channels.

3. This report is based on fieldwork conducted in these communities for approximately eighteen months between August 1981 and September 1983 and for several weeks during the summer and fall of 1986. Initially, I lived in San Andrés and made frequent visits to La Paz. In both places, rapport was established with community members. My wife and I participated in community activities in both locations, regularly visiting households and taking part in community celebrations. Special attention was paid to recording patterns of aggressive behavior and parent/child interaction. For the last twelve months of fieldwork, we maintained residences in both locations, and after initially spending more time in La Paz to compensate for more time previously spent in San Andrés, we switched from one community to the other on a weekly to biweekly basis. This allowed me to remain informed on current events and to conduct research activities in both places. The profiles of the two communities offered here primarily reflect the 1981–1983 field project, and of course social conditions should not be assumed to have remained constant over subsequent years, especially given the magnitude of social and economic change occurring throughout Mexico.

4. Such informal mechanisms of aggression control are also reported for other groups. For example, gossip is discussed by Robarchek (1988:n. 5) for the Semai; Hollan (1988:58) for the Toraja; and Romney and Romney (1966:67) for the Mixtecans of Juxtlahuaca. Pastron (1974) and Hollan (1988) discuss denial for the Tarahumara and the Toraja, respectively. The issue of avoidance is considered by Pastron (1974:389) for the Tarahumara; Hollan (1988:54, 64) for the Toraja; Sorenson (1978) for the Fore; Draper (1978:43) for the !Kung; and Robarchek (1979:106) and Dentan (1978:130) for the Semai. The association of illness with anger and/or aggression is treated by Dentan (1978:97) for the Semai; Hollan (1988, especially pages 59 and 62) for the Toraja; and Romney and Romney (1966:71) for the Mixtecans. Also, fear of sorcery and witchcraft is listed by Romney and Romney (1966:67) and Hollan (1988:58) as well as by Sorenson (1978:13) for the Fore.

5. Sixteen questions relating to child discipline taken from longer, structured interviews are analyzed here. Analyses are performed on eighteen interviews from La Paz and on thirty-one from San Andrés. All respondents from both locations were fathers, and none of the respondents were from the same compound. Only males were chosen to be respondents for two reasons. First, many women in both places did not speak Spanish with enough fluency to provide answers to all of the questions. Second, restrictive patterns of male/female interaction in San Andrés presented a situation wherein the interviewing of females by males was neither socially acceptable nor advisable. Nor did it seem appropriate to hire female assistants under such conditions. The mean age of the fathers in both samples was forty years ($t = .833$; $p < .70$, 2-tailed). Additional details are reported in Fry (1993).

6. Specific methodological details are provided in Fry (1986, 1988, 1990). In brief, the samples were similar regarding characteristics such as age of parents, number of siblings, age order within the family, and economic standing within the community. Children were observed for a total of 150 hours, which averages to about three hours per child. Following Altmann (1974), focal individual sampling was used, and observations were narrated into a tape recorder carried in a small backpack or recorded on paper using a shorthand notation scheme. I recorded a run-

ning commentary of behavior engaged in by focal children using previously defined behavioral categories. After the initial period of accustomization, children did not pay much attention to me.

✦ References

Aldis, Owen
1975 *Play Fighting.* New York: Academic.

Altmann, Jeanne
1974 Observational Study of Behavior: Sampling Methods. *Behaviour* 49:227–267.

Bandura, Albert
1973 *Aggression: A Social Learning Analysis.* Englewood Cliffs, NJ: Prentice-Hall.

Black, Donald
1984 Social Control as a Dependent Variable, in *Toward a General Theory of Social Control,* Donald Black, ed.: 1–38. Orlando: Academic Press.

Blurton Jones, Nicholas
1972 Categories of Child-Child Interaction, in *Ethological Studies of Child Behaviour,* Nicholas Burton Jones, ed.: 97–127. Cambridge: Cambridge University Press.

Briggs, Jean
1978 The Origins of Nonviolence: Inuit Management of Aggression (Canadian Arctic), in *Learning Non-Aggression,* Ashley Montagu, ed.: 54–93. New York: Oxford University Press.

Dentan, Robert
1968 *The Semai: A Nonviolent People of Malaya.* New York: Holt, Rinehart, and Winston.
1978 Notes on Childhood in a Nonviolent Context: The Semai Case (Malaysia), in *Learning Non-Aggression,* Ashley Montagu, ed.: 94–143. New York: Oxford University Press.

Draper, Patricia
1978 The Learning Environment for Aggression and Anti-Social Behavior among the !Kung (Kalahari Desert, Botswana), in *Learning Non-Aggression,* Ashley Montagu, ed.: 31–53. New York: Oxford University Press.

Flanet, Veronique
1977 *Viveré, Si Dios Quiere.* Mexico City: Instituto Nacional Indigenista.

Fried, Jacob
1953   The Relation of Ideal Norms to Actual Behavior in Tarahumara Society. *Southwestern Journal of Anthropology* 9: 286–295.

Friedrich, Paul
1972   Political Homicide in Rural Mexico, in *Anger, Violence, and Politics*, I. Feierabend, et al., eds.: 269–282. Englewood Cliffs, NJ: Prentice-Hall.

Fry, Douglas
1986   An Ethological Study of Aggression and Aggression Socialization among Zapotec Children of Oaxaca, Mexico. Ph.D. dissertation, Anthropology Department, Indiana University.
1987   Differences Between Playfighting and Serious Fighting among Zapotec Children. *Ethology and Sociobiology* 8:285–306.
1988   Intercommunity Differences in Aggression among Zapotec Children. *Child Development* 59:1008–1019.
1990   Play Aggression among Zapotec Children: Implications for the Practice Hypothesis. *Aggressive Behavior* 16:321–340.
1992   "Respect for the Rights of Others Is Peace": Learning Aggression Versus Non-Aggression among the Zapotec. *American Anthropologist* 94:621–636.
1993   The Intergenerational Transmission of Disciplinary Practices and Approaches to Conflict. *Human Organization* 52:176–185.

Fry, Kathy
1989   Women's Status and Their Contribution to the Household Economy: A Study of Two Zapotec Communities. Master's thesis, Anthropology Department, Indiana University.

Greenberg, James
1981   *Santiago's Sword: Chatino Peasant Religion and Economics*. Berkeley, CA: University of California Press.
1989   *Blood Ties: Life and Violence in Rural Mexico*. Tucson, AZ: University of Arizona Press.

Hollan, Douglas
1988   Staying "Cool" in Toraja: Informal Strategies for the Management of Anger and Hostility in a Nonviolent Society. *Ethos* 16: 52–72.

Huesmann, L. Rowell
1988   An Information Processing Model for the Development of Aggression. *Aggressive Behavior* 14:13–24.

Kearney, Michael
1972   *The Winds of Ixtepeji*. New York: Holt, Rinehart and Winston.

Levy, Robert
1978   Tahitian Gentleness and Redundant Controls, in *Learning Non-*

Aggression, Ashley Montagu, ed.: 222–235. New York: Oxford University Press.

Morrissy, E. P.
1978   Conflict Resolution in an Antiviolent Town: Preliminary Observations. Paper presented at the meetings of the International Society for Research on Aggression, Washington, D.C., Sept. 22–23.

Nader, Laura
1969   Styles of Court Procedure: To Make the Balance, in *Law and Culture in Society,* Laura Nader, ed.: 69–91. Chicago: Aldine.

Nash, June
1967   Death as a Way of Life: The Increasing Resort to Homicide in a Mexican Indian Town. *American Anthropologist* 69:455–470.

O'Nell, Carl
1969   Human Development in a Zapotec Community with an Emphasis on Aggression Control and Its Study in Dreams. Ph.D. dissertation, Department of Anthropology, University of Chicago.
1972   Aging in a Zapotec Community. *Human Development* 15:294–309.
1975   An Investigation of Reported "Fright" or a Factor in the Etiology of *Susto* "Magical Fright." *Ethos* 3:41–63.
1979   Nonviolence and Personality Dispositions among the Zapotec. *Journal of Psychological Anthropology* 2:301–322.
1981   Hostility Management and the Control of Aggression in a Zapotec Community. *Aggressive Behavior* 7:351–366.
1986   Some Primary and Secondary Effects of Violence Control among the Nonviolent Zapotec. *Anthropological Quarterly* 59: 184–190.

Paddock, John
1982   Antiviolence in Oaxaca, Mexico: Archive Research. Paper presented at the meetings of the American Society for Ethnohistory, Nashville, TN, Oct.

Parnell, Philip
1978   Village or State? Competitive Legal Systems in a Mexican Judicial District, in *The Disputing Process: Law in Ten Societies,* Laura Nader and Harry F. Todd, Jr., eds.: 315–350. New York: Columbia University Press.
1988   *Escalating Disputes: Social Participation and Change in the Oaxacan Highlands.* Tucson, AZ: University of Arizona Press.

Pastron, Allen
1974   Collective Defenses of Repression and Denial: Their Relationship to Violence among the Tarahumara Indians of Northern Mexico. *Ethos* 2:387–404.

Robarchek, Clayton
1979　Conflict, Emotion and Abreaction: Resolution of Conflict among the Semai Senoi. *Ethos* 7:104–123.
1980　The Image of Nonviolence: World View of the Semai Senoi. *Federated Museums Journal* 25:103–117.
1988　Ghosts and Witches: The Psychological Dynamics of Semai Peacefulness. Paper presented at the meeting of the American Anthropological Association, Phoenix, Arizona, Nov. 16–20.

Romanucci-Ross, Lola
1973　*Conflict, Violence, and Morality in a Mexican Village.* Palo Alto, CA: National Press Books.

Romney, Kimball, and Romaine Romney
1966　*The Mixtecans of Juxtlahuaca, Mexico,* Six Cultures Series, Vol. IV. New York: John Wiley and Sons.

Selby, Henry
1974　*Zapotec Deviance.* Austin: University of Texas Press.

Smith, Peter, and Kathryn Lewis
1985　Rough-and-Tumble Play, Fighting, and Chasing in Nursery School Children. *Ethology and Sociobiology* 6:175–181.

Sorenson, Richard
1978　Cooperation and Freedom among the Fore of New Guinea, in *Learning Non-Aggression,* Ashley Montagu, ed.: 12–30. New York: Oxford University Press.

Steinmetz, Suzanne
1977　The Use of Force for Resolving Family Conflict: The Training Ground for Abuse. *Family Coordinator* 26:19–26.

✦ 6

"Why Don't You Kill Your Baby Brother?" The Dynamics of Peace in Canadian Inuit Camps

Jean L. Briggs

The title, "Why Don't You Kill Your Baby Brother?" may come as a shock as the heading for an article about peace. Yet, as Jean Briggs shows, the teasing of children among the Inuit has a role in preparing them for a community life that is generally peaceful. We use the term *generally* because Inuit culture has been far from entirely peaceful. "Murder was known in many—perhaps all—Inuit societies, and in some it seems to have been a very frequent occurrence," writes Briggs. Today, too, even when camp life is tranquil, suspicion and fear are not far from the surface. The dynamics of peace and conflict management include such techniques as joking, reassurance, discretion, and isolation. What emerges very powerfully from Briggs's empathic treatment of Inuit life, however, is that peace may have a dark side. One would wish that a small community of closely related individuals would be held together by perception of mutual interest and the love and respect that emerges from long association. These qualities are abundant among the Inuit. But it appears that they are not sufficient. In their human, and therefore imperfect world, the peace is also maintained by institutions that generate (and yet contain) fear, anger, and distrust. How common is this pattern? It may be very general. Certainly, in this volume, we have several examples: Thomas Gregor examines the fear and antagonism that is linked to peaceful, intervillage politics among the Mehinaku of Brazil (Chapter 10); Clayton Robarchek looks at the anxiety that lies behind Semai harmony (Chapter 7); and Robert Dentan explores the ambivalent relationships of members of peaceful "enclaved" societies (Chapter 3). Human relationships are inherently ambivalent. Opposition and antagonism may coexist with and even help to construct systems of peace and nonviolence.

—THE EDITORS

✦ In selecting aspects of cultures for analysis, there is always the danger of focusing attention on matters of concern in one's own society, rather than in the society under study; in danger of reformulating the world of others in one's own terms. How to manage conflict in such a way as to avoid or minimize its socially disruptive consequences is certainly a problem that is salient to many of us who live, with a strong sense of helplessness, in the midst of poorly controlled violence of all sorts and with the threat of destruction on a massive scale hanging over us.

However, I found conflict to be of major concern also to the Inuit, with whom I lived in small, isolated, and apparently peaceful camps. The threat of violence, the scale of potential destruction, seems vastly different in their case, when looked at from outside the society by someone burdened with a sense of planetary doom, but perhaps it is not so different in the imaginations and experiences of Inuit themselves.

Inuit life, like life in the Western world, is rife with opportunities for hostile engagement, and the Inuit I knew were painfully aware of this fact. I think that conflict was writ large for them, both because they tended to have a very pervasive fear of aggression and because every individual was equally responsible for keeping the peace. I elaborate these points below and describe the ways in which these Inuit dealt with the conflicts and the potentials for conflict in their lives.

The data on which this chapter is based are drawn from my experience between 1963 and 1980 in two camps in the Canadian Northwest Territories—one camp, Utkuhikhalik, in the Central Arctic; the other, Qipisa, on Baffin Island in the Eastern Arctic. I cannot claim that the particular concatenation of circumstances, of behaviors and attitudes, that I observed in these camps obtains across the entire Inuit culture area from Alaska to Greenland and throughout the entire known history of that area. A comparison of Inuit groups shows striking resemblances in many respects; but, also, equally striking diversity, which inhibits facile generalization—not least in the area of aggression management. Readers of Canadian Inuit ethnography, my own *Never in Anger* (1970) in particular, have sometimes concluded that Inuit are always and everywhere pacific. Nothing could be farther from the truth. Murder was known in many—perhaps all—Inuit societies, and in some it seems to have been a very frequent occurrence (e.g., Rasmussen 1932: 17). Feuding was an obligation in some societies (e.g., Oswalt 1967: 184–185; Spencer 1959: 71) and there were cases in which the community took it upon itself to dispose of a person who was widely feared; for example, a recidivist murderer or someone who was violently insane. In Alaska, moreover, both Inuit and the cognate Yuit or Yup'ik (Siberian Eskimo) are known to have made war, not only on their Indian neighbors but also on other Eskimo groups (Oswalt 1967: 185–188).

Attitudes—that is, ideas, emotions, values—concerning aggression cannot, of course, be deduced directly from behavior. Similar behaviors may, in theory, be supported by quite different complexes of ideas, values, and emotions, whereas different behaviors may arise from very similar values and feelings. It is hypothetically possible that historically warring and feuding Inuit societies might have had views and feelings about aggression that were profoundly different from those of other Inuit groups, but I think it is more likely that a comparative study would discover that Inuit societies were linked by a family of resemblances, a complicated and not at all tidy pattern of shifting similarities and differences among groups.

My reasons for thinking this are threefold. First, Inuit in widely separated parts of the Arctic have recognized themselves in the generalizations I have made about "Inuit" psychodynamics, based on my observations in two small camps in the Northwest Territories. Secondly, although Utkuhikhalingmiut and Qipisamiut are geographically far apart and their living conditions are to some extent diverse, the differences in the way they construe their worlds can be seen as variations on common themes. And thirdly, the social experiences that produce motivational and interactional patterns, not only in the case of Inuit but, I would venture to say, in all societies, tend to be so complex that it would be difficult to reproduce exactly the same combination in any two environments; and the motivational patterns themselves, equally complex, must be subject to different pulls in the different situations that various groups encounter. Thus, it is possible that warring groups might recognize as their own, at least in part, the attitudes of Utkuhikhalingmiut and Qipisamiut and, in the ordinary run of everyday life, they might have managed conflict in similar ways. It is also possible that Utkuhikhalingmiut and Qipisamiut under other circumstances might have feuded or even made war without changing their complicated values and feelings very significantly. They certainly recognized violence against *individual* human beings as a distinct possibility in some circumstances.

This chapter, then, should be read as an illustration of one very ingenious and often effective Inuit way of organizing and controlling the knotty human problem of aggression. Though much of the analysis may apply far beyond the boundaries of the camps from which I draw my data, I should not want it to be read as a statement about "Inuit culture." I shall describe the ways in which I saw conflict managed and the factors that I thought gave rise to that management in the two camps in which I lived. The larger questions concerning similarities and differences between these camps and other Inuit communities will have to remain open.

✦ The Camps

First, some background information about the two groups,[1] to put in perspective their ways of dealing with conflict. The Utkuhikhalingmiut, in Chantrey Inlet at the mouth of the Back River, were isolated from Western society until comparatively recently; whereas the Qipisamiut, in Cumberland Sound on southeast Baffin Island, participated in whaling enterprises at the end of the nineteenth century and have had continuous contact with Westerners of one sort or another since then. As I have mentioned, the physical and social situations of the two groups at the time I lived with them were in some ways different and in other important respects similar. Both groups were seasonally nomadic and lived in camps about one hundred miles distant from the nearest settlements, Gjoa Haven in the one case, Pangnirtung in the other. To my eye, a major difference between them was that one was more prosperous than the other. The Utkuhikhalingmiut, in their river environment, lived primarily on fish, and their small cash income came from trapping foxes during the winter. The inventory of their household goods was small, and shortages of fuel, ammunition, and store-bought food were common. The living conditions of the Qipisamiut were much less austere than those of the Utkuhikhalingmiut. Whereas the Utkuhikhalingmiut lived in snowhouses in winter, the Qipisamiut lived in double-walled tents, *qammat* (singular, *qammaq*), that were insulated by a thick layer of Arctic heather between the two canvas walls. Unlike snowhouses, which drip unpleasantly if the indoor temperature rises above the freezing point, these tents could be heated up to 70–80°F with seal-oil lamps. The Qipisamiut also had a more varied diet than the Utkuhikhalingmiut. They hunted seal and harp seal, beluga, and caribou, as well as fish, birds, and eggs in season. Cash income came from sealskins and was ordinarily sufficient to provide expensive items such as tape-recorders, phonographs, shortwave radios, and so on, in addition to the essentials: food, clothing, fuel, ammunition, snowmobiles, boats, and boat motors. The Utkuhikhalingmiut knew about the more affluent conditions in which the eastern people lived, but they did not appear to feel deprived. As one young man remarked: "If I get twelve foxes this winter, I can buy everything I want."

The camp composition and the patterns of movement of the two groups were very similar. At the time my fieldwork was done, there were about thirty-five Utkuhikhalingmiut living in Chantrey Inlet and between fifty and sixty-five Qipisamiut in Cumberland Sound. Both groups were composed of bilaterally related kin—a core of close relatives together with a few other families who were related to the core in various ways. In both groups, the core comprised an old man, some of his married daughters and their families, and his other unmarried children of both sexes. Numbers fluctuated from year to year as less centrally related families joined or separated from the main group. They also fluctuated seasonally, because families tended to disperse in spring and summer and rejoin one another in the autumn at a central, winter camp. In the seasons of dispersal, the various families might live within sight of one another or at much greater distances, and lines of division within the group were reflected in the camping patterns. Men from the various camps met one another quite frequently while out hunting or fishing, but the women and children seldom saw those camped far away.

Among the Qipisamiut, households tended to be nuclear whenever sufficient building material or empty *qammat* were available—and some effort
was made to find separate space for young couples after they began to bear
children. Utkuhikhalingmiut households also tended to be nuclear during
the summer, but in the winter, an occasional joint snowhouse was built,
perhaps for added warmth as well as for increased sharing of food, work,
and sociability.

Among the Utkuhikhalingmiut, there were no acknowledged group
leaders. Each household head directed his own household but no others. In
the case of the Qipisamiut, however, the senior man—who was father,
grandfather, grandfather-in-law, or father-in-law of all but one of the other
men in camp—was recognized as "leader" by almost all these younger
men. In everyday matters of whether or not to hunt and where and what, the
elder exercised authority only over his own household members; but in
long-range decisions, such as whether to move to Pangnirtung or not, people deferred to his wishes, and when he moved his household to a new, sea-
sonal campsite, others tended to follow, at least to the general vicinity of
his camp. No household head was sanctioned if he made his own decisions
in such matters; deference was voluntary, but, phrased as loyalty, it was
nevertheless often there.[2]

Both groups had minimal contact with the outside world. As most Inuit
were already settled in communities, there were no neighboring camps.
Men travelled into the nearest settlement every month or so during the winter to trade skins for the store goods that they needed in their camp life.
Qipisa men, who were equipped with snowmobiles and powered boats,
were able to trade also in other seasons, when weather and ice conditions
permitted, but the Utkuhikhalingmiut, who had only dog-sleds for long-dis-
tance transportation, were cut off from Gjoa Haven altogether for six
months at a time. Women and children of both groups made the long journey rarely—usually once a year, in the summer, in the case of Qipisamiut;
less often among Utkuhikhalingmiut, because winter travel was arduous
and summer travel impossible.

The trading trips were almost the only contact the two groups had with
the larger world, except for occasional visitors: Inuit from the settlement
who were out hunting; officials from the settlement on official visits; and,
in the case of the Utkuhikhalingmiut, groups of sports fishermen who were
flown in by charter airlines in July and August. Individuals from both
groups had been sent out to hospitals, and a few of the children in each
group had had a little schooling. On the whole, however, both groups lived
quite self-sufficiently, adjusting minimally to Western culture, except for
the practice of Anglicanism and the incorporation of such material goods as
were useful to life in a hunting camp. As far as I could tell, the quality of
interpersonal relations in the camps, and the patterns of conflict management that I shall describe in this chapter, had been little, if at all, influenced

by Western contact. Patterns of childrearing, too, showed little outside influence and were variations on common themes of Inuit practice, which were—and are—found throughout the Inuit culture area, from Alaska to Greenland.

✦ Fear of Aggression

I said that I thought one of the important motivating factors underlying the very stringent control of many forms of aggression, which I observed both in Utkuhikhalik and in Qipisa, was a pervasive fear of aggression. Pervasive fears rarely have simple origins or dynamics, and the fear of aggression that I saw among these Inuit was no exception. Its roots, I think, can be sought in various circumstances of their lives and in the culturally constructed ways in which those lives were organized. Subsistence patterns, social organization, rules governing social interaction, and the cognitive-symbolic-emotional dynamics of Inuit culture and psychology all played a role in the development and maintenance of fear.

First, these Inuit were hunters, and they identified symbolically with the animals they hunted. This identification was classically expressed by a shaman whom Birket-Smith quotes as saying: "Life's greatest danger . . . lies in the fact that man's food consists entirely of souls" (1959: 166)—souls that could revenge themselves if killed, as humans would want to do if they were not well treated. I am not sure that Qipisamiut and Utkuhikhalingmiut still believed that animals had souls, which needed to be treated with respect and gratitude, but they, too, in many ways clearly expressed identification with animals. They attributed thoughts and feelings to them; they believed that a person who had committed suicide and therefore couldn't rest peacefully in another world was reincarnated in animal form; they imagined words in the calls of birds; and sometimes they responded to animals emotionally as if they were human. Children played with puppies as if they were babies, cuddling, "nursing," and backpacking them; they dragged seal foetuses across the floor, crying "maaaa maaaa"—the stereotypic rendition of a cry of pain; and I heard women murmur to a wounded gull-chick as it fluttered toward the water the same sympathetic endearments they would murmur to an injured child. Such identification cannot help but create a sense of danger when violence is directed toward the creatures one identifies with, especially when, as often happens, the perpetrator of violence is oneself. Children not only "adopted" and cuddled puppies, they also killed superfluous newborn pups with gusto, dashing them against boulders, dropping them off cliffs, or throwing them out to sea. And the wounded gull-chicks to whom those endearments were murmured had been shot, for sport, by the same women who cooed at them sympathetically as they fell.

Physical violence directed against animals is, of course, a real and necessary part of a hunting life, and it is visible to all. In our camps, weapons were everywhere to be seen and were frequently tested in the immediate vicinity of camp. Boys were trained from infancy to enjoy killing, and in Qipisa at the age of four or five they might—with the assistance of their elders—shoot their first big game animal.

Human beings were also occasionally the victims of violence. Accidents were a common occurrence; suicide was a familiar form of death; and all adults knew stories about murders and attempted murders, a few of them committed by people they knew personally. Some of these tales may have been true, others may have been fantasies woven out of suspicion and fear, but whatever their origin, they engendered fear.

A second fact of camp life that could have been related to fear of aggression was the very high value that was placed on the autonomy of every household head and on noninterference with others' behavior, since associated with these values was the absence of an elaborated system of interpersonal controls.

Fear of aggression was also inculcated in various ways during the process of socialization. I will discuss these at some length later on.

The last factor that I want to mention is the practice of emotional control—especially denial and nonexpression of hostile and resentful feelings. The knowledge that one is oneself covering up such feelings can make one suspicious and fearful of what others might be feeling and thinking. It might also lead to a dangerous accumulation of feeling. As one woman said to me: "A person who never loses his temper can kill if he does get angry."

Seen from the point of view of the Inuit individuals I know, I think the problem of conflict management is best phrased as a problem of keeping relations smooth; that is, keeping people happy, satisfied, unafraid, so that they will have no reason to be aggressive. This point of view was expressed very clearly by one old man who was listening to a radio broadcast of a hockey game. Hearing the cheers of the spectators, he said: "They're happy; I guess *they* don't make war." I saw the same emphasis on smoothness of relationships in expressions of approval for persons who were "patient" (*ningngasuit-*), "ready to accommodate" (*angiqsarait-*), and "stable" in mood and behavior, "never changing" (*su'ragunnangngit-*).

✦ Organized Management Strategies

This chapter focuses on the common, ordinary mechanisms of conflict management that I saw in operation every day in camp life, but the workings of which have not previously been analyzed. Usually, discussions of Inuit methods of social control have focused on more dramatic and organized "events," such as communally sanctioned murder, various forms of duel, and the eliciting of confessions. All of these were, historically, known in Utkuhikhalik and, because their distribution was widespread from Alaska to Greenland, I think it likely that they were known also in Cumberland Sound, the area of which Qipisa is a part. With one exception, which I note below, I did not observe these formal mechanisms. Most of them have perished. I was told about some of them, and others are well described in the literature. For the sake of completeness, I remind readers of these other methods, here.

I have already mentioned the occurrence of murder in Inuit communities. Sometimes it was committed impulsively; sometimes it was a matter of self-defense; and sometimes it was an obligatory act of vengeance. Thus, it can be seen both as an expression of conflict and as a response thereto. Impulsive murders—which are frequent—now seem to be committed mostly under the influence of alcohol. Feuding has stopped, and so, to a large extent, has the practice of killing dangerous people in self-defense. Instead, reliance is placed, when possible, on Western institutions. The police are called in to deal with murderers, and medical authorities are requested to remove the violently insane. I did know of one case in the 1960s in which an insane woman was killed because the camp in which she was living was so remote that Western authorities were beyond call.

Perhaps the most famous Inuit technique for dealing with conflict was the song duel. Song duels have been reported in Greenland, Alaska, and Canada (Weyer 1932: 227–228). In such contests, the offended parties exchanged scathing songs while an amused audience looked on. A most perceptive article on this subject was written by Eckert and Newmark (1980). Some of the songs that the authors analyze come from Utkuhikhalik, and my own summary remarks, below, on the institution of song dueling draw heavily on their work. I suppose that the disappearance of the song duel can be attributed to the influence of missionaries, many of whom condemned what they perceived as dangerously pagan festivities, associated with immoral activities.

Various forms of physical duel, such as mouth-wrestling and boxing, which were formerly known in the Utkuhikhalik area, have also disappeared, or been reduced in importance. The technique of mouth-wrestling is beautifully illustrated in one of Balikci's Netsilik films, *At the Winter Sea-Ice Camp* (1967), but in that film, wrestling is represented as merely a form of gaming—which, indeed, it often was and sometimes still is—quite apart from the role it played in the management of conflict.[3] Shoulder-boxing was described to me by a man who grew up in a Netsilik community near Utkuhikhalik. In this ritual, which, like the song duel, was performed in a festive context, two men (I think, never women) alternately dealt each other single blows on the shoulder until one or the other gave up, out of pain.

Shamans used to deal with crises, such as famines or epidemics, that affected the whole community by eliciting confessions concerning taboos broken. When a confession had been obtained, the shaman would recommend measures to be taken to reconcile the offended powers who had caused the catastrophe (Birket-Smith 1959: 151). Another sort of public performance occasioned by wrongdoing, which I have not seen mentioned in the anthropological literature, was described by a man who grew up in the northern part of Baffin Island (Muckpah 1979). Muckpah says that when marital problems disturbed the community, one person would be delegated to give the miscreants a tongue-lashing at a feast to which the whole community had been invited. The couple who had disturbed the peace would be humiliated, and at the end would be "told to keep a harmonious relationship" (1979: 41). This technique is still occasionally used: I observed it, in Qipisa, just once.

Interestingly, though most of these indigenous, formal devices for restoring social balance have vanished, the principles underlying them remain alive. They are, by and large, the same principles that govern the informal techniques that I describe below. Anticipating my argument, I draw attention to the following points. The confrontations in the various kinds of duel and in the other public performances were carried out in festive or playful contexts. Moreover, the conflict was never clearly in focus, in all its particular, controversial detail. The accusations made were formulated in vague or very general terms, if they were formulated at all. The man who told me about the shoulder-boxing did not mention that accusations were made, and in confessionals conducted by shamans, the audience merely waited for the "guilty" person to come forward and make explicit the faults that the shaman had only hinted at. The case was similar in song duels. A successful song utilized metaphor and allusions and avoided argument and self-justification, and the countering song was not a rebuttal or a defensive statement, which might escalate the quarrel; rather, it was a counterattack on some other subject—just as the countering shoulder-blow "equalized" rather than "argued against" the original blow. The conflict never took the form of a logically linked series of propositions, which could have built either to a firm conclusion concerning right and wrong, with its residue of a disgruntled loser, or to an all-out battle between factions, each competing to have their version of truth recognized or to destroy the opposition. These would have been unbalanced solutions. At the end, some people would have belonged to the community more solidly than others. As it was, when the duel or the feast was over, the conflict was supposed to be over, too, and offenders were reincorporated fully into the community. I think readers will find resonances of these qualities in the informal workings of social control that I now describe.[4]

✦   Principles Underlying the Management of Conflict

The problem of conflict management can be examined from a variety of angles. One can look at the ways in which conflict is prevented, the ways in which it is expressed, and the ways in which it is resolved.

The ways in which Utkuhikhalingmiut and Qipisamiut managed all these aspects of the problem in daily camp life were, in both camps, based on the same principles. These principles were avoidance of serious confrontation, reassurance, and pacification. Justice and punishment were foreign ideas. And though winning and losing were part of the fun in competitive play, serious conflicts were not seen in these terms. What was important was the preservation and/or restoration of peace. Eckert and Newmark (1980: 209) argue that the aim of a song duel was to reestablish a "stable ambiguity" in which nobody won and nobody lost.

Prevention of Conflict

Not surprisingly, Utkuhikhalingmiut and Qipisamiut were actively concerned to prevent conflict, to avoid confrontations that might engender bad feelings; and they had many ways of doing this.

First, they were extremely cautious, both about putting themselves forward (making claims for themselves) and about making claims on others. An immodest person or one who liked attention was thought silly or childish. Utkuhikhalingmiut commented with amusement: *"Huuhugilaaqtuq"* (he thinks he's somebody). Qipisamiut said: *"Qaqayuq"* (he likes being the center of affectionate attention and shows off in response to it). Respected persons were reticent about their own accomplishments. They were realistic about their skills but did not call attention to themselves and were certainly not boastful.

Avoidance of making claims on others took many forms, some of which might seem rather extreme to many Westerners. Direct requests were either avoided altogether or were phrased extremely modestly and considerately: "I just want (need) a little bit. Do you have enough? It's not your last? No no, that's too much." Often, requests were phrased as benevolent, made on behalf of someone else, usually a child, more rarely an old or sick or exceptionally needy person. In other words, the very high value that these Inuit placed on nurturant behavior was invoked. Both giver and asker bathed in its light, appearing as virtuous people.

Another very common way of asking for something was to phrase the request as a joke, so that if the recipient of the request wanted to refuse, both parties could pretend that there was no serious content to the interaction. In other words, there was no confrontation and there were no hurt feelings.

In addition to avoiding or minimizing direct requests, both

Utkuhikhalingmiut and Qipisamiut avoided making promises, and they rarely issued direct invitations, either. A promise might be broken and cause resentment. An invitation might be refused, and as a result, the feelings of the inviter might be hurt. Or invitees might feel they had to accept in order not to hurt the feelings of the inviter, which would create awkward feelings all around. So plans were formulated tentatively: people said "maybe" they would do this or that, rather than making definite commitments, and invitations were phrased as statements of what the speaker himself was going to do: "I'm going clamming." People addressed were free to follow or not as they pleased. Often, no statement at all was made: one noticed what others were doing and followed or not at will.

Still another way of avoiding possibly offensive confrontations was not to ask questions about another's mental or physical condition—that is, about motives, thoughts, feelings, or health. This was especially true of open-ended questions that might put a person in the awkward situation of having either to invent an answer or to refuse to answer altogether. It was proper to respect a person's privacy and autonomy with regard to the control of information. "Why?" was one of the rudest questions one could ask. If people wanted to know why I was silent, they might ask: "Are you feeling hungry? Tired? Sleepy? Homesick?" But if I said "No" to all the items in the standard repertoire, they would stop asking. The assumption was that if people wanted others to know something, they would tell them. The initiative was left to the holder of the information to communicate it. One did not ordinarily ask questions about another's plans, either. Even the head of a household might wait for his adult son to take the initiative in informing him of his hunting or travel plans. I have more than once asked a young man's father (his "leader") whether his son was planning to go with some others on a certain trip that was being discussed, only to have the father reply: "He hasn't told me yet."

So far, I have been describing ways of avoiding conflictful confrontations by respecting the autonomy and privacy of others: being indirect, discreet, not putting oneself forward, not making claims on others, or attempting to influence them. Another way of avoiding confrontations was to deny that one was unhappy, angry, dissatisfied, resentful—to "forget" the situation and "try to be happy," as Inuit from various parts of the Arctic have said to me. A very frequently used technique was to turn the situation into a joke; to laugh at it. I once observed a teenage Utkuhikhalingmiut girl teaching this attitude to her six-year-old niece. The latter was sulking because of something her younger sister had done. The aunt, noticing this, asked her niece: "Are you annoyed because of what your sister has done?" And when the child admitted that she was, her aunt said, "That's not annoying, it's funny."

But a resentful person was not the only one who might try to turn a difficult situation into a joke. People who had caused others to become unhappy or resentful—by saying something critical or by refusing an ever-so-modest request—might also deny that their offensive behavior had been serious; and by pretending that their behavior was frivolous—even when it was not—they would try to reassure the offended individuals that they had no reason to be upset.

Reassurance is another very important Inuit technique of avoiding conflict. In addition to pretending that meaningful behavior was meaningless—"only a joke"—Qipisamiut and Utkuhikhalingmiut made great efforts to be helpful, obliging, and considerate (*nallik-*). They made an effort to anticipate and meet the needs of others, so that the latter never had to be demanding. A good deal of the "welcoming" behavior that non-Inuit visitors notice in Inuit and attribute to simple warmth and good nature is motivated by the wish to reassure possibly dangerous and powerful strangers that they have nothing to fear: that Inuit are willing to help them, so that they will have no reason to attack or mistreat the Inuit, either. I have mentioned already that these Inuit believed that a major motive for aggression was fear, and that the only safe person was a happy one.

Causes of Conflict

Of course, these methods of keeping people happy and relationships smooth did not always work. In fact, though they prevented some resentments and conflicts from arising, they created others. For example, resentment could be created when people failed to take the initiative that others silently expected or wished them to take; when they failed to perceive others' needs, spontaneously, or neglected to offer voluntarily the information that others wanted to have or felt was their due. Moreover, when people withheld or denied negative feelings instead of expressing them, they left a wide field for others to imagine all that was not being expressed; and, as I have said, imagination is likely to be vivid when one is aware of all the thoughts and feelings that one is oneself suppressing.

Interpersonal relations in Inuit society are often not at all smooth. There are many causes of disagreement, discontent, and resentment in Inuit society, as there are in other societies. As is evident from the examples I have given, two major sources of trouble in these camps were envy and jealousy and the associated feelings of deprivation and loneliness. Generous though they were, these Inuit were extremely possessive of both material goods—including, very importantly, food—and people; and individuals were extremely inclined to compare what they did not have with what others did have and to feel aggrieved by the comparison.

Another major cause of conflict that I observed—especially between parents and adult children, and between spouses—was the question of where to live or camp, and with whom. This problem is perhaps particularly important in nomadic society, where alternatives are numerous and living patterns are flexible and changeable.

Disagreements also arose within each gender concerning matters related to work: who was to do what and with whom. I had the impression that this was a more important problem for men, who needed to have companions in the hunt, and who were sometimes dependent on large equipment, such as boats and motors, which were always owned by one person and used in conjunction with others.

"Serious" Methods of Coping with Conflict

The methods used to deal with problems when they arose were in keeping with the principles of avoidance, indirection, and reassurance that I have described.

One method was by hinting. Ruupi[5] might mention in conversation with Ilisapik that Aluki had said Ilisapik had not visited her (Aluki) for a long time; or that Aluki wonders whether Ilisapik brought any cigarettes with her when she came home from her trip to the settlement. Then Ilisapik might take the hint and visit Aluki or give her some cigarettes.

Prayer and sermons were also used on occasion by these very Anglican Inuit. The sermons were mostly directed at me, because I wasn't sufficiently sensitive to subtler methods of correction (see, for example, Briggs 1970: 257); but prayer, in the course of the Sunday services that were conducted by the Qipisa camp leader, was directed at one of the young men of the camp, who sometimes spoke loudly and angrily to his wife.

I have mentioned that a person who never got upset was very highly valued. A person who did get upset easily, one who "took things seriously" (*pivik-*) was not approved of. Nevertheless, it did sometimes happen that angry accusations were made directly. Even then, however, people refused to escalate a conflict by arguing or by taking sides.

If the angry person was a child, a fool, or the female anthropologist, this refusal to participate was rationalized by the belief that getting angry is childish and that it is demeaning to lower one's own behavior to a childish level. Instead, others laughed and turned the incident into a joke; tried to reassure the angry person that "it's nothing to get angry at, have some tea"; commented disapprovingly: "*You* get angry easily"; or just ignored the angry behavior. There is, however, an interesting exception to this principle of pacification, which I will describe below.[6]

If the angry person was not defined as "childish" in mentality and was therefore feared, people would again take care not to participate in or escalate the conflict, but in this case the motives were different. People might stand aside, be silent, or retreat, owing to a fear of dangerous consequences. If answering back did not further anger an already angry opponent, it might frighten him or her. As I have said, fear was thought to be as dangerous as anger, since a frightened person might attack in self-defense.

I observed a striking example of these attitudes one day while a number of people were trying to haul a heavy boat out of the water. The rope slipped and struck a man named Eliya painfully in the face. Eliya stood silently, recovering, for a few moments and then said loudly to Paulusi: "If you hadn't let go, this wouldn't have happened!" Paulusi said nothing, and they continued to haul in the boat. But Paulusi's wife, who had also been helping with the boat, silently left the group, went home, and had a severe asthma attack, which lasted for some hours. It was eventually cured with the help of her family, who came to pray and sing hymns with her; and she later told me that the attack had been caused by her fear of Eliya's anger. Eliya, in the meantime, left on an extended hunting trip and was gone for several days.

Eliya's departure was an instance of a very common way of dealing with anger; namely, isolating it. If the angry person did not remove himself for a while, as Eliya did, he might withdraw into silence or physically leave the house; alternatively, all those who witnessed the incident might leave, so that the angry person was left alone. Later, the person who was angry might try to reassure the victim of his annoyance that he had meant nothing by what he said, that he had not been angry at all but only "joking."

Occasionally, isolation of the angry or easily upsettable person might be more than temporary. Ostracism is an extreme form of withdrawal, but even this behavior might be so subtly performed that the ostracizers could not be faulted. They would appear warmer and more nurturant (*nallik-*) than ever—to the untutored eye—as if to say: "The problem is not our fault. The problematic person has gotten angry or upset for no social reason, just from 'himself' (*imminik*)."

If a person was greatly feared—if, for example, he had killed a person or threatened to do so, or if he was violently insane—he would be isolated in another way. Either he would be left to live alone while the others moved away; or, in the case of the murderer, he himself might move away and live alone, because he knew that he was feared and that a person who was feared might be killed. And indeed, the most serious of the "serious" modes of dealing with conflict was to kill the difficult person. The decision might be made either by one frightened individual or by the group, to prevent a killing on the part of the feared person. As mentioned above, a modern alternative is to ask the police, or sometimes the medical authorities, to intervene and to imprison or hospitalize the dangerous person.

It is clear that withdrawal serves a variety of functions. It is a way of preventing conflict before it happens; a way of expressing disapproval or fear in the presence of conflict; a way of solving or dissolving the conflict; and, finally, a way of sanctioning the persons who caused the disturbance, since being isolated is a very unpleasant experience, especially for people who do not enjoy solitude and are very sensitive to public opinion and very disturbed by disturbances of the peace.

"Playful" Methods of Coping with Conflict

The other major way of coping with conflict—joking—serves all the same functions that withdrawal serves.

The distinction between *serious* and *playful,* between *pivik-* and *pingnguaq-,* was very important to Utkuhikhalingmiut and Qipisamiut. I have said that they valued a happy person because they believed that a happy person was not likely to create conflicts. A happy person would not make others afraid, and therefore he would be liked. He would also be safe, they said, because if others liked him, they would not be inclined to attack him. People frequently insisted that they did not wish to be frightening (*iliranaq*), and in part their desire to be unfrightening was self-protective.

One way to prove that one was a happy person was to laugh and joke a lot, and Utkuhikhalingmiut and Qipisamiut did laugh and joke a lot. Indeed, I think in many contexts this was the preferred mode of interaction. To be "serious" had connotations of tension, anxiety, hostility, brooding. To "think too much" was considered dangerous, both to one's own health and to the health of others, since it was believed that concentrated thought could kill. On the other hand, it was highest praise to say of someone: "He never takes anything seriously."

I have presented joking so far as a means of avoiding confrontation, a means of reassuring both the joker and others that there is nothing to fear. But joking was also a means of airing grievances and keeping them in the forefront of everybody's consciousness without appearing to do so. It was a means of testing responses to a grievance without appearing to do so, and a means of sanctioning others—criticizing or humiliating them—without appearing to do so. In other words, because of its ambiguity, joking was not only a means of *avoiding* confrontation but also a means of *confronting*—without committing oneself to the "serious" and therefore frightening consequences of confrontation.

It was a very powerful means of confronting because, as long as one was defined as "joking," one did not need to limit oneself to presenting one's grievance in realistic terms. One could exaggerate and dramatize, threaten to pull a person's hair, burn down his house, steal from him, or kill him. Joking was also powerful because the exaggerations and dramas, the playful threats, resonated in the recipient of the joke with real vulnerabilities and fears, which had been aroused by past experiences and which provided strong motives for resolving the conflict.

I still have a vivid memory of an occasion in Qipisa on which joking was used to deal with my annoyance. I was making bannock, a sort of fried bread, one day, when two teenage girls came in to visit. Anna was fifteen,

Lucy fourteen. At one point I had difficulty in picking up one of the newly fried bannocks. It was too hot to pick up by hand, but it kept slipping off my pocket knife and finally fell into a puddle of water on the side platform of my tent. I swore—in English—stabbed the bannock with my butcher knife, and finally succeeded in moving it to where I wanted it.

When I swore, Anna, who understood a few words of English, whispered to Lucy: "She scolded." When I looked at Anna suspiciously, she smiled at me. Then Lucy said to me, smiling: "Are you angry, Yiini?" Immediately, I recalled with most unpleasant vividness a time sixteen years earlier in Utkuhikhalik when my irritability had caused me to be ostracized (1970: 285–299), so I smiled back and said, "Not at all!" Lucy, smiling in a manner that looked to me "amused," said: "Please fight." Somewhat startled, I said: "What?" Lucy said: "Attack us." I asked: "Why?" Lucy: "Because we'll cry." I: "Because you want to cry?" Lucy: "If you attack us, I'll push your seal-oil lamp over," and she demonstrated how she would shove it. Her smile never changed. I said in a mild voice and with a smile: *"Aijai!"* (an exclamation of fear). The girls said to each other: "Let's go to Maata's house." They went out and didn't return until the end of the evening, several hours later.

It is clear that these "jokes" hinted at power relationships and at violent behaviors, but the latter were rarely or never actualized. In the case I just described, what I feared—ostracism—had in fact happened, though in a faraway camp, in a time before my interlocutors were born. But in many cases, the fears were originally aroused not in serious experiences but in playful ones, when the frightened person was a child and adults were playing with him or her as an object. And so we come to the question of socialization.

✦ Socialization[7]

Why did these indirect, playful ways of keeping the peace work? Socialization for the management of conflict in a style appropriate to life in Qipisa and Utkuhikhalik involved several interrelated lessons. I will present them sequentially, but they were not learned sequentially.

First, it is obvious that in any society one has to learn one's place in the social system, which means—in terms of our categories—learning relations of belonging and of power: who will support one and who won't; who is Us and who is Them; who has the power and/or the authority to injure and to sanction. A system of classification more psychologically real to Qipisamiut and Utkuhikhalingmiut might be: who is frightening, socially (*iliranaq*) and/or physically (*iqsinaq*) vs. who is happy (*quvia-*), accommodating (*angiqsarait-*), unchanging (*su'ragunnangit-*), and helpful (*ikayurumayuq*). In other words, with whom does one need to be most circumspect and obliging, and with whom can one be most expressive and relaxed?

In Qipisa and Utkuhikhalik, it was also necessary to learn the dramas of everyday life; that is, learn to recognize—and, indeed, to anticipate ahead of time—situations that might lead to conflict: the dangerous situations in which people might feel envy, jealousy, anger, or resentment. One also had to learn the appropriate ways of defusing those situations; that is, the appropriate values, behaviors, and feelings to display.

What is perhaps less obvious is that one also had to learn to think and feel like an Inuk, not only to behave like an Inuit. In other words, one had to learn the appropriate vulnerabilities and sensitivities that would make the dramas *work* in predictable ways. It was not enough to recognize dangerous situations; one had to fear them.

These fears and associated sensitivities were of several sorts. One had to learn to fear aggression and conflict; that is, learn to anticipate and fear their consequences. One had to learn to fear being the center of attention: fear putting oneself forward. One had to learn to associate these situations with self-exposure and the possibility of ridicule and rejection, or possibly even physical attack, so that one would be motivated to avoid conflict and to be conciliatory. One also had to learn to suspect serious meanings in joking remarks—to perceive, interpret, and fear hints, both about the wishes of others and about the possibility of sanction.

In other words, one had to build up a backlog of emotional experience before it was needed, so that when a conflict occurred, indirection would work: the aggrieved person's grievance would be heard, even if it was only jokingly alluded to, and the person who caused the grievance would be motivated to pay serious attention to it.

So, how did children learn to recognize potentially dangerous situations and how to deal with them? How did they learn the appropriate psychological sensitivities when adults did everything in their power to keep conflicts from occurring and, when they did occur, tried to make them seem other than what they were? How could children learn to fear the possible consequences of aggression and conflict in a society in which children were rarely or never aggressed against in a serious mode—in anger or as a punitive measure—and often were given what they wanted when they screamed for it? A society in which even adults rarely aggressed against each other in serious mode and were pacified more often than not? How could children learn to fear being the center of attention when they got a lot of gratification from being the center of everyone's affectionate attention? How could they learn to suspect and fear hidden meanings when they were benignly treated and cherished? And how could they learn to fear sanctioning power that was very rarely exercised?

One answer to all these questions is—perhaps predictably—through play. I have said that adults expressed in jokes—sometimes dramatic jokes, like Lucy's—all sorts of grievances and violent fantasies that could not be expressed seriously. They did something similar when playing with children. All the problem areas of adult life were dramatized in vividly exaggerated form in interactions with small children. I call these interactions games, because, if asked, adults would claim to be "only playing" (*pingnguaq-*, *uqangnguaq-*); but they dealt with very real problems—all the ones that caused conflicts: envy, jealousy, possessiveness, doubts about belonging and being loved. They dealt also with fears of many kinds—of being abandoned, attacked, humiliated, loved too much—fears that both caused conflict and motivated people to solve conflicts.

I think that, in part, the adult players were relieving their own feelings when they played; but, often, the children who were played with had the same problems as the adults. Indeed, since the games were consciously conceived of partly as tests of a child's ability to cope with his or her situation, the tendency was to focus on a child's known or expected difficulties. If a child had just acquired a sibling, the game might revolve around the question: "Do you love your new baby sibling? Why don't you kill him or her?" If it was a new piece of clothing that the child had acquired, the question might be: "Why don't you die so I can have it?" And if the child had been recently adopted, the question might be: "Who's your daddy?"

Often, too, I think the games were a way of suggesting problems to children: they structured and interpreted the children's world for them, so that they began to feel envy, jealousy, possessiveness, doubts, and fears that they did not feel before, in the situations in which Inuit expected those emotions to be felt.

The children, of course, did not know that the adults were playing when they asked these dangerous questions. Consequently, the games were very hard work for them. Because this is so, and because the questions tend to shock Westerners who hear about them, I think it is worthwhile to digress here: to put the games in the larger context of the children's other experiences with their adult caretakers, and to show how they worked.

Utkuhikhalingmiut and Qipisamiut, by and large, loved babies and small children very much and gave them a great deal of sensitive care and attention, nursing or feeding them when they were hungry, putting them gently to sleep when they were tired, comforting them when they were unhappy, holding and cuddling them a great deal of the time when they were awake, chanting to them over and over again special affectionate refrains that wove strong dyadic bonds between them and their caretakers, and always including them in the company and activities of others, both children and adults. Several times I heard older women chide young mothers for failing to pick up a baby or a small child as soon as it woke. They considered the mother's behavior careless and unfeeling. Parents expressed momentary annoyance, now and then, when a child was obstreperous or disobedient; but rarely did they express anger. To be angry with a child was demeaning. It demonstrated one's own childishness, and one older woman told me that, as an educational device, it was thought likely to backfire and cause a child to rebel. When it did happen, it was strongly disapproved.

In any culture, socialization is a multifaceted process. Adults in Qipisa and Utkuhikhalik frequently instructed children verbally concerning proper social behavior, telling them what they should and should not do. Often, they rewarded a small child's good behavior with an affectionate nod or comment; and, once in a while, they created some other pleasant experience in support of an approved value. But older children were not given much praise: they were not thought to need it. Qipisa people, unlike Utkuhikhalingmiut, sometimes raised their voices at children; but scolding, which was heard as an expression of anger, was disapproved of. Instead of insisting that children obey instructions and punishing them if they didn't, adults had various other options. They might ignore the misbehavior, remind the child of proper behavior, laugh, or make a disapproving sound, a wordless *moo*.

Most important of all in the context of this discussion, they might question the child and create dramas of the sort I have mentioned. This they did repeatedly every day. A central idea of Inuit socialization is to "cause thought": *isumaqsayuq* (Stairs, 1989: 10). According to Stairs, *isumaqsayuq*, in North Baffin, characterizes Inuit-style education as opposed to the Western variety. Warm and tender interactions with children help to create an atmosphere in which thought can be safely caused, and the questions and dramas are well designed to elicit it. More than that, and as an integral part of thought, the dramas stimulate emotion.

Thought and feeling are inevitably related in any culture, because emotions always provide the motives for thinking; and, conversely, thought defines emotions and makes it possible for us to experience them. But whereas we downplay the importance of this relationship and even like to imagine that emotions and rational thought are in opposition, the Inuit that I observed utilized the relationship in powerful ways, creating intense emotions as a means of stimulating thought, including the most pragmatic and "rational" varieties.

So, while interaction between small children and adults was consistently good-humored, benign, and playful on the part of the adults, it taxed the children to—or beyond—the limits of their ability to understand, pushing them to expand their horizons, and testing them to see how much they had grown since the last encounter.

Facing Children with Issues

The issues that children were presented with in the playful dramas were dangerous, as we have seen. It would be hard for a child not to be threatened when asked who she would like to live with on the death of her mother; or when told that his father is never coming back from his hunting trip; when asked whether he is as lovable as his elder brother, or why she doesn't kill her baby sister. Such issues must strongly motivate children to learn to deal with them in some manageable way. The emotionally powerful words, voices, and gestures of the dramas drew and held the attention of the children I observed; and, repeated day after day in a variety of contexts, I think they helped children to trace paths from one context to another and to construct social and psychological worlds of meaning that, in their cognitive and emotional complexity, were closely related to the everyday dramas of adult life in Qipisa and Utkuhikhalik.[8] The issues might grow in salience over time, accumulate and shift meanings as children acquired more experience with them, and they probably faded in importance as children learned appropriate ways of dealing with them, and as other, more immediately troublesome problems took their place; but their emotional power was such that they never disappeared altogether. The attitudes and feelings, social characters and skills, that the dramas helped to create were of lifelong duration and governed conduct in all the varied contexts of everyday life.

The emotional power and, thus, the educational efficacy of the dramas derived from a number of characteristics. For one thing, children were active participants in the dramas, which were performed not only *for,* but unwittingly *by,* the children. And it was the children who had to make sense of them—a point to which I shall return. Moreover, dramas were highly personalized in several ways. On any given occasion, one child—or at most two, in interaction with each other—would be played with, and usually the attention of every adult present was focused on the drama, either as audience or as participant, supporting the main adult performer. The problems that were presented were of personal concern to the child played with, because they were geared to that child's own stage of development, and because the formulations of the drama made use of the child's own individual fears and wishes, understandings and misunderstandings, which were known to, or suspected by, the adult players. Often a drama focused on a troublesome transition that a child was going through—weaning, adoption, the birth of a sibling—and investigated his or her feelings about that transition.

Adult players did not make it easy for children to thread their way through the labyrinth of tricky proposals, questions, and actions, and they did not give answers to the children or directly confirm the conclusions the children came to. On the contrary, questioning a child's first facile answers, they turned situations round and round, presenting first one aspect, then another, to view. They made children realize their emotional investment in all possible outcomes, and then allowed them to find their own way out of the dilemmas that had been created—or perhaps, to find ways of living with unresolved dilemmas. Since children were unaware that the adults were "only playing," they could believe that their own decisions would determine their fate. And since the emotions aroused in them might be highly conflicted and contradictory—love as well as jealousy, attraction as well as fear—they did not always know what they wanted to decide. "Oops! I almost agreed!" exclaimed one three-year-old, mounting guard over her mixed feelings when a neighbor she liked threatened her by inviting her, insistently and in tender tones, to come and live with her.

Sometimes adults might give a child a clue that he, or she, was on an appropriate track: "Now she [the child] is beginning to just smile!"; or, a broader hint, "Do you imagine he [the tormentor] doesn't love you?" But if the child failed to pick up the clue, the adults were not likely to point out the road more clearly. Instead, they would wait for the child's understanding to mature "by itself." Children might temporarily avoid a too-difficult decision by refusing to respond to the questions or, more amusingly, by abruptly changing the subject with an exclamation like: "POP goes the weasel!" or "One-two-three GO-O-O!" or "My daddy has a nice little long penis!" But in the long run, there was no escape. The adults kept presenting the issues and testing the child's responses until the child consistently fell within the limits of the range recognized as adult.

In short, active learning was assured by focusing on one child at a time and making that child the protagonist in a drama; by tailoring the drama to the child's special situation, state of feeling, and understanding; by making the ground that the child had to tread seem perilous and, thus, important to tread carefully, but at the same time, introducing the play when the child was not upset, not feeling imperiled and resistant to learning; by expecting the child to develop her or his own resources to formulate and deal with issues; and by continuing to test that development until the child consistently demonstrated adult behavior in the face of temptation to be nonadult.

The training was hard, but in most cases, the ground was not really shaking under the child's feet. Since the adult players were usually not themselves angry or afraid, they were perfectly in control of the situation,[9] and I think that children did tend to perceive the safety as well as the danger. Though they might yell in wordless protest, stare in fear, or raise an arm threateningly, they did not develop permanent terrors of the neighbors who offered to buy or adopt them or who invited the puppy to bite off the penis.

From another point of view, the games actually enhanced the children's safety even while they elicited their fears. They relieved children of the burden of carrying their painful, dangerous, antisocial feelings alone, and they indirectly suggested solutions for those feelings. The adult who, with no sign of fear, asked a little girl why she did not kill her baby brother instead of carrying him, on the one hand recognized the possibility that the child might want to kill; on the other hand, she was demonstrating that such thoughts were not so terrible that they had to be hidden, and that she trusted the child not to act on them. Most importantly, she was also giving the child an opportunity to realize that she enjoyed nurturing that baby brother and did not entirely want to kill him.

The qualities engendered in these dramas—acute watchfulness, sensitivity to the messages of others, a tendency actively to correlate experienced events and draw conclusions from them—had many uses, in both social and physical worlds. Elsewhere, I have argued that, through these means, children learned both a flexible, experimental, problem-solving approach to life (1991a) and a strong attachment to important values (1979). Here I focus, of course, on lessons more directly relevant to problems of conflict management. Let me give now some examples of games that I think contained such lessons, and point out what children might have learned from them. I want to emphasize that I am presenting only fragments of these games, am choosing from among many variants on the same themes, and am outlining only a few of the many possible lessons that could be contained in these games. I do not assume that all possible lessons were perceived by all children on every occasion on which a given game was played; only that some lessons might be picked up by some children on some occasions, and that any lesson that *was* perceived would be reinforced by many other games on many other occasions.

Example 1. A mother put a strange baby to her breast and said to her own nursling: "Shall I nurse *him* instead of you?" The mother of the other baby offered *her* breast to the rejected child and said: "Do you want to nurse from *me*? Shall *I* be your mother?" The child shrieked a protest shriek. Both mothers laughed.

Some of the lessons that children might learn from this game are: (1) that they belong to mother; (2) that they *want* to belong to mother; (3) that the person they belong to will feed them; and (4) that the person they belong to, and want to belong to, could be taken away. In other words, they could learn to be a little bit uneasy about their life situations; and they could learn that it is very important to belong, but that it is not quite certain that they can keep what they want.

Such uneasiness could in turn have several effects: (1) it could make children watchful to see whether people have intentions to deprive them; (2) it could make children cling more strongly to mother—that is, could focus them on keeping what is theirs; and (3) it could make children anxious to please mother.

It is easy to see how such feelings can *create* conflicts, through suspicion and resentment of the imagined intentions of other people. But if the same feelings of suspicion and resentment are projected onto others—*"they feel suspicious of me"*—then the lesson taught by the game could ultimately be an awareness that such feelings are dangerous, and thus the groundwork is laid for a tendency to conciliate others as well as mother.

Example 2. An aunt held out a piece of bannock and jam to her one-year-old niece, who happily reached out for it. The aunt slapped the child's face lightly. The child cried and was cuddled and nursed by her mother. The aunt held out the bannock again . . . and the sequence was repeated until the child no longer reached out for the bannock but instead looked at her aunt warily.

From such a game children might learn (1) some doubts about the benignity of the outside world—about the wisdom of expecting or demanding to be given things, and about the power of others to sanction undesirable behavior. They might also learn (2) a little watchfulness, suspicion about hidden meanings, and perhaps (3) a little fear of aggression, too.

All of these feelings could become motives for being reticent, not putting oneself forward, not making claims that might cause conflict. (The aunt confirmed that undemandingness was what she was trying to teach.) And, as I have suggested, a feeling of suspicion might encourage one to become watchful of people's behavior and to learn to read complex meanings in apparently simple messages.

But perhaps the most interesting—because least obvious—way of learning to avoid conflicts is illustrated by the following example.

Example 3. An aunt put her niece's hand on the head of another child (both of them were three years old) and whispered: "Pull his hair." As the niece didn't immediately pull, her aunt did it for her, with adult strength. The victim shrieked and hit the aggressing child, who hit back. The conflict between the children became a battle royal. Adults urged them on and laughed: "Look, look! She's going to hurt him!" But before the children could do serious damage to each other, the adults stopped them by distracting their attention with the offer of a bottle of milk.

Some of the lessons that might be learned from this game are: (1) that aggression hurts; (2) that adults consider aggressive behavior comical and childish; (3) that pacification is comforting and feels better; and perhaps also (4) that it is better not to be noticed than to be playfully made the center of attention and laughed at.

✦ Conclusions

These were not the only kinds of experience that taught the plots of everyday life and the emotions and behaviors appropriate to them; but they were important ones, because they were highly charged with emotion, and therefore, I have suggested, children were strongly motivated to pay attention to the messages contained in them. The questions children were asked, the behaviors that were suggested to them, and the comments that were made about their behavior in the context of a game all focused their attention on the aspects of the event that the adults considered important and relevant, and suggested or reinforced appropriate emotional and behavioral reactions.

By arousing and focusing on antisocial and anxious emotions, games created possibilities for conflict that might not exist otherwise; but they also created the imaginative ability to empathize with others' feelings, or to project one's own feelings onto others, and it is partly this ability that makes it possible to anticipate conflict situations. In addition, and most importantly, the games helped to create the fears that made conflict situations not only recognizable from afar but also dangerous to the well-being of the children themselves, and thus motivated them to avoid or resolve those situations. As in a shadow show, they demonstrated the dangers inherent in the inappropriate reactions and awakened the children's imagination, so that thereafter, if they seemed to be in danger of really misbehaving, it was only necessary to hint—jokingly—at experiences they had had before they were sure how to interpret adult behavior in its complex mixture of seriousness and joking. All that was necessary was to reawaken doubts. And those doubts were easily awakened, not only because the original experiences were powerful but also because the games taught children to rely on their own senses in interpreting their own experience, to be watchful, alert to hidden meanings and intentions, and to keep testing others, as adults had tested them in childhood. One young woman, from a different part of the Arctic, demonstrated this attitude clearly when she said, discussing my analysis of these dramas: "Whenever an adult says something to me, I ask myself, 'Why did she say that? What did she mean?'"

Finally, the games taught the appropriate responses to conflict. I have pointed out how children might learn to withdraw in response to being catechized, tested, and laughed at in play. That is one way in which they were able to defend themselves against being played with, and, as we have seen, withdrawal was one of the main ways in which adult Utkuhikhalingmiut and Qipisamiut dealt with—and deal with—conflict situations.

A child's other alternative was to learn to play actively; that is, to respond in the playful mode to being played with. The games were, themselves, models of conflict management through play. And when children learned to recognize the playful in particular dramas, people stopped playing those games with them. They stopped tormenting them. The children had learned to keep their own relationships smoother—to keep out of trouble, so to speak—and in doing so, they had learned to do their part in smoothing the relationships of others.

✦ **Notes**

Although this chapter draws on impressions I have absorbed on all of my field trips (1960, 1961, 1963–1965, 1968, 1970, 1971, 1972–1973, 1974, 1975, 1979–1980), the data on socialization dramas is taken primarily from observations made between 1974 and 1980, when my work focused directly on those interactions. I am grateful to the Canadian Department of Indian Affairs and Northern Development, the National Museum of Man (now the National Museum of Civilization), and Memorial University of Newfoundland for their support of these later trips. Earlier versions of the paper were read at the Hebrew University of Jerusalem and Bar-Ilan University (1981), the University of Copenhagen (1983), the University of Chicago (1984), and the University of Tromsø (1987). Comments and questions received on all those occasions helped to develop and clarify my thinking. Gratitude of a special sort goes to the Inuit with whom I have discussed my analyses and who have encouraged me by recognizing my interpretations as true to their experience.

1. When I was socialized as an anthropologist, it was our custom to write in the present tense—of course, with appropriate disclaimers—even when the situation that was being described had changed. I participated—of course, with appropriate disclaimers—in that tradition. Now, however, the current concerns about the limits of "authorial authority" [*horrid term*] have infected me. In this chapter, I change my practice and write in the past tense, even though much of what I describe is alive and well in many parts of the Arctic.

2. There was one man in the camp who did not consider the old man his leader; namely, the man who was not a member of the leader's family. This man was himself elderly, though, I think, younger than the leader. He and his wife lived in the camp because two of their sons had married into the group. The elder son had married a daughter of the leader, and the younger had married one of the latter's granddaughters. Interestingly, though the sons helped their father a lot in various ways—hunting with him, providing him with food—nevertheless, in matters of camp movements they deferred to their father/grandfather-in-law, not to their father, who came and went quite independently of the rest of the camp.

3. A Netsilik man who was participating in the regional games held in his area in the summer of 1992 told me that mouth-wrestling had been excluded from those games on the ground that it was "too violent."

4. As I mentioned, my analysis of the workings of the song duel is drawn from that of Eckert and Newmark (1980). I would point also to a fine paper by Morrow (1990: 141–158) for a similar but more far-reaching exposition of the fundamental philosophical concerns that underlie conflict-management behavior, and much other behavior, too, in Inuit and Yupik societies: ideas about the indeterminate and experiential nature of knowledge and the proper uses of knowledge in the service of

maintaining the "balanced dynamic tension of the world" (1990: 155). Morrow's analysis, like that of Eckert and Newmark, greatly enriches my own.

5. All personal names used in this paper are pseudonyms.

6. See Example 3 in the section, Socialization.

7. Though here, as elsewhere in the chapter, I limit myself to the past tense and to the scene that I observed, discussions I have had with Inuit from various parts of the Arctic indicate clearly that the educational process I observed in Qipisa and Utkuhikhalik closely resembles that found today in a number of other widely dispersed Inuit communities, from Alaska to Greenland. The socialization dramas, in particular, which play an important part in this paper and in all my work, are very much alive, not only in communities from Alaska to Greenland, but also, in many cases, in southern cities, where Inuit are bringing up children. Their stability across time and space is amazing. Though, of course, one can't necessarily assume that their effects will be the same in all the environments in which they occur, it would be a great mistake to assume that they have died, together with the camps where I observed them.

8. For a more extensive discussion of this process of creating meaning, see Briggs 1991b.

9. One woman told me that teenagers sometimes did not play the games appropriately: they lacked sufficient self-control. She added (speaking in English): "I have to watch myself, because I could begin to enjoy myself too much."

✦ References

Balikci, Asen
1967   *At the Winter Sea-Ice Camp.* Montreal: National Film Board of Canada.

Birket-Smith, Kaj
1959   *The Eskimos.* London: Methuen.

Briggs, Jean L.
1970   *Never in Anger: Portrait of an Eskimo Family.* Cambridge: Harvard University Press.
1979   The Creation of Value in Canadian Inuit Society. *International Social Science Journal* 31(3): 393–403.
1991a Expecting the Unexpected: Canadian Inuit Training for an Experimental Lifestyle. *Ethos* 19(3): 259–287.
1991b Mazes of Meaning: The Exploration of Individuality in Culture and of Culture Through Individual Constructs, in *The Psychoanalytic Study of Society,* L. Bryce Boyer & Ruth Boyer, eds., vol. 16. Hillsdale, N.J.: Analytic Press.

Eckert, Penelope, and Russell Newmark
1980   Central Eskimo Song Duels: A Contextual Analysis of Ritual Ambiguity. *Ethnology* 19(2): 191–211.

Morrow, Phyllis
    1990   Symbolic Actions, Indirect Expressions: Limits to Interpretations of Yupik Society, *Etudes Inuit Studies* 14(1–2): 141–158.

Muckpah, James
    1979   Remembered Childhood, in *Ajurnarmat,* International Year of the Child Issue on Education, Nov. Inuit Cultural Institute.

Oswalt, Wendell H.
    1967   *Alaskan Eskimos.* San Francisco: Chandler.

Rasmussen, Knud
    1932   *Intellectual Culture of the Copper Eskimos.* Report of the Fifth Thule Expedition 1921–1924, vol. 9. Copenhagen: Gyldendal.
    1931   *The Netsilik Eskimos: Social Life and Spiritual Culture.* Report of the Fifth Thule Expedition 1921–1924, vol. 8, nos. 1 & 2, Copenhagen, Gyldendal.

Spencer, Robert F.
    1959   *The North Alaskan Eskimo: A Study in Ecology and Society.* Bureau of American Ethnology Bulletin 171. Washington, D.C.: Bureau of American Ethnology.

Stairs, Arlene
    1989   Self-Image—World-Image. Paper read at the First Conference of the Society for Psychological Anthropology, San Diego, CA.

Weyer, E.
    1932   *The Eskimos.* New Haven: Yale University Press.

✦ 7
Ghosts and Witches:
The Psychocultural Dynamics
of Semai Peacefulness
Clayton A. Robarchek

The Semai are arguably the most peaceful people known to anthropological literature. Among the Semai peace is not relative: it is virtually absolute. Clayton Robarchek finds the basis of the Semai peace in the nature of the individual's relationship to the group. More than in most human communities, the individual Semai is intensely dependent on the group for a sense of personal security. A violation of group harmony is perceived as a threat. In a tightly structured argument, Robarchek explores the relationship of the individual to the larger group by examining the culture of ghost beliefs. He explains why the Semai are afraid of ghosts but unafraid of witches. Along the way, he gives us a clear picture of the nature of the Semai peace. Notice that the relationship of Semai individuals to their group resembles that of the peaceful enclaved societies described by Robert Dentan in Chapter 3.

—THE EDITORS

✦ The Semai Senoi, hunters and swidden gardeners of the mountains of peninsular Malaysia, are one of the most peaceful societies known. Men do not fight one another; husbands do not physically abuse their wives, nor parents their children; children seldom fight among themselves; and assault, rape, and murder are virtually unknown. Intragroup raiding and feuding has never been known to occur; nor has warfare with outsiders.[1] The typical response, both individual and social, to threat is flight. Analyses of Semai world view and belief systems have revealed a culturally constituted reality where people are essentially powerless in a universe of overwhelming malevolence: a world where helpless men, women, and children are ceaselessly beset by a terrifyingly malevolent universe of beings—human and nonhuman, material and immaterial—whose nature it is to prey on them (Robarchek 1979a, 1980, 1986; Robarchek and Robarchek 1988, 1992).

This chapter examines the psychocultural dynamics of Semai ghost beliefs, their relationship to this image of reality, and their role in constituting and maintaining a behavioral environment where violence is essentially precluded as an option in human relations. The ethnographic present in the description that follows represents Semai society and culture as my wife and I found it in 1973–1974, when we conducted our first field study. Brief data from a second study in 1979–1980 are presented in an epilogue. For reasons that will become apparent, I want to begin this consideration of Semai beliefs with a discussion of a belief complex that they do not have: witchcraft; i.e., the belief that there are members of society who have both the power and the intention to cause harm to their neighbors by magical means (cf. Spiro 1969).[2]

Because witch beliefs are so common in the ethnographic record, and because they share many similarities wherever they are found, anthropologists have devoted considerable effort to attempting to understand and explain them. These explanations have usually taken one of two forms: explanation in terms of the content of the beliefs themselves, or in terms of their psychological and social functions. Space constraints preclude an extended discussion of the ethnography and ethnology of witchcraft here, but a few examples will suffice to introduce some of the hypotheses that have resulted.

Kennedy (1969) has attempted to account for the widespread similarities in the content of witch beliefs by seeing the witch image as symbolically representing the inverse of proper human values: almost an incarnation of evil. This inversion of human social values is expressed in the witch's typical reversal of normal human behavior: witches are homicidal, cannibalistic, and often incestuous or otherwise sexually perverse; they kill their own kin, they prowl at night, they fly through the air or travel through the ground, and so on. They are, according to Kennedy, "almost a pure representation of what psychoanalysis calls the id—the cauldron of subconscious, socially prohibited human drives and motives which Freud postulated as universally striving for expression" (1969: 168).

This view of the witch image as a symbolic expression of forbidden human impulses is compatible with psychological-functional analyses of witch beliefs in which the witch image is seen as a means by which impulses, especially hostility, that are socially disapproved or threatening to the self-image may be projected and expressed in a socially acceptable form (e.g., Kluckhohn 1944; Nadel 1953: Spiro 1967, 1969).

Social-functional analyses focus on the functions that witch beliefs serve for society as a whole. Beatrice Whiting's classic cross-cultural study of witchcraft beliefs (1950) illustrates this approach. She classified a sample of societies in terms of the presence or absence of "superordinate social control," i.e., social institutions with the coercive power to enforce proper behavior and punish transgressions. She found the absence of superordinate social control to be highly correlated with the belief in sorcery, which she saw as an alternative means of maintaining social control in the absence of superordinate coercive authority.

As I noted at the outset, witchcraft beliefs are not significant in Semai culture; yet, other things being equal, there are several reasons for expecting that they should be.[3] For example, Semai fit perfectly Whiting's definition of groups lacking in "superordinate social control"; that is, there are no social institutions with the power to coerce and enforce proper behavior. Each band has a headman; however, his authority is limited to his powers of persuasion, and there is no indigenous political organization above the level of the band.[4] Even more generally, Semai culture holds that no one has the right to force anyone to do anything that he or she does not want to do. Even small children cannot be forced to obey their elders if they do not wish to (cf. Dentan 1968, 1978; Robarchek 1977, 1979b).

Yet, while the Semai have no superordinate social control, neither do they have witches, which is even more surprising in view of the fact that witchcraft beliefs are widespread in Southeast Asia, including among groups to whom the Semai are linguistically related and with whom they share a common cultural substrate (see LeBar, Hickey, and Musgrave 1964). Benjamin (1968), for example, reports homicide by sorcery among the closely-related Temiar, whose territory adjoins that of the Semai to the north; and the surrounding Malays, from whom the Semai have borrowed numerous cultural elements, have a highly developed complex of witchcraft beliefs (Skeat 1900; Endicott 1970), of which Semai are well aware. Nonetheless, among Semai themselves, a concern with witchcraft is virtually nonexistent.

Are the Semai somehow psychologically and/or culturally "resistant" to the witchcraft beliefs that are important to other groups in the region, and if so, how? One possible explanation is that such beliefs are somehow fundamentally incompatible with other elements of the Semai psychocultural system, and this I believe to be the case. Of particular importance in this equation are two interrelated psychological and cultural themes—helplessness/dependence and danger/fearfulness—that are central to Semai world view (Robarchek 1979a, 1980, 1986).

✦ The Nature of Reality

From the perspective of individual psychology, two deeply learned cognitive and affective orientations underlie and give subjective credibility to the cultural expressions of a conception of a world of helplessness and danger. During enculturation, individuals acquire a conception of themselves as powerless in a hostile and malevolent world that is essentially beyond their control. They also acquire a set of behavioral dispositions—habits—that, together with these cognitive and affective orientations, lead people, in times of distress, to seek and to expect aid and comfort from kin and fellow band-members (see Robarchek 1977, 1979a for detailed discussions of this enculturative process). The result is that dependence (with its reciprocal, nurturance) becomes a major structural dimension in most social relationships, both among human beings and between them and the supernatural world.

This orientation in human relations can be seen clearly in the pattern of responses to an oral sentence-completion test that I used to explore attitudes and values (see Robarchek 1980, 1986 for detailed discussions of the application of this test). To the item, "If (s)he is in difficulty, (s)he . . . ," the overwhelming majority of respondents (seventeen of eighteen) said, "seeks (or gets) the help of others." To the item, "if (s)he is afraid, (s)he . . . ," the modal response was, "gets a friend, relative to accompany him/her." (Note the respondents' spontaneous equation of fear, which implies danger, with being alone.) To the item, "When (s)he is hungry, (s)he . . . ," the modal response was "Asks someone for food." The implication of all this is clear: when a person is stressed, he or she seeks and finds support in the nurturance of others.

This attitude of dependency is complemented by a reciprocal responsibility to provide nurturance. This is revealed in another set of sentence-completion items directed toward eliciting normative conceptions, definitions of "goodness" and "badness." There were six of these items:

"They praise him/her because (s)he . . . "
"If (s)he is a true friend, (s)he . . . "
"(S)he is a good person, (s)he always . . . "
"(S)he is angry at his/her friend/relative because . . ."
"(S)he is a bad/evil person, (s)he always . . . "
"His/her kin reject him/her because (s)he . . ."

Of 102 value-related responses to these items, only three were not directly related to two core values: nurturance (the giving of physical, material, or emotional support) and affiliation (the maintenance of harmonious interpersonal relations). Further analysis showed that the ideal of "goodness" is primarily defined positively in terms of nurturance: helping, giving, and so on.

"Badness," on the other hand, is defined almost entirely in terms of behaviors inimical to affiliation: getting angry, quarreling, fighting, and so on. This emphasis on maintaining harmonious interpersonal relations within the kindred and residence group reflects the crucial role played by the localized band, *hii'*—the inclusive "we, all of us here together": kindred and residence group—as the only refuge from, the only protection against, the omnipresent dangers that lay siege to every individual and every community.

Because of the tangled web of interlocking kin obligations generated by bilaterality, becoming embroiled in a dispute inevitably jeopardizes relations with with one's own kin as well as with others in the community, calling into question the integrity of the band and threatening the only source of nurturance and security in a hostile and dangerous world. The fear of alienation from kindred and community is, in fact, of major significance in social control, acting as a deterrent to antisocial behavior or to any behavior that might precipitate conflict. This fear is clearly expressed in the responses to another of the sentence-completion items: "More than anything else, (s)he is afraid of. . . ." The modal response, more frequent than "dangerous spirits," "tigers," and "death" *combined* (all of which were cited), was "becoming embroiled in a dispute."

Thus, the intense dependency strivings characteristic of individuals, together with the central place of the kindred and band as the ultimate sources of nurturance and security, make it essential that relations within the band be free of overt suspicion and hostility. Any overt expression of anger between band members, even a few sharp words, is, in fact, grounds for invoking formal procedures that are directed toward healing such breaches and restoring amicable social relations. The image, and to a very large extent the reality, of the group as benevolent and nurturant must be maintained (Robarchek 1977; 1979a,b; 1986).

✦ **The Nature of Humankind**

One of the most important aspects of any society's reality is the people in it. For Semai, there are two kinds of people: *hii'* and *mai. Hii'* are, as we have seen, "we, all of us here together," kin and coresidents, the group of a hundred or so people with whom life is bound up from birth to death. These are the only people whom one can truly depend upon and trust, who will provide food in times of illness or injury, and who will summon the band's "spirit kin" to combat the illness-causing attacks of malevolent supernatural beings. The rest of the human world—Semai from other areas as well as other aboriginal peoples and other ethnic groups—are *mai.*

Mai are potentially dangerous, and relations with them should be kept to a minimum. A Semai aphorism succinctly expresses the appropriate attitude: *"hal mai, hal mai; hal hii', hal hii'"* (literally, "their affairs are theirs; our affairs are ours"); i.e., "Do not become involved in the concerns of outsiders!" The malevolence of *mai* is both symbolized by and given concrete form in bogeymen beliefs, such as *mai kahnoh kuui,* the "cutting-off-head strangers," foreigners—outlanders or even strange Semai—who wait in ambush in the forest to cut off Semai heads to sell to Malays or other lowlanders who are believed to use them in magical rituals (Robarchek 1979a, 1986).

188   ✦   *Clayton A. Robarchek*

This fundamental dichotomy of we and they—kin and strangers, nurturance and malevolence, security and danger—that defines the human world characterizes the nonhuman world as well, where an identical dichotomy exists in the distinction between *gunik* and *mara'*. *Mara'* are "they (*mai*) who eat us," dangerous beings who may or may not have material form at any given time. These beings may be tigers, leopards, and other dangerous animals; or the *mara'* that lives in the ground, who twists and shrivels limbs; or the tree *mara'* that reaches down with its long, gibbon-like arms to seize and break the neck of a person's "soul," bringing death within hours; or any of a hundred others. Whatever their embodiment or mode of attack, *mara'* are everywhere, waiting only the opportunity to inflict injury, illness, and death.

Gunik, on the other hand, are the band's allies against these forces, benevolent "spirits" who can be called upon to aid human beings in times of trouble, especially in treating illness. *Gunik* were once *mara',* but they have joined *our* human society and become kin (they may, however, still be *mara'* to other bands). *Mara'* become *gunik* by coming to a man or woman in a dream, teaching the dreamer a song, and asking to become a member of the dreamer's family. Henceforth, the *gunik* calls the dreamer "father" or "mother," and the dreamer's children "sibling." By singing the song, they can summon the *gunik* from its home in the forest to aid its human kin, especially by seeking out and eliminating the sources of their illnesses and warding off the attacking *mara'* (Dentan 1968; Robarchek 1977, 1986).

These images (see Table 7.1) are cognitively, affectively, and morally isomorphic, and what they define is a world where the only security is in *hii',* in the band and its spirit kin. All else is danger and death.

It should now be clear why Semai do not have witches: the witch image would confound these two classes of entities and attributes. Socially, the witch would be in the left-hand column of Table 7.1: a kinsman; a

Table 7.1   Semai Psychological Dichotomy

hii'	*mai*
We	They
Kin	Non-kin
Band-members	Foreigners
Gunik	*Mara'*
Nurturance	Hostility
Affiliation	Conflict
Security	Danger
Good	Evil

Note: The column on the right describes and defines the world outside the band, the world within which each Semai settlement maintains its precarious existence. The column on the left represents the only security in this world of overwhelming danger.

band-member; one of us. Morally and behaviorally, the witch would be in the right-hand column: the embodiment of malevolence and evil. Since *hii'*, the group, is central—the sole source of nurturance and security in the cognitive maps of individuals—it is essential that the image of the group as benevolent and a source of succor be maintained. The suggestion that some band-members are actually witches, malevolent beings dedicated to the destruction of their friends and kinsmen, would conflict directly with the image of the band as the only reliable source of security in an otherwise malevolent universe. Spiro (1967), for example, shows how the Burmese belief that one in seven persons is a witch results in a pervasive climate of fear, suspicion, mistrust, and hostility in Burmese peasant communities. In a Semai band, such perceptions would menace the sole source of security, the residence group, and thus would be intolerably threatening to individuals, attacking the very bedrock of personal identity and security and leaving individuals alone and defenseless against the omnipresent hostility and danger lurking without.

There is, however, another belief system in Semai culture—one that is, in many ways, isomorphic with the belief in witchcraft, but that differs from it in ways that are clearly dependent upon and reflective of the unique cultural context in which it occurs: this is the Semai belief in ghosts. Before examining the content of these beliefs, however, we first need to understand where ghosts fit in Semai cosmology and ontology. This entails the introduction of several other concepts.

✦ Semai Ghosts

Semai ghosts, like witches elsewhere, are unequivocally malevolent and homicidal. They seek to kill humans, especially kinsmen. When a death occurs, they come in droves to eat the corpse. They prowl around the houses in the night, scratching at the thatch and trying to gain entry. The houses must be shuttered tightly at dusk and the cooking-fires kept burning to keep them from attacking the survivors. Even in the daytime, they ride the mists and storm clouds or lurk in the forest in the vicinity of their graves, placing across the trails gossamer threads that enter the body on contact, causing fever and weakness. Even the ghosts' baleful stare causes sickness; their touch is like ice, and it brings sickness and death.

In addition to their homicidal natures, they exhibit a number of other characteristics typical of witches: cannibalism, for example. Humans are their "meat," and they attack and kill in order to devour their victims' bodies. Also like witches, much of their behavior is the obverse of normal human behavior: fire is their water, blossoms are their fruit, they wear their backbaskets upside down, they fly through the air or travel through the ground, and so on (cf. Dentan 1968).

Also like witches, ghosts are (or rather, were) friends and kinsmen; members of the band. However, since they are *mara'* and were also *hii'*, they have the potential to confound the categories of reality, and thus the two images must be compartmentalized and kept separate. If Semai were forced to confront the paradox, it is to be expected that a good deal of cognitive dissonance might be generated by the perception that those people who were helpful, friendly, and supportive (and most people do approximate this ideal most of the time) when they were alive become, after their deaths, homicidal ghosts bent on killing and devouring their friends and kin.[5] A conversation that I had with a friend on this point shows the psychological necessity of maintaining the separation of these two images and, ultimately, the need to avoid any imputation of hostility within the group.

A neighbor and I were discussing ghosts and encounters with them one afternoon, and he recounted an experience of some years before when he was chased by a ghost. As background for the story, he described the place where it happened, the cloudy, misty day, the grave nearby, the person buried there, and the circumstances of his death (a youth who had bled to death after accidentally chopping off his fingers with a parang). It was abundantly clear from this account that he implicitly believed that the ghost that had chased him was the ghost of this boy. A bit later, I raised the question of why good people become evil ghosts. He thought for a long while, and then offered the following explanation: the ghost that we fear, he said, the *mara'* that attacks us if we go near a grave, is not the ghost of the person whom we buried there; rather, it is a strange ghost, a foreigner. After death, the ghost of our covillager goes elsewhere to live in some other grave, and a strange ghost (*mai*) from outside our territory comes and takes up residence in the vacant grave. It is this foreign ghost that we fear and that seeks to kill us.

This was clearly an ad hoc rationalization constructed on the spur of the moment, since it was at variance with everything else that I had been told about ghosts before (or afterwards, since I tried unsuccessfully to get the same explanation from others and, some months later, from him). Still, the fact that such a rationalization was offered is revealing. It appears that these discrepant perceptions (ghosts=evil; *hii'*=good; but ghosts=*hii'*) are ordinarily compartmentalized and kept separate, and thus evoke no dissonance or threat. When forced to confront the paradox, however, my friend produced a new schema that once again isolated both perceptions, thus protecting and maintaining the image of the band and its members as benevolent and nurturant.

The ghost is also distanced from its human precursor, and thus from *hii'*, by Semai ethnopsychological theory. This holds that human beings have three animistic "essences," none of which corresponds to the Western concept of "soul" or "spirit." These essences are collectively called *"ruai,"* a term that is both a generic and a specific. The taxonomic relationships among these are shown in Table 7.2. The three specific "essences" are *"ruai," "klook,"* and *"kitmoic."* *Ruai* is a tiny, immaterial manikin that resides behind the forehead. Sometimes symbolized as a bird, it is somewhat birdlike in its characteristics: flighty, irrational, and easily frightened. It is also not solidly fixed in the body; it can and often does flee the body, as when startled by a loud and unexpected thunderclap. Dreams are primarily the adventures of the *ruai* as it wanders during sleep. It is the seat of human irrationality and irresponsibility, and thus often does things in dreams that the person would not do when awake. The *ruai* may stay away from the body for days or even weeks without severe consequences other than lassitude and a general malaise. If it is captured or killed during its wanderings, however, the person will waste away and ultimately die (cf. Dentan 1968).

Table 7.2 Taxonomic Relationships of Animistic Essences

Ruai		
Ruai	*Klook*	*Kitmoic*

Klook is a much more substantial essence. It resides in the heart and is the source of rationality and consciousness. The *klook* can also leave the body, which results in loss of consciousness, and it may also have dream experiences. Separation of the *klook* is a much more serious matter than the wanderings of the *ruai,* since the body lies comatose. Death will follow if it does not return within a few days (cf. Dentan 1968). Together, the *ruai* and *klook* constitute the personality of an individual.

Kitmoic is the ghost. The *kitmoic* however, does not exist during the lifetime of an individual but comes into being only after death, generated from the decomposing corpse in the first six days following burial (cf. Dentan 1968). The *ruai* and *klook* go elsewhere after death, to a flowery place of coolness and shade, or deep into the earth, to the Stone of Life. Only the *kitmoic* remains, to prowl the earth in search of human flesh. Here, once again, the malevolence of *kitmoic* is separated from the benevolence of *hii';* these homicidal ghosts, although they are *mara'* that are *of* our neighbors and kinsmen, are not *in* them.

Nonetheless, Semai ghosts, like witches, are especially appropriate as vehicles and objects for both the projection and direct expression of hostile and other forbidden impulses that arise within the group, since they closely approximate those people—neighbors and kin—toward whom such feelings are likely to be held (cf. Spiro 1952).

Ghosts can also serve as objects for the direct but socially approved expression of hostility since, like witches, they can be killed. Following the death of of an infant in our settlement, I took part, along with several other men, in an abortive ghost-killing expedition. The evening following the burial, we waited at the grave-site with our parangs, to ambush the ghosts that would come to feast on the body. One of our number had a ghost as a *gunik* and would have been able to see them if they appeared, but they had apparently been repelled by a piece of burning rubber placed at the grave by the bereaved mother to keep them away. Nevertheless, in the classic mold of the witch-hunt, such direct action taken against ghosts provides a focus for the diffuse but powerful emotions aroused by a death in the community.

Ghosts, with their inversion of human values, thus stand, like witches, as the antithesis of humanity: an objectification of pure evil. Unlike witches, however, they are no longer members of the group and thus give no cause for fear and suspicion of one's neighbors. The source of the perceived hostility and threat is placed outside the group of living human beings and is, thereby, no threat to social relations or to the image of the group as benevolent and nurturant. The image of *hii'* is protected and maintained (cf. Spiro 1952, 1953).

In summary, what I have tried to do here is to provide a glimpse into the culturally constituted world of the Semai—a world where danger and death are omnipresent, where lone individuals are helpless, and where only through the support and nurturance of the community is survival possible. Within this environment of meanings, people organize their activities, conceive of their options, and live their lives. Here, any overt conflict or even attribution of hostility threatens to rend the encompassing net of interpersonal relations, negating the most fundamental Semai values and threatening to set individuals adrift in an overpoweringly hostile and dangerous world. Beliefs about the natures of human and nonhuman beings, including ghosts, are part of the cultural constitution of this reality, both reflecting and shaping social relations. In the reality thus constituted, the social and psychological implications of violence have essentially precluded it as an option in normal human relations.

✦ Epilogue

More recent data cast additional light on this analysis. In the years intervening between our first study in 1973–1974 and our most recent fieldwork in 1979–1980, vast changes had taken place, many as a result of a Malaysian government policy to "resettle" Semai and other aboriginal peoples in permanent villages and, by encouraging or forcing them to take up rubber-planting or other market-oriented activities, to draw them into the economic and political sphere of the Malaysian state. This, coupled with strong pressures on aboriginal peoples to adopt Islam, has amounted to a systematic policy of ethnocide—a policy whose effect has been largely to destroy the self-sufficient subsistence economies, forcing the people into the labor market and, thereby, freeing the land, timber, water, and other resources of the forest territories that they and their ancestors have occupied for millennia to be converted to the ends of "development," a process that is proceeding apace both in peninsular Malaysia and in Malaysian Borneo.

Among the most far-reaching of these changes was the shift in the subsistence system from swidden gardening to wage-labor on the plantations and other enterprises that are invading this traditionally Semai region. At the insistence of the Malaysian government, the pattern of shifting cultivation and impermanent residence has now largely been replaced by permanent villages. This is leading to the collapse of the swidden cycle and a loss of subsistence self-sufficiency as more and more men and women now work for wages. One result has been that daily life, which was formerly almost completely focused inwardly on the interdependent and essentially self-sufficient community, is now increasingly involved with *mai*: employers, government bureaucrats, other laborers, and so on. These people, who can not be trusted or relied upon, who are known to lie, cheat, and to exploit the Semai and their resources for their own advantage, now occupy a central place in the concerns of most Semai, but they are outside that community of kinsmen that once provided all-encompassing nurturance and security against the outside world.[6]

As the social field becomes more complex, as *mai* become more significant figures in daily life, and as dependence upon and conflicts with them become more common, the witch image, formerly latent in Semai culture, may be emerging to give concrete form and substance to these conflicts, and to give expression to the emotions that they arouse.

This is evidenced by the fact that, in 1980, two deaths that had occurred since our previous visit were attributed to sorcery by Malays. These Malays, allegedly angered because the two men had refused to sell them *durian* fruit that had already been promised to a Chinese trader with whom the group has a long association, were said to have retaliated by putting spells on (or poison in) food or drink that was consumed by the two Semai. Violent gastrointestinal attacks quickly caused their deaths.

The witch image of foreignness (since they still do not exist within the band), malevolence, and evil corresponds with perceptions of the increasingly salient *mai*, and becomes a vehicle both for the explanation of misfortune and, given the strongly internalized controls on the direct expression of hostility, for its projection.

Moreover, I expect that incidents of direct aggression and violence by Semai will increase, as individuals, especially younger people, further their involvements with the outside world. An increasingly external orientation necessarily entails a corresponding decrease in the significance of the band as the sole reference group and the sole source of the senses of security and identity, lessening the internalized controls on violence provided by the traditional value-set and the self images that it informed (cf. Robarchek 1986). Additionally, people will have more opportunities to observe and to learn the uses of violence, and to come to see it as a behavioral option.

Unhappily, something of the sort already appears to be happening. In 1980, we heard rumors of fistfights involving boys from more acculturated lowland settlements, and of one or two shootings. Dentan (1988b) also reported a murder by a Semai of a Chinese shopkeeper who had cheated him and taken his wife. It is only to be expected that as Semai conceptions of their reality change from the traditional images that I have tried to sketch here, becoming more and more consonant with the images held by the outside world, and as they are increasingly exploited and abused by that world, they will increasingly adopt the instrumental conception of violence that seems to be characteristic of most of the rest of humanity.

✦ Notes

Analysis of these data and their application to questions of peacefulness and warfare were supported by research grants from the Harry Frank Guggenheim Foundation, whose support and encouragement is gratefully acknowledged.

1. The sole documented exception to this is the participation of some Semai in an aborigine military regiment and in Home Guard units originally organized by the British colonial administration during the insurgency that followed World War II. This is discussed at some length in Robarchek and Dentan (1987). There is also a Semai myth of a war with the Malays, which may or may not describe an actual historical occurrence (cf. Dentan 1988a).

2. The conventional distinction between witchcraft and sorcery is not relevant to the discussion that follows and both are encompassed here under the term *witchcraft*.

3. I say "not significant" rather than "nonexistent" because the Semai do recognize that there are Malay witches, and that a rejected lover might go to one of these for a love-charm, or, possibly, for a spell to cause the ex-lover to fall ill. There is also a spell that can be recited over food to cause illness, and a person who has been seriously wronged can ask *Jenang* (a rather vaguely conceived ancestor-being) to cause the person to fall ill. Most people, however, doubt that this would really work; and, in all of these cases, the spells are said to work only against one who has committed a real offense against the aggrieved party. Most people, in fact, emphatically deny that any of these events ever really happen, and (in 1973–1974) I heard of no cases where any of these spells were considered as causes of any illnesses or deaths. The point here is not that Semai deny the possibility of witchcraft but, rather, that it is simply of no practical or psychological importance to them.

4. There are now, and were then, of course, the Malaysian state and national

governments, but in 1973–1974 these had little direct influence in the day-to-day life of the more remote Semai settlements, such as the one where we lived.

5. This should not be taken to mean that life in a Semai hamlet is completely blissful and serene (cf. Robarchek and Dentan 1987). There is resentment, jealousy, backbiting, malicious gossip, and most of the other petty conflicts that plague human communities everywhere. Nonetheless, most people, most of the time, do live up to their social obligations as Semai culture defines them.

6. Even though the band is losing its all-encompassing psychological salience, as people become more involved with non-band-members on an individualized basis, there remains a strong desire to maintain the generalized reciprocity that both symbolizes and expresses the community's nurturance and coherence (cf. Robarchek and Robarchek 1988). With the abandonment of swiddening, however, generalized food-sharing becomes increasingly difficult to maintain, and now a major (possibly *the* major) cause of indebtedness is the purchase, on credit, of quantities of rice and dried fish for the purpose of sharing within the community.

✦ References

Benjamin, Geoffrey
    1968   Headmanship and Leadership in Temiar Society. *Federation Museums Journal* XIII: 1–43.

Dentan, Robert K.
    1968   *The Semai: A Nonviolent People of Malaysia.* New York: Holt, Rinehart and Winston.
    1978   Notes on Childhood in a Nonviolent Context: The Semai case, in *Learning Non-Aggression,* Ashley Montagu, ed. Oxford: Oxford University Press.
  1988a   The Rise, Maintenance and Destruction of Peaceful Polity. Paper presented before the 1988 annual meetings of the American Association for the Advancement of Science, Boston.
  1988b   CA Comment. *Current Anthropology* 29:4(625–629).

Endicott, Kirk M.
    1970   *An Analysis of Malay Magic.* Oxford: Clarendon Press.

Kennedy, John G.
    1969   Psychosocial Dynamics of Witchcraft Systems. *International Journal of Social Psychiatry* 15(3):163–178.

Kluckhohn, Clyde
    1944   Navaho Witchcraft. Papers of the Peabody Museum: 24.

LeBar, Frank M., Gerald C. Hickey, and John K. Musgrave
    1964   *Ethnic Groups of Mainland Southeast Asia.* New Haven: Human Relations Area Files.

Nadel, S.F.
1953   Social Control and Self-Regulation. *Social Forces* 31: 265–273.

Robarchek, Carole J., and Clayton A. Robarchek
1988   Reciprocities and Realities: World Views, Peacefulness and Violence among Semai and Waorani. Paper delivered before the 87th annual meeting of the American Anthropological Association, Nov. 16–20, Phoenix, AZ.

Robarchek, Clayton A.
1977   Semai Nonviolence: A Systems Approach to Understanding. Ph.D. dissertation, Dept. of Anthropology, University of California, Riverside.
1979a   Learning to Fear: A Case Study of Emotional Conditioning. *American Ethnologist* 4(4):555–567.
1979b   Conflict, Emotion and Abreaction: Resolution of Conflict among the Semai Senoi. *Ethos* 7(2):104–123.
1980   The Image of Nonviolence: World View of the Semai Senoi. *Federated Museums Journal* 25:103–117.
1986   Helplessness, Fearfulness and Peacefulness: The Emotional and Motivational Context of Semai Social Relations. *Anthropological Quarterly* 59(4):155–204.

Robarchek, Clayton A., and Carole J. Robarchek
1992   Cultures of War and Peace: A Comparative Study of Waorani and Semai, in *Aggression and Peacefulness in Humans and Other Primates,* James Silverberg and J. Patrick Gray, eds. New York: Oxford University Press.

Robarchek, Clayton A., and Robert K. Dentan
1987   Blood Drunkenness and the Bloodthirsty Semai: Unmaking Another Anthropological Myth. *American Anthropologist* 99(2):356–365.

Skeat, Walter W.
1900   *Malay Magic.* London: Macmillan.

Spiro, Melford
1952   Ghosts, Ifaluk and Teleological Functionalism. *American Anthropologist* 54:497–503.
1953   Ghosts: An Anthropological Inquiry into Learning and Perception. *Journal of Abnormal and Social Psychology* 48(3):367–382.
1967   *Burmese Supernaturalism.* Englewood-Cliffs, NJ: Prentice-Hall.
1969   The Psychological Function of Witchcraft Belief: The Burmese Case, in *Mental Health Research in Asia and the Pacific,* William Caudill and Tsung-Yi Lin, eds.: 245–258. Honolulu: East-West Center Press.

Whiting, Beatrice
1950   *Paiute Sorcery.* Viking Publications in Anthropology, 15. New York: Wenner-Gren Foundation for Anthropological Research.

✦ 8

Peace and Power in
an African Proto-State

George Park

This chapter presents a general theory of peace, using ethnohistorical and ethnographic data from the Kinga of southwestern Tanzania. George Park maintains that peaceful and aggressive societies may be permutations, one of the other. Among the simple, bush Kinga, aggression is expressed through warfare and accusations of witchcraft. The Kinga of the more complex proto-state, however, express emotions of aggression and fear indirectly, in a "theater" of aggression. This more "peaceful" society thereby manages competition and conflict as a sublimation of aggressive behaviors. As such, the line between "aggressive" and "peaceful" cultures becomes more difficult to draw.

—THE EDITORS

✦   This chapter has the premise that conflict is the stuff of politics and appears in sublimated form as constituted authority. If the business of politics is the sublimation and not the neutralization of disordering forces in society, we should not be surprised at the appearance of highly organized violence (war) even in societies that know very well the value of peace. The case considered is an East African, Bantu-speaking society with chiefly institutions. It is situated in a region—southwestern Tanzania—that appears to have had a stable and restrained war-pattern before about 1840 (Park 1988). So far as space has allowed, I use the method of controlled comparison (Eggan 1954) within that region to illuminate circumstances of my case. Fieldwork was done in the early 1960s, but the war-pattern I discuss was directly remembered only by my oldest informants. The ethnic group best described in the literature of the region is the Nyakyusa (Wilson 1950, 1957, 1958, 1959, 1977). My own descriptive ethnographies of the Kinga are in preparation for publication.

Until it was quietly taken over by German mercenary troops at the end of the nineteenth century, the Kinga proto-state, in its mountain setting, remained remote from much of the disruption that affected the region in late precontact times—disruption by roving Ngoni armies from the far south, Arab slavers from the coast, and several local conquest states bent on plunder. It is critical to my argument that, while chiefly institutions are found in some form through most of the region, their development is uneven.[1] Islands of complexity comprise a *political* archipelago; that is, a political superstructure rises at a series of court centers, to well above the mean level of institutional complexity for the region. At a distance from the centers and their court culture, conditions favor something closer to "ordered anarchy." This is the regional bush-culture. The war pattern there revolves around self-help. Only the more developed courts were able to suppress it, favoring a monopoly of legitimate coercion, an early marker on the road to statehood. The scope of suppression was usually ill-defined in the best of cases—a matter of what we may call feudal or premodern boundary maintenance.

Cross-cultural studies of war, witchcraft, and political evolution are many, and have helped us establish a broad basis for understanding a case like that of the Kinga, where the three phenomena intertwine. But a discussion of that literature would be proper in another place. I have explained elsewhere (Park 1974) how I conceive the relation between systems of transactional, mechanical, and authoritative sanctions. My analysis of Kinga institutions is consistent with that scheme and the finding that most societies rely on all three types of sanction, but favor only one. Kinga culture does *not* confirm Whiting's exploratory finding ([1950] 1971) that witchcraft beliefs fall away with the emergence of "superordinate justice" or "superordinate punishment"; but it does help to illuminate the problem she had with her African cases. Witch-finding was a major service of the royal courts in Kingaland. The courts had symbiotic relations with the egalitarian bush communities that they dominated and served. The conventional wisdom that held (and maybe holds) all cultures to be naturally integral has to be questioned when we are teasing out the meaning of variables like peace and nonviolence with respect to one culture. Complex wholes derive their complexity from internal opposition and contrast, and Kinga culture bridged a lot of categories important in cross-cultural sociology.

My initial distinction is between *direct* and *indirect action.* I take it from Ortega y Gasset (1932), who applied it to the occasional breakdown of social order into violence during the years that were to issue in the Spanish Civil War. War, unlike riot, is a thoroughly organized form of action, but both are *direct* in Ortega's sense. The semantic implications of the distinction can best be grasped by reviewing some conceptual pairs that it sorts out (see Table 8.1). Note, in the table, that the implied transmutation of terms can be conceived as *sublimation*—a term that psychologists apply to the appearance of a socially acceptable habit, following the suppression of an unacceptable one, the unacceptable being judged ancestral to the acceptable. Confirmation of this psychiatric judgment would be found in neurotic breakdown, if the actor reverted under stress to the predicted ancestral form of unacceptable behavior. In a sociological context, the parallel would be the *evolution* of institutions entailing indirect action, and reversion to the corresponding direct forms under conditions of crisis, social disruption, or anomie.

Table 8.1 Sublimation as It Can Be Read into Conceptual Pairs

Direct Action	Indirect Action
War	Positive peace
Vengeance	Wergild
Loot	Profit
Riot	Remonstrance
Assault	Civil action
Reprisal	Indemnification
Insult	Irony
Risk	Insurance
Domination	Superordination
Revolution	Reform
Rape	Seduction
Hate	Malice

Note: For each pair, the *indirect* entry can be regarded as a transform of the *direct*. The implied transmutation can be conceived as sublimation.

A glance at the pair-list in Table 8.1 may be enough to suggest that well-entrenched social and semantic structures are crucial to either the historical or the developmental (individual) transformation of direct into indirect action. When we speak of cultural *complexity,* we are referring to the presence of such structures. They are the product, in any community, of gradual (and probably uneven) evolution. Conceiving of the accretion of complexity in this way brings its psychological and semiotic dimensions into focus. The notions of direct and indirect action are correlative and are meant to be taken relativistically. Striking someone may be indirect action in a clinical or ritual situation. Ortega y Gasset (1932) described social class as a massive system of indirect action, but more recent social critics have seen this system as a kind of repression amounting to psychological violence, perhaps even justifying physical counterviolence. The relevance of this to my African case is that, in political evolution, direct becomes indirect through sublimation. I argue that sublimation is the power-builder's trump card in developing a political superstructure. I do not hold that power produces any sort of aversion to direct action, only that it has more to gain and less to lose by the sublimation of aggression.

The Kinga free tradition ended with the inception of German control at the turn of the century. Kinga were a highland valley people with lingering memories of diverse origins and with a chiefly class. Any member of the class who distinguished himself as a political leader in a bush community might set himself up with a court. If it flourished, he would be recognized as ruler of a minor center within a *domain,* which was in turn a major center of one of the four *realms,* each ruled from a princely court village. In Kinga theory, war never occurred *within* a realm, though in a ritually constrained form it was chronic and (with occasional remissions) likely to remain so *between* realms. All local rulers able to call up arms on a nonkinship basis will here be treated as chiefly. Kinga recognized the three ranks implied above. Using a loosely feudal terminology, we may term them lords (minor and major, in the tributary domains) and princes. But each ruler had his own court, however humble, and his own men, however few. A lord had to be jealous of his lieutenants; a prince had to be jealous of his lords. To hold the realm together, a prince needed the reputation for strength associated with leadership in war, and had to monopolize it. Only in the prince's name could the massed fighting force of the realm be brought together. But this did not entail the suppression of volunteer raids on *ethnically external* herds. These raids might be sponsored by any local ruler on behalf of his court and were essential aids to power-building.

Though the growth of cultural complexity has many dimensions, I focus on just three: *law* and *witchcraft* will throw a backlight on *war.* To look at war alone would strip it of the semantic and institutional context we need for understanding. I begin with law.

✦ Building Power Through Dispute-settlement

Kinga law was unwritten but not unformulated. If not uniform, it was open to a strain toward standardization, as any healthy system of law must be. Local rulers at all levels heard cases. Major disputes could be passed on to a higher court or taken there by dissatisfied litigants. Access to the legal services of a powerful court was through social access to its officers. This entailed acts of obeisance and suitable prestations. These acts confirmed a status difference, not between chiefly and commoner classes, but (since a prince would not staff his court with likely rivals) between officers of the court and suppliants of either class. In effect, the suppliant made obeisance to power, not rank. In the hearing of a case, any elder with the respect of his peers might speak out. Elder one day, suppliant the next, a man symbolically put his autonomy at pawn with his spear when he sought the justice of the court. When it came to approaching the prince himself, or a powerful lord the suppliant crept like a dog and whined in a child's or woman's voice, disclaiming manliness.

Law is a function of indirect action. A litigant will be full of the justice of his case, but before he can win by way of the law he forswears his right to settle a dispute by direct action. The hard and permanent structure here is a semiotic one. And it inheres between self and society, not between persons. As an institution, the court of law effects a pattern of sublimation whereby personal indignation and anger are transformed, through the perceived self-interest of the litigants, into a celebration of established power.

Codification as a feature of law is a product of courts that must appear to deal evenly with litigants, and the decay of law can be a mark of tyranny. But, in turn, the existence of a widely known, codified system of law supports a just court's majesty, from which authority must spring. Whereas law, especially in Bantu studies, has usually been treated as the sublimation of self-help and feud, witchcraft has been described as though its political context were either absent or simply accidental. We may find it natural that colonial authorities banned trials of witches from the courts. Europeans had long since concluded that witchcraft was unreal. But they introduced a new and confusing source of crime for the courts to handle. It became a crime to identify oneself or accuse another as a witch. So elders in the Kinga courts were expected to repudiate their own folk beliefs about evil. The courts risked seeming irrelevant to people who were still convinced their worst troubles were caused by secret enemies. The difficulty of implementing the European policy, intended as nothing short of semiotic surgery, was not as great for Kinga as for more anxiety-ridden peoples sharing the regional culture; but we have to doubt that a court system could have been built up in this region by a prince insensitive to mystical fear. Power is not built by ignoring undercurrents, and fear is the most notorious wildcard in the chiefly game—even more so than sex. Witchcraft cases can hardly be handled by self-help, because intrepid action by one group against another, based on the bare allegation of an individual, will settle no scores. Crimes of secrecy and intrigue were the bread and butter of a princely law court, if only because the local, less formal courts lacked the aesthetic distance—the majesty and consequent *moral authority*—to resolve them. By casting interpersonal conflict in mystical terms, witch beliefs set up the need for formal types of procedural intervention. Without it, justice could not be seen to be done. My argument is not that witchcraft in itself favors political order but that—ironically—power can be built more readily by sublimating (rather than neutralizing) what seem to be forces of entropy. Throughout the region, the special *manner* that goes with political power, that quality of self-possession in a strong leader that a European might call charisma, is recognized as witchcraft.

✦ The Sublimation of Angst

The sudden experience of fear demands action—fight or flight. But the experience of fear is always modified by learning, and in situations where the socially proper response to fear is *indirect* action, "fight or flight" comes closer to being "put up or shut up." The aggressive response may be a formal challenge leading to formally constrained combat or to litigation, and the response of withdrawal may range from negotiated exit to ritual acts of acceptance, resignation, or supplication. Sociologically, the sublimation of direct into indirect action appears as a process of institutionalization. A rough approximation to "watching" history (seeing it happen) is to be gained by sampling communities in a region where institutionalization has gone much farther in some places than others. Hence, in the ethnographic region of southwestern Tanzania, the sublimation of angst can become an all-but-visible process.

First, it is necessary to distinguish between the two contexts for witchcraft—bush and court. On the one hand, as a phenomenon of bush-culture, this famous African ideology of witchcraft is folklore. It constitutes a channel for public accusations of enmity but provides no set denouement. Resolution has to be improvised. On the other hand, in court-culture, witchcraft fears are sublimated into politically manageable notions and converted to spectacle.

In bush-culture, throughout the region, wherever court influence is negligible, self-styled ritual specialists claim that they can divine evil intent. Commonly, the folk prefer to consult distant specialists. In search of anonymity, they readily cross the ethnic and linguistic borders so important to anthropologists. The specialist they consult is likely to be a pedlar of counteractive medicines, so he seems to be selling material products as well as information. What they do when they have his mystical weapon in their kit bag is their own responsibility, and in the bush-culture, resorting to this kind of indirection may more often than not help trouble just to blow over. Time, care, and money have been invested. Their sick daughter recovers, and they congratulate themselves on having acted wisely. But recovery is not a foregone conclusion, and when it does not happen and mutterings break out into emotional accusation, the stage is set for violence—reversion (regression) to direct action.

The difficulty of dealing with witchcraft allegations in an egalitarian community made the bush-culture vulnerable to intervention by the princely court. Witch beliefs constitute a mode of analysis and a code of conduct (Marwick 1965; Mair 1969; Harwood 1970). When feuding in this mystical code begins to threaten the general peace, procedural intervention is thought to be legitimate. At Kinga court centers, all ritual specialists were drawn into the local officialdom. Techniques of divination were elaborate, and investigations of witchcraft could end in a dramatic execution. One diviner brought before the Germans in the early years of this century readily confessed to condemning men to death but successfully entered the plea of the *apparatchik*: under new orders he would do otherwise. It is no exaggeration to say that, within Kinga court-culture, the ideas of justice and atonement were reduced to formal procedure and law. In the bush-culture this was not the case, but cases that could not be settled in the bush community were referred to the court, which was always anxious to extend its power through the routinization of an appellate process. The best way to see the bush-culture scenario worked out is by sampling ethnic groups in the region that had not been brought under chiefly courts.

The prime information source for witchcraft at the level of folklore in the region of southwestern Tanzania is Gulliver's study of the Ndendeuli. "Ndendeuli thought and said that an accused witch and his accuser could not continue to be neighbours" (1971: 161). The rhetoric of witchcraft in a bush-culture provides for the open expression of distrust: the making conscious and public what had been unconscious and private—an impending break in the primary, fiduciary community, in the local settlement. If the breach is not healed it will grow. The formation of factions begins at the first airing of suspicion, when some are seen to support and others to reject an accusation by innuendo. Successive incidents of trouble, if they confirm the alignment of distrust, will decide the time and lines of schism. Then only spatial dissociation—which in the conditions of the bush means exit by a dissident group, sometimes following violence—will constitute a resolution. Throughout the scenario, action tends to be direct, led by protagonists free to express the feelings that are provoking them.

In its sublimated form in Kinga court-culture, witchcraft is abstracted from the level of folklore and spontaneous feeling to that of official procedure. Accuser and accused may face a poison ordeal (most often with the substitution of dogs) with approximately equal objective probability of loss. This arrangement is such that, half the time, an accusation will be rebuffed; and half the time, the accused will be found culpable.[2] The full force of the ordeal is concentrated in the political theater that the court has composed from the troubled lives of its subjects. On such an occasion, who would miss the show? And whatever the outcome, who could miss the point that ordinary folk cannot govern themselves? A prince who failed to drive that home could call a war and have no takers.

There are other societies in the region that represent a midway stage between Ndendeuli and Kinga. Harwood (1970) shows that the Safwa, like the Nyakyusa (Wilson 1950), conceive that the mystical power of witches is shared by rulers who use it not to do evil but to punish it. That this power has a double edge need not oblige us to call it (with Harwood) morally neutral; yet the political culture of the Safwa or the Nyakyusa can be said to have achieved only a modest sublimation of the angst behind witch beliefs. Safwa wanted the ordeal to effect either reconciliation or a clean break within a patrilineage when it was riven by dispute (Harwood 1970: 114f.). Nyakyusa antagonists usually obtained the sanction of a chief before proceeding, but took the ordeal from a private specialist. Each side would be backed up by a small party of witnesses, in much the same manner that Europeans would stage a duel. In both cases—Safwa and Nyakyusa—the aim of the ordeal is to bring an ill-defined issue to a head. Usually the denouement is left to be worked out privately. In this, kin groups may take the lead.

If the case causes general public concern, a Nyakyusa chief may intervene after a verdict has been reached in the forum of public opinion. The culprit can be ostracized and/or have cattle confiscated. The community may be fed in a feast of atonement. The difference between this and the Kinga scenario is theater. Spontaneous feelings are still prime movers in the Nyakyusa version. The ordeal is taken voluntarily and the chief is disinclined to flaunt his power. In Wilson's catalogue (1950: 198ff.) of thirty-eight cases for which details could be obtained, the most frequent outcome was that the accused witch simply moved away. In three cases, the chief confiscated cattle, but in two of those cases the chief himself or a member of his family was the supposed victim; i.e., the chief was the accuser. We have here a rough quantitative measure of the position of one ethnic group on the continuum between bush and court, between direct and indirect versions of the witchcraft institution.

To make political theater out of witchcraft is to move a quantum step beyond what is reported for the Nyakyusa. For the Nyakyusa, the sublimation of spontaneous affect is effected primarily through the institutionalized procedures of divination. Where dramatic values are attained the best scenario is that one party becomes the scapegoat. The result: one person exits from the group and there is promise of atonement for the others. The message of the Kinga prince—*Vengeance is mine!*—remains unuttered in Nyakyusaland, even should one of the antagonists succumb to the poison ordeal, for the drama is played out *in the bush,* not at court.

When (below) we come to look at warfare, it will again be worth comparing the Kinga and Nyakyusa, for the dramatic requirements of battle for the two societies matched exactly, in spite of the greater centralization of authority among Kinga. The ecological settings differed, as did the ethnic contexts, perhaps more than the political cultures. The same priorities in variant circumstances produce variant institutions, which are often better seen as instruments, not embodiments, of culture. While the formal patterns of doing battle in both lands were identical, the consequence of war for the Nyakyusa was a form of predatory expansion through the hiving off of junior chiefs to seek their fortunes without ties to the past (Wilson 1950; Charsley 1969). Nyakyusa, like Alur far to the north (Southall 1954), expanded by providing chiefly services to nearby, politically less-developed bush communities. The Kinga pattern was more consistent with fixed territories and the consolidation of rule within them.

✦ War, Peace, and Power

There were no pacifists among Kinga, unless they were women—and women had no political voice. For men, it was un-Kinga to fly from a situation that called for fighting, to talk peace when the other side was talking war, or otherwise to be seen avoiding physical confrontation. If Kinga institutions provided a reasonably secure life for a settled population in a militarized region, it was not popular or chiefly policy to strip war of its glories. Yet Kinga warriors did fly from combat in situations where non-Kinga would have kept right on. To understand this, we need to look at the relevant institutions in emic (i.e., Kinga) perspective. Though, in ordinary talk, men would abhor slaughter, they loved warfare at its best. And they took care to keep it so by transcendental means.

I have elsewhere described how it was that Kinga priests from the four warring realms felt that they must cooperate in an annual religious ceremony that had attributes of pilgrimage, procession, and retreat (Park 1966). To do this, they had to enjoy close, cross-boundary ties; and by this cooperation, they deepened those ties and negotiated necessary redefinitions of the Kinga political charter. At home, a priest lived and cooperated closely with the secular leaders of the court. He was a full-fledged member of his local officialdom, even to the point of sometimes traveling with the tax-and-justice squads that regularly visited outlying settlements to adjudicate disputes, collect tribute, and confirm loyalty. The priest, as diviner, would be of particular value in a witchcraft case; but he also acted as a magistrate. Some priests claimed to be members of the chiefly class, but others remembered an autochthonous, prechiefly origin as rain-priests in a bush-culture. The more elaborate the power system of the court, the more politicized was the calling of priest.

To what extent did the priests, with their extended ambience, help to keep the peace? They introduced procedural interventions into this "internal" or controlled warfare that so limited the fighting between Kinga realms that slaughter hardly could take place. A prince would never consider going to battle without proper ritual preparations. Medicines must be administered to all the warriors—not as we administer pills but in a solemn and theatrical manner. The battleground must be ritually prepared. Priests on each side used medicines to put boundaries on the no-man's-land within which level-field fighting might take place.

An ordinary warrior wore his shield and a clutch of spears on the left arm. When he ran out of spears, he had no choice but to flee if the battle turned on him. But let an attacker chase him into his home territory, crossing the medicine boundary, and the pursuer's knees would "turn to water." In such circumstances, war is something staged, not waged.

There are no contemporary observations of Kinga formal warfare on record, but the folk memory was keenly alive at the time of my fieldwork thirty years ago. This memory agrees so well with MacKenzie's (1925) notes on the Nyakyusa version that interested readers may wish to consult that source. The two parties line up face to face at about the range of a very heavy javelin. Spears cannot be thrown effectively from the line, but invective can. The preliminary moves are dancelike: warriors display their paint, furs, feathers, and leaping skills. When a foolhardy mood has been established, braves will begin to charge forward in threatening manner to dare the enemy spear.[3] From time to time, the challenge will be taken up by a brave on the other side, and spears may be exchanged. A solid hit on the shield draws a roar of applause from the ranks. An adroit turning of a well-aimed missile does the same. With time taken out for relaxing and freshening up, the battle can last all day. Usually, it is when men begin to tire and overdo their parts, when the theatrical surface wears thin and the field is in disarray, that someone will be severely or even mortally wounded. Then the battle has been won and lost. The two sides retire, the one to feast and the other to find consolation in quiet company.

Kinga youths of warrior age went about in ringlets made with red clay, using it as body paint as well, in the well-known Maasai style. For dancing, their ornamentation was gay, for warfare fierce; but the movements in the two forms of theater were not unrelated. The point of ringlets is to give greater life to body movement, as all dramatic ornament does, but especially to amplify the effect of facial expression. War was communicative even while it was assertive.[4] The losing prince had often not lost much: his team may have been winning theatrically before the accidental wounding of a player forced him to withdraw. He could renew the battle if he chose another day. But if formal warfare was virtually indecisive, what was the purpose Kinga saw in it?

All through the bright, dry season, when spirits were high and men could best be spared from work in the fields, an important Kinga court was an armed camp. The main business of the bachelor warriors was to be warriors; just as the main business of the modern standing army is—simply—to stand; that is, to be there in some suggestively visible way with its arrays of tanks, planes, and missiles. The Kinga court staged war games at home the way a Western school will stage contact sports. Formal engagement with a rival court was the high form of this military theater, as the annual contest with a rival team will be for a high school. But to carry the analogy further, we would have to suppose that these high school pupils were from time to time raiding the premises of their rivals by night, carrying off valuable spoils.

Not all attacks were staged, however. Kinga parties sometimes raided one another by stealth, without the procedural interventions of formal warfare. Under the cover of night, attacking in the grey of dawn, volunteers would steal cattle and sometimes women. The spoils belonged to the court.

For the young braves, sufficient prize was the glory won. If they brought booty and had not lost a man, a public triumph was staged on their return. Even without such triumph, the daring of their deeds was not lost upon peers or elders. Stolen cattle were for the royal herds, for feasting the court. Stolen women were for men of power, to be taken as concubines to bear a man's child and raise it to weaning. Then the child would remain while the woman was returned. The gains of war at this informal level—flesh, in more than one form—were appropriate to the more direct action entailed.

✦ Political Theater

A longing for justice, fear of malice, and craving for mastery are themes of Kinga experience that the court-culture magnified and sublimated to the purposes of power. The pyramidal system of the four realms, so long as it could be maintained, meant that power was balanced. Theater, alone— "mere theater"—could never have managed that. Political theater is staged *in* the world of its audience because it is enacted *by* its audience. There is drama before your eyes as others psych up and make their moves, but there is drama also in the part you play for others to see. Under the ritual, ornament, and spectacle, what propels the drama is mortal danger.

Law, witchcraft, and war revolve around mortal danger. The comparatively spontaneous emotional life of the bush-culture has the character that sociologists used to identify with "primary groups." When feelings are expressed as they occur, they do not build into strategies of indirection and subversion. There is a normal, episodic play of self-assertion and catharsis in intimate affairs that builds not structures but understandings. In the social psychology of yesteryear, the neurotic forms of intimacy that, in the literature and cinema of today, may seem normal were dismissed as pathologies. When I was a student, Robert Redfield used to speak of the building up of a moral order in communities, distinguishing that from the "technical order" that comprises the social structure; and Horace Miner talked of normative (as opposed to functional) integration. The difference in perspective between their time and ours reflects more than the opening of scholarly eyes by research. It is harder today to find social space that is open; to find a primary group that feels free to go its own way. The twentieth century has seen hamlets everywhere gathered into villages, and villages into towns. In the bush-cultures of the African world we are reconsidering here, circumstances (prior to the Tanzanian government's villagization program) usually allowed people to move away from conflict. Those who seemed to be choosing to make trouble for their neighbors could be obliged to move, if the mechanisms of open accusation generated a consensus. But political power depends on integrative structure; thus, it moves a community and its institutions away from a pattern of open consensus and spontaneous self-assertion toward one of sublimation.

If the Kinga political system tended toward a balance of power and a trivialization of war at the summit, war went beyond the charade. The land was seriously invaded at least three times during the nineteenth century. On those occasions, war was waged without ritual constraints and decided by the balance of slaughter. Early in the years of German rule, a movement of armed rebellion swept the region, drawing in the eastern realm of Kingaland. At German command, an army from the western realm proceeded to decimate the eastern population. Any male of any age who could be hunted down was slain; women were abducted. The graphic reports I recorded of this civil war a half-century later attested to its truly uncivil ferocity and the responsibility for this of the individual Kinga fighters. In the condition of mercenaries, under simple orders unhedged by ritual constraints, their efficiency as killers was second to none in the region.

One of the nineteenth-century invasions was mounted by a Hehe or Hehe-Bena horde seeking cattle, women, and children to swell distant herds and settlements. Details are lost to memory, except for one: After enemy forces had withdrawn with what loot and captives they could take, men who had fled into the woods emerged to find companions standing like scarecrows on the field of battle. What they saw as they approached was a gruesome form of impalement. Kinga remember this particularly because the exaggeratedly heterosexual Hehe are contemptuous of their neighbors' sexual practice. But above all, Kinga remember because the scene speaks to them of an alien mentality. Why would men act this way? It is not the cruelty but the displaced sexuality of it that Kinga feel went beyond code.

As war games may have real consequences, dreams can turn to nightmares when the civic balance is lost. Raised from early boyhood to be tough and go all-out for victory in games of contact and combat, Kinga men took to fighting as second nature. *But Kinga men are not aggressive.* They are predominantly easygoing, humorous, and gregarious. Some African schools in southwestern Tanzania, as my children can attest, can be fiercely repressive, even violent communities. Kinga schools, by contrast, were beautifully harmonious. Freudians might like to know that Kinga boys (and, separately, girls) are not subjected to sexual fears and frustrations. Their fierceness cannot be doubted, but it comes as *second* nature. It is an act.

Kinga youths like to shine. You see this in their dancing, minstrelsy, hunting, and sports. Egalitarian norms were strong, but heroes transcended the norms, just as a prince must do, with rites of installation and burial that conferred divinity upon him. One of the wrinkles of formal combat most readily recalled was the institution of the champion. A prince might hire a noted warrior from another realm or a neighboring ethnic group to stand as his champion in drawn battle. If his hero lost, the prince had lost—that was the institution. What propelled such a formal war was not patriotic fervor but admiration for the art of war—the art that most perfectly expressed political mastery.

The popularity of champions tells us much. Kyelelo the Cruel was a usurper-prince whose grandson, at the time of Tanganyikan independence, was still ruler of the western realm. Tales about this dark hero were to be heard in all the realms but his own—and the reason for this was not unpopularity at home—far from it—but that the dramatic impact of the tales was comparable to that in England of Shakespeare's stuff on Richard the Third. These stories would not play on Kyelelo's home stage. On the other hand, oral history in neighboring realms paints his as a time of unlawful war, when the benevolence of fraternity among princes broke down. In law, all Kinga were treated as equals, but in fantasy they knew a hierarchy of mastery. Heroes of battle were adored, as were masters of the dance and song. Court-culture was fueled by dreams of glory and grandeur. While all remained in balance, the nightmares of slaughter that the system had to generate remained only that. The rise of chiefly politics binds the many more tightly together because it binds them to a common danger. The art of politics is balance, but in the faltering of that art, its scaffolding of indirect action falls away, and in the hands of an unstable hero the genius of war will raze the world.

In vulgar Freudianism, the unconscious is a horny, brutal, self-destructive homunculus in the human machine, and sublimation is a mechanism that, by deflecting crude and primary instincts, makes civilized society possible. "Do you really believe," asks Freud ([1920] 1943: 131) in the midst of World War I, "that a handful of unprincipled place-seekers and corrupters of men would have succeeded in letting loose all this latent evil, if the millions of their followers were not also guilty?" The troublesome thing about that is, not just the terrible truth in it, but the stickiness of Freudian guilt, from which it seems our hands will not be cleansed. It may be that Ortega y Gasset's terms of discussion, carefully explored, could point a way out of these woods.

Violence is the breakdown of social routines that do not merely serve our needs but shape them. Because of what they do to and with human needs, some social routines are more likely than others to break down into violence. War patterns are of this kind. The Kinga had a "safe" pattern. It stands up under scrutiny where (for instance) the untraditional, late-nineteenth-century Hehe pattern in the same region fails. Kinga could argue, as modern nation-states do, that their whole military capability was justified as defense. Perhaps it was. Their courts were flourishing, productive centers, attractive to youth. Their elites were attentive to morale. But banging the big drum and blowing the long trumpet for war, staging a month of beer and battle games, or feasting and feting happy young raiders on their maiden return with purloined cattle, was at best a dangerously indirect way of keeping the peace.

✦ Notes

1. Aidan Southall (1954, 1988) has discussed the political phenomenon in question under the title of the *segmentary state.* Power is "pyramidal," in that primary power is exercised *locally* and the hegemonic power of a central segment (village, chiefdom) over lesser segments grades down to a minimal influence over marginal settlements, where loyalty is retractable. I prefer for the Kinga case the bland label *proto-state,* as the variety and plasticity of institutional structures is greater than a single model would suggest. In this chapter, I am more concerned with political culture, which shows greater uniformity, than social structure, dealt with elsewhere (Park 1988).

2. If both dogs die the verdict is general skulduggery. The court is usually glad to wash its hands of the matter. If both vomit and live, the verdict is general absolution. The court will be slow to hear any renewal of accusations from either side. If only one dog lives, the owner of the other has been placed at the mercy of the court. If the specialists who brew the poison always aim for a clear decision, they will, in the long run, find the potency that is most likely to spare one and kill the other. This makes the chances even.

3. The Kinga sword (not a stabbing spear; the sword was meant for slashing) was a rarity. The idea was to tease an opponent out of his spears, then rush him with a weapon hidden in your shield. Surviving examples have been handed down in lordly lines, but there seems to have been no ritual prohibition on ownership. In youth, a lord should have distinguished himself as a leader in fighting. When the sword's use was mimed for me, the point was to score by putting your enemy to flight, not by cutting him up—he would not stay around for that. (Much less would he follow the victor home as captive, in the fashion of Middle American proto-states.)

4. The techniques of war evolve within a *region,* because a superior technique, once introduced, has to be adopted quickly by neighboring peoples. In this case *superior* refers especially to confirmation of chiefly authority, not territorial conquest. Elsewhere in the region, after the initial Ngoni intrusions of 1840 and the acceleration of slave-trading in following decades, new and more destructive forms of war were evolving.

✦ References

Charsley, S. R.
    1969   *The Princes of Nyakyusa.* Nairobi: East African Publishing House.

Eggan, Fred
    1954   Social Anthropology and the Method of Controlled Comparison. *American Anthropologist* 56:743–763.

Freud, Sigmund
[1920] 1943   *A General Introduction to Psycho-analysis,* Joan Rivière, trans. Garden City, NY: Garden City Publishing.

Gulliver, P. H.
1971   *Neighbours & Networks.* Berkeley, CA: University of California Press.

Harwood, Alan
1970   *Witchcraft, Sorcery, & Social Categories among the Safwa.* London: Oxford University Press.

MacKenzie, D. R.
1925   *The Spirit-Ridden Konde.* London: Seeley, Service.

Marwick, M. G.
1965   *Sorcery in Its Social Setting.* Manchester, UK: Manchester University Press.

Mair, Lucy
1969   *Witchcraft.* Toronto: McGraw-Hill.

Ortega y Gasset, José
1932   *The Revolt of the Masses.* New York: W. W. Norton.

Park, George
1966   Kinga priests: The Politics of Pestilence, in *Political Anthropology,* Marc J. Swartz et al., eds. Chicago: Aldine.
1974   *The Idea of Social Structure.* Garden City, NY: Doubleday.
1988   Evolution of a Regional Culture. *Sprache und Geschichte in Afrika* 9: 117–204.

Southall, Aidan
1954   *Alur Society.* Cambridge, U.K.: W. Heffer & Sons.
1988   The Segmentary State in Africa & Asia. *Comparative Studies in Society & History* 30 (1): 52–82.

Whiting, Beatrice Blyth
[1950] 1971   *Paiute Sorcery.* Viking Fund Publications in Anthropology 15. New York: Johnson Reprint.

Wilson, Monica
1950   *Good Company.* London: Oxford University Press.
1957   *Rituals of Kinship among the Nyakyusa.* London: Oxford University Press.
1958   *Peoples of the Nyasa-Tanganyika Corridor.* University of Capetown.
1959   *Communal Rituals of the Nyakyusa.* London: Oxford University Press.
1977   *For Men and Elders.* New York: Africana.

✦ 9
Words in the Night: The Ceremonial Dialogue— One Expression of Peaceful Relationships Among the Yanomami

Jacques Lizot

French anthropologist Jacques Lizot has lived regularly with the Yanomami people in the Venezuelan Amazon for more than twenty-three years. The unusual depth of his experience is reflected in the complexity and richness of Yanomami life that he reveals in his writings, including this chapter. Here he offers a refreshing approach to the Yanomami by focusing on the ceremonial dialogue as one expression of the nonviolent and peaceful side of their society. Like hospitality and gift giving, the ceremonial dialogue is an example of the exchange and reciprocity that are so fundamental to the social structure of the Yanomami. Accordingly, Lizot's analysis provides important new insights into peace as well as war among the Yanomami.

—THE EDITORS

✦   The Yanomami ceremonial dialogue is a cultural event of great importance. Integrated into the social system of exchange and reciprocity, it contributes effectively to the establishment and maintenance of peaceful relationships. When it is combined with a cosmological vision and a symbolic system, it transforms the mythological expression of a world *prior to society;* and in this manner it reveals the actual foundations of that society. As a linguistic code, this ceremonial dialogue proposes a synthesis of indigenous notions about man: the relationships between the sexes, sickness and death, and peace and violence; in brief, a synthesis of concepts about the nature of man and society and of man in society. By revealing a fundamental structure, in which the operator is the system of exchanges and reciprocity according to various codes and modalities, it compels the student to examine the foundation of what Sponsel refers to in the introductory chapter of this book as "the dialectic of peace and warfare." To the question: "What is warfare?" one can answer only after defining what peaceful relationships are. This is because, from peace to warfare, there is no radical break; only a transformation, a passage from one modality of reciprocity to another, through this capital, fatal accident that is a man's murder.

Chagnon's (1988) sociobiological analysis of Yanomami aggression fails to explain warfare, among other reasons, because it ignores the details of the social and cultural context. His approach reduces warfare to an individual biological phenomenon, a simple expression of man's violence; a perverse consequence of an alleged biological adaptation of which aggression was at the same time the result and the price to be paid. No! Warfare and peace are, first and foremost, sociological facts and the expression of a social structure. As Mauss ([1923] 1966) said, these are total social facts; namely, they simultaneously affect the economic, social, and political realms, as well as the system of collective representations as expressed in mythology, ritual, symbolic code, men's notions, their vision of the world, their intellectual activities, and, finally, their language.

In the abundant literature written about the Yanomami, the ceremonial dialogue is hardly mentioned. The nocturnal form (*wayamou*) has, in fact, drawn more attention than the diurnal form (*himou*). The best descriptions are those of Cocco (1972: 326–330) and Shapiro (1972: 149–151). Two other authors, however, have given us their interpretations. Neither is an anthropologist. For the ethologist Eibl-Eibesfeldt (1971), a large portion of the dialogue is unintelligible. Its unique function, in his account, is to offer and claim goods: the Yanomami spend the entire night declaring to each other: "Give me, I give you" (*gib mir, ich gebe dir*) (1972: 774). The thesis of the linguist Migliazza (1972) is more elaborate, but no less fallacious: he suggests that the dialogue is conducted in an archaic language that was once spoken by the entire ethnic group. In his account, language would have survived, in spite of its subsequent evolution into several dialects, in order to facilitate communication between communities that do not understand each other anymore. It would serve as a lingua franca, learned, spoken, and understood by the men only. Migliazza argues that diglossia is a characteristic of the Yanomami linguistic situation, and he does not hesitate to cite and correct Ferguson's (1964) definition of this term. Neither the ethologist nor the linguist provide any data to support their viewpoints. These failed, premature, explanatory attempts make it seem inviting to look at (related) works concerning other ethnic groups.[1]

Those works are few in number. Folk (1963: 216–230) describes a variant of the ceremonial dialogue from the Wawai and states that this ritual is confined to north of the Amazon. Another, sociological, analysis of the dialogue, as it appears among the Trio, was carried out by Rivière (1971) and it is very enlightening. I will return to it. Urban's more recent (1986) contribution takes on the aspect of a comparative analysis. He notes the

existence of a ceremonial dialogue among the Jivaro (*shuar* and *ashuar*) in
Ecuador, Kuna in Panama, and Shokleng in Brazil. In general, Urban's
analysis is disappointing. True, he talks about solidarity and reciprocity
concerning the ceremonial dialogue, but the former term is inadequate and
not very appropriate, while the latter he fails to link to a particular type of
social organization.

According to Rivière, the ceremonial dialogue reflects both the general
status quo and contemporary Trio political structure. It serves as regulator
in disputes and permits appeasement when there are conflicts. This is the
means by which the Trio, whose residential communities are distant from
each other, establish and maintain peaceful relationships. When we compare the Trio with the Yanomami, with regard to social and political organization and the function of the ceremonial dialogue, we find that there are
both obvious similarities and very large differences. (These will appear,
below, little by little.) The Yanomami ritual seems to be the expression of
an underlying structure, located at a deeper, more fundamental level. It possesses extensions at the level of mythology and cosmology that the Trio ritual does not appear to possess. Like Rivière, I am convinced that the meaning of the statements in the dialogue is a fairly secondary aspect (at a
certain level of analysis only), and that its primary function is not to transmit messages.

I must first broadly characterize the social organization of the
Yanomami. As will be seen, the ceremonial dialogue is part of it, and my
analysis will frequently refer to the dialogue. The Yanomami kinship
vocabulary is of the Dravidian type. It essentially rests on four principles of
opposition: distinction of generations, distinction of gender, distinction
between two large categories of relatives (blood relatives and affines), and
distinction of the relative age among blood kin of Ego's generation
(Dumont 1975: 85–100). The distinction of filiation and affinity crosses all
of society. Marriage is prescribed between cross-cousins (children of mother's brother and children of father's sister), and affinity is a relationship
between groups that perpetuates itself from generation to generation. The
parents of the bride normally select their son-in-law, who is compelled to
work bride-service for them. The duration of this service is variable, but it
is seldom less than three years. A strong avoidance governs the relationships between a son-in-law and his parents-in-law. The simultaneous
exchange of sisters between brothers is rather uncommon: when it does
occur, there is no bride-service. The latter is performed only in exchange
for a future bride. The core sociopolitical unit is the residential community.
Within the same dwelling, it consists of a number of families linked to each
other by either consanguineous or affinal ties.

Ideally, each residential group consists of at least two factions—the
factions being divided by a latent antagonism. The members of a faction
are joined in consanguineous relationship, whereas their relationship with

the opposing faction is affinal. Thus, the factional organization of the residential community coincides more or less with the distinction made between kinship by blood and kinship by marriage. The core of a faction is normally formed by a group of cognates sharing the same ancestry, their wives, and children. They live close together, with their hearths side by side. In the dwelling, a faction occupies a well-defined section. As I noted above, the stable core of the faction, which consists of descendants of a shared ancestor (brothers and parallel cousins), may be joined by sons-in-law who are carrying out bride-service or who are in uxorilocal residence. They may even be joined by outside families. As part of their political game, factional leaders attempt to attract new elements to enlarge their faction.

Within the residential community, decisions are made by an informal council set up by factional leaders and the most elderly men of the community. The leaders arouse their group. They often serve as intermediaries in political relationships. During rituals and ceremonies, they take responsibility for the feasts. They are enterprising men, of great intelligence. They are also brave and skillful hunters, knowledgeable of the natural environment and of the resources of the local geography. Between the different factions, as well as the latent antagonism there reigns a mutual emulation. As a political unit, the residential group sticks together and forms a common front in conflicts, but it is also marked by internal divisions between the social subunits and also between individuals. Within the community, services and mutual gifts of food and goods make up the essential part of daily relationships. Individuals, family groups, and factions are welded by continual transfers. When it is necessary, or when he feels the need, an elder makes a public harangue (*patamou*). He may want to convince villagers of the necessity of a decision involving the support of others (for example, make clean new gardens, repair the dwelling, or go hunting/camping in the forest); or he may want to express his opinion, and/or suggest rules of behavior to younger people. Elders and leaders are diplomats: without any power of coercion, they strive to convince by word and by example. Their authority is moral.

Consanguineous relatives are frequently scattered among several neighboring communities that are opposed to other factions with which they also establish alliance relationships. These close, neighboring communities, generally located within a day's walk, develop by fission from a common community of origin (Lizot 1984). They have frequent contacts and exchanges, and represent, quite accurately, what Rivière (1971) calls, among the Trio, an agglomeration. The maximum social density is, indeed, located at this level. Among the Yanomami, the unit is called *yahitherimi;* less frequently it is referred to as *ahetetherimi.*[2] Within the *yahitherimi* unit, relationships are generally, although not always, peaceful. Each residential group in the *yahitherimi* unit maintains privileged relationships for its own advantage. These relationships are sometimes exclusively commercial, and sometimes affinal, and extend to more distant residential communities. Distance causes the ties to be looser, contacts less frequent, and the social density weaker. It can be seen that Yanomami social organization is based on discrete groups that can nevertheless fit into each other, or even gradually encroach on each other. Individuals, family groups, blood and affinal kin, factions, the community, the *yahitherimi* unit, and finally groups beyond are united and linked by exchange and reciprocity assuring the system's cohesion. It is this totality that will henceforth be referred to as the social structure.

✦ **The Ceremonial Dialogue: Form and Content**

The Yanomami distinguish mainly two varieties of ceremonial dialogue. One is diurnal (*himou*), and the other nocturnal (*wayamou*). Contrary to what Shapiro (1972) and Urban (1986) say, there are no "strong" or "weak" forms. Strictly, from a formal point of view, there is no difference between them. Considerably more than the *wayamou,* the *himou*[3] is a ritualized form for extending invitations or for expressing urgent requests. Like the *wayamou* (see below), the *himou* may help resolve conflicts and restore peace. In contrast to the *wayamou,* in which young people can (and must) participate, the *himou* is utilized only by middle-aged men and active elders. During a feast, the *himou* takes place on two occasions[4]—first, to signal to the guests that they must reach the hosts' dwelling at a specific time; second, to invite the guests to enter the dwelling. The *himou* also takes place during a funeral rite called *paushimou.*[5] In this rite, cinerary gourds are distributed to the kin of the deceased and, precisely at this moment, the *himou* takes place. The kin are responsible for the gourds. Later, during the feast, they must distribute them among other kin for the crushed bones of the deceased to be consumed in a gruel of cooked ripe bananas.

The other form of the dialogue, the *wayamou,* takes place during the night on the occasion of a visit or a feast. It does not take place when the guests are *yahitherimi;* only when they belong to more distant communities, with whom, it must be remembered, contacts are rare, making opportunities for exchange less frequent. This confirms the particular status of the *yahitherimi* and leads to the eventual function of the *wayamou* in social relationships. At this level, there is a correspondence between the revealing role of the local political organization of the Trio and Yanomami ceremonial dialogues. One must nevertheless draw attention to an exception to this rule that in fact confirms my hypothesis. When ties between members of the *yahitherimi* deteriorate and there is a threat of open conflict, it is common for the communities involved to explain themselves during a *wayamou.* In this case, the dialogue enables the expression of grievances in all openness. The speaker has the right, and even the duty, to say anything he wants to his opponent, using the most offensive terms: accusing him in the most brutal way, insulting him, treating him like a coward, threatening him, and challenging him (see Appendix: F18, F19, F20).[6] The rules of the *wayamou* require that the opponent listen meekly, without taking offense at what is being said, since each person speaks in turn and there is, in that way, the right to answer back. It is amusing to listen to the speaker, who repeats, unperturbed (more or less completely), insults that were originally destined for him. In this case, the *wayamou* serves both as an expression of conflicts and as a means of opposing them: by conjuring the threat of declared hostility, it restores peace. A Yanomami expresses this clearly during the dialogue that is given in fragments in F19 of the Appendix, saying in effect: "The Yanomami argue among themselves; they express in all openness what they have to say to each other and then they calm down: their anger subsides."

A typical prelude to a *wayamou* might go as follows: Some men, after a long, hurried journey (perhaps they slept along the way), finally approach the dwelling they intend to visit. They stop, unpack from their belongings a ball of *roucou* (the yellowish red dyestuff made from the pulp that surrounds the seeds of the annatto tree), some feathers, and down. They paint their bodies and anoint their faces and chests, and fasten on skin armbands. They stick feathers into rods attached to their earlobes and, by way of pendants, hang skins—from the septicolor (*Tangara chilensis*) or cotinga (*Cotinga nattererri*). Then, very carefully, they help each other to apply white down to their hair and to the tail of a saki monkey (*Chiropotes satanas*) that each has tied to his forehead. When they are ready, they cross the threshold of the dwelling, to be welcomed by shouts, whistles, and the sounds of arrows being banged against bowshafts. They position themselves, standing, with impassive faces, at the very center of the central area. Elders approach to examine them, recognizing them under their patterns of dyes and feathers, and invite them next to their hearths. They lay down on designated hammocks, saying not a word. They appear stiff, expressionless; their quivers are placed against their chests. They are offered a chew of tobacco and soon they are given food. Now, a few words are exchanged. Nightfall arrives. Soon, even nearby objects are hardly visible. The *wayamou* begins. First, young people arrive. As the night progresses, older, then still older men follow. The ceremonial dialogue will terminate at dawn's first light, when the shiniest stars toward the east are growing dim.

The dialogue takes place at the periphery of the central area. In rainy weather, it is held under the extension of the roof's canopy. The two participants face each other, occasionally standing, occasionally squatting, and sometimes supporting themselves with a bow. At all times, however, the body leans—now to the left, now to the right, accompanying the sequences of the *wayamou*. The hands rhythmically strike the chest, the thighs, or the buttocks. The volume, tone, and tempo increase or drop, slow or accelerate. The sections of the dialogue, whether spoken or sung, are linked together. Body motions accompany and emphasize the articulated sections. Occasionally, the voice drops and the tone becomes that of conversation, even of confidence. A host initiates the dialogue. The guest answers with near repetition what has been said. Then the guest takes the initiative. He "answers back" (wã kôãmai). The host in turn replies. Each person speaks for approximately half an hour.[7] Speaking from his hammock, another host joins the two participants. His voice, which is low and muted to begin with, becomes louder and louder. The participating guest acknowledges him without much delay, and the latter leaves his hammock (*ithou*), replacing his companion in front of the guest. A second guest similarly replaces the first one and so on throughout the night. (The chain of participants, showing the roles of each individual, is summarized in Figure 9.1.)

Figure 9.1   Structure of Participation in the Wayamou

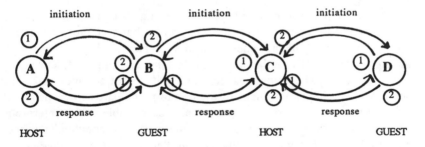

The figure shows speech rotation of the first two hosts and the first two guests in the ceremony. The sequence is continued as further hosts and guests take the places of the earlier participants. The arrows show the direction of the words addressed host-to-guest and vice versa. (After response 1, the guest speaks initiation 2, and so on.) There is also a spatial rotation—the second host, C, in spatial terms, taking the position of the first, A, and so on.

It is always a host and a guest that face each other. One improvises the speech and the other replies. The latter then "answers back." Hence, an exchange structure is established—in which the exchange elements are words. This structure, involving all the guests and all the hosts, throughout the night, I saw to be the invariable pattern. It is obvious to me—now.

However, because of my obsession to discover the *meaning* of what was being said (meaning that did not readily disclose itself), I was incapable at first of seeing it and venturing to believe that its interpretation could be independent of the words' meaning.

Because the *wayamou,* as an exchange of words, takes place in a friendly context, it contributes to the strengthening of ties between the participants and thus to the maintenance of peace. This is enhanced by the fact that it immediately precedes an exchange of gifts, just as the *himou* can herald a food offering or be a prelude to the distribution of cinerary gourds. *The ceremonial dialogue is both the exchange and the premise for exchange.* Indeed, with the coming of dawn, after the voices reciting the *wayamou* have stopped and the guests have taken a short rest and a light meal, a commercial transaction begins. This is the conclusion of the visit. As soon as it reaches its end, the guests will head for home. Their brief presence will have been the occasion for a continuous and intense exchange of food, tobacco, words, and goods, from hosts to guests and occasionally in the opposite direction. These exchanges, somewhat accelerated and contracted in time, compensate for the infrequent relationships between groups that live far apart.

The ceremonial speech is first and foremost a social relationship manifesting itself as a reciprocal exchange. The exchange is not of material objects, but words. This becomes even more apparent when young people participate. They recite; at the most they declaim. Lacking confidence, they never improvise. They repeat expressions and do not communicate with each other. The important thing for them is to participate and exchange. A large portion of the elders' exchange is also susceptible to this interpretation. Nevertheless, elders may exchange messages and communicate once and for all *by participating* in the *wayamou.* Perhaps they do engage in dialogue, and by occasionally interrupting each other for a moment, converse. What I attempt to illustrate here is that the question of knowing what is being discussed during the *wayamou* may lead an investigator astray, unless caution is used and unless the methodological choice consists of dissociating the problem of form from meaning. The form of the *wayamou* reveals its global significance: its nature is sociological, independent of the meaning of the words. In the ceremonial dialogue, the language can be completely disconnected from its communication function. What is being told may have nothing to do with an immediate reality. I do not argue that the problem relating to the meaning of the words in the *wayamou* is totally devoid of interest. But it is best to examine it apart; and in another way. This is what I now intend to do.

The Yanomami possess the rhetorical art. This rhetoric is powerful, full of eloquence and wit, occasionally difficult and subtle. They also have a sense for quick, sharp replies. They are masters of expression. The *wayamou* is a concentrate of Yanomami stylistic procedures: tropes are linked to one another, follow, and shove each other. They are dense and stunning. Speakers constantly use metaphor, metonymy, synecdoche, antiphrasis, and comparison. However, none of these stylistic procedures is specific to the *wayamou*. One encounters them in every serious conversation, and they belong to a level of elaborate speech utilized by elders (both men and women), publicly to evoke serious matters. Because of their difficulty, their accumulation in the ceremonial dialogue leads to a laborious, even impossible understanding to anyone not familiar with it. Young people must assimilate this form of expression little by little. Nevertheless, at this level of speech, some sense is generated. What are we comparing? What do the analogies and metaphors refer to? Levi-Strauss (1963: 345) writes: "Metaphor rests on the intuition of logical connections between a domain and other domains." Space precludes an in-depth analysis of the style and content of Yanomami ceremonial dialogue; however, I will attempt to describe the essentials in a few words.

The dialogue comprises numerous repetitions (see, for example, F1, F2, F3 in the Appendix), occasionally of an incomplete sentence, occasionally of a proposition, a word, or even a syllable. At times, the repetition introduces a new shade of meaning by adding a new grammatical element in the syntactic chain or via a syntactic modification. Sometimes a changed word results in an extension of meaning (F1, sentences 1–2; F2, sentences 5–6). These repetitions can be emphatic. More often they provide a pause before the introduction of a new theme. They enable the speaker to save time. One frequently encounters personal pronoun substitutions in the dialogue; "I" will be replaced by "he" or by "both of us" and "you" will be replaced by "both of you." This procedure is not restricted to the *wayamou*. It enables the speaker to distance himself from the designated person. Perhaps it emphasizes what is unreal in the speech. The desire to distance oneself is apparent when, for example, in daily life, a parent-in-law directly addresses a son-in-law by telling him "both of you" or "both of them." It is less brutal than "you" or "him," which are judged to be too direct. Substitution of a male kin term by its female equivalent is of more delicate interpretation. In this manner, the speaker will say "your wife" for "your brother-in-law," "your oldest sister" for "your oldest brother," and, in the vocative, "mother-in-law" for "father-in-law." Substituting a kin term by another of the same order produces the same effect in distancing oneself as the substitution of a personal pronoun by another. The former, however, may indicate something additional. Perhaps it indicates that, within the kinship system, gender distinction is believed to be less important, contingent in a certain way; whereas the opposition between filiation and affinity remains irreducible. This seems to be implied by Dumont's (1975) analysis of Dravidian kinship systems. Here again, the substitution of a kin term by its female equivalent is not confined to the dialogue: there are frequent examples in shamanistic practices.

The *wayamou* also systematizes a feature of everyday speech, especially when deceased individuals are evoked. Men are designated by names of objects that are typically male (arrow, lanceolate point, harpoonhead, quiver), and women are assimilated to female objects or activities (basket, calabash, water, forest) (F10, F11). To kill a man will be referred to as "shaking an arrowhead," "detaching a quiver," "breaking an arrow," "cutting a pole from a tree." As mortals, human beings are associated with the forest, trees, and dwellings; in other words, with corporeal elements in contrast to the immortal *hekura*[8] who are assimilated to rocks.[9] In order to evoke a cinerary gourd containing the remains of a woman, the speaker will refer to a component of the female costume; for example, a certain type of flower that women attach to the earlobe. If the speaker wishes to evoke the remains of a deceased man, a birdskin armband or macaw tail-feathers will be referred to. If the deceased was a shaman, he will be referred to as a diadem of feathers (*watoshe*). Men are thus assimilated to the world of animals and women to that of plants. Similarly, warfare is mixed up with hunting. Warriors are sometimes game animals and sometimes game birds. When a speaker refers to enemies who will be pursued, the mutum bird, the peccary, the agouti, and the deer will be named (F14). When reference is made to enemies for whom one is the prey, the jaguar or the puma will be named. A man will say to another man "I am your deer" or "I am your game" (F15). One is off to war the same way as one goes hunting for peccary by following its trail. The word to drive out (*hushuu* or *yashuu*) will replace to attack (*shurukai*). To go off to war also means to satisfy one's craving for meat (*naiki thao*). This manner of expressing oneself among the Yanomami is in perfect harmony with the metaphorical expression for murder, victims being "eaten" by their murderers. Occasionally, *wayamou* metaphors are less marked. More generally, one will refer to a ball of cotton as a predatory bird's egg (F21). Certain objects (rare) carry specific designations found only in the *wayamou*: *napëyoma* (the foreign woman, the white woman) will designate any manufactured object; *tisho hi* will be a bow (*hātō nahi*); *yāimorō uku* is a hot beverage the consumption of which is supposed to render the speaker more loquacious in the dialogue. However, these words are not numerous. One hardly encounters a word that touches archaism. One is really faced with a system of global representation that is not specific to the *wayamou*, but the *wayamou* expresses it systematically, thus making it more obvious.

If one now asks what is being discussed in the ceremonial dialogue, the reply will be: it is general and global. Any subject can be addressed, and the only limitations are those of the speaker's power of expression and familiarity with different aspects of culture. Some speakers are mediocre, others are masters, as much by their diction as by the extreme variety of themes they address and the beauty of their speech. Certain dialogues are focused on a unique subject. To compile a list would be to start something that would always remain incomplete. It is more significant to mention the most frequent themes. Speakers often talk about body paint (F1, F2), warfare, the hunt, relationships between the sexes, magical substances (hëri), witchcraft, and the exchange of food and goods. There are also declarations of bravery, and boasting (F16); and criticisms of violence and war (F17). Almost every dialogue refers to mythological episodes and cosmological conceptions (F4, F5). One of the most constant themes is that of the passage of the demons of dusk and morning (*weyari-harikari*), of *Titiri,* the demon of night, and of *Suhirina* (F6, F7, F8). These characters are important and I will refer back to them. During the dialogue, the participants constantly name rivers, mountains, rocks, and their surrounding topography. They constantly name the social groups in these places; the residential communities, and the groupings of communities or larger gatherings forming genuine subunits of population within the Yanomami ethnic group. One therefore constantly hears about the *shiithari* and the *parahiri* of strangers (*napë*), of people from upstream (*ora theri* or *hĩĩ theri*); above all, about the *waika* and the *shamathari* (F1, F3). This naming of the surrounding geographical and sociological space is an essential trait of the *wayamou.* It is interpreted below.

There is no dialogue that does not include a request for goods, but these requests are for the most part artificial: figures of speech that serve as reminders of the necessity for exchange. This can easily be demonstrated ethnographically: it suffices to note the goods that are requested during the *wayamou* and those that are, in fact, exchanged in the commercial transactions following the ritual, prior to the guests' departure. The correspondence is so small that it may be attributed to chance. The demands are as unreal and imaginary as the dye of the speaker of F1, when he says: "I obtained this bag of dyes from the *shamathari* . . . look at it . . . it is scented." However, the speaker came from the mountain and he had never visited the *shamathari.* There was no bag of dye to be seen; there was no fragrance to smell. In another text (Lizot 1990), a man from the mountain, where the only waterways are tumultuous torrents, requests an outboard motor and says: "I will abate its roar." This man does not have a canoe and would have difficulty in steering it. Will it be thought that his request is real? Of course not.

We can now understand why the young people do not fully engage in the dialogue and why they must train and learn it. At the level of verbal expression, it is a difficult exercise. The delivery is rapid; and all the Yanomami stylistic procedures are systematically used. One must have a good knowledge of the mythology, cosmology, toponymy, and surrounding social groups. The young people begin to train themselves around the age of fifteen. On rainy days, they can be seen swinging in their hammocks, reciting formulas of the *wayamou.* It is said that the *wayamou* stops the rain; and that it also shortens the night. It dispels diurnal and nocturnal darkness. The young take a role in the ritual only when they feel assured. They then appear at the very beginning of it: if they do not perform well, they are quickly replaced. A person who is incapable of participating in the dialogue, or who gets confused, is called *aka porepi*,[10] literally "speech of ghost." The same term designates someone who does not speak Yanomami very well or who does not speak at all, as in the case of very young children and strangers; and *wã porepi* means to speak incoherently. These two expressions, *aka porepi* (to speak like a ghost), and *wã porepi* (to be of ghost speech), are both built around the word *pore*, the ghost. The reason for the ghost's being associated with bad speech is to be found in mythology. *Poreawë* (Ghost) was the master of banana plants at a time when human beings—namely, the Yanomami—were deprived of them. One day, *Hõrõnami*, an ancestor who will be mentioned again, met *Poreawë* in the forest while taking cover from the rain and reciting the *wayamou*. *Poreawë* was carrying a heavy load of bananas. After inquiring what it was, *Hõrõnami* requested some seedlings. *Poreawë*, muddled (incapable of expressing himself correctly), delivered a long lecture on gardening and categorically refused the requested seedlings. *Hõrõnami* steals them from him (Lizot 1989a: 80–86). When introducing the ghost, shamans always make him speak incorrectly. Stinginess is therefore associated with bad speech; generosity with good speech. To speak correctly and to express oneself easily is called *aka hayuo* or *aka tao*. Individuals who are capable of participating well in the *wayamou* are called by those terms. The second term, however (*aka tao*), also designates a man who behaves himself well; someone who is hospitable and generous. The Yanomami, therefore, consider the exchange of goods and verbal communication (the exchange of words), to be equivalent. It will be seen below that such analogies are numerous and that they constitute a system in which the modalities of exchange and the codes are blended. The identity of these is recognized and conceptualized.

✦   The Origin of the Night: From Myth to Ritual

In primordial times, perpetual light prevailed. The sun remained at its zenith: man never saw dusk or nightfall. Hunters left, returned, cooked their game, and ate it; children pursued small birds; men and women slept anytime they felt fatigue and made love in the dwelling in broad daylight. Nobody thought of hiding in the forest; nobody got angry; nobody argued. It was perfect: a time when peace prevailed. Everything would have gone on like this, but the ancestors got tired of days that did not end. Also, nearby, they could hear, piercing, the demon *Titiri's* ceaseless moans. *Titiri* attributed names to mountains, hills, rocks, and waterways, and the first men listened to this terrifying voice. *Titiri*, the mutum (*Crax nigra*), was perched on a branch, leaning toward the ground under his own weight. All around him darkness prevailed. One day, *Hōrōnami* said: "My children, we must try!" Perhaps he thought that the night would come if *Titiri* were killed. Some young people left with blowpipes.[11] They missed *Titiri*, managing only to graze him. Nevertheless, for a short moment the night settled down and its associated sounds—screeching insects, croaking of toads— were heard. Then, daylight returned. "This is it indeed, this is what must be done," commented *Hōrōnami*. He then grabbed his blowpipe, got close to *Titiri*, and killed him outright. Night settled in. Some people were stranded in the forest and it was necessary to look for them by waving firebrands to light the way. *Titiri* transformed himself into the demon of the night. Supernatural beings burst from his chest and the *weyari-harikari*,[12] the demons of dusk and morning, sprang from his blood. Since that time, night has followed day. Walking from east to west, *Suhirina* is the first to reach midday. In the course of his travel, he slaughters all the animals he encounters. He is distantly followed by the *weyari*, who gather, cook, and eat the animals killed by *Suhirina*. They prefer the tough sloths.[13] Their passage foreshadows dusk. *Titiri*[14] follows them shortly after, when nightfall has just arrived. In the course of the night, but this time in the opposite direction, from west to east, these same beings follow the same route: *Suhirina* reaches the middle of the night, the *weyari*, now called *harikari*, show themselves just before sunrise, and *Titiri* appears with the first light of dawn. The night is the period of time between two passages by Titiri.

Before describing correspondences between the myth and the *wayamou*, I will provide more background. The forerunner of the demon of the night (*Titiri*) is the mutum. This is the preferred game bird of the Yanomami. Its wing feathers are used in the feathering of arrows. Men fashion armbands from the tuft, the skin of which is cut from the base of the beak to the base of the neck. The tuft's curly feathers and those from the belly are incorporated into the costumes of male Yanomami. The mutum's plumage—which is heavily contrasted, pitch black over the entire body, except on the belly where it is bright white—perfectly symbolizes the opposition of day and night (the day is to the night what white is to black). The mutum is intensively hunted during the dry season, particularly between December and February—the mating season for the bird. At about three o'clock in the morning, the male starts to cry (*miã ĩkĩĩ*), as the Yanomami say. Its song is six muted notes (the approximate number of words in a *wayamou* sequence), that are constantly repeated until daybreak. The hunters leave at about two or three in the morning and light their way with firebrands. Attracted by the song of the mutum, they stop under the tree where the bird is perched and at daybreak shoot their arrows.

Titiri is descended from the mythic bird. He is a supernatural being belonging to the category *yai thë*. He is anthropomorphic, his hair white and curled like the tuft feathers of the mutum. His penis is enormous and he mates with human beings while they sleep. He rips their skin with his monstrous appendage and robs them of their vital principle (*pei mi amo*).[15] The trail taken by *Titiri* is strewn with thorns that hurt his feet. At the same time *Titiri* perforates, with his penis, he is being perforated, by the thorns.

Two other characters of Yanomami mythology are the previously mentioned *Hōrōnami* and *Suhirina*. Both are skilled hunters. *Hōrōnami* appears in several myths[16] and seems to be associated with darkness and death. It is he who steals the banana seedlings from Ghost (*Pore, Poreawë*), when the latter is not willing to give. As already pointed out, he was at the origin of the night. He causes the metamorphosis of *Tatou* into an animal, thus confining him to a dark shelter.

It is worth emphasizing the cultural significance of the plantain banana. It is not only the most important food, since it accompanies numerous other foods, but the ashes of the dead are consumed in a gruel prepared with ripe, cooked bananas during "endocannibalistic" feasts. It is not coincidental that Ghost is the master of the banana plant: his presence refers back to the theme of death.

Suhirina (*suhi* is the scorpion) is the symbol of the perfect hunter. A good hunter or an excellent hunting dog is called *suhirina*. *Suhirina* is the hero of a myth of great importance: A shaman died and transformed himself into Moon, a cannibalistic supernatural being (*periporiwë,* moon spirit). In the night following his death, Moon[17] returned to devour the bones of his own corpse, which had just been burned. Caught while finishing his gruesome meal, he fled by climbing toward the sky as men shot arrows at him: all missed their target. *Suhirina* intervened when Moon was about to disappear behind the clouds. His arrow hit Moon and squirted his blood on the earth, where he transformed himself into armed men. They immediately slaughtered one another.

An in-depth interpretation of this theme will not be necessary. However, we must address the relationship between the ritual and the myth; or, more precisely, between Yanomami rituals and their mythology and associated beliefs. The connection from ritual to myth is neither direct nor simple. Kluckhohn (1942) refers to mutually interdependent links. More explicitly, Levi-Strauss (1958: 217) notes that "the correspondence between the myth and the ritual is a particular case of a general relationship between myth and ritual and among rituals." He adds that "the ritual and the myth are one and the same in a dialectical relationship" (1958: 265–266). This I will verify.[18] While the myth of the origin of the night may not exactly form the basis of the ceremonial dialogue ritual, it does at least provide the conditions for its realization: the arrival of the night; the creation of *Titiri* and of the *weyari-harikari*. The dialogue begins with *Titiri's* first passage at nightfall and ends with his second passage at dawn. Speakers in the dialogue, by naming mountains and waterways, like *Titiri* mark out a geographical space. The analogy between the six notes comprising the mutum's song and the six words of an average *wayamou* sequence has already been pointed out. The monotonous moan of the mutum *Titiri* also foreshadows the *wayamou* in an interesting way. Why, we may ask, is *Titiri's* moan frightening for the ancestors? Because this voice is solitary and the space it circumscribes by naming lies outside of time and is not oriented. Above all, it is empty. The mutum *Titiri's* death will not only cause the daily cycle (the night will follow the day and the day will follow the night), but also an orientation of space: from now on the sun rises in the east (*ora misi*), and sets in the west (*koro misi*). These two cardinal points constitute the axis where *Suhirina,* the *weyari-harikari,* and *Titiri* travel in both directions. The axis establishes a bipartition (north-south) of this space. Nor is this all. The *wayamou* does not limit itself to naming places in space and to proposing a toponymy. It populates this space; places social groups in it; humanizes it and socializes it. The different social groups are themselves polarized by the opposition of the *Waika* and the *Shamathari.* The former are distributed to the north and the latter to the south (among the central Yanomami). The *wayamou* space is doubly oriented. It is populated and stretches itself in the temporality imposed by the succession of night and day and lunar months. Briefly, it should be remembered that the designations *Waika* and *Shamathari* do not correspond to well-defined social groups, and they are not self-designations. Depending on his geographical position, each Yanomami is always at the same time *Waika* and *Shamathari,* while others are located more to the north or to the south. This orientation is approximate. It coincides roughly with north and south among the central Yanomami. However, it should be well understood that it is the opposition of social groups, respectively named *Waika* and *Shamathari,* that is significant, and that this opposition is sociological in nature. My conclusions are consistent with Levi-Strauss (1968: 156): "Myths about the origin of day and night conceptualize both space and time." The Yanomami conceptualize them via naming. Moreover, one can assert that, in the present case, myth and ritual are found vis-à-vis each other in a relationship of transformation.

Metaphorically, it is not exaggerated to state that *Suhirina* feeds (with game) the daily cycle represented by the *weyari-harikari,* and his presence in the system of representations is a reminder that there is no night without a moon. The moon may be visible in the sky, but its absence also reflects its presence. Yanomami women explicitly establish a relationship between the cycle of their periods and the lunar months: the same word is used to denote a woman having her period and the appearance of the new moon: *roo* (personal pronoun *he* or *she,* plus *to be seated*).[19] Recall the story: the blood of Moon, hit by *Suhirina's* arrow, is spilled on the earth where it transforms into warriors, who immediately engage in battle. The mythical origin of the moon is therefore simultaneously a mythical origin for warfare. The moon is thus doubly associated with blood: first, through the link

established by the Yanomami between its cycle and that of menstruation—
which is linked to procreation; second, through the blood of warfare and
violence—which is linked to death. It is therefore not surprising that a similar ritual, *unokai-mou,*[20] is simultaneously attended by women who are
having their first period and by murderers. Women procreate; and every
living being carries death from the moment of birth.

Among the Yanomami, when in mourning, women darken their cheek-
bones in black; and men paint themselves in black to go to war. Here we
see another relationship, and it takes us in the same direction. What I have
indicated, in a deliberately elliptical but momentarily sufficient manner,
agrees once again with what Levi-Strauss (1968: 60–105) writes in associating the monthly cycle with procreation and death. *Suhirina* and Moon
(the moon) convey this meaning in their own way. However, from the
mythical origin of the night to the origin of the moon the problem shifts on
several levels; and again, the question pertaining to the symbolism of col-
ors is raised. This question is directly relevant to my subject.

I have indicated that the contrast of black and white in the mutum's
plumage properly signifies the opposition of day and night, and I have suggested that black is to the night as white is to the day. It has just been stated
that black was also in a symbolic relationship with war and death. What,
then, corresponds to white? Logically, it must correspond to peace. This is
certainly the case, since warriors paint themselves in black, whereas visitors and participants cover their heads with white down. The opposition of
black and white and of day and night is apparent again. It will be recalled
that during the *wayamou,* a host with black hair—i.e., not wearing down;
black is the Yanomami natural color—faces a guest whose head, covered
by down, is white: night and day face each other. I can now complete the
system of opposition and argue that black is to white as the night is to the
day and warfare is to peace. I am solely interested in the semantic values of
black and white, but it is important to bear in mind that these values belong
to a larger system that includes red, associated with blood and life, and yellow, the connotations of which are ominous (old age, sickness). It is a system of four, opposing itself in pairs.

✦ **From Peace to Warfare**

Here I will take a step back in looking at the internal logic of the
Yanomami system. I have shown that the ceremonial dialogue was a reciprocal exchange, essentially peaceful in nature. What place does it occupy in
the totality of the system of reciprocal exchanges among the Yanomami?
And how is this system conceptualized by them? What, in other words, is
its global significance? Under its two forms (*himou* and *wayamou*), I argue
that the ceremonial dialogue is a modality for peaceful exchange and that

not all exchanges are peaceful. Among the Yanomami, the reciprocal exchange directs the whole system of communication and enables different social groups to form a structural totality.

In the following passage, the theory of reciprocity will be my starting point. According to Mauss ([1923] 1966), it is the obligation to give and to receive (to return also) that constitutes the foundation of peaceful relationships; and "exchange is the common denominator of a large number of social activities that are seemingly heterogenous." Commenting on the gift, Levi-Strauss (1966) writes that it is "the exchange which constitutes the primitive phenomenon, and the different products of the social activity (tools, manufactured products, foodstuffs, magical formulas, ornaments, dances, songs, and myths), are rendered comparable to each other by their common character to be transferable." He goes on: "They are often substitutable to the extent that different values can replace each other in the same operation" (1966: xxxiii).[21] Sahlins (1972: 236) warns against making the mistake of perceiving the exchange in terms that are exclusively material: it is, first and foremost, a social act.

What prevails within the Yanomami domestic group is what Sahlins calls generalized reciprocity. Elsewhere it is known as balanced reciprocity. In dealings with strangers, negative reciprocity abruptly ends the relationships. Between families and within the faction, exchanges of food and services predominate. The rules governing the distribution of game are strict. Day to day, the elders are in charge of these rules; the leaders take over during feasts and ceremonies. The hunter cannot eat the game he kills for fear of becoming a bad marksman (*sina*). Invitations to be fed and sheltered may be given to one or more domestic groups, a faction, or the entire community. It is always possible to request help from a relative in times of scarcity; when, for example, food is temporarily unavailable in the garden. The vocabulary on the subject is fairly substantial: *shoayou*, mutually to give shelter and offer food; *ni thāō*, to be offered food; *kahiki no kōāmai*, to give an offering of meat and an accompanying dish; *nowā ōhiāmou*, to ask to be invited in times of scarcity. Goods are exchanged from person to person, and the Yanomami have a passion for commercial transaction.[22] Every object has its history and this is often described in detail during the exchange. Every object that is given carries with it the impression, an immaterial mark, left by the donor (*imi no*). Two partners in a lasting exchange relationship are said "to have their arms interlocked" (*poko thapoyou*). Feasts, ceremonies, and rituals are occasions for exchanges. Shamanism is no exception to the rule: services are exchanged during an initiation; in a healing ceremony, hallucinogenic drugs are offered and received; and the shamans always offer each other spirits (*hekura*).

When a Yanomami dies, the series of funerary rituals is remarkable. Initially, the corpse is burned. Then, during a ritual called *paushimou*—the same as that to mark the end of a woman's seclusion after her first period and the end of a murderer's isolation—the bones are pulverized, and the gourds into which they have ben poured are distributed. Finally, the bone powder is consumed—sometimes on more than one occasion. These ceremonies are not only the occasion for feasts, however: the corpse of the deceased is an object for both exchange and consumption. Hence, Moon's eating of his own body is scandalizing: he removes himself from the exchange. Obviously, the exchange does not solely focus on material objects. I have found numerous cases and I expect soon to discover others. By extension, it can be said that everything is suitable for exchange. I have also indicated that certain modalities of the exchange are meant to consolidate the state of peace. They specialize in that sort of thing, so to speak: as Sahlins (1972: 239) writes, "to assure peace is not a sporadic event, a selective relationship set up between two groups, but a continuous process pursuing itself within society."

The Yanomami moral code is organized around two dominant virtues: generosity (*shi ihite*) and courage (*waitheri*).[23] This is no coincidence. The former implies frequent gift-giving; and the latter comprises the obligation to take revenge (*no yuo*); namely, to retaliate in kind, corpse for corpse. This is the implacable application of "an eye for an eye, tooth for a tooth." It is now clear that the relationship between generosity and courage rests on a close analogy and that these two qualities are governed by the same logic: that of the gift and the countergift, or in other words, the reciprocal exchange. Whereas one quality is definitely oriented toward peace, the other is oriented toward war. What do peace and warfare have in common? According to the Yanomami, to take revenge and to be brave is to retaliate in kind; to do to others exactly the same, no more no less, as they do. As I stated, corpse for corpse. To take revenge (*no yuo*) literally means "to seize the value." Children of both sexes are taught this lesson as soon as they are able to stand on their feet. For instance, when a child has been bitten or hit by another child, the mother or father, conscious of the strict application of the rule, forces retaliation in the same manner and at the same spot. Revenge is also taken on objects. The Yanomami bite the thorn that pricked them; they cut the sharp point that wounded them; they bite the lice that tormented them; they burn the head and the teeth of the wildcat that killed a dog. *Return insult for insult.* A victim of a destruction must in turn destroy. It is imperative to hit back when hit. Finally, one must avenge the dead.

Like the gift and hospitality, revenge and warfare are governed by the principle of reciprocity. The Yanomami associate generosity and courage because the two virtues are perceived as two modalities of exchange and reciprocity. The accomplished man must excel in the exchange. He must therefore be generous and take revenge at the same time. He is an accomplished man because he fully participates in the exchange under all its forms. The principle of reciprocity is of such importance in Yanomami culture that it is incorporated into grammar: the morpheme /-yo-/, a verbal suffix, is the reciprocal.[24] I have already indicated reciprocal verbs (*shoayou, poko thapoyou*, etc). There are others: *wã wayou,* to chat; *yimirayou,* to inquire about; *yahatuayou,* to insult each other; *yathëyou,* to treat each other as coward; *wãhã yuayou,* to name one another; *shëyou,* to fight each other with a stick; *si poayou,* to slap or hit each other with the flat part of the machete; *ninayou,* to shoot arrows at each other. All these verbs are reciprocal and gerundive. Reciprocity simultaneously covers the field of peaceful relationships, relationships based on violence, and, finally, warfare.

I have previously indicated that in a certain way and in a certain context, bad speech was an index of avarice; good speech, on the contrary, was an index of generosity. This is rendered possible because two levels of exchange are perceived as analogous. Thus, the "confusion" of the levels of exchange and the modalities of reciprocity reappears, and finds itself confirmed if the meaning of the words are addressed and some ethnosemantic analysis is carried out. Concerning the *wayamou,* I have indicated that *wã kõãmai* means "to answer back"; *kõãmai* means to return a borrowed object. Built the same way, *no kõãmai* is to assure reciprocity of a commercial exchange—"to return the value." The latter word also means to take blood revenge, to kill someone because of a murder (with relatives interposing). And *kahiki no kõãmai* means to give an offering of meat and an accompanying dish. The word *matohi* is remarkable in having several possible meanings: item of exchange or personal possession; the remains of a deceased person after cremation; what is used to kill, namely the weapons and the magical substances (*hëri*); and *rahaka toayou* means both mutually to exchange lanceolate arrowheads and to wage war. Similarly, *hiima toayou,* which literally means to exchange dogs, signifies to kill in order to avenge a dead person. To assure blood revenge is also expressed as *ãtãri shetekeprai*—literally, to divide a harpoon arrowhead into two. In this case, revenge appears under the guise of sharing.

To be in a state of war, to wage war, is *niyayou;* namely, to shoot arrows at each other. This is the most common word, but there are many others, all explicit in the idea they convey. To give a few examples: *na wayou,* to make love to each other; *totihayou,* to give each other pleasure; *ohëmayou,* to starve each other; *yahatuayou,* to insult each other; *wãhã wayoayou,* to tell each other stories. The indigenous idea that expresses itself mixes up insistently the levels of reciprocal exchanges, the codes, and the modalities. This is because this idea is global for the Yanomami and it retains, first and foremost, the principle. The reciprocal exchange simultaneously covers the field of peaceful exchanges, violence, and warfare, and this conceptualization corresponds very well with practice. The reciprocal exchange is indeed the first phenomenon: it cross-cuts all of the social structure. The different codes that are utilized and the various modalities of exchange are, as said by Levi-Strauss, interchangeable. Put another way, this means that peace (what we call peace, although the word does not exist in Yanomami) and warfare (strictly speaking, that word does not exist either) are both the same expression of the social structure. They are not perceived as antithetical but as a similar expression of exchange and reciprocity: nothing more than two modalities. To conclude, it can be asserted that the modeling of peaceful and hostile relationships emphasized by indigenous ideas and practices is fully consistent with the "nature" of warfare among the Yanomami: related communities (via filiation and affinity ties) are always those who wage war against each other, and every residential group currently at war once had peaceful relationships with its present enemies, and may be at peace in the not too distant future. In peace, as in war, the relationship of exchange is preserved: it is inherent to the social structure.[25]

✦ Appendix

The excerpts of the *wayamou* presented here are from a collection of texts in preparation (Lizot 1990). Each excerpt illustrates some aspect of the analysis in this chapter.

The excerpts are numbered within each paragraph for ease of commentarial reference.

F1: 1. I wish to draw a line on your face, 2. I wish to paint your face. 3. Among the *Shamathari,* 4. among the *Shamathari,* 5. I requested the container (of dye); 6. here is the container, 7. look at it, look at it; 8. make sure the dye is good, 9. you will blush, 10. you will become *hekura* (i.e., you will become shaman). 11. He smells good! COMMENT: This is a perfect illustration of the imaginary content of the discourse in the *wayamou:* there is no dye and the guest never went to the *Shamathari.*

F2: 1. I do not know how to paint myself, 2. calamity, aren't you going to say that? 3. Don't even mention it, 4. don't even mention it. 5. Let us trace a line on our forehead; 6. when you will have done it, 7. I will express my satisfaction! COMMENT: These fragments are a continuation of fragment 1.

F3: 1. Over there at the *Toshopo* waterfall, 2. at the *Toshopo* waterfall, 3. those who live over there (near the waterfall), 4. those who live over there, 5. from whom goods are requested because they have some, 6. they have not given items of clothing. COMMENT: *Toshopo* waterfall refers to the locality and to the social group living there.

F4: 1. Those who shot their arrows against the moon, 2. and the aggressive wasps, 3. and the aggressive wasps, 4. look at them go, look at them go. COMMENT: This passage hints at violence and warfare. The first sentence refers to those, including *Suhirina*, who shot their arrows against Moon (in the mythical episode). The second sentence refers to the "demons" of war, the *āiāmori*, a bloody and violent people of immortal beings who lick the blood from their wounds.

F5: 1. Do you know Thunder? 2. Do you really know him? 3. How is his head? 4. How is his head? 5. He lies down in a cotton hammock. COMMENT: This refers to cosmology. Thunder (*yāru*) lives in the "celestial disc" (*hetu misi*) accompanied by souls. He is the master of fruits. His hair is turned yellow and his body (his head) is covered by blisters.

F6: 1. The *weyari* who walk one after another, 2. they (the men) killed *Titiri*, 3. where the mutum "cried," 4. they killed him, 5. and his white down will transform itself into *weyari*. COMMENT: This fragment refers to the myth of origin of the moon, to the murder of the mutum, forerunner of *Titiri*, and the metamorphosis of his white down into *weyari*. This interpretation is a variant of the one presented in the text.

F7: 1. While the *weyari* push away my hands, 2. I wish to request goods, 3. I wish to request goods. 4. Do not think that I will say that. COMMENT: Another reference to the *weyari*, who prohibit the speaker from requesting goods as long as daylight has not appeared.

F8: 1. *Titiri* does not say: "And what if I stayed here a little longer and started to plant banana plants?" 2. He does not take leave for another day. 3. "He would tell himself gossip," he does not say he hurries even though his feet hurt. COMMENT: At daybreak this conversation concludes the *wayamou*, which draws to an end at the exact moment that *Titiri* arrives.

F9: 1. The men have dispersed habitations, 2. even though their dwellings are distant, 3. I keep them close by naming them. COMMENT: In the first sentence the word "trees" (plural) is the one actually used, not "men," a common substitution during the *wayamou*, particularly when the names of deceased individuals are evoked. In this fragment, the speaker states that he makes close (i.e., present) the habitations of humans by uttering their names.

F10: 1. Brother-in-law, "she lives over there," 2. do not say that. 3. "I keep the woman for good," 4. brother-in-law, do not say that, look this way, 5. and come back with her. COMMENT: During the *wayamou*, a host asks a guest to return a woman who fled. See comment in F11 for details of word-substitution. Here, the word for a variety of gourd is used to indirectly refer to a woman.

F11: 1. "Brother-in-law visits them and shows to them the woman," 2. this is what I will say, will say, will say. 3. "This is because they do not see her even for a moment, 4. this is because they do not see her even for a moment, 5. unfortunately they are angry," 6. Yes, in my dwelling, 7. if the woman will appear, 8. I will approach and ask: 9. "brother-in-law, what is your intention? 10. I will keep her, I will marry her, 11. is this really what you want to do?" COMMENT: This fragment of *wayamou* is the guest's response to the request in F10. In the first sentence, the woman is associated with a gourd (*āshito,* the plant that produces a certain type of gourd). Then, and successively, the woman is called a basket and water. In the eleventh sentence the expression *"amishi kōō"* (to drink) means to keep a woman to oneself; namely, to marry her.

F12: 1. Who in fact, 2. killed my relative, 3. and made him disappear?

F13: 1. To the youth who accompanies me, 2. to the one who accompanies me, 3. when I go to war, (I say): 4. "My child, 5. follow me closely, 6. it is me, it is me, 7. who will attack the enemies." COMMENT: This passage requires a complete deciphering. Literally, the meaning is: "To the youth who accompanies me when I go hunting, I say: "My child, follow me closely, I will drive out the peccaries." In this context the Yanomami word that means to look for game has the meaning of "to go to war"; the word for peccary [*Peccary:* a large mammal, resembling a pig—ED] is mentioned instead of "enemy," and the expression to drive out peccaries means "to attack the enemies."

F14: 1. Even under difficult conditions, 2. we will surely reach our enemy, 3. at least this is what you, Yanomami, calmly believe.

F15: 1. Because I think about it, 2. because I think about it now, 3. because your game thinks about it, 4. his words are as such. COMMENT: The speaker, having been threatened, designates himself to his interlocutor as his game.

F16: 1. Be quiet, 2. otherwise I will kill you. 3. Who will avenge you? 4. With my ax, 5. with the destructive power of my ax, 6. I will break your pelvis, 7. I will throw you in the water. 8. With the white men's cord, 9. with the cord, 10. I will strangle you. COMMENT: This is not a real threat. These are only words, at the most a declaration of bravery not addressed to anyone, and made in the context of a friendly encounter. Compare this with the tone expressed in F17, where the speaker is the same person, in the same *wayamou.*

F17: 1. These points that we keep at the tip of our arrows, 2. and that they intend to shoot (against some persons): 3. "They are well sharpened," 4. that, the Yãnoãmi do not say, 5. I never hear them say that. 6. "Be quiet, 7. be still each in your corner!" 8. this is what I finally say. COMMENT: The peaceful attitude of F17 denies the ostentatious boastfulness of F16, expressed by the same person. This is an explicit criticism of violence, and the same man will later add: "the arrows inflict pain and the *Yãnoãmi* do not think of it" (*Yãnoãmi* is a variant of Yanomami).

F18: 1. Go ahead, utter my personal name, 2. let us name each other, 3. this is what I will say, 4. this is what I will say, 5. this is indeed what I say. COMMENT: This *wayamou,* as well as those in F19 and F20, takes place in an atmosphere of conflict between two communities where relationships are deteriorating because of thefts, gossips, and mutual accusations. The two groups have gathered for the *wayamou* to provide an honest explanation leading to an appeasement. To name someone present is a very serious provocation among the Yanomami, and the speaker's genuine challenge will not produce a sequel.

F19: 1. When I will arrive, 2. I will immediately approach myself (to you). 3. Perhaps he will stop by each fire, don't believe that, 4. I will attack you immediately, 5. I will attack you upon arrival; 6. I was about to hit you on the ribs. 7. Listen to my words: 8. This is how the *Yãnoãmi* [Yanomami] argue, 9. then they calm, 10. then they calm down. COMMENT: This is the same context as F18, but the participants are different. As in F16, the speaker displays bravery, but this time the antagonism is real. What is being said is: The Yanomami say (during the *wayamou*) what they need to communicate to each other, in all honesty. Peace is then restored, each person is once again calm.

F20: 1. Son, stay awake, 2. inhalor of hallucinogens, 3. you are really ugly, 4. you are really ugly. 5. Coward, 6. here, on my back, 7. place your stinking fingers. COMMENT: This is the same context as F18 and F19. Here can be seen the level of verbal violence attained in a confrontation during the ceremonial dialogue in the event of a conflict among *yahitherimi*. However, there is no corresponding concrete act of violence. On the contrary, peaceful relationships are restored. Verbal violence averts armed conflict.

F21: 1. "Where is my cotton ball?" 2. they asked each other. 3. "Where is mine? 4. Will you give it to me?" 5. Tell me quickly, tell me quickly. 6. When I complete the ball, 7. I will bring it to you, 8. you will ask for it, 9. you will want it. COMMENT: This is a promise of exchange. It is often by putting an object in front of the recipient that an offering is made.

F22: 1. This red thing girding your loins [loincloth], 2. give it to me. 3. With the women who are here, 4. you have already made love with [your loincloth], 5. when I leave, I will get rid of the foul smell of the sexes, 6. it will certainly become clean. 7. What bears the name of soap, 8. add it [to the loincloth that you will give to me], 9. I will make the smell disappear, 10. and I will touch it with my penis [I will wear it]. COMMENT: The speaker never wears a loincloth. Note the two circumlocutions: This red thing girding your loins (F22.1.) and What bears the name of soap (F22.7.).

F23: 1. "Give me the thing belonging to the white men." 2. This is what you say. 3. Do not request without suggesting anything in exchange, 4. do not show yourself again empty handed, 5. you never give anything in exchange for what you take. 6. Don't imagine that I only talk, 7. aren't you leaving without having obtained anything? COMMENT: The speaker warns the guest who obtains goods by promising to bring something in exchange later and does not keep his promise. Here, the words have meaning. This is a genuine warning, even though this time, too, the guest will not leave empty handed.

✦ Notes

I am grateful to Frank R. Thomas, who translated my manuscript from French to English; to Ursula Thiele, who helped with the revision; and to the Spark M. Matsunaga Institute for Peace at the University of Hawaii, which provided a grant to Leslie Sponsel in support of the translation. Space limitations prevented the publication of the Yanomami texts of the dialogues, but these will appear in my subsequent publishing.

1. I saw a small collection of *wayamou* texts edited at the Max Plank Institute (ethology). The Yanomami transcription is highly defective: the sentences are butchered, and the translation is contrived. Nevertheless, it is from such documents that Eibl-Eibesfeldt (1971) concludes, for instance, that the *wayamou* is unintelligible and that a science of human ethology is supposedly created.

2. The words *yahitherimi* and *ahetetherimi* are nouns of similar form (*yahi-the-ri-mi* and *ahete-the-ri-mi*). Although their semantic fields partially overlap; they are not synonymous. *Yahi* and *ahete* respectively designate *dwelling* or *habitation* and *near*. The compound suffix, *therimi*, refers to a community or a grouping of persons. *Yahi*, therefore, refers to the residential identity of people who live in several neighboring communities, often stemming from a common community of origin. *Ahete*, on the other hand, stresses proximity. The first word is used much more frequently than the second.

3. *Wayamou* and *himou* are present-progressive verbs. In the text, through class transposition, I will utilize these words as nouns and will refer to the *wayamou* and the *himou*.

4. During a feast, the invited community may come from a distance greater than a day's walk. The entire group of men, women, and children travel this route in easy stages, subsisting along the way. On arrival, the guests camp out near the hosts' habitation and wait for the hunters to return and for everything to be organized, when the formal invitation to enter is given.

5. The *paushimou* ritual (from *paushi,* an element of body decoration, such as a feather or flower) is performed about ten days after the cremation of the body. The bones, hitherto kept in a basket (*yorchi*), are crushed into a fine powder that is then poured into gourds (*hishima*) and sealed with beeswax. The *paushimou* is in two parts: one is material and consists of making the bones edible and divisible (as described in the text); the other is symbolic and consists of transforming the bones into an element of display to enable the relatives of the deceased to decorate themselves—which is precisely the meaning of the word *paushimou.* For more information on the funerary ritual, see Clastres and Lizot (1978) and Albert (1985).

6. The letter *F,* followed by a number, refers to the fragments of *wayamou* mentioned in the Appendix.

7. The duration of each person's participation in the *wayamou* depends largely on the number of guests. When several are present, they relieve each other (this is compulsory), each person participating in several dialogues during the night.

8. The *hekura* are a class of supernatural beings opposed to another class called *yai the.* The *hekura* are the "spirits" of plants, animals, and certain natural phenomena. They are also mythological ancestors. Domesticated by the shaman, the

hekura becomes the shaman's assistant. The shaman himself is a *hekura* (the word also means shaman). By convention, I will translate *hekura* as spirit or shaman and *yai the* as demon.

9. For the association between wood and short life, see Levi-Strauss (1964:157–161).

10. A specific vocabulary is associated with the *wayamou:* e.g., *aka hārōprou* or *wā yakëi*, to muddle, to make mistakes while talking; *wā titiai*, to assimilate the *wayamou* expressions, to learn new themes; *wā karëhai*, to participate correctly.

11. Currently, the Yanomami do not use the blowgun, and its use is not attested in the recent past. Sorcerers (*ōkā*) shoot their evil substances with the help of a hollow tube twisted beneath fibers surrounding a dart—a device similar to a blowgun.

12. *Weyari* comes from *weyate*, dusk, and *harikari* from *harika*, morning. The suffix *-ri* (the same as that contained in *yahitherimi*) indicates a grouping of living beings, a people.

13. The sloths lead to the theme of a local night provoked by a sororal incest. See Lizot (1989a:57–59).

14. By regressive assimilation, *Titiri* comes from *mi titi*, night, darkness.

15. See Lizot (1976:173–177).

16. See Lizot (1989:36–38, 80–86, 109–144).

17. Moon—a male character.

18. For a lengthy discussion on the relationships between the ritual and the myth and the nature of the ritual, see Levi-Strauss (1971:597–611).

19. When having their period, women sit on a log with their back leaning against a hammock.

20. *Unokai* is a ritual state; *unokaimou* refers to the respect of taboos and their accomplishment. Without straying into giving a detailed analysis of this ritual, I wish to emphasize that my work suggests an interpretation that is very distinct from that proposed by Albert (1985) for the *Yanomame* ritual (his being supported by an erroneous etymology of the word). The fact that the ritual is carried out by women who are having their first period (and their husbands) and by murderers requires a global interpretation, explaining one case and then another. The myth of origin of the moon opens up another opportunity for analysis.

21. My emphasis.

22. For more details, see Lizot (1989b:228–238, 162–164).

23. The analysis of the word *waitheri* presented here in the context of the system where this value belongs, is an extension of the analysis that I made in another text (Lizot: forthcoming).

24. /-yo-/ is followed by a temporal marker, or the perfective. The concept *gift* is also incorporated into language construction. All the verbs with the meaning of sharing, or with this meaning attached under certain circumstances (to break, to pick, to take down, etc.) possess a series of ad hoc inflections indicating the removal of a piece from a larger whole, the division into two or more portions. Similarly, in the inflexions formed of compound suffixes *-ke-* indicates the one who offers, /-re-/ the one who takes or obtains, and *-pe-* the one who receives (Ego as speaker).

25. This study was just completed when I had the opportunity to read Ferguson's (1992) contribution: "A Savage Encounter: Western Contact and the Yanomami War Complex." The view is entirely foreign and does not make any sense in relationship to the problem of warfare among the Yanomami. Ferguson's theory is very rigid—a model that is perhaps applicable in certain cases and for certain types of wars. He selected what he needed in the literature to illustrate his theory (occasionally among the worst authors) and neglected what did not fit. Warfare among the Yanomami apparently bothers Ferguson, so he denies it.

✦ References

Albert, Bruce
  1985   Temps du sang, temps des cendres: representation de la maladie, systeme rituel et espace politique chez les Yanomami du Sud. Est. These de Doctorat, Universite de Paris X, Nanterre, France.

Chagnon, Napoleon A.
  1988   Life Histories, Blood Revenge, and Warfare in a Tribal Population. *Science* 239:985–992.

Cocco, Padre Luis
  1972   *Iyewei-teri. Quince años entre los yanomami.* Caracas: Escuela Tecnica Popular Don Bosco.

Clastres, H., and J. Lizot
  1978   La part du feu. *Libre* 4.

Dumont, Luis
  1975   *Dravidien et Kariera. L'alliance de mariage dans l'Inde du Sud et en Australie.* Paris: Mouton.

Eibl-Eibesfeldt, Irenaus
  1971   Eine ethologish Interpretation des Palmfruchtfest des Waika (Venezuela) nebts einegen Bemerkungen über die bindende Funktion von Zwieggesprachen. *Anthropos* 66:767–778.

Ferguson, Charles A.
  1964   Diglossia, in *Language in Culture and Society: A Reader in Linguistics and Anthropology:* 429–439. New York: Harper and Row.

Ferguson, R. Brian
  1992   A Savage Encounter: Western Contact and the Yanomami War Complex, in *War in the Tribal Zone: Expanding States and Indigenous Warfare,* R. Brian Ferguson and Neil L. Whitehead, eds.: 199–227. Santa Fe, NM: School of American Research Press.

Folk, Niels
1963   *Waiwai: Religion and Society of an Amazonian Tribe.* Copenhagen: Danish National Museum, Ethnographie Serie 8.

Kluckhohn, Clyde
1942   Myth and Ritual: A General Theory. *The Harvard Theological Review* XXXV.

Levi-Strauss, Claude
1958   *Anthropologie Structurale.* Paris: Plon.
1964   *Le cru et le cuit.* Paris: Plon.
1966   Introduction a l'oeuvre de Marcel Mauss in *Sociologie et anthropologie, Marcel Mauss:* ix–lii. Paris: Press Universitaires de France.
1968   *L'origine des manières de table.* Paris: Plan.
1971   *L'Homme nu.* Paris: Plon.

Lizot, Jacques
1984   *Les Yanomami Centraux.* Paris: Editions de l'Ecole Pratique des Hautes Etudes.
1985   *Tales of the Yanomami: Daily Life in the Venezuelan Forest.* New York: Cambridge University Press.
1989a   *No patapi tëhë/ En tiempos de los antepasados.* Puerto Ayacucho, Venezuela: Vicariato Apostolico.
1989b   Sobre la guerra. *La Iglesia en Amazonas* 44:23–34.
1990   Dialogues cérémoniels, in Textes Yanomami (T.2): 356–628. Manuscrito del autor.

Mauss, Marcel
(1923) 1966   *Sociologie et Anthropologie.* Paris: Press Universitaires de France.

Migliazza, Ernest C.
1972   Yanomama Grammar and Intelligibility. Ph.D. thesis, Indiana University.

Rivière, Peter
1971   *The Political Structure of the Trio Indians as Manifested in a System of Ceremonial Dialogue.* The Translation of Culture. London: Tavistock Publications.

Sahlins, Marshall
1972   *Stone Age Economics.* Chicago: Aldine.

Shapiro, Judith
1972   Sex Roles and Social Structure among the Yanomama Indians of Northern Brazil. Ph.D. thesis, Columbia University.

Urban, Greg
  1986 Ceremonial Dialogues in South America. *American Anthropologist* 88:371–386.

Wilbert, Johannes, and Karen Simoneau, eds.
  1990 *Folk Literature of the Yanomami Indians.* Los Angeles: Latin American Center Publications.

✦ 10

Symbols and Rituals of Peace in Brazil's Upper Xingu

Thomas Gregor

We are beginning to understand the institutional basis of peace. Cooperation and peace are linked to the exchange of goods and services, to intermarriage, and overlapping relationships, to divided loyalties, and to the absence of fraternal interest groups. What remains relatively little researched, however, is the role of expressive symbolism in the structuring of peaceful societies. The focus of this chapter by Thomas Gregor is on the symbolism of peace among the native peoples of Brazil's Upper Xingu. The ritual interaction of the Xingu tribes constitutes an implicit philosophy of peace. Gregor maintains, however, that Xingu ceremonial and its underlying meaning is more than simply an expression of political harmony. Xingu values and symbols of peace are so emotive, so stimulating of action, that they actually *generate* peaceful relationships and institutions.

Ironically, the ritual described in Gregor's analysis is a kind of war game in which the participants hurl insults and spears at one another. As in the societies described in Chapters 3, 6, 7, and 9 (by Dentan, Briggs, Robarchek, and Lizot), the Xingu peace is composed of elements of both alliance and opposition. Is the balance of attraction and antagonism a characteristic of peace systems? It may well be that peace is not so much an achievement as it is an uneasy process—balancing opposing sides of human nature.

—THE EDITORS

✦ What is the cause of war? On this question, the social sciences provide answers. Violent conflict may be adaptive for those who participate: they gain territory and property; they benefit from demographic adjustments; and they gain a reputation that is advantageous in defense against other warlike communities. War also meets personal needs. It displaces aggression, directing it to out-groups; it satisfies the need for prestige and honor; and it protects leaders from internal disaffection.

But what of peace? On this topic, unlike war, we know little, in part because peace is hard to find. War, on the other hand, is widespread. In fact, we could almost say that, among state-level societies, it is ubiquitous.

States usually have their origins in warfare and, once founded, war may be their principal business. Even if we confine our attention to relatively peaceful states, we find much evidence of organized armed conflict. Matthew Melko (1973) surveyed a large number of "peaceful empires" and found that they are "relatively rare in history." Moreover, Melko's study was possible only with a liberal definition of peace. All of the societies in his sample were militaristic beyond their own borders and kept standing armies.

Shifting our focus to smaller societies, peace is almost as hard to find. Keith Otterbein, in a cross-cultural study of war (1970), found only four nonwarlike societies in a sample of fifty. Richard Sipes, in a comparative study of warfare and sports, writes that "relatively peaceful societies are not easy to find. I had to investigate 130 societies to find eleven, of which five were rejected because of insufficient information" (1973: 68). The societies that are peaceful usually fit one of two social types. They are enclaved societies, such as the Hutterites and the Amish—as Robert Dentan describes in Chapter 3; or they are very small-scale, tribal societies, many of them hunters and foragers. Dentan believes that this group is largely comprised of refugee bands, whose experience with more powerful neighbors has been agonizingly traumatic.

Peaceful societies are rare. When looked at close up, many of them turn out to be not so peaceful. The !Kung bushmen in Africa, long known in the literature as "the harmless people" engage in feuds that take the lives of substantial numbers of people. Their homicide rate (approximately 41.9 per 100,000 population) is nearly four times that of the United States (10.7 per 100,000).[1] Until recently, however, anthropologists have de-emphasized the occurrence of violence in simple societies. Homicides appear to be rare events in very small communities even if, statistically, the rate of violent death is high (i.e., the period between deaths is relatively long). Moreover, many of the peoples in question eschew conflict and minimize it when it occurs (see Knauft 1987). We should not, however, underestimate the impact of killings in small societies. Though, in terms of time elapsing, they seem unusual, they are remembered for generations. Violent deaths may create an atmosphere of lethality and unpredictability, envenoming the psychological life of the society. Jean Briggs's discussion in Chapter 6, entitled *"Why Don't You Kill Your Baby Brother?" The Dynamics of Peace in Canadian Inuit Camps,* spells out the contradictions of potential violence in a generally peaceful society.

Peaceful societies are rare, and rarely completely peaceful. Peace, however, is more than a chimera that recedes as we move closer. If we are content to give up the search for the "gentle other" and look at relative—rather than absolute—peace, there remains much to be learned. Peaceful societies, it turns out, have special structures that control and manage conflict. Socialization practices, political organization, kinship, and expressive culture echo the same message of antiviolence.

The best known ways of promoting peace are behavioral and structural. Socialization, for example, has a profound impact on aggression in adulthood. Marc Ross (1986), using a large sample of cross-cultural data, shows that the best indicator of the presence and intensity of aggression is the neglect or abuse of children. Social and political organization are also crucial. The exchange of goods and intermarriage between local communities creates links between individuals that enlarge the political community and create a constituency that opposes conflict. Moreover, such contacts lead to the development of parallel institutions, common culture, and mutual understanding.

Among the least known of the bases of peace is the expressive symbolism of peaceful societies. In general, ideologies associated with war are more developed than those that express peace. Interest in warfare, feuding, and aggression infuse the mythology and symbolism of the worlds' peoples. Rarely does a philosophy of peace approach the complexity of *ahimsa* or *satraghya* of India (Nakhre 1976) or the varying concepts of nonviolence reviewed by Galtung (1981). Thomas Hardy once commented on the lower status of peace as an item of human interest: "War makes rattling good history, but peace is poor reading."

We can nonetheless discern an implicit philosophy of peace in the expressive culture of nonviolent tribal societies. Much of this philosophy is to be found in ritual, especially where ritual peacefully links separate political communities. The intention of this chapter is to examine the expressive and symbolic basis of peace in a tribal society, looking especially closely at ritual. The focus is on one of the world's more remarkable peace systems, that of the Mehinaku Indians and the neighboring tribes of the Upper Xingu region in central Brazil.

✦ The Mehinaku and Their Xingu Neighbors— Once Separate, Now Linked

The Mehinaku are one of nine single village tribes of tropical forest Indians living along the headwaters of the Xingu River in the Mato Grosso.[2] These communities speak different languages and at one time must have had strikingly different cultures. What is remarkable about the Xinguanos is that despite these differences they are generally peaceful, a fact that was noted by the first European observers in the region in the late nineteenth century.

As a result of substantial subsequent research among all of the Xingu language groups, the institutional basis of the Xingu peace is now clear. Of greatest importance is that the Xinguanos exchange goods and services and that they intermarry. Each village manufactures a trade specialty, such as hardwood bows (the Kamaiyura), ceramics (the Waura), shell necklaces and belts (the Carib-speaking tribes), and potassium chloride salt (the Mehinaku). These monopolies are minimally supported by access to special resources or strategically guarded secrets of manufacture and materials. The monopolies endure because trade itself is valued. According to a Mehinaku villager, "We have beautiful things that they want. And so we trade and that is good."

Due to regular intermarriage,[3] the Xingu tribes are linked by kinship. Bilingualism is common. Nearly all of the Xinguanos have kin, friends, and trading partners in other tribes, whom they visit and host. The Xinguanos also exchange services, such as shamanistic healing, and attend each other's inauguration and commemoration of village chiefs. The institutional basis of peace is so extensive that the original differences among the Xingu tribes have eroded. The politically autonomous tribes act somewhat like linguistically distinct and residentially separate ethnic groups within a larger social framework of common institutions and values.

A Self-sustaining Peace System

The Xingu peace system consists of interest in trade, the need for spouses, and joint ceremonial. These are institutions of sociative peace, in that they bring the villagers together in advantageous relationships and generate a common sense of community. The system is self-sustaining in that, once in place, the values of sociative peace intensify and broaden. Prestige goes to the chief who deals effectively with chiefs in other communities, to the trader with many partners in other villages, to the host with many interesting guests from other tribes, and to the shaman with an intertribal practice. Intertribal marriage leads to bilingualism, kin groups, and friendships that cross tribal lines—and, ultimately, to yet more intertribal marriages.

Intermarriage and the exchange of goods and services creates a positive basis for peace in the Upper Xingu. This peace is by no means absolute. The violent exceptions to the ethic of peace include the corporal punishment of children, spouse beating, rape (see Gregor 1990a), eruptions of pushing and shoving on the village plaza (rare), and, historically, retaliatory raids against warlike groups to the south of the Xingu basin (also rare).

By far the most important exception to the *pax Xinguana* is the execution of witches. Occurring once every ten to fifteen years among the Mehinaku, witch killings are a potentially explosive source of tension. On a few occasions, the villagers have teamed up with members of allied factions in other tribes to kill witches in their own and neighboring communities. Remarkably, in such instances, further killings rarely occur and the potential for feud is not realized. In only one instance in my records of witchcraft executions was there an immediate revenge killing, and this response ended the violence. In part, the dampening of conflict occurs because the aggrieved individuals resort to countersorcery instead of turning to violence. Their efforts continue until their anger wanes and they lose interest in revenge (Gregor 1977).

As is true of other peaceful, small-scale societies (Knauft 1987), the villagers try to put the deaths from witchcraft executions behind them. "Let it be" was one of my informant's comments in explanation of why he had not avenged the execution of a kinsman he loved.[4] The Xinguanos are consciously aware that violence is atavistic and threatens the continuity of the larger system of peace. Whenever witchcraft executions have brought them to the abyss of revenge warfare, they have been able to step back. Moreover, contrary to appearances, fear of witchcraft functions as a mechanism of *separative peace*. Separative peace keeps potential antagonists apart and prevents conflict. In the Xingu, witchcraft beliefs are a deterrent to misconduct. They insure courtesy. "Do you know him?" an informant asked while pointing out an older man. "He is a real witch. I said to him: 'I will be your friend.' If he were not my friend he would kill me. Therefore I pretend to like him." Since one cannot be sure who is a witch, a policy of appeasement makes good sense. Serious theft, intertribal vandalism, the robbing of fish traps, and other mischief are restrained because of fear of witchcraft.

As is true of the institutions of sociative peace, fear and the resulting pattern of deterrence, once in place, is self-generating. Fear of witchcraft, the practice of appeasement, and the friction inherent in intertribal relations lead to resentment. The system is so structured, however, that direct expression of resentment is both unmannerly and unwise. Instead, it is expressed obliquely in a host of vivid, out-group stereotypes and in the taunting and exploitation of spouses from other tribes and unwanted visitors. The victims nurse their resentments. The anger and friction developed by the system is projected onto out-groups. "The x tribe is angry with us," I was frequently told, the identity of x varying from occasion to occasion. The system of sociative peace is thereby balanced by the oppositional, centrifugal characteristics of Xingu life. There is always ample fuel to feed the fear and anger that smolder in the Xingu villages.

The Role of Symbolism

The examples of barter, intermarriage, ritual, and witchcraft suggest that the institutional basis of the Xingu peace system has two facets. Joined by kinship and common interest but separated by language, ethnic differences, and the fear of witchcraft, the Xinguanos keep the system delicately balanced. The balance, however, is constantly being tested. To maintain it, the Xinguanos need reminders that it is in their interest to meet the challenge.

However, many of the most significant peace-promoting behaviors occur at infrequent intervals. Trade and intermarriage, for example, are sporadic events that demand considerable commitment of resources and time. This raises a problem, since humans seem to require more frequent and less costly incentives if they are to remember who they are and how they ought to behave. It is here that ideology and expressive symbols serve the villagers. Unlike marriage, talk is cheap. Little more than talk, many of the values, images, and metaphors of peace are easily produced, easily transported, and easily renewed. They are, nonetheless, a fundamental basis of harmony. They provide a set of expectations about how others will respond to positive gestures and how they will react to provocation. Crucially, the symbolism of peace stands at the interface of cultural systems and systems of social action. It is embodied in mythology, ritual, language, rationales for institutions, and stereotypes associated with roles and social groups. These *dramatize* and *intensify* the underlying values and norms of peace; they *condense, idealize,* and *internalize* key values, thereby building moral and emotional messages into individuals' expectations and perceptions of behavior; and they create a shared, cognitive understanding of social relations in which nonviolence is expected and even inevitable. Ultimately, they structure a concept of a peaceful personal identity and what it means to be human.

✦ Symbols of Unity and Separation

In the Xingu, the overriding moral question about individuals, relationships, and cultures is the question of violence and nonviolence. So fundamental is this view of the world that it forms the basis for the first questions about anything in the environment that is new or unexpected, be it human, animal, or even a new artifact with a potential for harm. In 1985, for example, I took the Mehinaku chief on a tour of the zoo in Rio de Janeiro. His first question upon seeing a new animal was: "Is it ferocious [*japujaitsi;* an angry person] [or] is it peaceful [*awujitsi;* a good person]?"

The concept of the good is tied to peacefulness. A villager's reputation and moral worth depend on being circumspect in behavior, avoiding confrontations, and rarely showing anger. These behaviors are regarded as "harmonious" and aesthetically pleasing. In Mehinaku, the term for peaceful conduct is described by the same term (*ketepepei*) as that used for visually pleasing objects and suggests beauty and balance. In relationships, the *ketepepei* individual is outgoing, sociable, well-dispositioned. The good citizen is therefore peaceful in response to both the moral imperative of peace and the aesthetics of behavior. The violent man lacks the requisite sensitivity, killing and maiming others, often without motive, and becomes "ugly" in the process. He loses human status: is "not a person." Such individuals are said to be physically identifiable.

The philosophy of peace is the main principle of interaction among the Xingu tribes. Slightly different ideas code the behavior in different Xingu groups. Basso (1973) describes the Carib concept of *ifutisu*. The prevailing culture of the region, however, is that violence is ugly, dangerous, and inhuman, while peace defines what is human and morally valued. This ethic, with the exceptions already noted, is realized in behavior: Xinguanos are usually nonviolent. Moreover, in the villagers' view, breaches of the peace are exceptional and frightening. Children are lectured by their parents to avoid physical confrontations. Shamans use magical techniques to soothe angry children and to "weaken" the fury of non-Xingu Indians and Brazilians. No prestige is accorded to the warrior; nor is it to the killer of a witch. On the contrary, those who participate in a killing are stigmatized by what they have done and they must take ritual precautions to protect themselves from contamination. The overall pattern is one in which peace is the primary ethical principle of community life.

✦ Symbols of Violence and Separation

Peace in the Upper Xingu is dependent on the institutions and symbolism of sociative peace. Yet, as in most societies, the philosophy of peace does not stand alone. Rather it is contrasted with its opposite: violence, war, aggression, and anger. I have maintained that this mix of unity and separation that characterizes the relationship among the villagers strengthens the Xingu peace. The same may be said of the balance of symbols. Expressions of disengagement and opposition serve as foils for symbols of alliance and sociality. Displays of aggression and violence dramatize the ideology of peace, letting it be seen in relief.

That the villagers exemplify this perspective is readily apparent when they articulate their philosophy of peace. Ask an informant about why the Mehinaku are peaceful and the discussion inevitably shifts to the dangers of not being peaceful: the horrors of warfare and the ugliness of violence. The most dramatic symbols in the villagers' repertory are the *wild Indian* (*wajaiyu*), the *witch,* and *blood.*

The wajaiyu. The *wajaiyu* includes all non-Xingu Indians, especially those who in the past raided the villagers. From the Xinguano perspective, the *wajaiyu* is the antithesis of the civilized Xinguano, or *putaka:* "He beats his children. He rapes his wife. He shoots arrows at the white man's planes. He splits people's heads with clubs. He kidnaps children and burns villages. He kills his own kin. War for him is a festival."[5]

The villagers have good reason to fear and despise the *wajaiyu*. The Mehinaku chief still bears a scar from when he was ambushed and shot by a bowman from the Carib-speaking Txicao tribe. But the *wajaiyu* is more than a physical threat. He is a shadow figure, a screen upon which the villagers project their darkest imaginings about the human condition. As such, the *wajaiyu* puts the peaceful Xinguano into vivid relief. The villagers use the image of the *wajaiyu* to stress what is proper and civilized. An angry child will be ridiculed as a *wajaiyu*. In the men's house, in the center of the village, the men perform grotesque imitations of wild Indian speeches. A mother grooming her reluctant child says, "stop moving or you will crawl with vermin like a *wajaiyu*."

The witch. Another symbol, that of the witch, makes the same point but from the perspective of relationships within the village. According to the Xinguanos, there are no natural deaths. Witches cause, or at least abet, sickness and death. Although apparently a kinsman and a comrade,[6] the witch lacks the essential characteristic of humanity, that of empathy with his fellows. The witch, say the villagers, "does not feel sadness for other people's pain." In this he resembles the wild Indians beyond the borders of the Xingu reservations. Outside the pale of humanity, and not resonating with others' feelings, the witch is unpredictable and acts without motivation. In answer to the question, "Why does the witch want to kill people?" a villager typically responds: "How should I know! *I* am not a witch. The witch is not a *real* person." Like the wild Indian, the witch embodies impulses of anger and revenge that are forbidden to the peaceful, generous Xinguano: "If you don't give him food, he'll kill you. If he says: 'Give me a little salt,' you give it to him quick. If you don't give it to him you better hide it . . . the witch is mindless."

Blood. The final symbol associated with violence that we shall examine is blood. For the Mehinaku, and for most of the other Xinguano tribes, blood is a powerful and generally negative symbol. It evokes strong feelings of disgust and revulsion. When cooking fish and fowl, the Mehinaku take care that it is well done, to avoid bloodiness. All red meat other than monkey (a food that is profoundly ambivalent for the villagers) is taboo, in part because of its bloodiness. "We don't eat animals with blood," explain the Mehinaku, "and so our bellies are never hot with anger." Villagers who are bleeding, whether from injuries, ritually inflicted wounds, or menstruation, are potentially defiling. Killing is wrong, in part because it produces wounds and blood. No matter that it is the victim that bleeds, not the killer. And the corpse, an object of horror, is buried a long distance from the village. The blood is magically contaminating and defiling to the killers. It enters their faces and stomachs; it bloats their cheeks and abdomens and generates a foul odor. Even two decades after a witch execution, the physical signs on the perpetrators are recognizable: "Do you see him?" an informant whispers, pointing to a man who executed a witch more than twenty years before. "He is a killer. Look at the size of his stomach!"

There are magical methods of preventing contamination from violence. The killers may vomit and take medicines to eliminate their victim's blood. The moral stain that taints "a fiend for killing people," however, can never be wholly wiped clean. For years after the act, reminders of the deed surround the village. The victim's ghost stalks his grave and cries out in pain. To avoid the place where he was killed, the Mehinaku cut new trails through the forest. Passersby who hear the dead man's shrieks are haunted and fall ill.

The symbolism of blood as a contaminating fluid separates those who transgress from the civilized community. With the symbol of the witch and the wild Indian, it is part of a larger system of separative peace. These symbols are emotionally charged, perhaps beyond any others in the Xinguano repertory. Witches, wild Indians, and blood arouse intense emotions of hatred, disgust, and fear. Ironically, they also dramatize the values of peace and deter destructive conduct. Peace in the Xingu is thereby composed of sociative and separative elements which stand together in an uneasy balance. The result is one of the more remarkable peace systems thus far documented in the ethnographic literature. Let us now illustrate the symbolism of Xingu peace through one of its more dramatic expressions, the ritual of the Yawari.

✦ The Yawari Ritual

We know that the Xingu peace system dates at least from the time of the first recorded exploration, that of Karl Von den Steinen in 1887. The system is surely much older, since in Von den Steinen's time an elaborate ritual expression of peace was already in place. As we know it today, ritual in the Xingu is composed of intertribal and local ceremonies. Intertribal rituals undoubtedly began as small community rites that had the capacity to include others in wider networks of participation. If they were attractive to other groups, they were deliberately imported through the region. Today, all of the intertribal rituals bear the stamp of their local origins: the Xinguanos identify them as having begun among a specific tribe or linguistic group. The rituals include song texts from more than one language, reflecting their movement from tribe to tribe; and a few of the rituals are currently being promulgated and learned by new tribes who wish to include them in their repertory of rituals. This is the case of the Yawari,[7] originally a Trumái ritual, that the Mehinaku are currently learning. As Yaka, the Mehinaku chief, explained to me in 1989: "We Mehinaku don't yet know this ritual well. We have no Yawari singer. The Yawalapiti have one . . .

but not us. It is not our tradition. In the past I was taught the Yawari at the Waura. But the younger people still do not know it."

All of the Xingu intertribal rituals reflect elements of alliance and opposition. During the rituals, the villagers trade, dance and sing together, and visit one another as relatives and friends. They also wrestle competitively, take pleasure in the defeat of the visitor, and fear witches, thieves, and vandals from other tribes.

In the Yawari, the forms of alliance and opposition are particularly dramatic. The Yawari is a ritual in which members of opposed tribes pair off as kinsmen, but then hurl insults and subsequently wax-tipped spears at one another. It is a form of controlled warfare: of pleasure in others' pain; of biting verbal aggression; and of military displays of weapons and warriors. Yet it occurs in a highly regulated context of peaceful relations, kinship, and mutual pleasure.

The Yawari begins with a formal invitation to the chiefs of a neighboring tribe. This is delivered by ceremonial messengers (*waka*). The *waka* are part of the shared structure of ritual interaction among the Xingu tribes. They invite other tribes to the great ceremonies celebrating the inauguration of new chiefs and to the mourning rituals for those recently deceased. When the guests arrive at a host village for a ritual, the *waka* ceremonially lead them into the community, guide them through the phases of the ceremony, present them with gifts and food, and bid them leave when it is time to go. The *waka* symbolize the formal context of intertribal ritual and the friendly intent of the host tribe. In the Yawari, the *waka* do not take part in the hurling of insults and spears that are the focus of the ritual. Unlike the frequent informal visits between kin or traders, the *waka* raise the level of interaction to that of separate political communities interacting within the larger intertribal culture.

In August of 1989, the Mehinaku *waka* invited the Yawalapiti tribe to participate in a Yawari.[8] Typically, when relationships are tense between tribes, the *waka* are received only after they have been left languishing in the sun for several hours. The Yawalapiti, however, were on good terms with the Mehinaku. In short order, their chief emerged from his house and addressed the *waka* in a formal speech and then painted their backs with annatto dye[9] as a symbol of an accepted invitation.

In the Mehinaku village, the men had set to work making *atlatls*[10] and spears tipped with wax. Setting up a straw dummy in the center of the plaza, they hurled the spears at the target as part of their practice for the arrival of their neighbors.

When the Yawalapiti arrived, they set up camp just outside the Mehinaku village. The *waka* ceremonially led the visiting chiefs into the village and provided them with fish and bread made from manioc flour. That night within their camp, the Yawalapiti shamans sang the Yawari songs. Their chants and rattles, heard in the Mehinaku village, provided a mysterious backdrop to the ritual event. I emphasize that the Mehinaku and most of the Yawalapiti shared in this sense of the uncanny. Not only is the Yawari a new ritual for these Arawakan tribes, but as is true of most of the intertribal rituals, the meaning of many songs is unclear. In the Yawari, most of the songs are in Trumái, a linguistically isolated language that is the least widely known of the Xingu tongues. Aurore Monod-Becquelin, an ethnographer who has worked with the Trumái, has translated some of the Yawari songs as first-person representations of animals and spirits, a pattern that is characteristic of the other Xingu rituals. Much of the meaning is obscure, even to the Trumái, however, since many words are in other languages (Monod-Becquelin 1978: 8, 11). The Mehinaku find the meaning of the ritual not in the song texts but in the actual event of alliance and opposition that relates the two tribes.

The next morning, the villagers painted themselves with various patterns, representing jaguars, hawks, and eagles. Many other features of Yawari adornment (such as the use of black pigment) symbolize aggression and danger. However, the details of body paints and costume—as with the songs—are secondary to the larger structure of the ritual.

✦ The Ritual and the Relationship of Cousins

The Xingu peace system has an institutional base in the political and kinship organization of the Xingu tribes. To a large extent, however, peaceful relations between tribes is personally based. Individual relationships of bartering, entertaining visitors, and marriage choice are the foundation of the larger system. At times, relations between individuals become the symbolic model for larger relationships between tribes. Crucial to the ritual structure of the Yawari, as Monod-Becquelin has described for the Trumái (1978), is the relationship of cross-cousins.[11] Among the Xingu tribes, cross-cousins are potential marriage partners and in-laws. After a marriage, the relationship of same-sex cross-cousins is characterized by rules of extreme respect and obligation: a man must not say the name of his wife's brother and he gives him obligatory gifts of goods and labor. Such demonstrations of respect and obligation are a source of resentment as well as alliance. Within marriage, this hostility is suppressed or disguised in subversive gossip and innuendo; but when cousins are not related by marriage they will nonetheless express the tension of potential affinity through obligatory joking and mock insults.

Incorporating elements of both alliance and antagonism, the relationship of cross-cousins is an interpersonal model of the relationship of the Xingu tribes. In the Yawari, cross-cousins are the target of aggression.[12] In fact, ritualized antagonism toward these relatives is the defining event of the ritual. The Mehinaku chief explained:

You do not taunt other relatives. *Only* your cross-cousins. It is not like the ritual of mourning. In that ritual you wrestle with everyone, with your nephew, with your uncle, that is the tradition. Not so with the Yawari. People battle with their cross-cousins, not with anyone else. It would sadden others to battle with them. "Why have you shot me?" they would say.

In the 1989 Yawari, the Mehinaku and the Yawalapiti lined up in front of a straw dummy. Each individual took a turn shouting insults and striking the dummy with a wax-tipped spear. Typically, an insult began with a call of "Drooo!"—an imitation of the whizzing of a flying spear—and then the name of an intended victim, always a cross-cousin. The insults mixed humorous and occasionally cruel invective, much of which was sexual in nature or based on the cousin's habits or appearance. Some typical examples include, "Oh, my cross-cousin, you sex fiend, you are covered with boils!" or "Genital-hair woman!" or "Your penis is grotesquely large!" Some insults were bitingly sarcastic. One man, who was unable to attract a wife or lover, was told, "Oh, you have so many wives!"; another, often ridiculed for wearing shorts begged from Brazilian visitors, was reminded that "the skin on your thighs has turned white" (from being out of the sun).

Other taunts focused on personality traits, ridiculing the cross-cousin as stingy, angry, and untruthful. Although the mood was raucous, many jeers were genuinely offensive. Prominent individuals received special attention from the jokesters. The Mehinaku chief was belittled as stingy and unwilling to share the gifts that he had received from filmmakers then resident in the community.[13] Particularly noteworthy was that some taunts and jibes included innuendos of witchcraft accusations, which in the Xingu can lead to executions.

Many insults hurled by the villagers were intended not just for their cross-cousins, but for the entire opposing tribe. The Mehinaku were on the verge of leaving their community (located on a site that formerly had been loaned to them by their opponents). Hence the Mehinaku chief's taunt, directed to all of the visiting tribe: "Oh! My cousins! You told us that we could make our village here. I remember your speech. Now you are glad that we are leaving. Well, I am happy that you are sending us off!" The Yawalapiti responded: "Go ahead and get going to your new village. We want to burn your houses. Go off and so much the worse for you there!"

Hurling spears and insults at the straw dummy is regarded as the preliminary for the main event, which is throwing wax-tipped spears at people. A hit is a painful experience, as I can testify from having been struck by a stray spear as I was taking photographs. Like all periods of license in which normal rules are suspended, the Yawari is potentially dangerous. In the past, some men have concealed rocks and razor blades under the wax tips of spears. Even more threatening to the larger peace system, Yawaris have sometimes gotten out of hand and degenerated into vicious melees, as the Mehinaku chief recalls:

The Auiti tribe went to the Kuikuru. The Auiti taunted them: "Drooo, the Kuikuru are witches," they said. "The Kuikuru eat turtles (an unattractive food); they are fiends for turtle," they said. And therefore the Kuikuru hurled many spears and hit the Auiti. And the Auiti got the Kuikuru back. There were not many Auiti, but they were strong! Tak! Tak! Tak! The spears struck home. The Auiti grabbed the Kuikuru's spears and broke them. Not just cross-cousins did this, but everyone. It was a war! Then the Auiti went off. The chief, all the women, all of them, they went off. They were not given manioc bread [a symbol of the host-guest relationship]. They just went off.

Keeping the Ritual Peaceful

Events like these, though rare, show that the Yawari is a serious affair with a potential for aggressive contact between the Xingu tribes. The mechanisms that keep the ritual in control duplicate and model the devices that sustain the Xingu peace.

Of greatest importance is that the Yawari expresses aggression *within a structure of rules* and *in the presence of bystanders*. As the villagers repeatedly emphasize, the only appropriate target is a cross-cousin. Serious injury to one's cousin is prevented by the fact that he is partly protected by a small shield. Moreover, the spear must be tipped with wax and it must be thrown well below the waist. The rules of the event are such that aggressors and their targets change roles. If a villager inflicts too much harm he may find himself equally injured moments later.

In both the Yawari and ordinary life, the rules are enforced by bystanders, whose opinion has an impact on behavior. The chiefs have a special obligation to witness and respond to breaches of good conduct. They displayed controlled behavior and rebuked overly aggressive individuals (usually young men) in their group. The villagers say that it is the chiefs' fault if the Yawari degenerates into a brawl. In the larger Xingu world, bystanders also preserve the peace. Privacy is minimal, and an extraordinarily efficient gossip system exposes each individual to public scrutiny (Gregor 1977). The chiefs have a key role in the community in restraining aggression and modeling idealized nonviolent behavior (see Gregor 1990b).

In the Yawari, as in the case of the larger peace system, the villagers reflect on the nature of peace and violence. They are at pains to remind one another that Yawari violence is not serious. They encapsulate the event, deny that it is a significant breach of the peace, and tell the observer, who may be somewhat intimidated by the display, that: "We weren't really fighting each other. We were just teasing one another, it was just a game. . . . There is just a little sadness in it for the cross-cousin . . . (soon) the anger is over and you are kinsmen again." Significantly, the ritual closes with a reminder that the participants are, after all, friends and kin. The last contestants approach their targets and touch them as lightly as possible

254 ◆ *Thomas Gregor*

with their spears, signifying that their real intent has not been to do harm.[14]

The same self-aware attitude that constrains Yawari violence limits aggression among the Xingu tribes. The Xinguanos know that aggression, be it vandalism by young men, theft, or witchcraft killings, invites retaliation and threatens the Xingu peace. As in the Yawari, the villagers avoid serious aggression because it jeopardizes a larger and valued structure.

An additional restraint on Yawari violence is magical beliefs. Blood, we recall, is a defiling and dangerous substance. Bleeding and shedding blood are to be avoided. In the Yawari, many ritual precautions focus on the hazards of being struck and the danger of blood. The night before the event, the villagers avoid going to sleep, lest they have a dream that foretells being injured. One of the young men explained: "The Yawari is frightening. If you were to sleep your dream might not be good, you would be struck. . . . Yesterday we did not sleep and therefore they did not get us a lot. . . . In preparing for the Yawari, you do not sleep. It is dangerous and frightening!" At the ritual, injured participants induced vomiting to remove contaminating blood, and hopefully to prevent injury in the next Yawari. As in the more general beliefs about blood and aggression, these practices intensify the villagers' anxieties about violence, and thereby inhibit it.

Finally, the Yawari, like the larger Xingu system, incorporates many elements of highly valued sociative peace. These include the celebration of the cross-cousin relationship—a symbol of marital alliance as well as of opposition. The incorporative power of this symbol is best illustrated by the end of the ceremony, during which the Mehinaku women danced with the Yawalapiti men. Many other elements within the ceremony repeated the message of association and connectedness, including trading, visiting, and gossiping. The ritual is not only one of opposition and antagonism: it is also an expression of the warmth that binds the Xingu tribes.

◆ The Xingu Culture of Peace

The *pax Xinguana* is an extraordinary human achievement. Though they speak different languages, the tribes of the region have created a rich and enduring culture of peace. The system is founded on the institutions of sociative peace: intermarriage, trade, ritual, and peaceful values. In an ideal world, that would be sufficient. But all social life generates friction and resentment, and this must be taken account of in a peace system. The Xinguanos are noteworthy in that they have taken the darker side of human relationships and turned it to their advantage: opposition, fear, and conflict serve the larger system of peaceful relations. This pattern is particularly clear in witchcraft beliefs (which are among the most malign of human institutions). In the Xingu, these encourage courteous behavior. The pattern is also evident in symbols that contrast with, and thereby dramatize, peace, such as those of blood, witches, and wild Indians.

The symbolism of Xingu peace finds vivid expression in the Yawari. A rudimentary functionalist analysis might interpret the ritual as a safety valve that allows a direct expression of aggression in a system that normally constrains or deflects these feelings. I am sure that this explanation is at least partly correct: the villagers enjoy having the opportunity to inflict some pain on their friends and kinsmen. They see ritualized violence (including wrestling) as both expressing and vitiating anger. I would, however, go beyond this interpretation. The Yawari is not only a safety valve, it is a superb expression of the conflicting values that are at the heart of the Xingu system. The Xingu peace includes both separative and sociative elements—as does the Yawari. The dialectic works because symbolic expressions of the system (such as the Yawari) generate and sustain a view of the world that discourages violence. The rituals, metaphors, and symbolic devices we have examined have far-ranging implications for behavior. Together, they create an overwhelming symbolic structure that makes the Xingu peace intense, rich, and persuasive.

✦ Notes

I gratefully acknowledge support from the United States Institute of Peace (USIP grant 141–1–89) and the Harry Frank Guggenheim Foundation in preparation of this chapter.

1. In 1985, Detroit had a homicide rate of 58.2 per 100,000. Statistics are cited in Knauft (1987:464).

2. Between 1967 and 1989, I completed more than two years of fieldwork among the Upper Xingu tribes. Most of that time was spent with the Mehinaku, but I have also lived with the Yawalapiti, visited most of the other tribes, and worked with informants from all of the Xingu groups. The quotes in this chapter are from Mehinaku or Yawalapiti informants.

3. Approximately 35 percent of marriages are to members of other tribes.

4. Such killings are also restrained by the Xinguanos' uncertainty about how to identify witches. "I would not kill a witch even if he killed my sons," explains one of the Xingu leaders. "There is no way to know with certainty who is guilty. Most of those who have been killed were needlessly killed. Their deaths were ugly affairs."

5. It is well to note that, in recent years, the villagers have moved beyond these stereotypes to form alliances with the *wajaiyu* for the purposes of confronting threats to their lands.

6. All alleged witches are males.

7. A film of the 1989 Mehinaku Yawari is referenced under Gregor 1991. Additional descriptions of the Yawari ritual appear in Monod-Becquelin (1978), Galvão (1950), and Murphy and Quain (1966).

8. The description that follows of the Yawari ritual is condensed in that each

of the repetitive stages of the ceremony is not reported. The intention is to emphasize those portions of the ritual that deal with opposition and alliance between the Xingu tribes. The term *Yawari* is the closest Mehinaku approximation to the name of the ritual, which has been glossed as *Jawari* in the literature.

9. A bright red dye from the annatto plant is occasionally used for coloring by food processors in the United States.

10. According to Robert Carneiro (pers. com.) the Yawari's is the only use of the *atlatl*, a device for hurling spears, among native South American peoples.

11. The children of the mother's brother and the father's sister are cross-cousins.

12. Most of the villagers have so-called "classifactory" cross-cousins in all of the Xingu villages. These are individuals who in fact are very distant relatives, but act as if they were more closely related. Like true cross-cousins they maintain joking relationships. Even when many miles off, they are "remembered." After an explosive sneeze, a Mehinaku may jokingly exclaim: "Ah-ho, my cross-cousin!"—the Mehinaku equivalent of, "God bless you."

13. At the time, I was coproducing a film, *Feathered Arrows,* with the British Broadcasting Corporation. We had introduced many gifts into the community, as well as paying a substantial fee to the villagers. The issue of the fair distribution of these resources was a serious one.

14. Monod-Becquelin (1978) notes that the Trumái burn all the spears at the conclusion of the ritual.

✦ References

Basso, Ellen B.
   1973   *The Kalapalo Indians of Central Brazil.* New York: Holt, Rinehart and Winston.

Galtung, Johan
   1981   Social Cosmology and the Concept of Peace. *Journal of Peace Research* XVIII: 183–189.

Galvão, Eduardo
   1950   O Uso do Propulsar entre as Tribos do Alto Xingu. *Revista do Museu Paulista,* N.S. 6:469–477.

Gregor, Thomas
   1977   *Mehinaku: The Drama of Daily Life in a Brazilian Indian Village.* Chicago: University of Chicago Press.
   1985   *Anxious Pleasures: The Sexual Lives of an Amazonian People.* Chicago: University of Chicago Press.
   1990a   Male Dominance and Sexual Coercion, in *Cultural Psychology: Essays on Comparative Human Development,* James W. Stigler, Richard A. Shweder, and Gilbert Herdt, eds. Chicago: University of Chicago Press.
   1990b   Uneasy Peace: Why Xinguanos Don't Make War, in *The Anthropology of War.* Advanced Seminar Series of the School of American

Research, Jonathan Haas, ed., Cambridge: Cambridge University Press.
1991   *Feathered Arrows.* 16mm color film. British Broadcasting Corporation.

Knauft, Bruce M.
1987   Reconsidering Violence in Simple Human Societies. *Current Anthropology* 28:457–500.

Melko, Matthew
1973   *52 Peaceful Societies.* Oakville: CPRI Press.

Monod-Becquelin, Aurore
1978   Contribution to the Study of the Javari in the Xingu Culture. Unpublished manuscript.

Murphy, Robert F., and Buell Quain
1966   *The Trumái Indians of Central Brazil.* Monographs of the American Ethnological Society 24. Seattle: University of Washington Press.

Nakhre, Amrut
1976   Meanings of Nonviolence: A Study of Satyagrahi Attitudes. *Journal of Peace Research* 13:185–196.

Otterbein, Keith F.
1970   *The Evolution of War: A Crosscultural Study.* New Haven, CN: HRAF Press.

Ross, Marc Howard
1986   The Limits to Social Structure: Social Structural and Psychocultural Explanations for Political Conflict and Violence. *Anthropological Quarterly* 59:171–176.

Sipes, R. G.
1973   War, Sports and Aggression: An Empirical Test of Two Rival Theories. *American Anthropologist* 75:64–86.

Steinen, Karl Von den
1940   *Entre os Aborigenes do Brasíl Central.* Separata da Revista do Arquivo 34–58. São Paulo, Brazil: Departamento de Cultura.

✦ 11
Toward a Pedagogy of the Anthropology of Peace and Nonviolence

Leslie E. Sponsel

The body of literature on aspects of the anthropology of violence and war is both rich and rapidly growing, but little attention has been given to the anthropology of nonviolence and peace. In this final chapter, Leslie Sponsel provides a systematic inventory of this literature, listing available titles that are important for both teaching and research.

—THE EDITORS

✦ Both peace studies and anthropology include three basic components: research, education, and action. Each of these components is important. This book, intended as it is to stimulate teaching as well as research on anthropological aspects of peace and nonviolence, accordingly ends with some brief remarks and information toward a pedagogy of the anthropology of peace and nonviolence. A full reference to each of the citations given is in the resource list at the end of the chapter.

The resource list is in two sections—A. General and B. Anthropology. It is further divided into: Periodicals; Abstracts; Encyclopedias; Directories; Textbooks; More Specialized Books; Anthologies; Case Studies; Bibliographies; Literature Reviews; and Films and Videos.

The chapter also includes a sample syllabus. As in any course, the format may vary: it may be lecture, seminar, or a combination of these. The grade may be based on quizzes and/or examinations; book reviews (written and/or oral); library and/or field research papers (written, with brief oral summary in class); individual and/or group discussions of articles and/or books; a diary or journal wherein the students summarize class lectures and discussions, readings, and especially their reaction to these; or some combination of the above.

It is especially useful to use films, such as *Dead Birds,* the classic about traditional warfare in New Guinea among the Dani, or selections

259

from the following Yanomami titles: *The Yanomamo of the Orinoco, The Feast, Ax Fight, Magical Death,* and *Contact: The Yanomami Indians of Brazil.* A sequence of films that has proven especially effective as a special segment with a regional focus on New Guinea, Australia, and Oceania is *Dead Birds, First Contact, The Last Tasmanians, Angels of War, Halflife: A Parable for the Nuclear Age,* and *Tahiti Witness.* The *Meo* is a moving illustration, using the context of refugees from the Vietnam War, of the militarization of an indigenous society.

The course may have a topical, regional, and/or problem-and-issue focus. For instance, the course could be organized around these successive subjects: human nature, violence and war, nonviolence and peace, the transition from nonviolence/peace to violence/war, and vice versa. Another possibility is to use bibliographies on the anthropology of war and related matters, selecting a combination of themes from those works that include a convenient list or index of topics. Or the course might have a much narrower focus: a single specialized theme might be chosen; or a small selection (see below).

Although the wealth of literature on anthropological aspects of violence/war is growing, much less attention has been given to nonviolence/peace. Among very useful bibliographies on the anthropology of war, human rights, and related topics are Divale (1973); Downing and Kushner (1988); and Ferguson and Farragher (1988). Also see two cumulative indexes available for the advocacy journal, *Cultural Survival Quarterly.* So far, there is no general textbook on the anthropology of nonviolence/peace and/or violence/war. It has, however, proven illuminating for a class to read through one of the recent textbooks in peace studies (Barnaby 1988; Barash 1991). The instructor can bring out aspects that are relevant to anthropology, or vice versa. Although they are now a bit dated, the best reviews of the anthropological literature on war are Ferguson (1984) and Otterbein (1973) (see also Otterbein 1993). Chapter 1 of *The Anthropology of Peace and Nonviolence* is the first review of the literature of the anthropology of nonviolence and peace (see also Sponsel 1994b). A rich resource is the annotated bibliography of peaceful societies by Bonta (1993). Among encyclopedias, *The Encyclopedia of Cultural Anthropology,* which is due for publication this year (1994), has numerous articles on aspects of peace and nonviolence, and these could serve as a springboard for lectures or as articles for students to read and discuss. *The International Encyclopedia of Social Sciences,* although dated (1968), remains a useful source for overviews of key topics and concepts. Also especially useful are *World Encyclopedia of Peace* (Laszlo 1986) and the periodical, *Peace Review,* with its general and accessible articles. At least sixteen anthologies are now available, as are excellent, book-length, ethnographic case studies.

There are also excellent sources for exploring narrower aspects of the subject. Among textbooks on anthropology, for contrasting theoretical approaches to the anthropology of war, see Haas (1990); on cross-cultural conflict resolution, see Avruch et al. (1991). Other documented topics are cross-cultural analysis of war (Otterbein 1985); enculturation/socialization for nonviolence (Howell and Willis 1989; Montagu 1978); ethnic conflict (Horowitz 1985; LeVine and Campbell 1972; Montville 1990; Nash 1989); genocide (Kuper 1981; Staub 1989); homicide (Martin and Wilson 1988); the innate aggressionist position (Feilbeman 1987; Montagu 1976); the militarization of indigenous zones (Clay 1987; Ferguson and Whitehead 1992), nuclear armament and war (Bumsted 1985; Firth 1988; Kiste 1974; Turnbull 1972; Turner and Pitts 1986; Worsley and Hadjor 1986); the pacification of indigenous societies (Rodman and Cooper 1979); primate conflict resolution and peacefulness (DeWaal 1989; Mason and Mendoza 1993; Silverberg and Gray 1992; Smuts 1985); the role of anthropology in war (Goldschmidt 1979; Wakin 1992); and war in ecological perspective (Ferguson 1984; Vayda 1976).

It is useful to use an introductory general textbook on peace studies to provide background (Barnaby 1988; Barash 1991), then to move on to books on selected key topics (such as human nature or genocide) for exploration in greater depth. This can be followed by one or more anthologies, which will provide a broad, cross-cultural sample, and then book-length case studies to provide detailed coverage of particular cultures.

The rest of this chapter is devoted to the resource list and a brief outline of a sample course on the anthropology of peace and nonviolence. The course outline is given first:

✦ Sample Syllabus

The Anthropology of Peace and Nonviolence

I. INTRODUCTION
Introduction to course, peace studies, and anthropology.

II. FOUNDATIONS: HUMAN NATURE

Stevenson, Leslie
   1987   *Seven Theories of Human Nature*. New York: Oxford University Press.
Kohn, Alfie
   1990   *The Brighter Side of Human Nature: Altruism and Empathy in Everyday Life*. New York: Basic Books.
Montagu, Ashley, ed.
   1976   *The Nature of Human Aggression*. New York: Oxford University Press.

III. PRIMATE NONVIOLENCE AND PEACE

de Waal, Frans
  1989   *Peacemaking Among Primates.* Cambridge: Harvard University Press.
Smuts, Barbara
  1985   *Sex and Friendship in Baboons.* New York: Aldine de Gruyter.

IV. VALUES AND INSTITUTIONS OF PEACE AND NONVIOLENCE: A CROSS-CULTURAL SURVEY

Montagu, Ashley, ed.
  1978   *Learning Non-Aggression: The Experience of Non-Literate Societies.* New York: Oxford University Press.
Howell, Signe, and Roy Willis, eds.
  1989   *Societies at Peace: Anthropological Perspectives.* New York: Routledge.
Sponsel, Leslie E., and Thomas Gregor, eds.
  1994   *The Anthropology of Peace and Nonviolence.* Boulder: Lynne Rienner Publishers.

V. ETHNOGRAPHIC CASE STUDIES OF NONVIOLENT AND PEACEFUL SOCIETIES

Briggs, Jean L.
  1970   *Never in Anger: Portrait of an Eskimo Family.* Cambridge: Harvard University Press.
Dentan, Robert K.
  1968   *The Semai: A Nonviolent People of Malaya.* New York: Holt, Rinehart and Winston.
Howell, Signe
  1984   *Society and Cosmos: Chewong of Peninsular Malaysia.* New York: Oxford University Press.
Turnbull, Colin M.
  1983   *The Mbuti Pygmies: Change and Adaptation.* New York: Holt, Rinehart and Winston.

✦ Resources from Peace Studies

Periodicals

Aggressive Behavior. Issues from 1975 to date.
Bulletin of Peace Proposals 1970– .
Conflict Management and Peace Science 1985– .
International Journal on World Peace 1984– .
International Peace Research Newsletter 1963– .

Journal of Conflict Resolution 1957– .
Journal of Peace Research 1964– .
Journal of Peace Science 1973– .
Journal of Refugee Studies 1988– .
Peace and Change 1972– .
Peace Research 1969– .
Peace Research Society Papers 1964– .
Peace Research Reviews 1967– .
Peace Review 1989– .

Abstracts

Peace Research Abstracts 1964– .

Encyclopedias

Laszlo, Ervin, and Jong Youl Yoo, eds.
   1986   *World Encyclopedia of Peace,* vols. 1–4. New York: Pergamon.
        (Vol. 4 lists peace institutes, organizations, journals, and bibliographies.)
Levinson, David, and Melvin Ember, eds.
   1994   *The Encyclopedia of Cultural Anthropology,* vols. 1–4.
        Lakeville: American Reference Publishing.
Sills, David L., ed.
   1968   *International Encyclopedia of the Social Sciences,* vols. 1–20.
        New York: Macmillan.

Directories

Day, Alan J., ed.
   1986   *Peace Movements of the World.* Essex: Longman. Institute for
        Defense and Disarmament Studies
   1984   *American Peace Directory.* Cambridge: Ballinger Publishing.
Woodhouse, T., ed.
   1988   *The International Peace Directory.* Plymouth: Northcote
        House.

Textbooks

Barnaby, Frank, ed.
   1988   *The Gaia Peace Atlas.* NY: Doubleday.
Barash, David P.
   1991   *Introduction to Peace Studies.* Belmont: Wadsworth
        Publishing.

Wallensteen, Peter, ed.
1988 *Peace Research: Achievements and Challenges*. Boulder: Westview Press.

Anthologies

Ausenda, G., ed.
1992 *Effects of War on Society*. San Marino: AIEP Editore. Avruch, Kevin, Peter W. Black, and Joseph A. Scimecca, eds.
1991 *Conflict Resolution: Cross-Cultural Perspectives*. Westport: Greenwood Press.
Bohannan, Paul, ed.
1967 *Law and War: Studies in the Anthropology of Conflict*. Garden City: Natural History Press.
Downing, Theodore E., and Gilbert Kushner, eds.
1988 *Human Rights and Anthropology*. Cambridge: Cultural Survival.
Fried, Morton, Marvin Harris, and Robert Murphy, eds.
1968 *War: The Anthropology of Armed Conflict and Aggression*. Garden City: Natural History Press.
Foster, Mary LeCron, and Robert A. Rubinstein, eds.
1986 *Peace and War: Cross-Cultural Perspectives*. New Brunswick: Transaction Publishers.
Ferguson, R. Brian, ed.
1984 *War, Culture, and Environment*. New York: Academic Press.
Ferguson, R. Brian, and Neil L. Whitehead, eds.
1992 *War in the Tribal Zone: Expanding States and Indigenous Warfare*. Santa Fe: School of American Research Press.
Haas, Jonathan, ed.
1990 *The Anthropology of War*. New York: Cambridge University Press.
Halpern, Joel M., ed.
1993 "The Yugoslav Conflict," Special Issue of *The Anthropology of East Europe Review* 11 (1–2):3–126.
Howell, Signe, and Roy Willis, eds.
1989 *Societies at Peace: Anthropological Perspectives*. New York: Routledge.
Lang, Hartmut
1992 The Anthropology of Conflict. *Zeitshcrift für Ethnologie* 1990, Band 115.
Mason, William A., and Sally P. Mendoza, eds.
1993 *Primate Social Conflict*. Albany: State University of New York Press.

Montagu, Ashley, ed.
  1978 *Learning Non-Aggression: The Experience of Non-Literate Societies.* New York: Oxford University Press.
Nettleship, Martin A., et al., eds.
  1975 *War: Its Causes and Consequences.* Chicago: Mouton Publishers.
Nordstrom, Carolyn, and JoAnn Martin, eds.
  1992 *The Paths to Domination, Resistance and Terror.* Berkeley: University of California Press.
Otterbein, Keith
  1993 *Feuding and Warfare: Selected Works of Keith Otterbein.* New York: Gordon and Breach.
Reyna, S. P., and R. E. Downs, eds.
  1993 *Studying War: Anthropological Approaches.* New York: Gordon and Breach.
Riches, David, ed.
  1986 *The Anthropology of Violence.* New York: Basil Blackwell.
Rohl, Vivian J., M. E. R. Nicholson, and Mario D. Zamora, eds.
  1992 *The Anthropology of Peace: Essays in Honor of E. Adamson Hoebel.* Willamsburg: Studies in Third World Societies Publication no. 47, vols. 1 and 2.
Rubinstein, Robert A., and Mary LeCron Foster, eds.
  1988 *The Social Dynamics of Peace and Conflict: Culture in International Security.* Boulder: Westview Press.
Silverberg, James, and J. Patrick Gray, eds.
  1992 *Aggression and Peacefulness in Humans and Other Primates.* New York: Oxford University Press.
Turner, Paul R., and David Pitts, eds.
  1986 *The Anthropology of War and Peace: Perspectives on the Nuclear Age.* Granby: Bergin and Garvey.
Worsley, Peter M., and K. Buenor Hadjor, eds.
  1986 *On the Brink: Nuclear Proliferation and the Third World.* London: Third World Communications.

More Specialized Books

Bumsted, M. Pamela, ed.
  1985 *Nuclear Winter: The Anthropology of Human Survival.* Los Alamos, NM: Los Alamos National Laboratory.
Clay, Jason W., ed.
  1987 Special Issues on Militarization and Indigenous Peoples. *Cultural Survival Quarterly* 11(3–4).

de Waal, Frans
  1989   *Peacemaking Among Primates.* Cambridge: Harvard University Press.
Feilbeman, James Kern
  1987   *The Destroyers: The Underside of Human Nature.* New York: Peter Lang.
Firth, Stewart
  1988   *Nuclear Playground.* Honolulu: University of Hawaii Press.
Goldschmidt, Walter, ed.
  1979   *The Uses of Anthropology.* Washington, D.C.: American Anthropological Association special publication.
Horowitz, Donald L.
  1985   *Ethnic Groups in Conflict.* Berkeley: University of California Press.
Kiste, Robert C.
  1974   *The Bikinians: A Study in Forced Migration.* New York: Holt, Rinehart and Winston.
Kuper, Leo
  1981   *Genocide: Its Political Use in the Twentieth Century.* New Haven: Yale University Press.
LeVine, Robert A., and Donald T. Campbell
  1972   *Ethnocentrism: Theories of Conflict, Ethnic Attitudes, and Group Behavior.* New York: John Wiley.
Martin, Martin, and Margo Wilson
  1988   *Homicide.* New York: Aldine de Gruyter.
Montagu, Ashley
  1976   *The Nature of Human Aggression.* New York: Oxford University Press.
Montville, Joseph V., ed.
  1990   *Conflict and Peacemaking in Multiethnic Societies.* Lexington: Lexington Books.
Nash, Manning
  1989   *The Cauldron of Ethnicity in the Modern World.* Chicago: University of Chicago Press.
Otterbein, Keith
  1985   *The Evolution of War.* New Haven: Human Relations Area Files Press.
Rodman, Margaret, and Matthew Cooper, eds.
  1979   *The Pacification of Melanesia.* Ann Arbor: University of Michigan Press.
Silverberg, James, and J. Patrick Gray, eds.
  1992   *Aggression and Peacefulness in Humans and Other Primates.* New York: Oxford University Press.

Smuts, Barbara
 1985   *Sex and Friendship in Baboons.* New York: Aldine de Gruyter.
Staub, Ervin
 1989   *The Roots of Evil: The Origins of Genocide and Other Group Violence.* New York: Cambridge University Press.
Turnbull, Colin
 1972   *The Mountain People.* New York: Simon and Schuster.
Vayda, Andrew P.
 1976   *War in Ecological Perspective: Persistence, Change, and Adaptive Processes in Three Oceanic Societies.* New York: Plenum.
Wakin, Eric
 1992   *Anthropology Goes to War: Professional Ethics & Counterinsurgency in Thailand.* Madison: University of Wisconsin Center for Southeast Asian Studies, Monograph No. 7.

Case Studies of Nonviolent and Peaceful Societies

(See sample syllabus on page 261, and Bonta 1993).

Case Studies of Violent and Warlike Societies

Boehm, Christopher
 1987   *Blood Revenge: The Enactment and Management of Conflict in Montenegro and Other Tribal Societies.* Philadelphia: University of Pennsylvania Press.
Chagnon, Napoleon A.
 1992   *Yanomamo.* Fourth edition. New York: Harcourt Brace Jovanovich.
Hallpike, C. R.
 1977   *Bloodshed and Vengeance in the Papuan Mountains: The Generation of Conflict in Tauade Society.* New York: Oxford University Press.
Heider, Karl
 1979   *Grand Valley Dani: Peaceful Warriors.* New York: Holt, Rinehart and Winston.
Kiefer, Thomas W.
 1972   *The Tausug: Violence and Law in a Philippine Muslim Society.* Prospect Heights: Waveland Press.
Koch, Klaus-Friedrich
 1974   *War and Peace in Jalemo: The Management of Conflict in Highland New Guinea.* Cambridge: Harvard University Press.

Meggitt, Mervyn
 1977 *Blood Is Their Argument: Warfare Among the Mae Enga Tribesmen of the New Guinea Highlands.* Mountain View: Mayfield Publishing.
Rappaport, Roy A.
 1984 *Pigs for the Ancestors: Ritual in the Ecology of a New Guinea Tribe.* Second edition. New Haven: Yale University Press. Second edition.
Romanucci-Ross, Lola
 1973 *Conflict, Violence, and Morality in a Mexican Village.* Chicago: University of Chicago Press.
Vayda, Andrew P.
 1960 *Maori Warfare.* Wellington: Polynesian Society Maori Monographs No. 2.

Bibliographies

Bonta, Bruce
 1993 *Peaceful Peoples: An Annotated Bibliography.* Metuchen, N.J.: Scarecrow Press.
Candland, Christopher
 1992 *The Spirit of Violence: An Interdisciplinary Bibliography of Religion and Violence.* New York: Harry Frank Guggenheim Foundation.
Divale, William Tulio
 1973 *Warfare in Primitive Societies: A Bibliography.* Santa Barbara: ABC Clio.
Downing, Theodore E., and Gilbert Kushner, eds.
 1988 *Human Rights and Anthropology.* Cambridge: Cultural Survival.
Ferguson, R. Brian, and Leslie E. Farragher, eds.
 1988 *The Anthropology of War: A Bibliography.* New York: Harry Frank Guggenheim Foundation, Occasional Paper Number 1.

Literature Reviews

Ferguson, R. Brian
 1984 *Introduction: Studying War,* in *Warfare, Culture and Environment,* R. B. Ferguson, ed.: 1–81. New York: Academic Press.
Otterbein, Keith F.
 1973 *The Anthropology of War,* in *Handbook of Social and Cultural Anthropology,* John J. Honigmann, ed.: 923–958. Chicago: Rand McNally.

Sponsel, Leslie E.
1994a *The Mutual Relevance of Anthropology and Peace Studies*, in *The Anthropology of Peace and Nonviolence*, Leslie E. Sponsel and Thomas Gregor, eds. Boulder: Lynne Rienner Publishers.
1994b *The Natural History of Peace*, in *Peace Systems*, Thomas Gregor, ed. (forthcoming).

Directories

Rubinstein, Robert A., and Mary LeCron Foster, eds.
1988 *Directory of Anthropologists Working on Topics of Peace, International Security, and Conflict Resolution.* Gainesville, FL: Commission on the Study of Peace, International Union of Anthropological and Ethnological Sciences.

Periodicals

Human Peace Quarterly (CSP/IUAES) Gainsville, FL: Dr. Paul Doughty, Department of Anthropology, University of Florida, Gainesville, FL 32611.

Films and Videos

Angels of War (World War II in New Guinea).
Ax Fight (Yanomami of Veneuzuelan Amazon).
Contact: The Yanomami Indians of Brazil.
Dead Birds (the Dani of New Guinea).
Feathered Arrows (intertribal peace in the Upper Xingu)
First Contact (New Guinea).
Halflife: A Parable for the Nuclear Age (bomb testing in indigenous territories).
Magical Death (Yanomami).
Marshall Islands: Living with the Bomb.
Moonblood (Yanomami).
One World or None (written and directed by Ashley Montagu).
The Africans—Part 5.
The Feast (Yanomami).
The Meo (Hmong refugees in Laos from the Vietnam War).
The Survival of the Species—The Making of Mankind, Part 7.
Yanomamo of the Orinoco.

✦
The Contributors

JEAN L. BRIGGS is a professor of anthropology at Memorial University of Newfoundland. She has conducted extensive field research with the Inuit in the Northwest Territories of Canada. This research is the basis for her *Never in Anger: Portrait of an Eskimo Family* and *Aspects of Inuit Value Socialization.* Beyond her interest in studying Inuit interpersonal dramas (illustrated in her contribution to this volume), Briggs is also studying the psychological aspects of cultural upheaval in both Canadian Inuit and Siberian Yupik communities.

ROBERT KNOX DENTAN is a professor of anthropology at the State University of New York in Buffalo. His pioneering work in the ethnography of the Semai is the basis for his book *The Semai: A Nonviolent People of Malaysia.*

DOUGLAS P. FRY is an assistant professor of anthropology at Eckerd College in Florida. He has conducted extensive field research with the Zapotec of Oaxaca, Mexico, and within schools in the United States, focusing on interdisciplinary approaches to the study of aggression, the socialization of aggressive and prosocial behaviors, and conflict-resolution techniques.

WALTER GOLDSCHMIDT is professor emeritus at the University of California in Los Angeles. He has conducted extensive field research in East Africa. He is editor of *The Uses of Anthropology,* a volume that includes case studies of applied anthropology in World War II and other contexts.

THOMAS GREGOR is a professor of anthropology and chair of the Department of Anthropology at Vanderbilt University in Nashville, Tennessee. He has conducted extensive field research with the Mehinaku of the Xingu in the Brazilian Amazon. This work forms the basis of two books, *Mehinaku: The Drama of Daily Life in a Brazilian Indian Village* and *Anxious Pleasures: The Sexual Lives of an Amazonian People.* He is editor of the forthcoming multidisciplinary anthology, *Peace Systems.*

271

BRUCE M. KNAUFT is an associate professor of anthropology at Emory University in Atlanta. He has conducted extensive field research with the Gebusi of the Western Province of Papua, New Guinea. His publications include the books *Good Company and Violence: Sorcery and Social Action in a Lowland New Guinea Society* and *South Coast New Guinea Cultures: History, Comparison, Dialectic* and major articles on sociality and human evolution in *Current Anthropology.* He has been awarded research fellowships from the Center for Advanced Study in the Behavioral Sciences and the Harry Frank Guggenheim Foundation.

JACQUES LIZOT is a research associate with the National Scientific Research Center and the Laboratory of Social Anthropology in Paris, France. He has resided almost continuously with the Yanomami of the Venezuelan Amazon for more than twenty-three years. He has numerous publications in French, Spanish, and English, including *Tales of the Yanomami: Daily Life in the Venezuelan Forest.*

ASHLEY MONTAGU is a pioneer in exploring biological and anthropological aspects of aggression, war, nonviolence, peace, and related phenomena. Among the numerous books he has written or edited, the most relevant to this volume are: *On Being Human; The Direction of Human Development; Growing Young; Learning Non-aggression; Touching; Love; The Natural Superiority of Women; The Peace of the World; The Elephant Man; The Dehumanization of Man* (coauthor Floyd Matson); *Darwin, Competition and Cooperation; The Nature of Human Aggression; Man's Most Dangerous Myth: The Fallacy of Race;* and *Statement on Race.* He wrote and directed the film, *One World or None,* which has been described as one of the best documentaries ever made.

GEORGE PARK is a professor of anthropology at the Memorial University of Newfoundland. He has conducted fieldwork in both northern Norway and East Africa. His work in Africa included two years among the Kinga in southwestern Tanzania. He is preparing to publish a major ethnography on the Kinga.

CLAYTON A. ROBARCHEK is an associate professor of anthropology at Wichita State University in Kansas. He has conducted extensive comparative field research with two very different societies, the Semai in Malaysia and the Waorani in the Ecuadorian Amazon. Respectively, these societies have been described as *extremely nonviolent* and *violent.*

LESLIE E. SPONSEL is an associate professor of anthropology at the University of Hawaii, where he directs the Ecological Anthropology Program. He was also a founding member of the Spark M. Matsunaga

Institute for Peace. He has conducted field research in the Venezuelan Amazon with the Sanemá, a northern subgroup of the Yanomami; and in southern Thailand, where he was able to compare adjacent Buddhist and Muslim communities. He is editor of *Indigenous Peoples and the Future of Amazonia: The Ecological Anthropology of an Endangered World* and coeditor of *Tropical Deforestation: The Human Dimension* (both forthcoming).

Index

✦
About the Book

At a time when war and other forms of violence seem to be ubiquitous and increasing, this refreshing book provides some hope by looking at the brighter side of human nature. Though not ignoring violence and war, the authors focus on nonviolence and peace by analyzing a broad sample of indigenous societies. Included are the Mehinaku of Brazil, the Zapotec of Mexico, the Inuit of the Canadian Northwest Territories, the Semai of Malaysia, and the Kinga of Tanzania. There is also a chapter on the Yanomami of Venezuela—usually characterized as highly violent—in which the peacefulness of everyday relationships is emphasized.

The introductory chapters of the book review the mutual relevance of anthropology and peace studies, as well as the evolution of cooperation in human prehistory. A cross-cultural comparison of peacemaking and the institutions of peace likewise helps to frame the work.

In exploring neglected aspects of nonviolence and peace, this unique collection will find a broad readership: among scholars, in courses in anthropology and peace studies, and with a more general audience.